Rural Sociology

Rural Sociology

An Analysis of Contemporary Rural Life

ALVIN L. BERTRAND, Editor *1918*

Professor of Sociology and Rural Sociology
Louisiana State University

and ASSOCIATES

McGRAW-HILL BOOK COMPANY, INC.

New York   *Toronto*   *London*   1958

List of Contributors

Wilfrid C. Bailey, coauthor: 9
  Division of Sociology and Rural Life, Mississippi State College

Ward W. Bauder: 10 and 22
  Farm Population and Rural Life Branch,
  Agricultural Economics Division, Agricultural Marketing Service,
  U.S. Department of Agriculture, Iowa State College

Alvin L. Bertrand: 1–3, 8, 12–14, 23, and 26
  Departments of Sociology and Rural Sociology,
  Louisiana State University

William S. Folkman: 20
  Department of Rural Economics and Sociology,
  University of Arkansas

Robert K. Hirzel: 27
  Department of Sociology,
  University of Maryland

Charles R. Hoffer: 19
  Department of Sociology and Anthropology,
  Michigan State College

Harold F. Kaufman, coauthor: 9
  Division of Sociology and Rural Life,
  Mississippi State College

Olen E. Leonard: 4 and 11
  Director, Northern Zone,
  Instituto Interamericano de Ciencias Agricolas, Havana, Cuba

Bardin H. Nelson: 6 and 7
>   Department of Agricultural Economics and Sociology,
>   Texas Agricultural and Mechanical College

Paul H. Price: 5
>   Departments of Sociology and Rural Sociology,
>   Louisiana State University

Harald A. Pedersen: 18
>   International Cooperation Administration,
>   U.S. Overseas Mission, Pakistan

Irwin T. Sanders: 28
>   Departments of Sociology and Rural Sociology,
>   University of Kentucky, and
>   Associates for International Research, Inc.

Robert L. Skrabanek: 16
>   Department of Agricultural Economics and Sociology,
>   Texas Agricultural and Mechanical College

James D. Tarver: 17
>   Department of Sociology and Rural Life,
>   Oklahoma State University

Joseph S. Vandiver: 21
>   Department of Sociology and Rural Life,
>   Oklahoma State University

Sloan R. Wayland: 15
>   Department of Sociology, Teachers College,
>   Columbia University

Eugene A. Wilkening: 24 and 25
>   Department of Rural Sociology,
>   University of Wisconsin

Preface

This book is the outgrowth of numerous discussions with teachers of rural sociology regarding the special requirements of courses in this discipline. The major objectives and the special features of the volume, as well as the organization and style, are the products of these discussions.

Two major objectives have been kept foremost in mind throughout the preparation of this book. The first stems from the fact that many students who take rural sociology are getting their initial introduction to the field. Quite often they come from schools whose curricula afford little opportunity for acquaintance with any of the social sciences, much less sociology. Not unusually they are well advanced in their undergraduate studies. In addition to this group of students, these courses customarily enroll sociology majors and other students with social science backgrounds. The purpose, then, was to prepare a volume suitable for use as a first course in sociology, with regard to theoretical grounding, and interesting and stimulating to more advanced students, in terms of new material and special emphasis.

The second major objective was to present American rural society of today as it is, dynamic and transitional. Accordingly, the idea that swift change is taking place can be said to be the central focus of the book. The impact of population shifts, technology, modern means of communication, formal education, and contemporary agricultural policy is directly and indirectly pointed out throughout the volume. Indeed, any other approach would be highly misleading concerning the present-day rural scene in the United States.

At least three features of this book set it apart from previously published texts in rural sociology. First, an entire introductory section, as well as major parts of several later chapters, is devoted to general sociological theory. This has been done not only to provide orientation for the beginning student but to emphasize the fact that rural sociology abides by the principles of all sociologies. The application of these principles to rural life is, of course, the final aim of each discussion.

The second feature of this book is its emphasis on current research.

vii

One of the purposes of inviting a number of contributions was to take advantage of the first-hand knowledge of research specialists. The studies available, including the many Agricultural Experiment Station studies, have been carefully explored. In this connection, current research findings have been used both to expand old concepts and understandings and to provide new ideas and principles.

The third unique feature, which does most to make this book different from its predecessors, is the inclusion of several chapters dealing with topics not heretofore treated in rural sociology or, for that matter, in general sociology texts. A substantial portion of Part VI, which deals with social change, falls into this category.

One problem of semantics must be mentioned. Throughout the text, the word *rural* has been used in such expressions as *rural areas, rural society, rural world,* and *rural people,* where the reference is for the most part to the rural-farm segment of the population and the area it occupies. At times, however, it will be clear that the total rural population or area is involved. This alternative has been used in lieu of the labored and often misleading word *farm.*

The book has been planned and implemented by the senior author and editor, Alvin L. Bertrand. Cognizant of the usual problems of symposiums, he asked and received the full permission and cooperation of the contributing authors in coordinating, standardizing, and integrating the various chapters. This has been a challenging and difficult task because space limitations made it necessary to delete passages that represented diligent research and careful presentation and contained ideas and illustrations dear to the authors' hearts. Whatever resultant shortcomings the book may have in organization and style should be charged wholly to the author-editor.

Acknowledgment is due so many colleagues, former teachers, students, and others for their direct and indirect assistance that listing is precluded. Sources and references are, of course, acknowledged in footnotes where appropriate. Contributing authors have also acknowledged special assistance in their various chapters. The senior author and editor must, however, gratefully acknowledge the continued encouragement of Professor Homer L. Hitt, former Head of the Departments of Sociology and Rural Sociology at Louisiana State University. Without his support, it is doubtful whether this work could have been brought to a successful conclusion. No small debt is also owed Mrs. Anna Godso, who cheerfully and competently typed and retyped the manuscript through its various stages. The senior author and editor's wife worked beside him through the many long hours necessary for the inevitable revising, editing, proofreading, and indexing. His appreciation can be measured only by those who have shared a similar experience.

ALVIN L. BERTRAND

Contents

x   *Contents*

PART ONE

Introduction

Part One is a general and theoretical introduction to the subject of rural sociology. In Chapter 1, sociology is defined, its nature as a science discussed, and its problems listed; and rural sociology is identified as a specialized application of sociology. In Chapter 2, a theoretical orientation for the study of society is provided in a discussion of the nature of social organization and rural social organization. Chapter 3 sets forth the cause and nature of rural-urban differences and, in so doing, provides justification for the specialized study of rural sociology. Chapter 4 offers something new in rural sociology texts; in order further to prepare the student for understanding the uniqueness of rural society, it affords insight into the psychosocial setting of this society as seen in rural values and norms.

CHAPTER 1 *Introduction*

Since rural sociology is a specialized application of sociology, it is necessary to study it in this perspective. Sociology is classified under the general heading of social science. It appeared as a special discipline when it became clear that the traditional social sciences did not tell the whole story of human behavior. Economists concerned themselves with social behavior in the production, distribution, and consumption of wealth, and psychologists interested themselves in the study and measurement of individual human differences. However, each of these disciplines dealt more or less exclusively with its own aspect of social life, and the same was true in the other social sciences. Sociology as a study arose because of the need to treat human relationships in their entirety. Strangely enough, this need was felt by men in various widely separated disciplines more or less coincidently. It is quite significant that early sociologists were recruited from such diverse fields as history, biology, philosophy, economics, and natural science.

These statements provide a clue to the definition of sociology. It is simply the scientific study of human relationships. No other discipline focuses attention primarily on human relationships per se, and it is thus that sociology differs from all other studies. In other words, the sociologist interests himself in human relationships simply because they are social in nature and not because they are related to economic, political, religious, or other types of activity. This is not to say that the sociologist ignores the other social sciences in seeking insight into specific problems. All social sciences, although they maintain their distinct points of view, deal with social life and have an aspect of unity. The scope of sociology and its relation to other disciplines will be apparent throughout this book.

THE NATURE OF SCIENCE

Sociology has been identified as a science by definition. This claim has sometimes been questioned by persons not familiar with the meaning of science or sociology. Because of such questions, it is pertinent to review here the definition of science and its methods.

In essence, the term *science* is used to denote a systematically organized body of knowledge obtained through the use of the scientific method. Stated in a simpler way, science consists of factual explanations of the world in which we live; it postulates certain characteristics of the natural order, and it could not exist if there were no system or order in natural phenomena. Likewise, there would be no science without intelligent men—scientists—to look for and catalogue natural laws.

The Scientific Method

The procedure followed in determining and classifying regularity in nature is called the *scientific method*. As indicated above, only that information obtained by applying the scientific method can be dignified by the name science.

The scientific method involves four major steps. The first is the identification of a problem worthy of investigation. It need not be a problem in the pathological sense; rather, it is a goal the attainment of which would represent progress of some sort. Problems can be definitely identified only after a thorough review of the literature and an exhaustive study of the work of others.

The second step is the formulation of a *hypothesis,* or a statement that expresses the belief that one condition or thing is related in a specific way to another condition or thing. A *working hypothesis* is one that can be tested for its truth. Quite often preliminary observations indicate that certain relationships do exist between phenomena of various sorts. These discoveries are called *theories* until more definite proof is obtained. Thus Einstein's theory of relativity will remain a theory until someone appears who is wise enough to devise a means of verifying it. Theories constitute a valid part of science.

The third step in the scientific method is the empirical testing of the relationships hypothesized or theorized. Two major kinds of mental activity are involved in the testing of relationships: *observation* and *inference*. The former may include bare observation (of phenomena that cannot be controlled, such as the family life of a tribal group) or controlled observation (such as is possible under experimental conditions in a laboratory). *Inference* is defined as a process of logical reasoning from known facts to unknown facts. Two types of inference may be employed: *Deduction* is defined as reasoning from the general to the particular, or the kind of mental activity used by Sherlock Holmes; and *induction* involves the opposite process, or reasoning from the particular to the general. Through inference one can determine from observation of one member of a group what the behavior of other members is likely to be in given situations.

The last step in the scientific method is the classification and description, in an orderly fashion, of what has been tested and observed. When the elements possessing common attributes have been placed in a class, given a name, and described so carefully that recognition is unmistakable, the scientific method has been carried to its logical end.

Techniques of the Social Sciences

All sciences utilize certain techniques for the validation of hypotheses and theories. These techniques vary somewhat from one discipline to another, and persons working in one occasionally question the validity of procedures used in others. In these circumstances, it is important to remember that all methods that can pass valid tests of causal relationships are worthy.

In the social sciences, some of the general techniques used are (1) the statistical method, which shows quantitative relationships; (2) the field-survey method, which involves the gathering of information at first hand through interviews or questionnaires; (3) the case-study method —the study in detail of one or a small number of cases considered typical; (4) the historical method—the tracing of the growth and continuity of social processes; and (5) the cartographic method—the use of graphic forms to make perplexing data meaningful.[1]

When the existence of certain relationships in natural phenomena has been verified by acceptable techniques, scientific knowledge has been gained. Each relationship may be called a *law* or *principle*, as, for example, the law of falling bodies in physics. The task of a scientific sociology is to discover principles in human relationships.

SOCIOLOGY AS A SCIENCE

Since human activity is patterned or ordered in a way that is similar to the patterning of natural phenomena, it is possible to have a science of human relations. Naturally, this patterning was observed long ago, but it was not studied scientifically until recently.[2] Auguste Comte (1798–1857) is often called the father of this study, and it is he who coined the term *sociology*.

Patterning of activity is observable in the things that humans do as

---

[1] For a detailed discussion of these techniques, see: Homer L. Hitt, "Scientific Method in Urban Sociology," in T. Lynn Smith and C. A. McMahan (eds.), *The Sociology of Urban Life*, New York: The Dryden Press, Inc., 1951, pp. 25–31.

[2] Otis Durant Duncan, "Rural Sociology Coming of Age," *Rural Sociology*, 19:2, 1954.

members of a given society. All the student needs to do in order to convince himself of this fact is to analyze his own behavior or that of his fellows for a day. The extent to which even the layman can predict the behavior of his fellows will be a surprising discovery. Dress, eating habits, observance of traffic laws, classroom behavior, etc., are all predictable to a large extent. The fact that *individual* behavior cannot always be correctly predicted is sometimes the basis for questioning of the predictive capacity of sociologists. The fallacy of this criticism lies in the fact that sociology is not concerned with individual behavior but rather with group behavior. Furthermore, prediction in sociology must be based on knowledge beyond that required in the sciences dealing with natural phenomena. The four general concepts or ideas of the so-called "exact" sciences—regularity, structure, function, and change—do not suffice for the social sciences. A fifth general concept or idea must be added. This is the concept of "meaning," [3] which refers to the fact that individuals act, not according to rigid, unchanging patterns, but according to their interpretation of the situation. The same situation, depending on cultural conditioning, may have a different meaning for two individuals. Thus, when confronted with similar circumstances or problems, a person reared in a rural-farm area may react quite differently from a person brought up in an urban area. To illustrate, a preschool child from the city, when asked where milk comes from, will probably answer, "the milkman," whereas the farm child will know that the source of milk is the cow. Prediction in sociology, therefore, can be made with more accuracy if one is familiar with the cultural background of the group being studied.

Social scientists are often criticized for the lack of preciseness of their predictions, the implication of these criticisms being that prediction is more exact or precise in the natural and physical sciences. A moment's reflection reveals the fallacy of such contentions. Admitting that human behavior can only be predicted within certain limits at best, social scientists note that physical scientists were far from predicting successfully the power of the hydrogen bomb, that biologists can predict the behavior of genes and chromosomes only within very narrow limits, and so on.

Sociology as a Generalizing Science

Sociology concerns itself with general and recurrent relationships rather than unique ones. The study and exposition of the unique and the particular are left to other sciences, which have a special interest in such phenomena. To illustrate, history is an individualizing discipline, in contrast to sociology, which is a generalizing discipline. Thus, historians

[3] John W. Bennett and Melvin M. Tumin, *Social Life*, New York: Alfred A. Knopf, Inc., 1948, p. 82.

have as their proper task the study of the unique features of past happenings. The historian who happens to discover a particular way in which one war or one religion or one government differed from others at a given time and place has made a contribution to his field of study. In contrast, the sociologist, working within the framework of a generalizing science, is credited with a discovery only when he succeeds in bringing to light social phenomena that are repeated in time and space, i.e., recurrent and predictable in all wars, all religions, or all national entities. In explaining social relationships, sociology naturally draws upon and synthesizes information from many other fields. This is true, of course, of many disciplines, and it does not invalidate their claim to being specialized studies.

The Problem of Objectivity. Unlike the physical scientist, the sociologist and other social scientists are personally involved in the phenomena they investigate. In other words, the sociologist deals with religion, family systems, government, and many other institutions and customs toward which he has a personal orientation. For this reason, a great deal of his training as a sociologist is concerned with achieving objectivity, or overcoming preconceived ideas, emotional biases, and tendency to make ethical judgments.

This problem of objectivity is further complicated by the fact that the prejudices of others are also involved. Because of the nature of his studies, the sociologist is confronted with an "audience" that feels qualified to speak with authority on his findings. In other words, everyone considers himself to be well informed on what is right and wrong in human relationships, forgetting that he has only limited cultural participation for guidance. The social investigator may thus feel a subtle pressure to come up with the "right" answers in terms of what is expected by the group. This type of pressure is more likely to come into play on matters charged with strong feeling, such as race relations, religion, and so on. Fortunately, strong pressure of this sort is rare, and in the long run the truth usually prevails. Nevertheless, the sociologist is confronted with a special problem that should be recognized by all students in the field.

Achieving scientific objectivity does not, of course, mean that one has to give up his moral or religious convictions. Quite to the contrary, sociology as a science is concerned only with such facts as the attaching of moral significance to certain actions or behavior by a given society, or the different ways in which people worship their god or gods, and like questions. Sociologists as scientists can never say what is good or bad, moral or immoral, ethical or unethical *in itself*. They can use these labels only within the context of a given culture. The point is simply that matters of this nature can be studied objectively but they cannot be judged good or evil by scientific means. This fact makes it possible for the scientist to reconcile his religious and other beliefs with his scientific investigations.

RURAL SOCIOLOGY AS A SPECIAL SOCIOLOGY

As we saw in the introduction to this chapter, sociology as a study constitutes a single unit. Nevertheless, like other sciences, it is divided into general and special areas. The basis for division is the fact that general sociology concerns itself with properties and interactional relationships common to all social phenomena, whereas special sociologies limit themselves to a special class of phenomena chosen for intensive study. Rural sociology can thus be classed as a special sociology.

In its broadest definition, rural sociology is the study of human relationships in the rural environment. This definition correctly implies that it is no more nor less than the sociology of life in a rural setting. This fact has led T. Lynn Smith to suggest that the systematized knowledge of rural social relationships could more aptly be called the *sociology of rural life*.[4]

Lowry Nelson succinctly delineates the scope of rural sociology by describing its three dimensions as follows: [5]

It comprehends not alone the delineation of the areas and sub-areas of community life, considered in the horizontal aspect; but includes as well the myriad forms of association within the spatial framework. In this latter aspect it describes all those functions which make up the associational life of rural man. Thus it is a discipline of great breadth—as wide, indeed, as the forms of associational life are varied.

It has not only breadth, but also "length." It cannot be content with mere description and analysis of the community as it appears in cross section; it must take cognizance of time as well as space. It recognizes that the community, as of the present, is the result of a long period of cultural change and cultural accumulation. In other words, every community has a history and is in large measure the product of an evolutionary process. The student of rural society must have a time perspective concerning his data. Such a perspective involves knowledge of the forces, both internal and external, which in the past have helped to shape the social phenomena of the present. Thus the discipline has "length" as another important dimension.

The third dimension is "depth." If we are to understand fully the social life of mankind, we need to know more about the nature of the individual himself: his needs, his drives, his motivation, his attitudes, and all of those subtle and elusive—though all-important—forms of covert behavior. What it is

[4] T. Lynn Smith, *The Sociology of Rural Life*, 3d ed., New York: Harper & Brothers, 1953, p. 10.

[5] Lowry Nelson, "Rural Sociology—Dimensions and Horizons," *Rural Sociology*, 10: 131, 1945.

that produces the forms of response in individuals and groups; how and why responses differ in time and place; how are folkways and mores changed (e.g., the substitution of one food habit for another); how are value-systems modified; and how can these subtle processes of interaction be measured and described— these are but a few of the questions involved in the quest for knowledge along the third dimension.

The Use of the Term Rural

Although the term *rural* is used often and glibly, the average student would find it difficult to give a satisfactory definition of the concept. This is true despite the fact that the rural and urban segments of the population present great contrasts. The difficulties of making a clear-cut distinction between the two population groups arise from at least two major problems. The first is the impossibility of utilizing simple statistical categories in delineation. The second is that it is almost impossible to categorize rural-urban differences. For example, it is difficult to determine whether a given borderline characteristic should be classified as rural or urban.

Despite these difficulties, fairly satisfactory definitions of rural and urban populations have been devised. The most widely used in the United States is that of the Bureau of the Census, which bases its distinctions on the criteria of size, incorporation, and density. According to the new definition adopted for use in the 1950 census, the urban population includes: [6]

. . . all persons living in (a) places of 2,500 inhabitants or more incorporated as cities, boroughs, and villages, (b) incorporated towns of 2,500 inhabitants or more except in New England, New York, and Wisconsin, where "towns" are simply minor civil divisions of counties, (c) the densely settled urban fringe, including both incorporated and unincorporated areas, around cities of 50,000 or more, and (d) unincorporated places of 2,500 inhabitants or more outside any urban fringe.

Obviously this definition is an arbitrary one and as such is subject to criticism. Nevertheless, it represents the best effort so far to delineate the rural and urban population aggregates, and it provides a satisfactory point of departure for statistical and cultural comparisons.

In the United States census, the rural population is divided into two groups, *rural-farm* and *rural-nonfarm*. The latter includes ". . . all persons living outside urban areas who do not live on farms." [7] Obviously, the remainder of the rural population, those living outside urban areas

---

[6] U.S. Bureau of the Census, *1950 Population Census Report*, P-C1, 1953, p. viii.

[7] The *Census of Agriculture* uses criteria slightly different from those of the *Census of Housing* in deciding which residences are farms. See: Calvin L. Beale, "Farm Population as a Useful Demographic Concept," *Agricultural Economics Research*, 9:109–111, 1957.

and working on farms, is classed as rural-farm. This is the group about which we are primarily concerned in this book, although some attention will be given to each rural population group.

When considering populations for which statistical information is not available, two criteria taken together may be used to determine rurality. The first is residence. People living in areas of relatively low population density (compared to others in their locality) will generally be identified as rural. The second criterion is chief source of livelihood. Individuals or populations obtaining all or a substantial part of their income from agricultural enterprises may safely be classed as rural-farm. Generally speaking, the chance is very great that persons deriving their income from agriculture or living in the less densely populated areas, or both, are bona fide ruralites. There are, of course, exceptions, and the student should exercise his own judgment in connection with those individuals or groups that satisfy the criteria but obviously are not rural-farm or rural-nonfarm residents.

Questions for Review and Discussion

1. What is the fundamental goal of science?
2. Can sociology legitimately be called a science? Explain your answer.
3. What steps are involved in the logical development of the scientific method?
4. Explain what is meant by the statement that "meaning," in addition to facts based on observation, is necessary for prediction in sociology.
5. Why is objectivity a particularly difficult problem for the sociologist?
6. Explain the relationship of special sociologies to general sociology.
7. Define rural sociology.
8. Distinguish among the urban, rural-nonfarm, and rural-farm populations.
9. Name and explain the more general techniques of the social sciences.
10. What is meant by the statement, "Sociology is a generalizing science"?

Selected References for Supplementary Reading

Bennett, John W., and Melvin M. Tumin: *Social Life,* New York: Alfred A. Knopf, Inc., 1948, chap. 5.

Cuber, John F.: *Sociology: A Synopsis of Principles,* 3d ed., New York: Appleton-Century-Crofts, Inc., 1955, chaps. 1–3.

Lundberg, G. A.: *The Foundations of Sociology,* New York: The Macmillan Company, 1939, chaps. 1 and 2.

Nelson, Lowry: *Rural Sociology,* 2d ed., New York: American Book Company, 1952, chap. 1.

Smith, T. Lynn: *The Sociology of Rural Life,* 3d ed., New York: Harper & Brothers, 1953, chap. 1.

Taylor, Carl C.: "Sociology and Common Sense," *American Sociological Review,* 12:1–12, 1947.

CHAPTER 2 *Social Organization and*
Rural Social Organization [1]

As we saw in Chapter 1, sociology as a study is based on the fact that human behavior is characterized by regular and recurrent patterns. This fact makes social interaction (interstimulation and response) the key concept in sociology.

The Nature of Social Organization

The term *social organization* is used to describe the vast, complex network of patterned human behavior within a society. In this chapter an attempt is made to show how societies are organized, and the student will find much of the basic theory of sociology in the review of the structural-functional aspects of society included here. Without this background it is impossible to understand sociologically the many facts presented.

Social organization is essentially a dynamic concept. The *patterns* of *human relationships* are constantly changing, even if they are, in varying degrees, regular and predictable. Therefore, it is necessary to regard social organization both as a condition and as a process.[2] In this connection it is possible to study, on the one hand, the structure, or framework, of social action and, on the other hand, the dynamics, or process, of social action. Both will be considered in the discussions that follow.

The Concept of Society. Social organization will be more meaningful to the student who understands the basic term *society.* As everyone knows, in common parlance the word may be used to refer to a group of

[1] The author is indebted to Dr. Clarence A. Storla, Jr., formerly Graduate Assistant in the Department of Sociology, Louisiana State University, for his assistance in the preparation of this chapter.

[2] For a detailed presentation of this point of view on the nature of social organization, see: J. O. Hertzler, *Social Institutions,* Lincoln, Neb.: University of Nebraska Press, 1946, p. 13.

11

elite or upper-class people or to a formal association of persons interested in a common cause, such as the Society for the Prevention of Cruelty
to Animals. However, to the sociologist, who uses the term in a technical
sense, a society is ". . . that group within which men share a total common life." [3] Put in another way, a society is simply a collection of people
with a "we" feeling who are sufficiently organized to carry out all the
conditions necessary to living harmoniously together.

In identifying societies, the student must be careful to look for three
characteristics. There must be (1) an aggregate of individuals, possessing
(2) a sense of belonging and cooperation, in (3) a more or less permanent association. Thus, the crowd at a football game or attending a lecture, although it is an aggregate of persons, could not be classified as a
society because their association is temporary.

It may be noted that in many quarters, the term *society* is roughly
synonymous with the word *nation*. In this sense, it is quite correct to
speak of American society or French society. However, it is equally
appropriate to refer to tribal or similar groups as societies.

Role and Status. Everyone is familiar with the fact that each individual
simultaneously plays a variety of roles in society. For example, one person may be a male, a parent, a school teacher, and many other things at
one and the same time. Obviously, the complexity of the particular society
determines the number of different positions individuals may hold. However, even in simple societies there is considerable differentiation of
individuals and groups on the basis of such things as age, sex, kinship,
and knowledge. This network of positions, along with the differential
participation of members of groups in the total culture (because of their
different positions), is termed *social differentiation*, and it reflects the
structural aspects of society.

The position of a person in the social group determines the nature
and amount of his responsibilities and obligations as well as his superior-
inferior relations to other members of the group. The sociological name
for a social position in its relationship to others is *status*. This meaning
of the term is to be distinguished from the popular use of the term to
mean a great amount of prestige. [4]

Status should not be thought of as synonymous with the individual
who occupies the position to which it is attached. It is simply the collection of obligations, responsibilities, and rights associated with a certain position in a given society. For example, certain rights and duties in
each society are associated with the status of males or of females, and

[3] Ely Chinoy, *Sociological Perspective,* New York: Doubleday & Company, Inc.,
1954, p. 21.
[4] John W. Bennett and Melvin M. Tumin, *Social Life,* New York: Alfred A. Knopf,
Inc., 1948, chaps. 6 and 7.

these remain independent of any one male or female. In fact, millions of individuals may occupy the status and enjoy essentially the same rights and responsibilities.

Each individual occupies a great number of statuses at one and the same time, and these statuses are continually changing. Thus one person may occupy the status of husband, father, skilled worker, and so on, at one time. At another time he could be a widower, a grandfather, and an unemployed person. Statuses change more or less automatically with age, education, prestige, and economic well-being.

Individuals come to occupy statuses in two entirely separate ways. One group of statuses is acquired at birth without effort on the part of the individual. Such positions carry with them *ascribed status.* Through ascription, the infant automatically gets such statuses as social class, race, sex, and age. A great many statuses, however, are thrown open to competition and come to the individual only after effort on his part. These positions bring *achieved status.* Achieved status is exemplified in the positions occupied by doctors, lawyers, governors, flag-pole sitters, and farmers. The more complex the society, the more opportunity each individual has to achieve a variety of statuses.

Obviously, each status carries with it certain rules that guide the social relationships of the occupier with others. The pattern of behavior expected of those who occupy given statuses is defined as *role.* Social roles are prescribed for every status, and interaction becomes predictable to the extent that individuals behave in accordance with the norms of their roles. *Social norms* are defined as required or acceptable behavior in a given situation. Role is the expected behavior associated with each status.

As a rule, social roles in a given society fit together with reciprocal obligations, such as those between husband and wife or employer and employee. So long as customary patterns are followed, society moves along smoothly; but when customary roles are not followed, relationships become strained. This is true because other members of society are at a loss to understand, evaluate, or predict the behavior of a member whose actions are contrary to those expected of a person occupying his status. For example, small-town school teachers and ministers violate certain expected behavior patterns at the risk of their tenure.

Social Stratification. As we saw in the previous section, each individual occupies several statuses in society. The total number of statuses a person holds makes up what is termed his *station.*[5] Within each society there are many persons who occupy roughly the same station and thus divide the population into horizontal layers, or strata. The term *social stratification* is used to describe this phenomenon. Persons in the upper

[5] Kingsley Davis, *Human Society,* New York: The Macmillan Company, 1949, pp. 91–92.

strata of society enjoy more prestige, honor, wealth, and authority, generally speaking, than persons in the lower strata. The symbols of class vary, however, and family background rather than wealth and power may loom as the most important factor in determining one's class position in certain places.

Movement from one social class to another is called *vertical social mobility*. Those societies that encourage such movement by providing many avenues for social climbing are said to have an *open-class* system. In our society, for example, a person may move from one class to another through success in such things as economic endeavor, education, religion, politics, athletics, and the armed services.

The system in which a person's class position is determined solely by birth and nothing he can do will enable him to change classes is referred to as a *caste* system. The classic example is the social system of India, where the rules of caste forbid marrying outside one's caste and restrict one's association with members of other castes to certain types of relationships.

It is important to observe that social classes have no formal organization. This fact makes it difficult to determine which class a given person belongs to. Generally, a combination of objective criteria (such as income, organizational membership, and positions of authority) and subjective criteria (such as the evaluation of a person's position by his acquaintances) is used to determine class position. Obviously, the number of strata, the symbols of class, and class mobility vary from one segment of a society to another. This will be brought out in the chapter dealing with rural social stratification.

Social Groups. With the concepts of status, role, and social stratification in mind, we may turn logically to the concept of the social group. This concept is central to the understanding of social organization; in fact, many sociologists claim that the study of human groups is essentially the study of social organization. When various statuses and roles interlock in a pattern of interaction within a society, a social group comes into existence. Chinoy defines and explains the social group as follows: [6]

A social group is a number of persons linked together in a network or system of social relationships. Its members interact with one another in a more or less standardized fashion, that is, according to norms or standards accepted by the group. Their relationships and interaction are largely based upon a set of interrelated roles and statuses. They are united or held together to a greater or lesser extent by a sense of common identity or a similarity of interests which enables them to differentiate members from nonmembers.

[6] Chinoy, *op. cit.*, p. 29.

In identifying a social group, the student must look for three characteristics. First, there must be a plurality of persons (two or more). Second, there must be definable interaction directed toward attaining common goals. Third, the members must possess a sense of solidarity, or what might be termed a "we" feeling. Groups that do not possess these characteristics are given other names; for example, groups such as students having a B average, owners of sports-model automobiles, or working wives would be called statistical aggregates or categories rather than social groups. One should not get the impression that such groups are not sociologically significant. They may have a great deal of sociological relevance, but they do not fall in the classification of a social group.

Groups are commonly classified according to the nature of the characteristics that draw them together. These may be such things as physical, residential, or interest characteristics.[7] *Elementary groups* are held together by one tie or bond, whereas *cumulative groups* are held together by a great many ties or bonds.[8] Some groups are short-lived, whereas others perpetuate themselves for long periods of time. The members of some groups meet in face-to-face contact; in others interaction takes place through shared activity (usually representing specialized interests) which unites the group but does not require intimate personal contact among the members. Groups in which contact is face-to-face are called *primary groups* and are illustrated by families and play groups. Shared-activity groups are called *secondary groups* and are exemplified by national labor unions and professional societies.

This terminology was developed by Charles H. Cooley, but other sociologists have used different terms to convey essentially the same meaning. Emile Durkheim described groups held together by a division of labor (shared activity) as *organic* in nature. If they maintained cohesion because of a homogeneity of characteristics of the individual group members, Durkheim said they were organized on a *mechanistic* basis. Ferdinand Tonnies used the terms *Gemeinshaft* and *Gesellschaft*, the former referring to those group relationships that develop unconsciously or subconsciously and the latter to those groups entered into deliberately for the achievement of recognized ends.[9]

Groups can also be distinguished as *formal* or *informal*, the distinc-

---

[7] For a much more detailed discussion of social groups, see: John L. Gillin and John P. Gillin, *Cultural Sociology*, New York: The Macmillan Company, 1948, p. 220.

[8] Pitirim A. Sorokin, Carle C. Zimmerman, and Charles J. Galpin (eds.), *A Systematic Source Book in Rural Sociology*, vol. I, Minneapolis, Minn.: University of Minnesota Press, 1930, pp. 306–310.

[9] Pitirim A. Sorokin and Carle C. Zimmerman, *Principles of Rural-Urban Sociology*, New York: Henry Holt and Company, Inc., 1931, p. 514.

tion between these types being that formal groupings have been deliberately and systematically set up to perform certain functions and operate according to certain established rules of procedure. Sociologists generally call such groups *associations*.

Locality groups are shaped by social relations chiefly dependent upon areal setting, that is, location or residence. People living in communities, neighborhoods, and regions provide examples of locality groups.

Interest groups have some common objective as a central unifying force. The farmers' cooperative is a type of interest group. The various types of groups important in rural society will be discussed in detail at the appropriate place in the chapters that follow.

The Nature of Culture

No doubt the student who has read this far has wondered how groups continue to operate, considering the complicated relationships among individuals in them. The answer to this question is found in the nature of culture. Culture explains to a very great extent the regular and recurrent patterns of human behavior. It also accounts for the standardization of behavior within groups and societies.

In its technical sense, the term *culture* does not refer to such things as art, literature, and music exclusively, nor does it connote the quality of being well versed in the nicer etiquette of the group. Such meanings are limited to popular usage. In its scientific sense, culture refers to those parts of man's environment which are man-made. Tylor's definition makes this point clear. "Culture is that complex whole which includes knowledge, belief, art, morals, law, custom, and any other capabilities and habits acquired by man as a member of society." [10] To facilitate understanding and analysis, culture is often divided into its material and nonmaterial components. The former includes the physical objects of a culture along with their use. Thus automobiles, skyscrapers, footballs, and the like would be classed as aspects of material culture. Nonmaterial culture includes the part of man's environment which does not have a physical structure, or a structure that can be felt or seen. Such things as religious beliefs, political ideologies, marriage customs, and taboos are identified as aspects of nonmaterial culture. There are certain universal elements in all cultures which are important enough to discuss under separate headings. These include folkways, mores, and institutions.

Folkways and Mores. The numerous behavior patterns that account for orderliness in man's social life arise out of culture. These patterns or habits were recognized and first named by William Graham Sumner. [11]

---

[10] E. B. Tylor, *Primitive Culture*, 1871, p. 1; reprint of 7th ed., New York: Brentano's, 1924.

[11] William Graham Sumner, *Folkways*, Boston: Ginn & Company, 1906.

Folkways are defined as commonly accepted rules of conduct that are not compulsive. Mores, on the other hand, are the "must" behaviors, and conformity to these patterns is enforced in various ways by the greater society. In other words, the person who violates a folkway will merely be considered eccentric, radical, or extremist, and although he may experience some social pressure in the form of gossip or ridicule, there will be no positive action to bring about conformity with established practices. To illustrate, a man who does not have his hair cut will elicit many raised eyebrows, whispered remarks, and even forthright observations but will not be forcibly constrained to go to the barber.

Mores carry much stronger sanctions than folkways, for society looks upon these behaviors as moral and necessary for the survival of the group. Because of this interpretation, the person who violates a mos is subjected to more positive expression of disapproval. It is significant that the mores are generally expressed in the legal codes of the group. Thus laws dealing with murder, stealing, adultery, and the like are found in almost all national legal codes. Some mores, of course, are not codified. For example, it would be unusual to find in any part of the United States a law dealing with classroom attire. Nevertheless, the girl presenting herself for class in a Bikini bathing suit would most certainly be violating a mos, unless she was a model in certain art classes.

Folkways and mores are differentiated along a continuum and are not sharply opposed, as might be supposed. In many instances it is difficult to determine whether a given act falls within the realm of folkways or of mores. The fact that many folkways are constantly changing to mores and vice versa is testimony to this and is the basis for continual study of culture.

Social Institutions. To understand fully the concept of social organization, one must see society as a group of persons among whom a set of institutions provides a framework for all activity.

In the parlance of social scientists, institutions are *systems of social relationships* for meeting various felt human needs. These systems include clusters of folkways, mores, and laws applying specifically to particular needs. The needs around which institutions center are derived from biological functions and from the prevailing culture. To illustrate, it has been pointed out that the biologically derived human needs, such as the sex drive and reproduction, form the basis of the institution of the family. Similarly, man's need for food, clothing, and shelter has given rise to economic institutions. Other needs, not biologically rooted, provide an equally important basis for social institutions. For example, man's concern with the supernatural brought religious institutions into being, and his need for social control led to the creation of governmental institutions. Educational institutions are the result of man's wish to better himself. Although there are other areas of institutional activity, the social institutions mentioned above are recognized as the major ones.

The social institution is an abstraction and must be recognized as belonging to the same category as government, love, and other abstractions. The student should be careful to distinguish between the institution, which is an abstraction, and the specific organizations and groups through which the institution is expressed. For example, the University Baptist Church of Collegetown, U.S.A., includes a specific congregation and certain rituals and ceremonies. At the same time, however, it manifests many values and activities characteristic of the Christian religion (an institution) in the United States.

Persons maintaining social relations are often too vaguely associated to be classified as social groups or social institutions. The term *collective behavior* is used to refer to groupings such as publics, crowds, and social movements.

Social Systems

The student will find reference to *social systems* in some of the discussions in this book.[12] Essentially, the concept of the social system is that of a complex web of social relations beyond primary groups. The term refers to integrated social interaction at various levels. It can be applied to a number of individual persons, interacting in society as a whole and in social groups, according to the expected behavior patterns in a given culture. In some ways it carries connotations similar to those of the term *social institution*.[13]

Social Processes

Social processes constitute a basic concept in the understanding of social organization. This concept is important because it comprises the dynamic element of society: in other words, the social processes constitute the moving aspect of social organization.

Social interaction may be looked upon as the genus and social processes as the species of social action. As individuals and groups come

[12] This usage reflects preference for the terminology of the functional school. An introductory text is not the place to discuss the various theoretical approaches in sociology, and this work, by virtue of its many authors, is not bound to the concepts of any one school. For a discussion of the approaches of the various schools, see: Nicholas S. Timasheff, *Sociological Theory, Its Nature and Growth*, Garden City, N.Y.: Doubleday & Company, Inc., 1955.

[13] The social-system approach is discussed in Stuart A. Queen, William N. Chambers, and Charles M. Winston, *The American Social System*, Boston: Houghton Mifflin Company, 1956, and in Robin M. Williams, Jr., *American Society*, New York: Alfred A. Knopf, Inc., 1951, chap. 3. For the social-system approach in a rural-sociology textbook, see: Charles P. Loomis and J. Allan Beegle, *Rural Social Systems*, New York: Prentice-Hall, Inc., 1950.

together and jockey for statuses, strive for goals, and manipulate one another to achieve the things the society values, interaction (reciprocal contact) takes place. It may be noted that unless there is interstimulation and response there is no interaction; and there must be communication between two individuals or groups before interaction can come about. Whether it is verbal, gestural, or otherwise symbolic, communication elicits understanding and response from interacting parties.

Certain forms of social interaction noticeably occur again and again with great regularity and uniformity. These types of interaction are designated *social processes*. Most sociologists classify social processes under two headings, *solidary* and *antagonistic*. Such processes as cooperation, accommodation, and assimilation are classified as solidary, and competition and conflict are listed as antagonistic.

Although these processes are to be discussed in detail as they apply to rural society, it is well to note that they cannot be separated completely. Interaction is so complex and all-inclusive that it is impossible to identify a type of behavior with only one process. In other words, almost all specific situations contain behavior that represents more than one process.

Social Control

Thus far, we have had a great deal to say about the order that exists in human society. However, we have not as yet mentioned the procedures through which individuals and groups are led to conform to the norms, or behave according to expected patterns. *Social control* consists of many processes by which the greater society enforces conformity to the patterns of behavior it considers to be right and good. It ensures the maintenance of social organization.

Social control operates at two different levels. Once the standards of right and wrong (moral norms) are set by the society, the individual may be kept in line by *informal* or *formal* control. Informal control is maintained by such forces as conscience, ridicule, and ostracism, and formal control by laws, rules, codes, and regulations.

Through the use of social controls the normative systems of behavior become so deeply ingrained in the individual that he is generally unwilling to behave counter to expectation. Compliance is never complete, however, and when deviation occurs, society quickly has recourse to its sanctions to bring the deviant back into line or to remove him as a menace to the welfare of the society.

Social Change and Social Disorganization

Although the rate of change varies from one society to another, no society is completely static. *Social change* refers to alterations in social organization. Many factors associated with social change are of interest to the sociologist. He is concerned not only with the factors that initiate and impel change and with the type and rate of change but also with the results of change. When social change is rapid and unguided, the result is often *social disorganization.*

Social disorganization exists when the equilibrium of society implied in social organization is disrupted. It comes about primarily because individuals and groups begin to work at cross purposes and thus defeat the objectives of the society. The consequences of social disorganization are often called *social problems.* Thus a social problem exists when a majority or an active minority within the society no longer regards the customary solution to problems of behavior relations as the best. Race relations, for example, did not become a problem until customary practices came to be regarded as morally wrong by a substantial number of people in the United States.

The concepts of social disorganization and social problems must be regarded as relative, since there are always some persons in every society who hold views and behave contrary to the majority practice. In so far as these persons bring about uncoordinated and disruptive activity, a perfect state of equilibium (organization) cannot exist. Thus, in many societies there are constant attempts to *reorganize* social interaction and combat social disorganization. The term *social planning* is associated with efforts in this direction.

Rural Social Organization

It must be remembered that the framework of social organization is the same in every society, although its functioning may vary somewhat from one society to another. The student is no doubt already aware of many differences between rural and urban social organization. In this connection, it should be understood that, although rural people work at many different occupations, the nature of agriculture as an occupation gives rural life its peculiar flavor. Three special features of agricultural endeavor seem to account in large part for the many differences in rural social organization as compared to urban social organization.[14] We shall review these features here and discuss them in detail in Chapter 3.

1. The farmer must have land in order to pursue his occupation. Because of this need, many of his interpersonal relations are concerned with obtaining and using land. Therefore, a good part of rural soci-

[14] The late Dwight Sanderson used the term *rural social organization* to mean the application of sociological knowledge to the betterment of rural life. In the language of this chapter, such efforts would be labeled *rural social reorganization.* See: Dwight Sanderson, *Rural Sociology and Rural Social Organization,* New York: John Wiley & Sons, Inc., 1942, p. 18.

ology is devoted to questions pertaining to how people hold, divide, and settle on the land. Included under this aspect of rural social organization are such topics as social patterns of farming, tenure arrangements, and land division. Each of these topics will receive careful study in subsequent chapters.

2. The farmer does his work in the open air, in close association with living, growing things but in relative isolation from other persons. This is the second of the factors that account for the variation between rural and urban social organization. This feature of rural life accounts in great part for the personality traits of rural people, as will be pointed out in Chapter 3. It is no accident that ruralites are more outspoken, trustful, and individualistic than their city cousins. But they are much less skilled in personality manipulation than urbanites, many of whom depend on the good graces of others for their very survival. The farmer lives close to his work at all times and is dependent on the capriciousness of nature for success. Both facts tend to give him a philosophy of life different from that of the urban dweller.

3. The third factor affecting social organization is the low man-land ratio in rural areas. The number of people available to support institutions such as the church and the school is relatively small. The low density of population also accounts for the fact that the persons who live in a given area are in continuous association with one another, since they belong to many of the same organizations. This close and continuous association leads to primary group relationships and is manifested in community and neighborhood patterns. All in all, the low density of population in rural areas is responsible for many of the unique characteristics of social institutions, social processes, social differentiation, social mobility, and social control.

The features listed above set the stage for the remainder of this volume. With the exception of Chapter 3, which defines the basis of rural-urban differences, the chapters that follow are devoted to the description, analysis, and discussion of specific phases of rural social organization.

Questions for Review and Discussion

1. Define rural social organization.
2. Why is it necessary to have an understanding of the technical meaning of society to study social organization?
3. Differentiate between society and culture.
4. Differentiate between role and status.
5. Why can American society be described as having a high degree of vertical social mobility?
6. What are the prerequisites for a social group?
7. How do folkways differ from mores?

8. Define, identify, or describe the following: (*a*) social processes, (*b*) social interaction, (*c*) social control, (*d*) social disorganization, (*e*) social problems, (*f*) a social institution.

Selected References for Supplementary Reading

Bennett, John W., and Melvin M. Tumin: *Social Life,* New York: Alfred A. Knopf, Inc., 1948, part II.

Bossard, James H. S., Walter A. Lunden, Lloyd V. Ballard, and Lawrence Foster (eds.): *Introduction to Sociology,* Harrisburg, Pa.: The Stackpole Company, 1952, chap. 28.

Broom, Leonard, and Philip Selznick: *Sociology: A Text with Adapted Readings,* Evanston, Ill.: Row, Peterson & Company, 1955, chaps. 2–4.

Lundberg, George A., Clarence C. Schrag, and Otto N. Larsen: *Sociology,* New York: Harper & Brothers, 1954, chaps. 6, 8, and 9.

CHAPTER 3

The Nature of
Rural-Urban Differentials

Sociologists and anthropologists have demonstrated to us that differences in personality and culture are not inborn. If they were, there would probably be little cultural variation from one population aggregate to another. Man is, however, born with an anatomy, physiology, and neural structure which set certain limits to his social behavior. In addition, the range of his actions is limited by his geographic as well as his social and cultural environment. All three types of influence come together in the socialization process and account for the unique characteristics of a given individual or group. The peculiar nature of these influences in the rural setting accounts for rural-urban differences as well as for variations among rural groups. These differences and the factors that give rise to them are explored in some detail in this chapter.

The Socialization Process

Socialization has been defined as the process by which the human organism is made into a person. Put in another way, it is the conversion of the infant from his original state of nature to his ultimate state as a "civilized" human being. It is an interactional relationship manifested primarily in the major social institutions. Through contacts such as those in the family, the church, the schools, and the economic world, the individual acquires the social and cultural traits that make him a functioning member of society. The folkways, the mores, and other cultural requirements, such as ideals, ideologies, attitudes, and values, are learned by the individual as he becomes socialized. In order to speed the learning process and to ensure conformity to accepted standards, a complicated system of rewards and punishments is continually in operation even in the simplest society. For example, in family groups everywhere the child is scolded or otherwise punished for disobedience or improper behavior. In contrast, he is praised or rewarded for conducting himself in the proper and accepted way. Those persons who fail to become socialized to the extent that they violate the mores are forcibly removed from the group as a menace; punishment, confinement to jail, and execution are some of the methods used to protect society from these unsocialized individuals. Less serious offenses are handled in different ways according to the custom of the particular groups. The account below tells how Amish parents in Pennsylvania solved a problem in the socialization of Amish youth.[1]

Amish parents, like other parents, find it a real problem to keep liquor completely out of the hands of young people. The nature of this problem, and an interesting attempt of the elders to cope with it, are illustrated by what is referred to as the "hotel deal" in Intercourse. At this town, where the young people usually gather on Sunday evenings before they go to the singings, there was a "hotel" until about three years ago; that is, an establishment in which liquor was sold. Against repeated instructions and admonitions, some horses and topless buggies continued to gather there and young men and their companions refreshed themselves before going to the singings. The Amish parents met several times to discuss the problem, and when a man was found who was willing to convert the "hotel" into a feed mill but lacked the required capital, they subsidized him. . . .

As we have seen, three major environmental influences—geographical, social, and cultural—account in the main for differences in behavior or socialization between groups and individuals. A knowledge of the special characteristics of the rural world is necessary to understand the difference between rural and urban societies. We shall base our discussion on the concept of the *rural-urban continuum.*

The Rural-Urban Continuum

There is some controversy among rural sociologists as to whether rural-urban differences occur in dichotomous fashion or along a continuum. Proponents of the former, more conventional theory hold that differences between the two populations are categoric in nature and in direct opposition to one another. Proponents of the continuum theory feel that rural-urban differences occur in relative degrees in a range extending between the two polar extremes of rural and urban. This view has received increasing attention in recent years and seems to the writer to be the more tenable position.[2] As T. Lynn Smith points out, rural

[1] Walter M. Kollmorgen, *The Old Order Amish of Lancaster County, Pennsylvania,* Washington: USDA Rural Life Studies, 4:81, September, 1947.

[2] For example, see: C. P. Loomis and J. A. Beegle, *Rural Social Systems,* New York: Prentice-Hall, Inc., 1950; I. A. Spaulding, "Serendipity and the Rural-Urban Continuum," *Rural Sociology,* 16:33, 1951; and John L. Haer, "Conservatism-Radicalism and the Rural-Urban Continuum," *Rural Sociology,* 17:343, 1952.

and urban characteristics do not exist in a vacuum.[3] The major characteristics of the one shade or blend into those of the other as the observer moves from the core areas of either.

In this chapter, rural-urban differences are discussed as matters of degree along a scale connecting two polar extremes. This understanding does not weaken or invalidate the position that rural-urban differences are real and definite. Rather it demonstrates that environmental influences are closely correlated to differences between these two groups. The more nearly "rural" or "urban" the environment, the greater the difference characterizing the persons or groups included in it.

THE INFLUENCE OF THE GEOGRAPHIC ENVIRONMENT

The geographic environment has four major aspects: location, climate, topography, and natural resources. All four are important influences on human life. The discussion below is designed to show the several ways in which the physical environment impinges on rural life and accounts for rural-urban differences.

The Physical Setting

The first and most obvious of the geographic influences that account for cultural differences is the physical setting, which causes differences between rural societies in different locations and between rural and urban societies in the same general location. One has only to contrast the inhabitants of hot, humid climates with the residents of arctic regions, or the people who live on gentle, rolling plains with the inhabitants of mountainous areas, to see how the physical setting accounts for differences in human societies. At the same time, the relative abundance of sunshine, food, water, clothing, shelter, good soil, useful minerals, and attractive topography are all aspects of the physical environment and all influence human behavior. The many differences in culture between rural areas which are attributable to variation in the physical environment are so obvious as to make enumeration unnecessary.

Physical setting also accounts for rural-urban differences, even though both groups within a given locality are subjected to the same general environment. The differentials come about because the rural person usually faces nature in its unmodified extremes and must wrest his living directly from it. In so doing he develops customs, practices, and personality traits compatible with his struggle with nature. The urbanite, on the other hand, seldom comes face to face with the extremes of his physical environment. He generally works indoors instead of outdoors, and when he works outdoors he has many ways to protect himself.

[3] *The Sociology of Rural Life,* 3d ed., New York: Harper & Brothers, 1953, p. 17.

Obviously the physical setting does not in any sense account for all the differences between cultures. It merely sets limits beyond which man cannot go. Within these limits, there is room for a great deal of variation, as we shall see in the discussion that follows.

The Capriciousness of Nature

This second geographic influence does much to differentiate the rural personality from the urban. The farmer, dependent as he is on the vicissitudes of weather, has a built-in element of uncertainty in his endeavor. He must expect, upon occasion, to see much of his year's work wiped out by a cloudburst, a hailstorm, or a plague of grasshoppers. He knows that sometimes it will rain when he needs sunshine, whereas at other times the sun will shine day in and day out until it burns up his crops. The farmer is no stranger to late freezes and early frosts, and in areas of relatively high technology, he attempts to protect his tender plants and fruit with smudge pots and paper cups. The following description of one of the "black blizzards" of the Northwest in which whole farms are swept away brings home the force with which the natural elements sometimes strike the farmer.[4]

Only those who have been caught in a "black blizzard" can have more than a faint conception of its terrors . . . the dust begins to blow with only a slight breeze. As it continues to rise into the air it becomes thicker and thicker, obscuring the landscape and continuing to grow in density until vision is reduced to a thousand yards or less. If this is to be a real dust storm, a typical black blizzard of the Dust Bowl, the wind increases its velocity until it is blowing at forty or fifty miles an hour. Soon everything is moving—the land is blowing, both farm land and pasture alike. The fine dirt is sweeping along at express-train speed, and when the very sun is blotted out, visibility is reduced to some 50 feet; or perhaps you cannot see at all. . . .

Thus it is when the observer is within the area of a storm's inception. At other times a cloud is seen to be approaching from a distance of many miles. Already it has the banked appearance of a cumulus cloud, but it is black instead of white, and it hangs low, seeming to hug the earth. Instead of being slow to change its form, it appears to be rolling on itself from the crest downward. As it sweeps onward, the landscape is progressively blotted out. Birds fly in terror before the storm, and only those that are strong of wing may escape. The smaller birds fly until they are exhausted, then fall to the ground, to share the fate of the thousands of jack rabbits which perish from suffocation.

Because he has to struggle against and endure the caprices of nature, the farmer is generally a more practical man than the city dweller. At

4 Svobida Lawrence, *An Empire of Dust,* Caldwell, Idaho: The Caxton Printers, Ltd., 1940, pp. 83–84; quoted in: Earl H. Bell, *Culture of a Contemporary Rural Community: Sublette, Kansas,* Washington: USDA Rural Life Studies, 2:15, September, 1942.

the same time, this aspect of his environment makes him more religious and more superstitious, as one result of his efforts to come to an understanding with the inscrutable powers with which he deals.

Close Communion with Nature

In contrast to his city cousins, the farmer does his work in the open in close association with the sun, the open air, the soil, and living, growing things. Various studies have shown that this close contact with the outdoors has been an important factor in maintaining the health of the agriculturist at a higher level than that of the city dweller. Beyond this, the farmer's close communion with nature develops in him a feeling for the open spaces away from crowds. Characteristically, he feels ill at ease and uncomfortable if he has to remain cooped up by indoor work. He also comes to commune with plants and animals almost as if they were animate and human. He takes pleasure in walking through his rows of corn or his herd of cattle and speaks of them with pride and feeling. His city neighbor has difficulty understanding this aspect of his behavior and would seldom enjoy the isolation from humans which accompanies it.

The close contact of the ruralite with the soil tends to make him view land as the most precious of possessions. This is another way in which his close communion with nature tends to set him apart. In this regard the farmer is quite frequently at a loss to understand the real estate dealer's attitude toward his land as having only an impersonal dollar value. All in all, there are many personality traits of the farmer which can be traced to his close association with nature.

Relative Isolation

One of the most obvious features of rural life is the low density of population. Although this factor in itself does not constitute a geographic influence, it is included under this heading because the nature of agriculture forces a low man-to-land ratio. It may be noted that modern means of transportation have greatly reduced the relative isolation of ruralites. Nevertheless, the country person continues to spend a great part of his time away from population centers, despite his ability to travel to them with relative ease.

The semi-isolation of the country dweller tends to affect his personality and culture in ways that are traceable to his lack of frequent outside social contacts. This isolation has two facets. The first concerns the availability of means of communication. Until recently the great distances between rural homes made it impractical to introduce good roads and telephone service. And although these facilities are now available in most areas, some rural families still do not have them.

The second way in which low density of population affects rural life concerns the many services that can be supported only by fairly large population aggregates. Thus the urbanite takes for granted such things as hospitals, which the ruralite does not have ready access to and therefore uses less frequently. The rural person is, of necessity, more self-reliant than his city neighbor. Distance also accounts in part for the fact that country people participate less in educational and social activities, and it keeps their outlook somewhat provincial in nature as compared with that of the urban dweller.

THE INFLUENCE OF THE SOCIAL ENVIRONMENT

The second major influence in socialization comes from the social environment, which consists of the groups and individuals with which a person interacts. As we saw in discussing the difference between various kinds of social groups, the number and characteristics of the in-groups, primary groups, and secondary groups with which a person is associated determine to a large extent his personality and behavior. It has been wisely said that it is possible to tell what kind of person an individual is if one knows the groups to which he belongs. The individual's personality is molded by the patterns of behavior required in his family, play, neighborhood, and other primary groups. It is here that he learns loyalty, devotion, sympathy, respect, and cooperation. Secondary groups represent more casual contacts and do not influence the personality so strongly as primary groups. Nevertheless, they extend the range of social contacts far beyond the primary group and give the individual more freedom of expression.

The Predominance of Primary-group Contacts

It is easy to see how the person whose associations are usually with primary groups might experience less loneliness and frustration and perhaps even develop a better integrated personality than the person whose contacts were mainly with secondary groups. On the other hand, the person who is active in secondary groups will probably be less narrow and localized in his outlook on life. It is significant that this is one of the major differences between rural and urban societies.

Despite increasing contacts with the outside world, the family continues to dominate the lives of its members in rural areas. This is true partly because of the relative isolation caused by geographic factors. It is more closely associated with the fact that farming generally is a family enterprise. Despite some specialization and division of labor among members of farm families, all are aware of and take part in the greater endeavor. This fact tends to produce a solidarity among family members that exists in few other occupations. Outside the family, the rural person's contacts are likely to be centered in the neighborhood or community. Here again, the stage is set for intimate associations. The farmer's neighbors engage in the same occupation, go to similar churches and schools, and, in general, live the same kind of lives as he. This is scarcely ever true in the urban setting.

With his associations more or less limited to family and neighborhood groups, the rural person is generally considered to be less broadminded than his city cousins. He is customarily characterized as conservative and traditional in his outlook and practices.

Social Differentiation

Not only are rural social groups more likely to be of the primary type, but they are fewer in number and less complex than urban groups. These diverging social environments account for a great deal of the difference between rural and urban communities. The difference in number and complexity of groups, as Smith points out, is closely associated with the differing origins of the rural and urban populations.[5] The city population, including as it does a large proportion of immigrants, contains a great variety of racial and cultural elements that constitute many divergent groups and create great social differentiation.

The heterogeneity of the city does not, however, imply lack of coordination or integration. The city merely functions in a different way from the rural community. In the urban setting, social solidarity is of the organic type, with integration based on specialization and a division of labor. In the rural setting, solidarity is of the mechanistic type, with homogeneity the key to integration (see Chapter 2).

Social Stratification

Although the principles of class and caste are the same for both rural and urban areas, there are a great many differences in the operation of these principles in the two groups. First, with regard to the relative complexity of the two types of societies, there are generally fewer strata or classes in rural society. Second, generally speaking, social extremes are greater in cities than in rural areas. In this regard, with the exception of areas characterized by large holdings, the rural social classes tend to be intermediate, or middle class. In other words, one is less likely to find the extremes represented by the millionaire and the relief client in the country than in the city. On the other hand, it is interesting that the caste principle is more rigid in rural areas than in urban areas. In India, for example, caste relations remain intact in rural areas

[5] Smith, *op. cit.*, p. 26.

long after they have been discarded in the cities. This phenomenon again suggests the conservatism of rural populations.[6]

Social Mobility

The circulation of people within a given strata or from one social strata to another is referred to as *social mobility*. Although this type of mobility is by no means absent in rural society, it exists on a much smaller scale than in urban society. The fact that there are fewer social classes and fewer occupations accounts in great part for this phenomenon.

MacIver and Page point out the great difference in socialization brought about by these different degrees of social mobility. They state that with greater mobility comes greater uncertainty, and this in turn makes the city a place where the individual's career is less foreordained than in the country. They also note that the maximization of opportunity for change is reflected in the degree to which urbanites patronize various forms of gambling, including the risking of secure positions and incomes for new ventures.[7] This fact helps to explain why ruralites take a rather stoical view of life and are less venturesome in most ways than urbanites.

THE INFLUENCES OF THE CULTURAL ENVIRONMENT

The third major influence in socialization comes from the cultural environment. In a way, social influences are a function of cultural influences. The basis for differentiation, however, is that only individuals are culture bearers. Thus a distinction can be made between those socialization factors that exist purely because of differences in the composition of society and those that come about because of differences in cultural orientation.

The cultural, or man-made, environment awaits the new-born infant as surely as and perhaps in a more positive way than the geographic environment. Culture patterns establish definite limits to behavior—norms, or expected behavior patterns. In this way, each society indirectly selects the type of personality that will be most successful in it.

It is important to realize that, in spite of the uniform influence of culture, no two persons have exactly the same personality, even though they may live in the same society. The reason for this phenomenon lies in the fact that every person participates differentially in his culture.

[6] For a comprehensive discussion of this aspect of the rural world, see: Smith, *op. cit.*, pp. 28–29.

[7] R. M. MacIver and Charles H. Page, *Society, An Introductory Analysis,* New York: Rinehart & Company, Inc., 1949, p. 323.

Despite certain universal features that exert a more or less uniform influence, each person has certain areas of experience which are unique to him, because no culture is ever transmitted in its entirety. The more complex the society, the greater the chance for personality differences. With these facts in mind, we may examine some of the different cultural influences in rural and urban areas.

Simplicity of Cultural Expressions

It can almost be stated as a fact without exception that cultural expressions in the country are simpler in form than those in the city. The folklore, folk expressions, folk songs, folk dances, and other types of expression are much less complicated than the parallel urban expressions of culture. One is led to the conclusion that sophistication, in connection with culture, is a monopoly of city people. When folk culture finds its way to urban centers, it is dressed in "city clothes" and loses its original forthrightness and simplicity. The "culture shock" which the ruralite sometimes experiences when moving to the city is understandable in terms of the more complex cultural environment. Simple virtues and moral and ethical standards lose their rural simplicity in the city and no longer gain unquestioning adherence. This fact accounts in no small part for rural-urban personality differences.

Social Control

In rural areas, order is maintained essentially through informal means. Thus neighborhood gossip and other devices come into play when a member of a rural society violates a code. When the less violent means of control do not suffice, recourse is had to more severe punishment. In rural areas, those offended are much more likely to do the punishing than in urban areas. This phenomenon is reflected in crime statistics for both rural and urban groups; homicide and aggravated assault are relatively more frequent in the rural setting. The rural culture dominates the law-enforcing institutions to the extent that they are characterized by autonomy and familistic procedures. The account of how Amish parents took a hand in checking the misdemeanors of their sons is illustrative.[8]

By holding the purse strings Amish parents exercise a rather effective control over the activities of the children up to the time of their marriage. Few parents give their children much spending money. This form of control evidently led to some petty crimes a few years ago and it is interesting to see how the resultant problems were solved.

Several young men, who wanted spending money, secretly took a few chickens from their families' chicken barns and sold them. This was repeated several

[8] Kollmorgen, *op. cit.,* p. 81.

times until a loss was noted by the parents and was reported to legal authorities. The nature of the theft was discovered, but the findings were given to the parents only. The report is that an understanding was then reached between a local official and the parents concerning corrective procedure. The local official gave the boys a strong lecture and declared that each was fined $50 to be produced immediately. As was expected, the boys had to go to their fathers, explain the situation, and ask for the money. The local official, according to the report, secretly returned the fines to the fathers. This procedure proved very effective, for it required the boys to make amends with the township official, the parents, and the church.

In contrast, impersonal law in the hands of police, courts, and other regulatory agencies maintain social control in the city.

Variety of Knowledge and Skills Required

Farming requires a great variety of knowledge and skills, and the successful farmer must be a Jack-of-all-trades. Not only must he understand the operation and care of machinery and equipment, but he must have some knowledge of the requirements of soils, plants, and animals and the prevention of plant and animal diseases; and he must be something of an expert in farm management and marketing. These requirements make the farmer closely acquainted with many aspects of material culture. In contrast, the city person, although he may have a deep understanding of the one particular part of culture in which he specializes, has little opportunity to understand all the aspects of a complex business such as farming.

Levels and Standards of Living

Cultural usage is reflected to a large extent in the home. The absence or presence of certain items, such as washing machines and television sets (see Fig. 1), determines both the level of living and the degree of participation in the culture. Studies of this nature point up two things. The first is that rural areas enjoy a lower level of living then urban areas, on the average. This accounts in some measure for the urban attitude of superiority, which is almost universal. The second is the different emphasis on cultural items as a result of different needs or values. For example, the clothes the ruralite wears are designed for the work he does and are different from the clothes the urbanite dons for work. To carry this illustration further, the farmer might feel out of place wearing a dinner jacket to a party, while the average city dweller would not be at ease attending a social function attired in cowboy boots and a wide-brimmed hat, as many farmers and ranchers do. Beyond this, the relative simplicity and agricultural orientation of rural

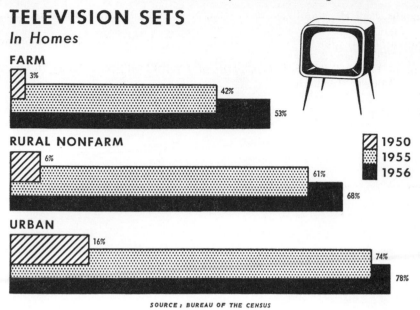

TELEVISION SETS
In Homes

FARM

3%

42%

53%

RURAL NONFARM

6%

61%

68%

1950
1955
1956

URBAN

16%

74%

78%

SOURCE : BUREAU OF THE CENSUS

U. S. DEPARTMENT OF AGRICULTURE NEG. 56 (10)-339 AGRICULTURAL RESEARCH SERVICE

Figure 1. Trends in television sets in homes in the United States, 1950, 1955, and 1956. The differentials between farm and nonfarm groups in the possession of television sets illustrates differences in cultural participation at given points of time.

culture does not bring to the attention of the ruralite many of the goods and services that the urbanite knows about and consequently feels he needs.

Questions for Review and Discussion

1. What does the social scientist have in mind when he refers to the socialization process?

2. Name and explain the influence of the three major environmental factors that account for differences in behavior between groups and individuals.

3. How might his close communion with nature affect the farmer's personality?

4. How are law and order usually maintained in rural society? In urban society?

5. What is meant by (a) the rural-urban continuum, (b) folk culture, (c) social mobility?

Selected References for Supplementary Reading

Kolb, John H., and Edmund de S. Brunner: *A Study of Rural Society*, Boston: Houghton Mifflin Company, 1952, chap. 1.

Landis, Paul H.: *Rural Life in Process,* New York: McGraw-Hill Book Company, Inc., 1948, chaps. 5–7.

Nelson, Lowry: *Rural Sociology,* 2d ed., New York: American Book Company, 1955, chap. 2.

Smith, T. Lynn: *The Sociology of Rural Life,* 3d ed., New York: Harper & Brothers, 1953, chap. 2.

CHAPTER 4 *Rural Social Values and Norms*

This chapter, the last in Part One, completes our introduction to the sociology of rural life. It is devoted to values and norms, which are of fundamental importance in understanding the behavior of individuals and groups.

Someone has said that man is a slave to his ideas. This means that each individual has a set of ideas that in large part determine what he likes and dislikes. Some of these ideas are developed in early associations with parents and siblings; others are learned in the everyday experiences of later life. Some are deeply fixed and seldom questioned; others can be easily replaced when the individual discovers more appropriate or satisfying ones. These ideas are shared by sets of individuals, or groups, which vary in size and in the intensity of the feeling that brings them into being. This sharing of ideas is basic to the functioning of modern society, for without it there could be no agreement as to what should be done or how it should be done; a chaotic state of affairs would prevail in society, each individual following his own ends and desires, which, all too often, would conflict with those of others.

Ideas as to whether objects or behavior are good, bad, desirable, or the like are called *values,* and the rules that govern action directed toward achieving values are called *norms.* People are expected to behave in accordance with the values held by the groups to which they belong, and this "expected" behavior is normative behavior. Farmers, for example, consider it of great importance that cattle other than their own shall not browse on their crops, and they share the expectation that each farmer will build fences and keep his livestock within them. Such effectively charged preferences constitute values, and the expectation as to what should be done is normative. A value then is an idea held by a group of individuals and indicating preference in a situation; and a norm is an idea that can be put in the form of a statement indicating what should be done under certain conditions. "It is the expected be-

35

havior of a number of men." [1] In discussing behavior, it is impossible to separate these terms, and for this reason they are considered together in this chapter.

INTERNALIZED VALUES AND NORMS

Although values and norms are learned, many of them become a part of the subconscious, so that they provide a basis for virtually automatic reaction. Many norms, for example, are not rules of behavior which have an independent existence apart from the individual; rather, they are internalized to the extent of being part of his make-up. Such norms form the basis for conscience, and violation of them can result in deep feelings of guilt or shame. The psychiatrist, in his efforts to aid the mentally ill, frequently tries to probe the patient's internalized values and norms in a search for conflicts among them which can produce personality disturbances.

This does not mean that each individual in a group or society possesses the same values and norms or that shared values are held with equal intensity. In fact, the opposite is true. Evidence for this is the fact that certain individuals suffer from nonconforming behavior more than others. Thus the magnitude of the reaction of a particular individual to nonconformity in his behavior is closely associated with the degree to which he has internalized certain norms associated with such behavior. A deeply religious person, for example, would probably experience more discomfort at the violation of a religious norm than would a person with less intensive religious training and with less conviction regarding the importance of religious sanctions.

Violations of norms may be either willful and deliberate or inadvertent. Generally, people do not choose to violate normative patterns of behavior, but circumstance and human frailty may prevent one's behaving according to his ideas. This disparity between ideal and actual behavior constitutes a serious barrier to the understanding of other peoples and cultures. In the field of political science it is well known that a group of people or a nation may be of uniform opinion on a particular issue but may behave in a quite unexpected way when given an opportunity to act, as in voting at the polls. A parent may tell his child what he should do under certain conditions, when he would actually be disappointed if the child did as he was told. Probably most mothers take some pride in the fact that their children do not behave in the schoolroom precisely as directed.

[1] George C. Homans, *The Human Group,* New York: Harcourt, Brace and Company, Inc., 1950, p. 124.

DOMINANT VALUES AND NORMS

The study of values is complicated, as we have seen, by the fact that individuals vary in the extent to which they assimilate values. In addition, it is further complicated by the fact that values vary in the intensity with which people adhere to them and in the diffuseness or specificity of their meaning. Some are of little significance; hence their violation elicits little individual or group sanction. Others, however, are considered basic to the welfare of the group, and their violation is censured accordingly. The former are generally values that concern preferences among alternate courses of action in everyday activities; that is, certain means to attaining certain ends are preferred over others. The more basic or "ultimate" values are considered good in themselves, and failure to behave in terms of them may be considered a threat to the well-being of the group. Among these are values associated with the more fundamental aspects of human welfare, such as honesty, respect for the rights of the individual, and a whole series of attitudes associated with sex and family life. A key to the nature of ultimate values lies in individual reactions to violations. It is usually the violation of the more deeply ingrained values that brings severe reproach from the group and if associated with guilt, personality problems for the individual.

Every group of people, whether they constitute a neighborhood or a nation, has a set of dominant or ultimate values within the framework of which the behavior of members is influenced or controlled. In our society, some of these dominant values include "the dignity of the individual, equality of opportunity, the right to life, liberty, and the pursuit of happiness, and growth of the free personality." [2] These values serve as a background for others, of less fundamental importance, which govern everyday behavior. Accepting, for example, the basic idea (value) that one should be permitted to pursue ends that will bring happiness would also entail acceptance of lesser values governing the selection of an occupation or of a spouse.

Accompanying the dominant values are a set of dominant norms, or rules that uphold the values. These norms serve as motivating forces influencing action in the desired direction. For example, people are expected to contribute to the welfare of the community whose benefits they enjoy. Those who can afford it may be expected to pay taxes to support the public school system and to provide for the building and maintenance of public roads, and definite rules are usually devised to assure that the "expected" actually comes to pass. The system of ulti-

[2] Robin M. Williams, *American Society,* New York: Alfred A. Knopf, Inc., 1954, p. 513.

mate or dominant values and the rules that prevent their being disregarded assure the individual that he can pursue his interests within the limits of group welfare. Without rules and values, this would not be possible.

CLASSIFICATION OF VALUES AND NORMS

For purposes of clarity and simplicity, norms may be classified as belonging to several types. This task is not easy, however, because the classifier tends to evaluate the data according to preconceived standards: meaning, for example, or the severity of the sanctions applied when the norms are violated.

The method commonly used for classifying norms is to divide them into the three broad categories described in Chapter 2: folkways, mores, and law. Folkways, it will be recalled, are informal rules of behavior based on habit and tradition. They are founded in usage, since they are the "folkway" of doing something. For example, there may be no *rules* concerning wearing shoes in a particular society, but if everyone who can afford it wears shoes, then wearing them is expected. In much of Latin America, a visitor to the house of a farmer may expect to be served coffee, whether the visit occurs in the morning, in the afternoon, or at night. There is no written rule about serving coffee, but it is expected, and most of the farmers would feel that their behavior was not proper if they did not conform.

Mores, too, are rules that have, for the most part, been handed down from parents to children as a part of their training. These rules, as we have already seen, are less flexible than folkways, since they are supported by religion and the religion-based morals with which they are associated. Because of their more fundamental linkage with group welfare, they are less likely to be violated than are folkways, and the violator incurs more drastic sanction. Individuals *must* conform to the mores. They provide the frame of reference for right and wrong. They are extremely rigid and are changed very slowly, if at all, since any threat to them is likely to be interpreted as endangering the group's very existence. Few individuals dare attack them directly. Some of the mores, such as those surrounding incest or parental responsibility for offspring, are not even open to free discussion. Some are converted into law in order to ensure enforcement.

Law is often the last step in the formalization of the rules of conduct, since not only are they made clear and explicit by appearing in written form, but machinery such as the police and the courts is established to see that they are enforced. Law is considered to be of basic importance to the functioning of society and the protection of the citizenry. Rules of law may be the formal result of action by courts or legislators, or they may be only implied and inferred from past action of the courts. These two types have been referred to as *enacted* and as *customary* law.[3]

THE FUNCTION OF VALUES AND NORMS

The study and observation of values and norms have, by the very nature of the subject, presented difficulties to researchers in the social sciences. Actually, sociologists are not yet in complete agreement on the legitimacy of trying to determine the specific nature of the values of society and their various levels of intensity. This does not mean that sociologists doubt the existence of values but rather that they raise questions about their concreteness and specificity. Is it possible, for example, to determine how much one desires a new car or new furniture in his house and whether either or both of these would be preferred to a piece of land or better health? A variety of conditions and situations, the influence of friends and associates, and the way one feels at a given moment may determine one's choice. Some of the extraneous factors influencing these choices are controllable, but most of them can be discovered only in experimental or laboratory situations.

The study of values is simplified somewhat by thinking of them not as isolated, individual ideas held by certain individuals and rejected by others but rather as interwoven in a system that, like a machine or an organism, is considerably more than the sum of its parts. Honesty, hard work, thrift, and independence may be generally diffused as values throughout the American scene; in varying degrees of importance, these values, in combination with a number of others, form a pattern, or configuration, which is characteristically American. The importance of any single value in the pattern will vary from one group or subculture of American society to another, but the variation will not be sufficient to change the configuration. The value orientation of a particular community of farmers in the Southwest may fail to include one or more of the dominant values of American society, or in the orientation a specific value may have an unimportant place; but if the remainder of the values of the configuration are present, the orientation can still be identified as American.

Within certain limits, the value system of a specific group will determine the behavior of the group in response to specific stimuli. American travelers in Latin America, for example, have frequently noted the centralization of action and thought in the capital cities of these countries

---

[3] Kingsley Davis, *Human Society,* New York: The Macmillan Company, 1949, p. 59.

and especially in the offices of the presidents of the countries and their advisers. This is in contrast to most parts of the United States, where localities are likely to regard their own resources as the basis for initiating action and then formulating the plans for carrying it out. In the Latin American countries, it would be an extremely arduous task to convince the people that they themselves should undertake the construction of a school or church. This, they would probably argue, should be left to the central government. On the other hand, residents of a Middle Western community might object if it were suggested that the Federal government should intervene in the construction of local schools and churches. The difference lies in the values held by the people. That which would be considered correct and proper in the one case would be interpreted as rash interference in the other.

During recent years, several studies concerning the function of values in the introduction of technology on the farm have contributed to our knowledge of values and their role in rural community life. It has been demonstrated that a specific set of values may be the key factor in the acceptance or rejection by a group of rural families of an innovation whose results have not been concretely demonstrated to the community. This phenomenon will be discussed at length in Chapter 25. A detailed study of two rural communities in the Southwest revealed that a whole series of diverging reactions of the two groups in concrete social situations were associated with their particular system of values. A Mormon community, for example, deeply prizing cooperation at the community level, was able to achieve enviable goals in building roads, paving streets, and constructing a gymnasium. Another community, of equal size and resources but valuing individual rather than community initiative, was unable to achieve these same goals. This does not mean that the value systems were completely different, for both were rural communities of the Southwest sharing many common American values. Rather, the difference was a matter of emphasis; one of the communities strongly emphasized cooperation, whereas the other had recourse to community action only as a last resort. In the words of the authors: [4]

While Rimrock [the Mormon Community] and Homestead share most of the central value-orientations of general American culture, they differ significantly in the values governing social relationships. Rimrock, with a stress upon community cooperation, an ethnocentrism resulting from the notion of their own peculiarity, and a village pattern of settlement (endorsed by the Church), is more like the other Mormon villages of the West. . . . The stress upon community cooperation in Rimrock contrasts markedly with the stress upon

[4] Evon Z. Vogt and Thomas F. O'Dea, "Comparative Study of the Role of Values in Social Action," *American Sociological Review*, 18(6):648, 1953.

individual independence found in Homestead. This contrast is one of emphasis. . . . In Rimrock, however, the expectations are such that one must show his fellows, or at least convince himself, that he has good cause for not committing his time and resources to community efforts while in Homestead cooperative action takes place only after certainty has been reached that the claims of other individuals upon one's time and resources are legitimate.

The receptivity of these communities to change was thus a function of their value systems.

The conclusions of a study of two New England communities were that the contrasting behavior of the communities was associated with their different sets of dominant community values. Changes effected in the two communities were invariably found to be associated with values involving community interest and responsibility. A conclusion of the study was that an understanding of the values of the communities provided a basis for understanding community behavior and even for predicting it.[5]

VALUE SYSTEMS IN AMERICA

Discerning visitors to the United States soon realize that the culture of the New World involves values that are in singular contrast to those of the Old. This should not be surprising in view of the contrasts in environmental conditions and the intermingling in the New World of culturally distinct groups that have come from every corner of the globe. It is not difficult to see these contrasts, but it is an exacting task to identify and describe them precisely. Many attempts to do so have called attention only to values of little importance; or the values were described at such a general and abstract level as to be of but little effective worth.

One European visitor who analyzed behavior in the United States came to the following conclusions: [6]

"Quantity" in America is not a fact, as with us; it is a value. To say that something is large, massive, gigantic, is in America, not a mere statement of fact, but the highest commendation.

In Europe, at least in intellectual circles, such terms as mechanical or machine-made are employed as terms of censure, which are opposed to "organic" or "artistic." In the same way the word "technique" seems often to savor of the superficial, unintellectual, and inartistic. The average American sets an absolute and positive value on technique. . . . Technique is not, as it would be in theory, a means to an end, but is becoming an end in itself.

[5] Richard E. Du Wors, "Persistence and Change in Local Values of Two New England Communities," *Rural Sociology*, 17:207–217, 1952.
[6] Richard Muller-Frecenfels, "The Mechanization and Standardization of American Life," in Logan Wilson and William L. Kolb, *Sociological Analysis*, New York: Harcourt, Brace and Company, Inc., 1949, p. 147.

These succinct statements about American culture may not be completely accurate; however, they suggest some of the charged preferences that motivate American behavior as seen by an outsider. In further identifying dominant American values, the same author finds that: [7]

In the case of "quantification" and "mechanization," as in that of typification, we are confronted by a different valuation. Distance, uniqueness, and originality are European values, which are foreign to the American. His values are the reverse of these—adherence to type, agreement, similarity. . . . There the only difference that counts is a man's quantitative achievements and success, which in the last resort is expressed in dollars.

One of the difficulties in identifying the dominant values in American culture is that many values carrying deep emotional significance are dominant only in certain regions, among members of particular ethnic groups, or even among certain classes. Some sociologists would probably argue that variations in the meaning of specific values between groups are so extreme that it is impossible to resolve the problem empirically. Are there valid criteria, then, for finding dominant American values? Actually, the answer is that many different sets of criteria could be used, and each would be valid if certain premises are assumed.

A large number of sociologists and anthropologists have compiled lists of values in American society. Three of these are as follows:

Classification No. 1 [8]

1. Monogamous marriage
2. Freedom
3. Acquisitiveness
4. Democracy
5. Education
6. Monotheistic religion
7. Freedom and science

Classification No. 2 [9]

1. Associational activity
2. Democracy (and belief and faith in it)
3. Equality as a fact and right
4. Local government
5. Practicality
6. Puritanism

[7] *Ibid.*, p. 150.

[8] John F. Cuber and Robert Harper, *Problems of American Society: Values in Conflict*, 3d ed., New York: Henry Holt and Company, Inc., 1956, pp. 486–487.

[9] Lee Coleman, "What Is American: A Study of Alleged American Traits," *Social Forces*, 14:498, 1941.

7. Uniformity and conformity
8. Freedom of the individual in ideal and in fact
9. Disregard of law; "direct action"
10. Prosperity and general material well-being
11. Emphasis on religion and its great influence in national life

Classification No. 3 [10]

1. Achievement and success
2. Activity and work
3. Moral orientation
4. Humanitarianism
5. Efficiency and practicality
6. Progress
7. Material comfort
8. Equality
9. Freedom
10. External conformity
11. Science and secular rationality
12. Nationalism, patriotism
13. Democracy
14. Individual personality
15. Racism and related group-superiority themes

Although these lists overlap at certain points, it is evident that they are not in complete agreement on the elements constituting the "core" of the American value pattern. However, this lack of agreement is less a contradiction than an indication that the configuration of American values is composed of numerous, sometimes heterogeneous, items, some of which may be absent or relatively dormant in a particular area or group. Although one could hardly doubt that local self-government, for example, constitutes a value in American culture, it would certainly rank higher in the hierarchy of values of certain rural communities than in other areas. Also, presumably certain values remain latent in particular communities or among specific groups until brought to the fore by special circumstances or crises considered to threaten the welfare or safety of the group.

Values and Norms of Rural America

Any attempt to define the system of values of rural America involves the question of whether or not it is legitimate to distinguish between the rural and urban civilizations. The point of view of the authors of this book was presented in Chapter 3. It may be repeated, however, that there are two distinct schools of thought associated with the idea

[10] Williams, *op. cit.*, pp. 388–440.

of a unique rural America. For example, one of the outstanding rural sociologists of the United States claims that "farm folk differ from urban people, and rural society from urban society" and offers substantial evidence to support this claim.[11] On the other hand, it has been argued that the terms rural and urban are no longer meaningful and useful when applied to the United States, since the country has now become culturally urban; i.e., the rural folk can no longer be distinguished in dress, speech, habits, and values from the urban. Although the nation is culturally more uniform now than in colonial times, those individuals who maintain that major differences have disappeared tend to overlook the fact that many rural areas in the United States still retain strict Early American values.

Numerous techniques have been devised to test the validity of rural-urban differences. Loomis and Beegle use sets of linear and polar devices in terms of which any group can be gauged.[12] The procedure is first to establish the values or value orientation and then classify groups in terms of them. This exercise accepts the premise of a rural-urban continuum, which was discussed in Chapter 3. Frequently urban, middle-class values are chosen as the standard or base values.

Application of this method reveals that rural family values are changing, following the pattern established by the urban families, and family relationships are becoming more "contractual" and impersonal in nature. Greater emphasis, for example, is placed upon farming as a business and less upon farming as a way of life. A commercialized market for commodities and labor replaces the old system of barter. Individual relations, especially those outside the immediate family circle, are becoming less personalized—i.e., of less concern to the group—with the concomitant result that violation of local norms becomes easier and censure and sanction for the violations less severe.

Another method of comparing values is the "trend to rationality" first treated by Max Weber.[13] According to Weber, man has come to depend more and more on his rational knowledge in carrying on his everyday affairs and less upon superstition, faith, and the supernatural. Thus tradition and custom play roles of decreasing importance in directing behavior, and confidence in empirical observations and analysis increases. Experimentation becomes the criterion for accepting innovations in farming and home practices, and economic efficiency, within limits of

[11] T. Lynn Smith, *The Sociology of Rural Life*, 3d ed., New York: Harper & Brothers, 1953, chaps. 2 and 3.

[12] For a theoretical treatment of this method, see: Talcott Parsons, *The Social System*, Glencoe, Ill.: The Free Press, 1951, pp. 36–45, 180–200, 350–351. For an attempt to apply scales within polar categories, see: Charles P. Loomis and J. Allan Beegle, *Rural Social Systems*, New York: Prentice-Hall, Inc., 1950, pp. 789–824.

[13] Max Weber, *Essays in Sociology*, translated and edited, with an introduction by H. H. Berth and C. Wright Mills, New York: Oxford University Press, 1946, p. 293.

costs, becomes the test of their worth. Rain becomes a consequence of air movements and pressure areas rather than the result of the good or poor behavior of the local people; planting time becomes a function of moisture and temperature rather than cycles of the moon, whereas plant diseases, insects, and pests are combated through the application of scientific methods that are available to those who care to acquire and use them.

Evidences of increasing "rationalization of life conduct" as defined by Weber are found in areas other than the purely economic, and it is in these areas that modifications of the value systems may find greatest resistance among the rural population. It is generally agreed, for example, that the recent decrease in birth rates in the Western World is due, in large part, to the effective use of birth-control devices, i.e., rational means of control.

The failure of rural families to follow immediately upon the heels of the urban, middle-class families in changing their values and accepting the associated new methods and techniques is the result of many factors, both rational and irrational. The acceptance or rejection of birth-control devices, for example, is associated with an assortment of factors, such as the economic value placed upon children, the availability of reliable educational information on the use or effectiveness of the devices, and the cost and difficulties associated with their use.

The restraining influence of deeply established values is generally evident when impending change touches upon such vital social areas as the family, the church, and the school.[14] This is particularly evident in the behavior of certain religious groups, such as the Mormons and the Roman Catholics, among whom sanctions regarding birth control are especially severe. Deep-seated religious values, reinforced periodically by the church, still operate so effectively in most Latin American countries that neither the urban nor the rural birth rate has shown appreciable decline, although information concerning birth-control devices is now circulated throughout these countries with little restriction.

A recent study conducted at the University of Kentucky, based upon numerous public-opinion polls, indicates that the differences in values between rural and urban America are much more evident in some areas than in others. Questions aimed at determining the opinions of farmers revealed that their views were at one extreme or the other as compared with other groups in the population. For example, they had the largest percentage favoring prohibition, wanting membership in the Communist party forbidden, and preferring standard to daylight-saving time. They had the smallest percentage, however, favoring social security for farmers, a national health program, universal military training, and Negro-

14 Loomis and Beegle, *op. cit.*, p. 72.

white equality in job opportunities.[15] In other areas their opinions as a group were not distinguishable from other segments of the general population.

Probably most students of the subject would agree that at present the trend of rural America is away from the traditional values that have so long characterized it and toward the more rationalistic values associated with the "urban middle class." This is certainly due in part to the inadequacies farm people are finding in their traditional values in meeting the exigencies of contemporary living. This, of course, is the basis for any sort of change, since only those innovations are inviting which promise to bring about more efficiently the same or some equally satisfying result. The trend in the United States, especially during the past thirty years, has been a constant, if somewhat sporadic, movement from the farm to the city. This obviously has forced major adjustments in the value orientations of the migrants which would make possible their assimilation into the normative structure of urban activities.

The dissemination of urban, middle-class values to the rural population has been aided tremendously by improved roads and transportation systems permitting easy contact between urban and rural peoples and greater economic interaction between farm and city. Town and city merchants have become increasingly aware of the buying potential of the farmer, who, with his increased agricultural production, has become more and more interested in factory-produced goods, which the press, radio, and now television have convinced him he needs. Although empirical evidence is lacking, one might well assume that a distinct set of values will soon be a memory rather than a fact in American rural life. This is an important conjecture in terms of understanding the rural life of the future.

With regard to the present, however, W. A. Anderson's studies of values in rural life, although limited to a sample of adults and youths in New York State, are extremely revealing. They clearly indicate the persistence of rural values to the present time. Through the use of an opinion scale, Anderson was able to determine that rural life was considered most favorable (1) for rearing children, (2) for healthful living, and (3) for obtaining the necessary facilities for a good level of living.[16] Thus, at the present time, the student must take into considera-

---

[15] Howard W. Beers, "Rural-Urban Differences: Some Evidence from Public Opinion Polls," *Rural Sociology*, 18:1–11, 1953. See also Eugene A. Wilkening, "Techniques of Assessing Farm Family Values," *Rural Sociology*, 19:38–49, 1954.

[16] Anderson's studies have been published as a series of Cornell University AES Memoirs and Bulletins and as Cornell University Department of Rural Sociology bulletins. For a summary of his findings, see: W. A. Anderson, *A Study of the Values in Rural Living*, part VII, "Summary," Ithaca: Cornell University AES Rural Sociology Publication 34, 1952.

tion distinct rural social values and norms if he is to understand fully the behavior of ruralites.

Questions for Review and Discussion

1. Define social values and norms, being careful to distinguish between the two.
2. What is meant by the term internalized values?
3. List the values dominant in your home community.
4. How do values account for the behavior of individuals in given situations?
5. List at least five "core" values in American society.
6. What are some of the differences between rural and urban values?
7. Do you think rural and urban values will continue to remain distinct? Defend your answer.

Selected References for Supplementary Reading

Beers, Howard W.: "Rural-Urban Differences: Some Evidence from Public Opinion Polls," *Rural Sociology,* 18:1–11, 1953.

Coleman, Lee: "What Is American: A Study of Alleged American Traits," *Social Forces,* 14:498ff., 1941.

Cuber, John F., and Robert A. Harper: *Problems of American Society: Values in Conflict,* New York: Henry Holt and Company, Inc., 1948, part III.

Green, Arnold W.: *Sociology,* 2d ed., New York: McGraw-Hill Book Company, Inc., 1956, chap. 8.

Williams, Robin M.: *American Society,* New York: Alfred A. Knopf, Inc., 1951, chap. 11.

The Rural Population and Rural Locality Groups

It is logical that the student's first questions regarding a population group center around its numbers and composition. Indeed, such information is basic to most types of sociological inquiry. After demographic facts (those pertaining to the study of human populations) have been ascertained, the spatial relations and locality groupings of the population take on significance for the student.

Part Two will present information on these subjects. Chapter 5 is devoted to a description of the composition and characteristics of the rural population of the United States and provides a foundation for many of the discussions that follow. Locality-group structure and function and neighborhood and community trends are discussed in Chapter 6. This discussion sets the stage for consideration of community-development programs in Chapter 7, which deserves the attention of all persons interested in community-improvement efforts. Chapter 8, the final one in Part Two, is concerned with the regional approach to the study of rural populations. It includes an introduction to regional theory, along with a description of the rural regions of the United States.

CHAPTER 5 *The Rural Population*

The basic element of a society is its people. An analysis of social life must, therefore, start with the population to which it is related. This chapter is designed to provide the student with basic demographic facts about the rural people of the United States, and these facts will constitute a frame of reference for the study of the various rural social structures and processes presented in subsequent chapters. The rural population will be analyzed demographically from four points of view: number and distribution; composition and characteristics; the nature of the vital processes among rural people; and rural population trends.

The material is presented in a precise and summary fashion, and a comparative approach is used to give the student insight into the basic differences between the major segments of the population of the United States. Thus comparisons are made between rural and urban or Negro and white populations where these are important. The data that serve as a basis for analysis are primarily from the 1950 census of the population of the United States and from the publications of the Bureau of Vital Statistics.

NUMBER AND DISTRIBUTION

Number: The Population of the United States Is Predominantly Urban.

The Bureau of the Census conducts annual surveys to determine major changes in the population of the United States. However, since these special surveys are not so detailed and reliable as the decennial censuses, the data in this chapter are primarily from the 1950 census.

In 1950, the population of the United States was 150,697,361 persons. Of this number, 20,048,350 (15.3 per cent) were farm residents. (The census estimate of April, 1957, placed the rural-farm population at 12.0 per cent of the total population.) As indicated earlier, the designation "rural-nonfarm" is used in the census to identify persons residing in the

51

open country and villages but not on farms. These persons numbered 31,181,325 (20.7 per cent of the total population) in 1950. Many persons consider the rural-nonfarm population as a component part of the rural society, although only a small proportion (8.5 per cent) of this group is related directly (by employment) to agriculture.[1]

The majority of the people of the United States are urban. The 1950 census indicated that almost two-thirds of the nation's people—96,467,686 persons—lived in cities at that time. This makes the urban way of life numerically dominant in modern American society.

Distribution: Farm People Are Concentrated in the South and in the Corn Belt.

The rural-farm population is of much greater relative importance in some areas of the country than in others. Table 1 shows the distribution of the population of the United States in 1950 by residence and region. An analysis of these data clearly shows that the East South Central region has the largest proportion of rural-farm people. In this region, farm persons made up 35.3 per cent of the total population. The West North Central region had the second largest proportion of farmers (26.5 per cent), followed by the West South Central (22.1 per cent), and the South Atlantic (21.9 per cent) regions.

Individual states with large proportions of their populations residing on farms in 1950 are Mississippi (50.3 per cent), Arkansas (42.0 per cent), and North Dakota (41.1 per cent). No other state had as many as 40.0 per cent of its people living on farms. However, six other states had more than 30.0 per cent of their populations classified as farm residents: South Dakota, North Carolina, South Carolina, Kentucky, Tennessee, and Alabama.

In some parts of the nation, the rural-nonfarm population assumes considerable importance. In the South Atlantic region, for instance, 29.1 per cent of the people were classified as rural-nonfarm residents in 1950. The Mountain states had the second largest proportion of their inhabitants in this classification (28.2 per cent). In the East South Central region, about one-fourth (25.6 per cent) of the people were rural-nonfarm residents.

From the standpoint of the individual states, West Virginia ranked first relatively in rural-nonfarm residents, as almost one-half (44.9 per cent) of its population was so classified. This high percentage probably reflects the importance of the coal-mining industry in that state. Vermont ranked second among the states in percentage (42.1 per cent) of inhabitants classified as rural-nonfarm. In only thirteen other states did the

[1] See: Luke Ebersole, *American Society*, New York: McGraw-Hill Book Company, Inc., 1955, p. 136.

Table 1. Population of the United States, 1950, by Residence
(New Census Definitions Utilized)

Area	Urban		Rural-nonfarm		Rural-farm	
	Number	Per cent	Number	Per cent	Number	Per cent
United States..................	96,467,686	64.0	31,181,325	20.7	23,048 350	15.3
New England..................	7,101,511	76.2	1,809,845	19.4	403,100	4.4
Maine......................	472,000	51.7	319,946	35.0	121,828	13.3
New Hampshire.............	306,806	57.5	179,266	33.6	47,170	8.9
Vermont....................	137,612	36.4	159,003	42.1	81,132	21.5
Massachusetts..............	3,959,239	84.4	651,299	13.9	79,976	1.7
Rhode Island..............	667,212	84.3	114,346	14.4	10,338	1.3
Connecticut.................	1,558,642	77.7	385,982	19.2	62,656	3.1
Middle Atlantic...............	24,271,689	80.5	4,503,683	14.9	1,388,161	4.6
New York..................	12,682,446	85.5	1,570,092	10.6	577,654	3.9
New Jersey.................	4,186,207	86.6	543,822	11.2	105,300	2.2
Pennsylvania...............	7,403,036	70.5	2,389,769	22.8	705,207	6.7
East North Central...........	21,185,713	69.7	5,510,241	18.1	3,703,414	12.2
Ohio.......................	5,578,274	70.2	1,515,265	19.1	853,088	10.7
Indiana....................	2,357,196	59.9	909,874	23.1	667,154	17.0
Illinois....................	6,759,271	77.6	1,189,709	13.7	763,196	8.7
Michigan..................	4,503,084	70.7	1,173,940	18.4	694,742	10.9
Wisconsin..................	1,987,888	57.9	721,453	21.0	725,234	21.1
West North Central...........	7,305,219	52.0	3,027,024	21.5	3,729,151	26.5
Minnesota..................	1,624,914	54.5	617,770	20.7	739,799	24.8
Iowa.......................	1,250,938	47.7	587,485	22.4	782,650	29.9
Missouri...................	2,432,715	61.5	658,442	16.6	863,496	21.9
North Dakota..............	164,817	26.6	200,332	32.3	254,487	41.1
South Dakota..............	216,710	33.2	182,485	28.0	253,545	38.8
Nebraska..................	621,905	46.9	312,170	23.6	391,435	29.5
Kansas.....................	993,220	52.1	468,340	24.6	443,739	23.3
South Atlantic................	10,391,163	49.0	6,158,176	29.1	4,632,996	21.9
Delaware...................	199,122	62.6	84,738	26.6	34,225	10.8
Maryland..................	1,615,902	69.0	543,623	23.2	183,476	7.8
Washington, D.C............	802,178	100.0				
Virginia....................	1,560,115	47.0	1,026,604	30.9	731,961	22.1
West Virginia..............	694,487	34.6	900,143	44.9	410,922	20.5
North Carolina.............	1,368,101	33.7	1,317,268	32.4	1,376,560	33.9
South Carolina.............	777,921	36.7	638,495	30.2	700,611	33.1
Georgia....................	1,559,447	45.3	922,696	26.8	962,435	27.9
Florida....................	1,813,890	65.5	724,609	26.1	232,806	8.4
East South Central...........	4,484,771	39.1	2,944,336	25.6	4,048,074	35.3
Kentucky..................	1,084,070	36.8	886,566	30.1	974,170	33.1
Tennessee..................	1,452,602	44.1	822,912	25.0	1,016,204	30.9
Alabama...................	1,340,937	43.8	760,313	24.8	960,493	31.4
Mississippi.................	607,162	27.9	474,545	21.8	1,097,207	50.3
West South Central...........	8,079,828	55.6	3,243,129	22.3	3,214,615	22.1
Arkansas...................	630,591	33.0	477,093	25.0	801,827	42.0
Louisiana..................	1,471,696	54.8	644,365	24.0	567,455	21.2
Oklahoma..................	1,139,481	51.0	540,804	24.2	553,066	24.8
Texas......................	4,838,060	62.7	1,580,867	21.8	1,202,267	16.8

Table 1. Population of the United States, 1950, by Residence (New Census Definitions Utilized) (*Continued*)

Area	Urban		Rural-nonfarm		Rural-farm	
	Number	Per cent	Number	Per cent	Number	Per cent
Mountain....................	2,785,888	54.9	1,430,508	28.2	858,602	16.9
Montana...................	258,034	43.7	197,051	33.3	135,939	23.0
Idaho.....................	252,549	42.9	171,128	29.1	164,960	28.0
Wyoming.................	144,618	49.8	89,207	30.7	56,704	19.5
Colorado..................	831,318	62.7	295,590	22.3	198,181	15.0
New Mexico...............	341,889	50.2	207,475	30.5	131,823	19.3
Arizona...................	416,000	55.5	256,673	34.2	76,914	
Utah.....................	449,855	65.3	158,387	23.0	80,620	11.7
Nevada...................	91,625	57.2	54,997	34.4	13,461	8.4
Pacific......................	10,861,904	75.0	2,554,386	17.6	1,070,237	7.4
Washington...............	1,503,166	63.2	602,026	25.3	273,771	11.5
Oregon...................	819,318	54.9	473,788	31.1	228,235	15.0
California.................	8,539,420	80.6	1,478,572	14.0	568,231	5.4

SOURCE: U.S. Bureau of the Census, *Census of Population: 1950*, vol. II, *U.S. Summary, General Characteristics*, part I, chap. B, table 58.

proportion of rural-nonfarm people exceed 30 per cent in 1950: Maine, New Hampshire, North Dakota, Virginia, North Carolina, South Carolina, Kentucky, Montana, Wyoming, New Mexico, Arizona, Nevada, and Oregon.

CHARACTERISTICS OF THE POPULATION

A study of the characteristics of a population is of fundamental importance in understanding the nature of social relationships. Very often, the basic causes of many of the problems of a society can be determined from an analysis of the characteristics of its people. In this section, the following major characteristics of the rural population of the United States are examined: residence, age composition, sex composition, racial composition, educational attainment, marital status, and occupation.

Residence: Less than One-eighth of the Total Population of the Nation Resides on Farms.

According to the latest census estimates, less than one-eighth of the nation's people are farmers. As indicated earlier in this chapter, in 1950 approximately two out of each three persons lived in the city, whereas only about one out of every five persons lived in a rural-nonfarm locality.

An analysis of the place of residence of the different racial groups reveals that whites are most urban and members of "other races" (exclusive of Negroes) are least urban. Negroes hold an intermediate position.

Place of residence by race is shown in Table 2. In 1950, 64.3 per cent of white people lived in the cities as compared to only 44.7 per cent of

Table 2. Residential Composition of the Population of the United States, 1950, by Race

Area	White		Negro		Other races	
	Number	Per cent	Number	Per cent	Number	Per cent
Total............	134,942,028	100.0	15,042,286	100.0	713,047	100.0
Rural-farm.......	19,715,254	14.6	3,158,301	21.0	174,795	24.5
Rural-nonfarm....	28,470,339	21.1	2,491,377	16.6	219,609	30.8
Urban..........	86,756,435	64.3	9,392,608	62.4	318,643	44.7

SOURCE: *Statistical Abstract of the United States, 1955*, table 25, p. 33.

persons of "other races" (exclusive of Negroes) and 62.4 per cent of Negroes.

As can be seen from these figures, persons of "other races" are the most rural, relatively speaking. The data for 1950 show that 24.5 per cent of these people lived on farms. Negroes are the next most rural group, 21.0 per cent of them living on farms in 1950. The white population of the United States resides on farms to a lesser extent than the other two groups mentioned above. Only 14.6 per cent of whites resided in rural-farm areas at mid-century.

Negroes reside in rural-nonfarm areas to a lesser extent than either whites or members of "other races," only 16.6 per cent of Negroes living in such localities in 1950. Nearly one-third (30.8 per cent) of those persons classified as members of "other races" and slightly more than one-fifth (21.1 per cent) of the whites lived in rural-nonfarm places at that time.

Age Composition: The Rural Population Is Short of People of Productive Age.

Figure 2 demonstrates the age structure of the rural-farm and rural-nonfarm populations as compared with the urban and the total populations of the United States. This graph shows age-sex pyramids as of 1950 for the entire nation and for the various residential groupings. An analysis of these age-sex pyramids indicates that basic differences exist in the age structures of rural and urban peoples. These differences can be

UNITED STATES, 1950

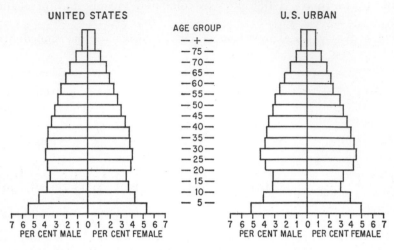

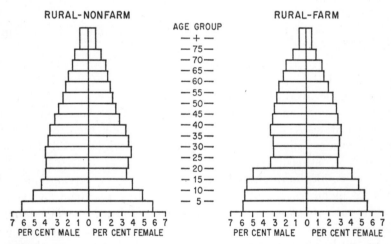

Figure 2. Age-sex pyramids of the population of the United States, by residence, 1950.

summarized as follows: (1) The rural-farm population contains the smallest proportion of people in the age group between 20 and 65 years of age. (2) The rural-nonfarm population has the largest proportion of persons 65 years of age and over. (3) The proportions 65 years of age and over in the rural-farm and urban populations are about equal. The basic difference is in the sex composition of the two groups. The urban aged population has a predominance of women, whereas the aged rural-farm population has a predominance of men. (4) The rural-farm population has the greatest proportion of persons under 20 years of age. The urban population has the smallest proportion of persons in this age group, and the rural-nonfarm population holds an intermediate position.

These differences in age structure have some definite consequences for rural and urban societies. When expressed in terms of dependency ratios (the number of persons under 15 years of age and over 65 years per each 1,000 persons between the ages of 15 and 65 years), these differential age structures mean that each 1,000 persons in the productive years of life in the rural-farm population support a considerably larger number of persons than their counterparts in the rural-nonfarm and urban populations. Specifically, the age-dependency ratios of the various groups are as follows: rural-farm, 787; rural-nonfarm, 637; and urban, 478. This fact alone could account in large measure for the differences between the levels of living prevalent among rural people and those of urban folk.

All residential groups have been experiencing a declining death rate, which is reflected in their respective age-sex pyramids. However, the most obvious influences are those of the recent increase in the birth rates (especially in urban areas) since the Second World War and the long-continuing pattern of rural-urban migration. The recent increase in the urban birth rate is evident in the large percentages of children in the urban population pyramids. Prior to 1940, the population of urban places had an extremely small proportion of children and was characterized by a birth rate that was not high enough to provide for the maintenance of the existing urban population. Growth taking place in cities prior to 1940 was due to the migration of young adults from the farms. In the fifties this phenomenon continues to account for the shortage of persons of productive age in the rural-farm population and the concentration of persons of this age in the urban population.

Sex Composition: There Are More Men than Women in Rural Areas.

The data show that in 1950, for the first time, the population of the United States was characterized by more females than males. In fact, at that time, there were only 98.1 males for every 100 females. This predominance of females, however, does not obtain for the rural-farm or rural-nonfarm segments of the population. Among those persons who live on farms, there were 109.8 men for each 100 women. The comparable figure for the rural-nonfarm population was 102.7. In contrast, a sex ratio of 94.1 indicates the numerical dominance of women in cities.

The same general patterns observed for the total population hold true for both major racial groups. Among the white urban population, there were only 93.5 males for each 100 females in 1950. In contrast, among the white rural-nonfarm population, there were 101.9 men for each

100 women, and in rural-farm areas the sex ratio for the white population was 110.2. Among urban Negroes the sex ratio was only 91.2, but in the rural-nonfarm and rural-farm Negro populations, the sex ratios were 107.1 and 102.5, respectively. Interestingly, among Negroes there is a higher sex ratio in the rural-nonfarm than in the rural-farm population.

Racial Composition: Proportionately More Negroes than Whites Are Rural Dwellers.

The population of the United States in 1950 was composed of 134,-942,028 white persons, 15,042,286 Negroes, and 713,047 persons of "other races." The percentages of the total population of each group were 89.6, 9.9, and 0.5, respectively. Table 3 shows the numerical and relative

Table 3. Racial Composition of the Population of the United States, 1950, by Census Divisions

Division	White		Negro		Other races	
	Number	Per cent	Number	Per cent	Number	Per cent
United States............	134,942,028	89.6	15,042,286	9.9	713,047	0.5
New England..........	9,161,156	98.4	142,941	1.5	10,356	0.1
Middle Atlantic........	28,237,528	93.6	1,875,241	6.2	50,764	0.2
East North Central....	28,543,307	93.8	1,803,698	5.9	52,363	0.3
West North Central...	13,576,077	96.5	424,178	3.0	61,139	0.5
South Atlantic........	16,041,709	75.7	5,094,744	24.1	45,882	0.2
East South Central....	8,770,570	76.4	2,698,635	23.5	7,976	0.1
West South Central...	12,037,250	82.8	2,432,028	16.7	68,294	0.5
Mountain.............	4,845,634	95.5	66,429	1.3	162,935	3.2
Pacific...............	13,728,797	94.8	504,392	3.5	253,338	1.7

SOURCE: *Statistical Abstract of the United States, 1955*, table 28, p. 35.

importance of each of these racial groups by census divisions. An analysis of these data clearly shows that Negroes are highly concentrated in three predominantly rural areas: (1) the South Atlantic region, where 24.1 per cent of the people are Negro; (2) the East South Central region, with 23.5 per cent of its population classified as Negro; and (3) the West South Central region, in which 16.7 per cent of the people are Negro.

New England and the Mountain region have the smallest proportions of Negroes in their populations. Persons of "other races" constitute significant proportions of the populations of only the Mountain and Pacific regions, and even there their numbers are small.

The largest proportions of nonwhites are found in Mississippi (45.5 per cent), South Carolina (38.9 per cent), Louisiana (33.1 per cent), Alabama (32.1 per cent), and Georgia (30.9 per cent). No other state had as much as 30.0 per cent of its population in this racial classification. On the other hand, three states (Maine, New Hampshire, and Vermont) had less than 1 per cent of their inhabitants classified as nonwhite.

Negroes are of the greatest relative numerical importance in the rural-farm population. The data presented in Table 4 show that 13.7 per cent

Table 4. Racial Composition of the Population of the United States, 1950, by Residence

Area	White		Negro		Other races	
	Number	Per cent	Number	Per cent	Number	Per cent
Rural-farm.....	19,715,254	85.5	3,158,301	13.7	174,795	0.8
Rural-nonfarm..	28,470,339	91.3	2,491,377	8.0	219,609	0.7
Urban.........	86,756,435	90.0	9,392,608	9.7	318,643	0.3

SOURCE: *Statistical Abstract of the United States, 1955*, table 25, p. 33.

of Negroes lived in rural-farm areas in 1950. They are of about equal relative importance in the rural-nonfarm and urban populations (8.0 and 9.7 per cent, respectively). The rural-nonfarm population has the largest proportion of whites in its population (91.3 per cent). As would be expected, the rural-farm population has the smallest proportion of whites, amounting to only 85.5 per cent, and the urban population was in an intermediate position with 90.0 per cent of its population classified as white. Persons of "other races" are of little significance in any of the three residential groups.

Educational Attainment: Urban People Have More Formal Schooling than Rural People.

United States census data indicate rather conclusively that the rural population, both open-country and farm, has less formal education than the population of urban places. At mid-century, among persons 25 years of age and over in the United States, males had completed a median of 9.0 years of schooling (see Table 5). Women, by comparison, had completed a median of 9.6 years. The white population in this age classification recorded greater educational attainment than nonwhites.

Table 5. Median Number of Years of Schooling Completed by Persons Twenty-five Years of Age and Over, United States, 1950, by Sex, Race, and Residence

| Area | Median number of years of schooling completed | | | | | |
| | Total | | White | | Nonwhite | |
	Male	Female	Male	Female	Male	Female
United States....	9.0	9.6	9.3	10.0	6.4	7.2
Urban..........	10.0	10.2	10.3	10.6	7.5	8.0
Rural-nonfarm...	8.7	9.0	8.8	9.3	5.1	5.9
Rural-farm......	8.6	8.5	8.4	8.7	4.3	5.4

SOURCE: U.S. Bureau of the Census, *Census of Population: 1950*, vol. II, *U.S. Summary, Detailed Characteristics*, table 115, pp. 236–243.

Among the former, the median years of schooling completed by males was 9.3 years and by females, 10.0 years. Comparable figures for nonwhites were 6.4 years for males and 9.2 years for females.

Among persons 25 years of age and over in the rural-farm population, the median number of years of schooling completed by males was 8.6 and by females 8.5. White persons in rural-farm areas are better educated than nonwhites. For example, in 1950, the median number of years of schooling completed by white males 25 years of age and over was 8.4. White females in this age group averaged 8.7 years. Comparable figures for nonwhites were 4.3 years for males and 5.4 years for females.

The rural-nonfarm population has a level of educational attainment more nearly approximating that of farm people than of urban dwellers (see Table 5 for comparative figures). Among persons 25 years of age and over in 1950, the median number of years of schooling completed was 8.7 for rural-nonfarm males and 9.0 for rural-nonfarm females. In this segment of the population, whites also have a higher educational attainment than nonwhites.

The lowest median number of years of schooling completed by persons 25 years of age and over in the nation is found among nonwhite males in rural-farm areas. The median years of schooling completed by persons in this category was only 4.3 years. Females of this residence, racial, and age classification also had the lowest attainment in the nation for members of that sex.

The data on median number of years of schooling completed by persons 25 and over also reveal that females have a greater educational attainment than males in each of the residence groups.

Marital Status: Fewer Rural-Farm Persons than Urban or Rural-Nonfarm Persons Are Widowed and Divorced.

In 1950, 26.4 per cent of the males 14 years of age and over were single, 67.5 per cent were married, 4.1 per cent were widowed, and 2.0 per cent were divorced (see Table 6).

Table 6. Marital Status of Persons 14 Years of Age and Over, United States, 1950, by Sex, Race, and Residence, in Percentages

Area	Total				White				Nonwhite			
	Single	Mar-ried	Wid-owed	Di-vorced	Single	Mar-ried	Wid-owed	Di-vorced	Single	Mar-ried	Wid-owed	Di-vorced
Males												
United States..	26.4	67.5	4.1	2.0	26.1	67.9	4.0	2.0	28.5	64.4	5.2	1.9
Urban....	25.0	68.6	4.1	2.2	25.0	68.8	4.0	2.2	25.7	64.4	5.2	2.4
Rural-non-farm...	27.0	66.7	4.4	1.9	26.5	67.3	4.2	1.9	32.8	59.8	5.9	1.5
Rural-farm...	31.2	64.0	3.8	1.0	30.8	64.3	3.8	1.1	33.6	61.5	4.3	0.6
Females												
United States..	20.0	65.8	11.8	2.4	19.9	66.2	11.2	2.4	20.7	62.0	14.6	2.7
Urban....	20.6	63.8	12.7	2.9	20.7	64.1	12.3	2.9	19.1	61.9	15.5	3.5
Rural-non-farm...	17.7	69.2	11.4	1.7	17.3	70.0	11.0	1.7	21.8	60.8	15.8	1.6
Rural-farm...	20.5	70.9	7.9	0.8	19.7	72.0	7.6	0.8	25.8	63.5	10.0	0.7

SOURCE: U.S. Bureau of the Census, *Census of Population: 1950*, vol. II, *U.S. Summary, Detailed Characteristics*, table 105, pp. 189–190.

When the analysis of marital status is made according to residence, it is found that rural-farm males have the largest proportion (31.2 per cent) classified as single and the smallest proportion (64.0 per cent) in the married category. By contrast, the males in the urban population had the smallest proportion in the single category and the largest percentage in the married classification. The data further show that males in the rural-farm population have the smallest proportions in the widowed and divorced categories (3.8 and 1.0 per cent, respectively). On the other hand, the urban male population is characterized by the greatest relative number of divorced persons, and rural-nonfarm males have the largest proportion of persons in the widowed category.

If the marital status of males 14 years of age and over is analyzed according to race, the same general differences as described for the total male population are found to exist. Among both whites and nonwhites, rural-farm males have the largest proportion of single persons and the smallest proportion of married persons.

The specific differences noted between the marital statuses of white and nonwhite males in the three residence groups are: (1) the non-whites have a larger proportion of males in a single status; (2) the whites have a larger percentage of males in a married status; (3) widowed non-white males are of relatively greater importance than widowed white males; and (4) generally, smaller proportions of nonwhite males are divorced than white males.

In 1950, one-fifth of the females 14 years of age and over in the United States were single, 65.8 per cent were married, 11.8 per cent were widowed, and 2.4 per cent were divorced (see Table 6). The most noticeable difference in the marital status of males and females is the much larger proportion of the women who are widowed. This circumstance prevails in each of the residential areas. The reason for this situation is the greater average length of life of women as compared to men, which means that large numbers of women must live out their later years in a widowed status.

There are some significant variations in the marital status of females in the urban, rural-nonfarm, and rural-farm populations. Females in the rural-farm population have the largest proportion in any residence group in the married status and the smallest proportions in the widowed and divorced categories. The rural-nonfarm population is characterized by the smallest proportion of single persons among its females 14 years of age and over.

Nonwhite females in the rural-farm and rural-nonfarm populations are single to a considerably larger extent than are their white counterparts. This is not the case in the urban population, however. The data in Table 6 show that white females in all three residential areas are married in larger proportions than are the nonwhite females. On the other hand, in each residential area, nonwhite females have a larger proportion in a widowed status than whites. In the urban population, a significantly larger proportion of nonwhite than white females is divorced.

Occupation: Ruralites Are Engaged in a Number of Jobs Other than Farming.

Although the majority of persons in the population who reside on farms are engaged in agriculture, other occupations also are followed by farm residents. In 1950, of the employed workers classified as rural-farm in residence, 70.8 per cent were occupied in agriculture. The second most important occupation of this residence group was manufacturing, in which 9.4 per cent were engaged. Persons engaged in the wholesale and retail trade made up 4.3 per cent of the employed persons reported as rural-farm. Construction was the fourth important occupation among persons in this residence category, with 3.1 per cent of the people on farms so employed. Individuals engaged in professional and related services constituted 2.7 per cent of the employed persons on farms in 1950. Other occupations in which rural-farm residents work are forestry and fisheries; mining; transportation, communication and other public utilities; finance, insurance, and real estate; business and repair service; personal services; entertainment and recreation services; and public administration. Of these occupations, persons engaged in transportation, communication, and other public utilities constituted the largest proportion, which was only 2.1 per cent. In none of the other occupations were as many as 2.0 per cent of the farm residents employed in 1950.

Persons residing in rural-nonfarm areas have different occupations from residents of farms. Only 8.5 per cent of the people in the rural-nonfarm population work on farms. The largest proportion of persons in the rural-nonfarm population is employed in manufacturing (25.6 per cent). The second largest group is engaged in wholesale and retail trade (18.0 per cent). Persons employed in construction (8.9 per cent) and in professional and related services (8.4 per cent) constituted the third and fourth largest groups in the rural-nonfarm population, respectively. Other occupations in which significant proportions of the employed persons in the rural-nonfarm population were engaged are transportation, communication, and other public utilities (7.4 per cent); personal services (5.9 per cent); mining (4.9 per cent); public administration (4.0 per cent); and business and repair service (3.1 per cent). Persons living in rural-nonfarm areas are also engaged in forestry and fisheries; finance, insurance, and real estate; and entertainment and recreation services. However, the proportions employed in these activities are very small.

These data indicate that the occupations of persons living in rural-nonfarm areas are very different from those of the rural-farm population. If the occupational composition of the rural-nonfarm population is compared with that of the nation as a whole, a very great similarity is observed. It seems likely that, in so far as occupational status is concerned, the people in the rural-nonfarm areas are in an intermediate position between the urban and farm populations. In this position, they are engaged to some extent in both urban and agricultural industries, a fact which accounts for the similarity of the occupational status of rural-nonfarm people and of people in the nation generally.

THE VITAL PROCESSES

Three processes determine the number and distribution of a population—births, deaths, and migration. These have become known to the demographer as the "vital processes," and they constitute a very important area of inquiry for persons interested in population change. We shall discuss each of these processes as it relates to the rural population of the United States.

Rates of Reproduction: Rural Families Continue to Have More Children than Urban Families.

The rural people of the United States have long had higher rates of reproduction than persons in the urban and rural-nonfarm areas. This has been so evident that the rural areas have been called the "seed-bed of the nation." In 1950, rural families continued to be the greatest producing unit in the population. Table 7 shows fertility ratios (the number

Table 7. Fertility Ratios, United States, 1950, by Race and Residence

Area	Fertility ratios *		
	Total	White	Nonwhite
United States......	403	404	396
Urban..........	362	366	327
Rural-nonfarm...	485	484	496
Rural-farm......	498	483	587

* The fertility ratio gives the number of children under 5 years of age per each 1,000 women aged 15 to 49 years.
    SOURCE: U.S. Bureau of the Census, *Census of Population: 1950*, vol. IV, "Special Reports—Fertility," table 34.

of children under 5 years of age per each 1,000 women aged 15 to 49 years) for the United States, by race and residence. These data show that there were 403 children under 5 years of age for each 1,000 women aged 15 to 49 years in 1950. When fertility ratios are studied by residence, it is seen that the city dwellers have the lowest rates of reproduction (a fertility ratio of 362) and the rural-farm people the highest rate (a fertility ratio of 498). The population in the rural-nonfarm areas has an intermediate status (a fertility ratio of 485) in so far as rates of reproduction are concerned.

The white population in 1950 had a slightly higher rate of reproduction than the nonwhites, 404 as compared to 396. However, this circumstance does not exist in the rural-nonfarm and rural-farm areas. In these localities, nonwhites have higher rates of reproduction than whites. The highest fertility ratio among any peoples in the nation is that of nonwhites in the rural-farm population (587). It is only in the urban population that the fertility of the nonwhites is less than that of the whites.

Until 1940, the population of the United States experienced a long period of declining rate of reproduction. Valid data regarding births are available from the 1920s. Although the practice of registering births was begun in 1915, complete data for the entire country were not available until 1933. Table 8 presents birth rates, adjusted for underregistra-

Table 8. Birth Rates,* Adjusted for Underregistration, United States, 1920–1955, by Race

Year	Births per 1,000 population		
	Total	White	Nonwhite
1920	27.7	26.9	35.0
1925	25.1	24.1	34.2
1930	21.3	20.6	27.5
1935	18.7	17.9	25.8
1940	19.4	18.6	26.7
1945	20.4	19.9	26.5
1950	24.1	23.0	33.3
1955	24.9	23.8	34.0

* Birth rates show the number of live births for each 1,000 persons in the population. The rates above have been adjusted by the Department of Health, Education, and Welfare for underregistration of births.

SOURCE: *Statistical Abstract of the United States, 1956*, table 56, p. 58.

tion, from 1920 to 1955, by race. A considerable decline in the birth rate is observed between 1920 and 1935, after which a substantial increase is recorded. In 1955, the birth rate had attained a comparatively high level, and this trend is characteristic of both whites and nonwhites. It seems apparent that the low birth rates of the 1930s were influenced somewhat by the economic depression of that time and that the increase that has occurred since 1940 reflects a change in values occurring as a result of the Second World War, the Korean War, and the prolonged period of prosperity that followed.

Although the extended decline in reproduction up to 1940 characterized both the rural and the urban segments of the population, the decrease in the rural areas was less precipitous than the decline in the cities. According to T. Lynn Smith, the fertility ratio of the urban population declined 34 per cent between 1910 and 1940 as compared with only 28 per cent among the rural-farm people.[2] However, the recent increases in reproduction have been less pronounced in the rural than in the urban areas. Smith reports that the fertility ratio of the rural-farm population increased only 25 per cent between 1940 and 1950 as compared with an increase of 69 per cent in the urban population.[3] These figures indicate that a substantial part of the increase in population during the decade of the forties is attributable to the increased fertility of city dwellers. This fact makes it seem likely that the long-prevailing differential in fertility between city and farm folk will eventually disappear.

Death Rates: Ruralites Continue to Live Longer than Urban Residents.

Traditionally, open country areas have enjoyed an advantage over cities from the standpoint of health. In the past, plagues and epidemics took their greatest toll in the cities. In recent decades, however, man has learned to control and regulate health conditions in urban areas, with the result that the mortality differentials between city and country have been diminished. Table 9 gives the death rates for the United States in 1953, by race and residence. The figures indicate the number of persons who die each year for each 1,000 persons in the population.

In 1953, persons who lived in cities died at a rate of 10.6 persons per 1,000 as compared with a rate of only 8.3 per 1,000 for the rural population. The death rate for the general population was 9.7 per 1,000 persons.

Nonwhites have a higher mortality rate than whites in the nation as a whole and in each of the residential areas. In the United States, nonwhites had a death rate of 11.0 per 1,000 persons as compared with only 9.5 for whites. In the rural population, nonwhites had a death rate of 9.1 as compared with 8.1 for whites. Similar figures for the urban population are 11.7 for nonwhites and 10.5 for whites .These data further indicate that rural white people have the lowest death rate in the population and that urban nonwhites have the highest mortality rate.

It should be pointed out that a differential in mortality rate prevails

[2] T. Lynn Smith, The Sociology of Rural Life, 3d ed., New York: Harper & Brothers, 1953, pp. 144–145.

[3] Ibid.

Table 9. Death Rates, United States, 1953, by Race
and Residence *

Area	Deaths per 1,000 population		
	Total	White	Nonwhite
United States...	9.7	9.5	11.0
Rural........	8.3	8.1	9.9
Urban........	10.6	10.5	11.7

* Definitions of *urban* and *rural* are based on the census of
1940. The populations for 1953 are calculated by linear in-
terpolation, using the definitions of residence of the census
of 1940.

SOURCE: *Statistical Abstract of the United States, 1956*,
table 72, p. 69.

between the sexes, women in the nation as a whole and in each of the
residential areas having a lower rate than men. Women in the United
States had a death rate of 8.1 in 1953 as compared to 11.1 for males.
A similar situation prevails among whites and nonwhites and among
urban and rural people.

*Migration: Farmers Move About Less than City Dwellers, But Many
Migrate.*

The third process affecting the number and distribution of a population is migration. Each year a considerable amount of moving is done
in the United States. Table 10 shows the mobility of the American population one year old and over in 1955, by residence. In this table the
1955 residence of each individual is compared to his residence in 1954,
yielding insight into the mobility of the entire population during the
preceding year.

Apparently, the rural-farm population is less mobile than either the
rural-nonfarm or the urban populations. The data in Table 10 show that
85.1 per cent of the rural-farm population one year old and over in
1955 were nonmovers. The rural-nonfarm population in this age classification was the most mobile: only 77.1 per cent lived in the same place
in 1955 as in 1954. In the urban population, 79.3 per cent were classified as nonmovers.

The data on migration show that the rural-farm population made proportionately fewer moves within the same county than did the rural-
nonfarm and urban populations. The same is true of moves within the

Table 10. Mobility Status of the Population 1 Year Old and Over, 1955, United States, by Residence

Mobility status (by comparison of 1955 and 1954 residences)	Population 1 year old and over, 1955							
	Total		Urban		Rural-nonfarm		Rural-farm	
	Number	Per cent	Number	Per cent	Number	Per cent	Number	Per cent
Nonmovers (lived in same house).................	126,190	79.6	80,650	79.3	27,470	77.1	18,070	85.1
Moved within the same county...........	21,086	13.3	14,092	13.9	4,979	14.0	2,015	9.5
Moved within the same state.............	5,511	3.5	3,242	3.2	1,587	4.5	682	3.2
Moved between different states.................	4,895	3.1	3,194	3.1	1,323	3.7	378	1.8
Abroad in 1954..........	927	0.5	546	0.5	283	0.7	98	0.4
Total...............	158,609	100.0	101,724	100.0	35,642	100.0	21,243	100.0

SOURCE: *Statistical Abstract of the United States, 1956*, table 36, p. 40.

same state and between different states. In each case, the rural-farm population had a proportionately smaller number of movers than did either the rural-nonfarm population or the urban population.

There are several specific migrations involving rural people which are of interest to the student of rural life in the United States. Two of these are rural-urban exchanges and movements of seasonal migratory agricultural workers. The first of these involves movements through which persons leave the farms and go into the cities and towns, or vice versa. The migration to the city apparently has been in process for many decades, although little data are available concerning it until the beginning of the twentieth century (see Fig. 3). The available data show that between 1930 and 1955 a net decline in the farm population occurred as a result of the rural-urban interchanges in all but four of these years. In 1931 and 1932 a net increase in the farm population occurred as a result of the Depression, which caused migration to the farms; in 1931 rural areas registered a gain of 156,000 people and in 1932 a gain of 607,000. In 1945 and 1946 the farm population also experienced a net gain, probably as a result of military demobilization after the Second World War. The increase totaled 846,000 persons in 1945 and 151,000 persons in 1946.

In the twenty-one years of the period since 1930 not accounted for above, more people moved to the city than moved to the country. In eight of these years, the net loss amounted to more than one million

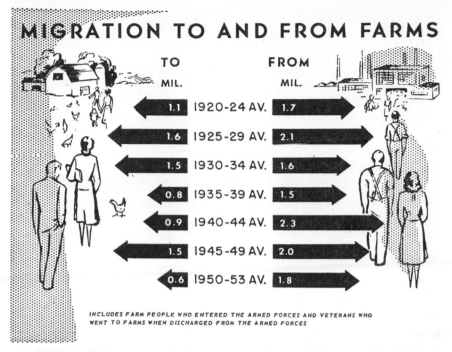

MIGRATION TO AND FROM FARMS

TO MIL.		FROM MIL.
1.1	1920-24 AV.	1.7
1.6	1925-29 AV.	2.1
1.5	1930-34 AV.	1.6
0.8	1935-39 AV.	1.5
0.9	1940-44 AV.	2.3
1.5	1945-49 AV.	2.0
0.6	1950-53 AV.	1.8

INCLUDES FARM PEOPLE WHO ENTERED THE ARMED FORCES AND VETERANS WHO WENT TO FARMS WHEN DISCHARGED FROM THE ARMED FORCES

Figure 3. Migration to and from farms in the United States, 1920–1953. (U.S. Department of Agriculture, Agricultural Marketing Service.)

persons. Losses of this magnitude occurred in 1941, 1942, 1943, 1947, 1949, 1950, 1952, and 1953. The greatest loss of persons in the rural-urban interchange occurred in 1942, when the farm population experienced a net loss of 2,975,000 persons.

There has been considerable interest in the selectivity of rural-urban migration. Attention has been given especially to the problem of determining the characteristics of the persons who leave farms and go to cities. Only two facts regarding the selectivity of this migratory movement have been more or less definitely established. These are (1) that the rural-urban migration is selective of young people and (2) that it is selective of females. The persons who leave the farm and move to the city are, for the most part, young people in their late teens or early twenties, and females tend to leave the farms in greater proportionate numbers than males. This selectivity of rural-urban migration for females is clearly reflected in the sex composition of the two areas, as shown earlier.

Attempts have been made to determine selectivity of rural-urban migrations in terms of such characteristics as education, health, physical vitality, race, and intelligence, but the research to this point has been inconclusive. Because investigations have turned up widely varying results, it must be assumed that selectivity of rural-urban migration on the basis of these qualities is not clearly patterned.

The number of persons involved in seasonal migratory agricultural work is not definitely known. The number of domestic and foreign migrant farm workers in 1956 is shown in Figures 4 and 5.[4] Most of the movements of seasonal workers begin in the South and progress toward the northern part of the nation, as a result of the variation in climate from north to south, which determines the time of harvest of the various crops. The following migratory streams are known to have existed in 1950: [5] (1) a movement from Florida to the Canadian border along the Atlantic coast, which includes migratory workers engaged in the harvesting of vegetables and fruits; (2) a movement commencing in Texas and moving northwest, north, and northeast as far as California, Montana, Minnesota, and Michigan, made up largely of Mexican and other Latin American farm laborers who harvest the sugar beet, cotton, and vegetable crops in these areas; (3) a movement with its origin in the Ozark and Appalachian mountain areas, extending westward to California, Washington, and Oregon and northward into Wisconsin, Michigan, and Ohio, including agricultural laborers employed in the harvest of miscellaneous crops; and (4) a movement in the Pacific Coast area, extending from California to Washington and made up of farm workers who harvest fruit and cotton.

RURAL POPULATION TRENDS

In 1790, when the first United States census was taken, the population of the nation was 3,929,214 persons. Of this number, 94.9 per cent (3,727,559 persons) were classified as rural residents. Thus, at that time the nation's population was made up of people who gained their livelihood principally through agricultural pursuits. In 1950 the situation was quite different. In the mid-twentieth century, as we have seen, the population of the nation was composed principally of urban dwellers.[6] The transition from a predominantly rural society to a predominantly urban one was completed in 1920, when, for the first time, the rural

[4] The Bureau of Employment Security of the U.S. Department of Labor publishes periodic counts of migrant farm workers.

[5] Lowry Nelson, *Rural Sociology*, rev. ed., New York: American Book Company, 1955, p. 138.

[6] According to the definitions of residence used in the census of 1940, the urban population was 88,927,464 in 1950, and urban persons constituted 59.0 per cent of the total. The figures quoted earlier are based on the new definitions of residence adopted in the census of 1950. It will be recalled that the urban population was given as 96,467,686 people, or 64.0 per cent of the nation's total.

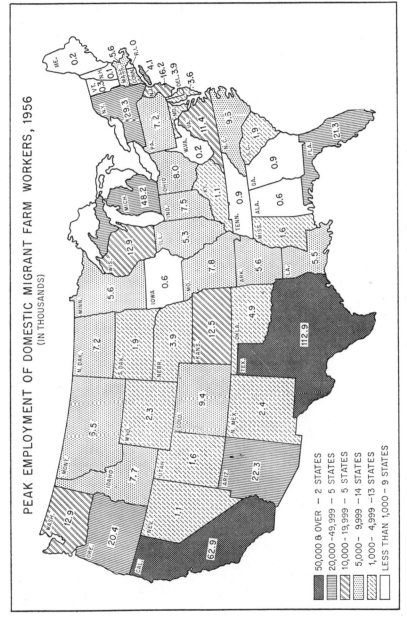

PEAK EMPLOYMENT OF DOMESTIC MIGRANT FARM WORKERS, 1956
(IN THOUSANDS)

50,000 & OVER — 2 STATES
20,000 - 49,999 — 5 STATES
10,000 - 19,999 — 5 STATES
5,000 - 9,999 — 14 STATES
1,000 - 4,999 — 13 STATES
LESS THAN 1,000 — 9 STATES

Figure 4. Domestic migrant farm workers employed at peak employment periods, by states, 1955. (U.S. Department of Labor, Bureau of Employment Security, Office of Program Review and Analysis.)

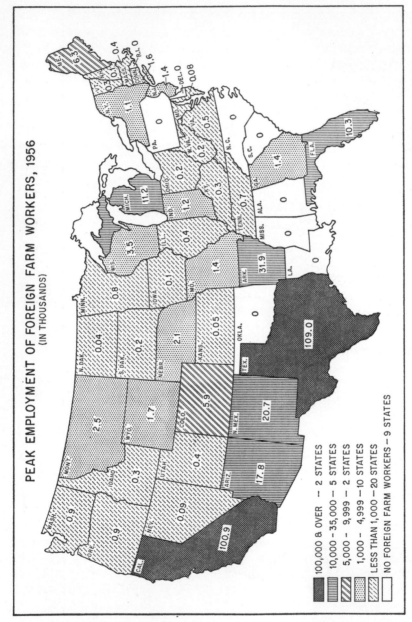

Figure 5. Foreign farm workers employed at peak employment periods, by states, 1956. (U.S. Department of Labor, Bureau of Employment Security, Office of Program Review and Analysis.)

population made up less than half of the total population (48.8 per cent).

Although the total population has undergone tremendous growth, this is not true of each of its residential segments (see Fig. 6). In fact, a substantial decline has occurred in the rural-farm population. In 1920, rural-farm people numbered 31,614,269 persons and made up 29.9 per cent of the total population. However, by 1950, the number of rural-farm residents, as shown previously, had declined to 23,048,350 persons

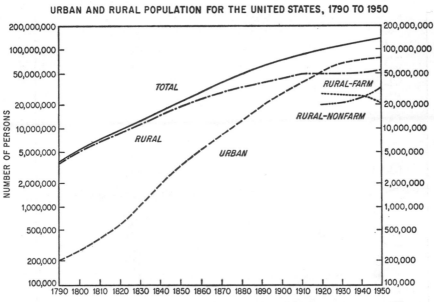

URBAN AND RURAL POPULATION FOR THE UNITED STATES, 1790 TO 1950

Figure 6. Trends in population growth of the United States, by residence, 1790–1950.

and constituted only 15.3 per cent of the population. In 1957 it was estimated that the farm population was down to 20,396,000 people. Figure 7 shows the change in farm population from 1920 to 1950 by states. The rural-nonfarm population, on the other hand, has experienced considerable growth. In 1920, persons residing in rural-nonfarm areas numbered 20,159,358 individuals and accounted for 19.1 per cent of the people in the United States. At mid-century the rural-nonfarm population had grown to 31,181,325 persons and made up approximately one-fifth of the population.

The study of trends in the growth of the American population clearly shows the rapid change from an agricultural population to a highly urbanized one. It will be interesting to see if this trend continues in the future and to discover what its implications are for the nation.

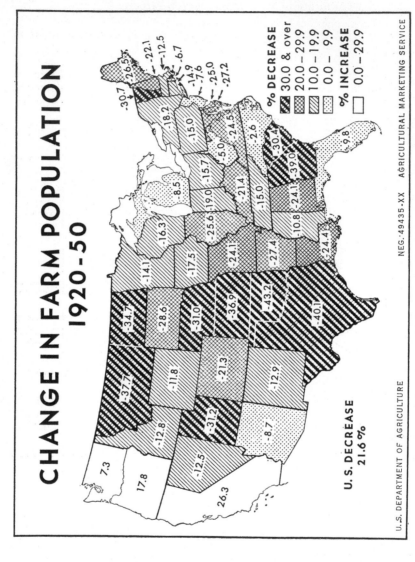

CHANGE IN FARM POPULATION 1920-50

% DECREASE
- 30.0 & over
- 20.0 – 29.9
- 10.0 – 19.9
- 0.0 – 9.9

% INCREASE
- 0.0 – 29.9

U.S. DECREASE 21.6 %

U.S. DEPARTMENT OF AGRICULTURE   NEG. 49435-XX   AGRICULTURAL MARKETING SERVICE

Figure 7. Change in the farm population of the United States, by states, 1920–1950.

Questions for Review and Discussion

1. What type of discussion would one expect in a chapter devoted to "demographic analysis"?

2. In order to acquaint yourself with the U.S. census volumes, do the following things: (a) Determine the increase or decrease in the population of the United States from 1920 to 1950. (b) Determine the residence composition of the population of your county. (c) Determine the racial composition of the population of your county.

3. Why is it important to study the demographic characteristics of a population?

4. Describe the differences in age structure of the urban and rural-farm populations of the United States.

5. List the important population trends in the United States.

6. Define, describe, or identify the following: (a) age-sex pyramids, (b) vital processes, (c) selectivity of rural-urban migration, (d) the sex ratio, (e) the dependency ratio.

Selected References for Supplementary Reading

Barnes, Harry Elmer: *Society in Transition*, 2d ed., New York: Prentice-Hall, Inc., 1952, chaps. 2–4.

Hitt, Homer L.: "Population Problems," chap. 2 in T. Lynn Smith and associates, *Social Problems*, New York: Thomas Y. Crowell Company, 1955.

Landis, Paul H., and Paul K. Hatt: *Population Problems: A Cultural Interpretation*, New York: American Book Company, 1954.

Nelson, Lowry: *Rural Sociology*, 2d ed., New York: American Book Company, 1955, chaps. 4 and 5.

Smith, T. Lynn: *Population Analysis*, New York: McGraw-Hill Book Company, Inc., 1953.

———: *The Sociology of Rural Life*, 3d ed., New York: Harper & Brothers, 1953, chaps. 3–9.

Thompson, Warren S.: *Population Problems*, New York: McGraw-Hill Book Company, Inc., 1953.

CHAPTER 6 *Neighborhood and Community*
Organization and Trends

Probably the first aspect of farm life that attracts the observer's attention is spatial relationships. The patterns of neighborhood and community organization in agricultural regions differ quite radically from those found in urban localities. The purpose of this chapter is to acquaint the student with certain major characteristics and trends of these locality groups.

Listed in order of size, the locality groups discussed in this book are the family, the neighborhood, the community, and the region. Since we shall discuss the organization of neighborhoods and communities in this chapter, the student should review the discussion of social organization in Chapter 2, especially the section dealing with social groups, as an introduction to the material that follows.

THE COMMUNITY

The term community has come to have a fairly clear-cut meaning, at least for rural sociologists.[1] The primary criteria of a community are the presence of ties or bonds that hold a group of spatially related people together and interaction among these people. Other characteristics include: (1) limitation of area, resulting in territorial proximity of the interacting persons, (2) common culture, or consciousness of kind, and (3) common behavioral norms within a shared social structure. Mercer has recently defined a community as "a functionally related aggregate of people who live in a particular geographic

[1] George A. Hillery, Jr., "Definition of Community: Areas of Agreement," *Rural Sociology,* 20:119, 1955.

locality at a particular time, show a common culture, are arranged in a social structure, and exhibit an awareness of their uniqueness and separate identity as a group." [2]

To understand the community, it is necessary to take account of social change.[3] The natural history of the community involves those forces leading to change or further development; thus it is by no means a static entity. Its members are constantly adjusting to changing conditions, new situations, and increasing demands. Part of this change in recent years has been individuation and specialization of interests. Formerly, the solidarity of the community was maintained by traditions, sentiment, prejudice, public opinion, and gossip. More and more, the community must maintain the loyalty of its members by means of the services it renders. The cohesive element has shifted from a mechanistic type of solidarity to an organic type (see Chapter 2). The rural community of today is thus a far cry from that of thirty or forty years ago.

The Community versus The Neighborhood

There is some difference of opinion within the field of sociology concerning the distinction between the neighborhood and the community. Most writers merely point out that it is very difficult to draw a precise line between the two. Carl Taylor, in one of his early works, states, "The community is the first social group in modern life that approaches self-sufficiency." [4] Taylor's definition, though it has been enlarged upon, has not been changed significantly up to the present time.

The traditional distinction between the two has thus been that the community represents a self-sufficient entity whereas the neighborhood does not. The question that arises from this statement is, "Under what circumstances is a social group self-sufficient?" A general answer that has been widely adopted is that a group is self-sufficient when it possesses most of the important social institutions. According to this criterion, a community is a group of people within a localized area containing a majority of the major social institutions. A group of people experiencing social interaction within a localized area with one or two social institutions as the focal point or means by which the area can be identified physically is thus a neighborhood. These are the definitions that are generally adhered to in this volume. The distinction is more

---

[2] Blaine Mercer, *The American Community,* New York: Random House, Inc., 1956, p. 27.

[3] Roy C. Buck, "Practical Applications of Community Research: Some Preliminary Considerations," *Rural Sociology,* 19:294, 1954.

[4] Carl C. Taylor, *Rural Sociology,* New York: Harper & Brothers, 1933, pp. 549–550.

easily understood if one thinks of the community as encompassing or containing a group, or cluster, of related neighborhoods.[5]

The neighborhood, to illustrate more fully, is an area within which borrowing occurs, where mutual aid is common, where first names are used, and where gossip takes place. The community, on the other hand, encompasses too large an area for these patterns to hold.

Geographical Setting

The general appearance of rural communities varies widely. There are, however, at least three recognizable spatial types, associated with the predominant forms of settlement found in rural areas. They may be characterized briefly as follows:

The Nucleated Agricultural Village Community. In terms of the number of rural people affected, the *nucleated-village* form of settlement is by far the most important in the world.[6] Its major characteristic is that the homes of farmers are clustered together, whereas their land is located away from the village. It is not unusual for animals and poultry to share their owner's quarters or to be housed nearby. The villages have a variety of shapes, some being round, others rectangular or irregular in shape. All such villages are characterized by a close-knit social organization fostered by residence proximity. Naturally, the fact that the farm lands are some distance from the farm homes is a disadvantage economically.

Examples of nucleated agricultural village communities are found in several places in the United States. The major concentrations are in New England, the Southwest, and Utah, but some of the plantations of the South offer a variation of this type of community. Figure 8 shows the general layout of a Mormon village in Utah. Note how one man's holdings may include several parcels of land some distance apart.

The Line Village Community. The second type of settlement pattern that gives rise to a unique type of community is known as the *line village*. Here, homes are in rows, generally on both sides of a stream or road, and the farm land is in long, narrow strips extending behind each house. It is obvious that this pattern was devised to retain the social advantages of residential propinquity and at the same time the economic advantages of living on one's own land. In the United States this type of community is traceable to French influence. Thus, examples of it are most prominent in southern Louisiana and in a few other places settled by the French.

[5] See: Irwin T. Sanders and Douglas Ensminger, *Alabama Rural Communities: A Study of Chilton County,* Montevallo, Ala.: Alabama College Bulletin 136, 1940.
[6] T. Lynn Smith, *Sociology of Rural Life,* 3d ed., New York: Harper & Brothers, 1953, p. 20.

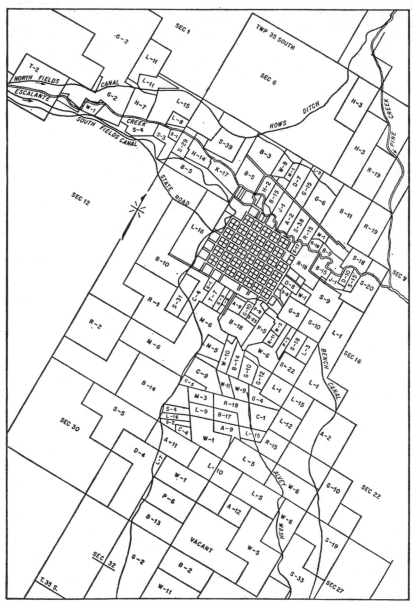

Figure 8. Diagram of the nucleated-agricultural-village pattern of settlement developed by the Mormons in Utah. Letters and numerals designate individual holdings. (From Lowry Nelson, *A Social Survey of Escalante, Utah,* Provo, Utah: Brigham Young University Studies, 1, 1925.)

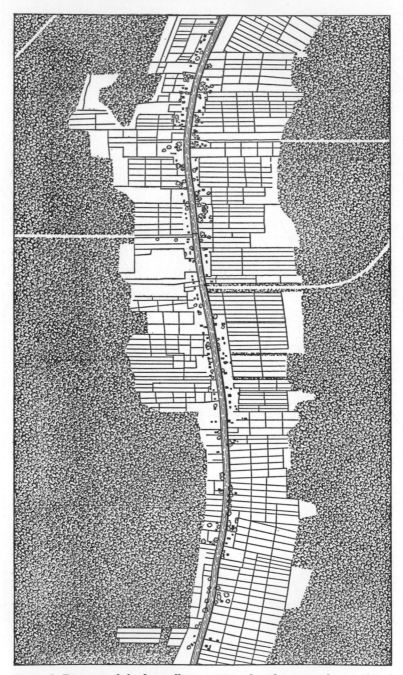

Figure 9. Diagram of the line-village pattern of settlement such as is found in South Louisiana.

Figure 9 illustrates the type of land holding found along Bayou Lafourche in Lafourche Parish, Louisiana.

The Open-country or Trade-center Community. The scattered-farmstead arrangement so common in the United States constitutes a third
type of community. The dispersed nature of settlement makes community boundaries harder to delineate than in the village types of settlement. However, through the procedures outlined in this chapter, neighborhoods can be delineated, and subsequently the several neighborhoods
that group together to form a community can be determined. Normally,
the community centers about a town or village where trading is done
and other services obtained. Figure 10 shows a typical community of
this pattern.

Each of these types of communities presents peculiar problems in

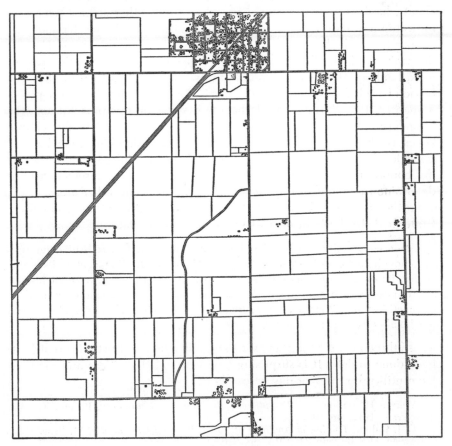

Figure 10. Diagram of the scattered-farmstead type of settlement pattern.
Note the community center at the top of the drawing.

terms of planning and development. In the United States, however, the predominance of the open-country type of community and neighborhood dictates that this type be given primary attention.

Early Studies of the Community

As early as 1912, Warren Wilson made a study of the evolution of the country community. He described the community as "that territory with its people which lies within the team haul of a given center." [7] His cognizance of the community as a locality group is seen in his observation that most of the farmer's social activities were confined to a definite geographic area—the locale to which he had primary access.

Galpin was the first sociologist to devise relatively precise methodology for determining community boundaries. He determined to find just how far the influence of each village reached. Toward this end he asked merchants, bankers, teachers, ministers, and various other service people to indicate on a map of Walworth County, Wisconsin, the most remote locations from which farmers came to do business or seek service. He also determined which village each family depended on for groceries, sale of milk, banking, dry goods, church, high school, etc. He then marked the home of each family trading at a particular village by sticking a pin in a map. A thread run around the outer edge of the pins formed the boundary of a service or trade zone.[8] His survey revealed twelve church zones, twelve trade zones, eleven banking zones, nine high school zones, seven local-newspaper zones, and many others. Galpin's method for locating boundaries of service units has been widely used by sociologists to determine the boundaries of neighborhood, trade, and other areas.

Further early clarification of the community concept came from K. L. Butterfield. In the light of his studies, Butterfield stated: [9]

A true community is a social group that is more or less self-sufficing. It is big enough to have its own centers of interest, its trading center, its social center, its own church, its own schoolhouse, its own garage, its own library, and to possess such other institutions as the people of the community need. It is something more than a mere aggregation of families. There may be several neighborhoods in a community.

These three men set the stage for the many community studies that have been done to date. It is surprising how many of their ideas and methods have utility for present-day researchers.

[7] Warren H. Wilson, *The Evolution of the Country Community*, Boston: The Pilgrim Press, 1912, pp. 91–92.

[8] C. J. Galpin, *The Social Anatomy of an Agricultural Community*, Madison, Wis.: Wisconsin AES Bulletin 34, 1915, pp. 3–6.

[9] Quoted in E. L. Morgan, *Mobilizing the Rural Community*, Massachusetts Agricultural College, 1918, p. 9.

THE NEIGHBORHOOD IN ITS CONTEMPORARY SETTING

The distinctive natures of the neighborhood and the community necessitate individual consideration of each. Community action and development are treated in greater detail in Chapter 7. In this section we shall review briefly the various approaches to neighborhood study and discuss the dynamics of neighborhoods.

How Neighborhoods Are Identified

At least three methods of identifying rural neighborhoods have been utilized. These methods are similar to those used in community studies.

Since a neighborhood is by definition a group of people who "neighbor" one another, the first and perhaps the most common method of identifying neighborhoods is simply to ask each family whom they look upon as neighbors and then use their answers as a basis for delineating their specific neighborhoods. A second method is to ask each respondent the name of his neighborhood and then mark the boundaries on a map as they are revealed by the responses. The third method was developed more recently.[10] It involves the identification of neighborhoods by the activities or interests common to a group of families.

Factors Related to the Persistence of Neighborhoods

Various research studies made during the past half-century indicate that neighborhoods come and go. Some die out permanently; others are reestablished. New ones develop, yet some of the old ones continue to exist. Kolb and Marshall found that factors related most closely to the persistence of neighborhoods were nationality, length of residence, and tenancy.[11] The more active neighborhoods were those in which at least 36 per cent of the families had heterogeneous nationality backgrounds. Ownership of land and longer residence in the neighborhood were also positively related to persistence.

A careful survey of the literature revealed that the quality most essential to maintenance of a neighborhood is "emotional unity," or the morale of the members. However, factors affecting the morale of one neighborhood may not affect the morale of another. In some neighborhoods, high morale appeared to be based on changes that linked the neighborhood closer to the greater community, making it a more effective functioning unit in a greater whole. In other cases, the consoli-

[10] John Kolb and Douglas Marshall, *Neighborhood-Community Relationships in Rural Society,* Wisconsin AES Bulletin 154, 1944, p. 35.
[11] *Ibid.,* p. 7.

dation or absorption of a central neighborhood institution by the greater community resulted in low neighborhood morale.

Forces that in general seem to have worked against the survival of strong rural neighborhoods are (1) the consolidation of schools and churches which previously served as neighborhood centers; (2) the increased acceptance of urban ways of life, which resulted in greater prestige for towns and cities and lower prestige for neighborhoods; (3) increased age, sex, and various other differentiations, which divide both family and neighborhood into more individualistic groupings; (4) increased migration, which served to diminish the significance of the kinship tie as a social bond; (5) the tendency of individuals to associate out-migration with general decline of the area or group; and (6) weakened social control in the neighborhood as a consequence of the operation of the preceding factors. It is paradoxical that these same factors may work to produce a stronger community, even though at the expense of the neighborhood.

In their case study of Hamilton County, Iowa, Jehlik and Wakeley made a thorough analysis of changes in rural organization. Part of their conclusion is as follows: "Frequent contacts outside the local community have decreased the frequency of neighborhood contacts. The more extensive contacts are based upon congeniality and choice rather than proximity." [12]

Will the Neighborhood Survive?

In view of recent trends, opinion is divided on whether or not the neighborhood will survive. If it is to continue to make a contribution as a social entity, it must do so by conscious purpose and not by drift. Those who would maintain the neighborhood believe that development techniques or procedures offer a solution to the problem of their decline. Others are not so confident of the value of neighborhoods in present-day society and doubt the wisdom of programs aimed at developing them.

Robin Williams observes that in a secularized, economically oriented culture with high mobility, local groups and family units assume a less prominent place in the total social structure. He concludes, nevertheless, that localistic primary groups are basic to the organization of American, as to any other, society.[13] Ryan, on the other hand, doubts that the neighborhood, from an organizational standpoint, has a place in modern society. He states: "The natural subunit of a community is the institu-

[12] Paul Jehlik and Ray Wakeley, *Rural Organization in Process: A Case Study of Hamilton County, Iowa,* Ames, Iowa: Iowa State College Research Bulletin 365, 1949, pp. 122–199.

[13] Robin Williams, *American Society,* New York: Alfred A. Knopf, Inc., 1951, p. 464.

tional or service group, not the neighborhood, and if community organization is desired, it would seem more reasonable to work through the subunits of the community rather than through extraneous groupings which partially reflect them." [14]

There is no doubt that emotionalism tends to creep into discussions concerning the neighborhood. However, many sociologists who are critically analyzing neighborhoods have recognized it and labeled it correctly. As Arthur E. Morgan puts it, "Fond memory may hark back to the old oaken bucket, but practical judgment prefers water under pressure." [15] It was apparently the failure of some individuals to recognize this tendency that led Frank D. Alexander, after careful study of the neighborhood and community concepts, to state: "There can be little doubt that the terms community and neighborhood have been used so loosely that they have lost their significance as scientific terms and should be abandoned for research purposes." [16]

A counterclaim is that organizational efforts to further the democratic process have a fertile field in those groups toward which the individual members have strong emotional feelings. Emotionalism that is a detriment to a research program may have some value in action programs. This seems, at present, one of the strongest crutches the neighborhood has to lean on.

Strengthening Neighborhoods

Action programs designed to improve neighborhoods are similar to community-development programs. Since community programs will be discussed in detail in Chapter 7, we shall mention them only briefly here.

Most neighborhood-improvement programs are based on the stimulation of self-analysis or social consciousness. The following are examples of recommendations for improving neighborhoods: (1) placing signs bearing the neighborhood name at significant crossroads; (2) placing signs bearing the name of each member of the neighborhood at the crossroad and at his home; (3) making a neighborhood self-survey; (4) distributing magazines containing feature stories on spectacular neighborhood developments; (5) showing motion pictures of spectacular neighborhood-improvement projects; (6) field trips to nearby neighborhoods; and (7) a wide variety of contests. If these programs gain the status of a social movement in the neighborhood, they will be a worthy area for research by rural sociologists and others.

[14] Bryce Ryan, "The Neighborhood as a Unit of Action in Rural Programs," *Rural Sociology,* 9:32, 1944.

[15] Arthur E. Morgan, *Community Service News,* 9, March–April, 1951, p. 61.

[16] Frank D. Alexander, "Locality-Group Classification," *Rural Sociology,* 16:237, 1952.

NEIGHBORHOODS AND COMMUNITIES IN PERSPECTIVE

Agriculture in the United States has evolved into a complex occupation and way of life. In some areas relationships among farm people have changed from those of the simple folk society characterized by intimacy and informality to those of the complex society marked by a high degree of formal, businesslike relations. These changes led T. Lynn Smith to state: "The net result of all this is to reduce greatly the rural-urban cultural differences. The greatest factor is, of course, the rapid diffusion of urban traits to rural areas." [17]

The older tendency to depend on primary groups such as the family and the neighborhood for social satisfactions is giving way to a new independence arising from the use of the automobile, hard-surfaced roads, and various other communicative devices. The individual may now be much more selective in his associations.

After a careful analytical study of changes occurring in rural locality groups, Bertrand sums up his findings by saying, "The rural neighborhood and community as traditionally defined have lost their identity, or are losing it. The neighborhood, as the smallest locality group and consisting of a few families in close communion and possessing a sense of belonging together, is now more an ideal than a reality." [18]

Slocum and Case, in presenting the implications of their research on neighborhoods, ask a most pertinent question: "Are we deluding ourselves about the prevalence and meaning of rural neighborhoods?" [19] They observed that it is quite possible for people at the county level to think of a locality as a neighborhood, even though the residents of the locality itself do not consider themselves to be members of such a neighborhood!

Traditionalists maintain that neighborhoods are the basis for moral unity in this nation; and it seems fairly evident that moral unity is the breeding ground for social ideals. However, the assumption that rural neighborhoods remain the strong centers of moral unity that they once were is questionable. Present evidence indicates that neighborhood contacts in the future, from the standpoint of both quality and quantity, will have little relationship to those characterizing the old concept of "primary group relationships." In view of this evidence, one is led to the conclusion that there is a continuing need for critical appraisal of the neighborhood and community within the context of rural social organization.

[17] Smith, *op. cit.*, p. 601.

[18] Alvin L. Bertrand, "Rural Locality Groups: Changing Patterns, Change Factors, and Implications," *Rural Sociology*, 19:176, 1954.

[19] W. L. Slocum and H. M. Case, "Are Neighborhoods Meaningful Social Groups?" *Rural Sociology*, 18:59, 1953.

Questions for Review and Discussion

1. What criteria do rural sociologists use to identify a community?
2. Distinguish between the concepts of the community and the neighborhood.
3. Explain how you would go about delineating a rural community.
4. Name and describe three types of settlement patterns characteristic of rural communities. Which type is predominant in the United States?
5. Do you believe the rural neighborhood of today will survive? Defend your answer.
6. How did C. J. Galpin contribute to the understanding of rural communities?
7. Discuss recent trends in rural communities and neighborhoods.

Selected References for Supplementary Reading

Hillman, Arthur: *Community Organization and Planning,* New York: The Macmillan Company, 1950.

Hoiberg, Otto G.: *Exploring the Small Community,* Lincoln: University of Nebraska Press, 1955.

Mercer, Blaine: *The American Community,* New York: Random House, Inc., 1956.

Morgan, Arthur E.: *The Small Community,* New York: Harper & Brothers, 1942.

———: *The Community of the Future,* Yellow Springs, Ohio: Community Service, Inc., 1957.

Sanderson, Dwight, and Robert A. Polson: *Rural Community Organization,* New York: John Wiley & Sons, Inc., 1939, chaps. 11–13.

Warren, Roland L.: *Studying Your Community,* New York: Russell Sage Foundation, 1955.

CHAPTER 7 *Community Development Programs*

Much of the recent activity of the Agricultural Extension Service and other agencies has been devoted to community betterment. In this chapter we shall discuss the objectives of community planning and development, citing the findings of some important research projects. Then we shall review a number of specific programs in this area, which is believed by many to represent the nation's greatest potential for the improvement of rural life.

THE SETTING OF COMMUNITY DEVELOPMENT PROGRAMS

Philosophy

The point has already been made that specialization has resulted in the production of terminologies, techniques, and interests that serve to set men apart as never before in human history. Differences among people are further accentuated by the struggle to achieve status in a highly competitive economy. The end result, as Fromm points out, is that modern man has difficulty finding meaning in the fragments that come into his hands. He does not have the necessary grasp to see the order or understand the relationships between the various apparently diverse ideals, ideologies, and actions with which he is confronted.[1] This development has led to disorganization rather than integration. Maston has gone so far as to say, "A civilization that is not integrated will have inner conflicts, confusion, and frustration."[2] Leaders of the community-development movement believe that democracy operating within the community can restore the core values, or integrating forces, of society. One of their spokesmen, writing about the vitality of democracy, observes, "It is a process by which free people in a free society are in com-

---

[1] Erich Fromm, *Escape from Freedom*, New York: Rinehart & Company, Inc., 1941, pp. 250–252.

[2] T. B. Maston, *A World in Travail*, Nashville: Broadman Press, 1954, p. 92.

munication with one another and together mold and control their own destiny at the neighborhood or community level." [3] The philosophy of community development, then, is that democratic procedures will flourish in the atmosphere of community life based on responsible participation by individuals working toward common causes. Poston expresses this philosophy clearly: [4]

Democracy is a process in which people are free to exchange ideas in a direct personal manner, to communicate with one another mentally and spiritually, and thereby to work out their own common destiny. If this process is blocked by policies and regulations that are determined from above, by institutions and organizations that are controlled from afar, by the separation of functions, by professional and specialized planners, by religious, social or economic barriers, or if it is blocked by any other barrier real or imaginary, then democracy cannot function. A free democratic society requires a certain environment in which to live. This is an environment of wholeness and social completeness, of stability, of self-control, of mutual sympathy and cooperation, of understanding and tolerance among heterogeneous interests. This environment may exist inside the local community, but if it does not exist there it cannot exist anywhere. In America there are still the resources—human and physical—with which to build such a community environment. They are in the skills, the knowledge, the very creation which has made the technological age. The job now is to make use of the freedom, the intelligence, and the resources that we have for the rebuilding of community life in order to preserve human values. In the trend toward specialization we have fallen into the habit of breaking up the community into a vast collection of carefully arranged compartments, each walled off and separated from the others. One is labeled business, another is agriculture, another is education, another is health, another is recreation, another is government, another is social service, another is religion, another is the home. The list is almost endless. Each of these compartments has become a special world in which there are further subdivisions. Then there are the organizational, special interest, and occupational groupings.

Although he was referring to the disciplining of special-interest groups rather than to the improvement of communities, President Eisenhower voiced essentially the philosophy of community development in his 1957 State of the Union message: "Freedom has been defined as the opportunity for self-discipline. Should we persistently fail to discipline ourselves, eventually there will be increasing pressure on Government to redress the failure. By that process, freedom will step by step disappear." [5] Thus the community-development movement as it has evolved in this country has as its object the organization or establishment of

[3] Richard W. Poston, *Democracy Is You*, New York: Harper & Brothers, 1953, p. 8.
[4] *Ibid.*, pp. 9–10.
[5] Dwight Eisenhower, "State of the Union," *U.S. News and World Report*, January 18, 1957, p. 109.

self-generating, self-disciplined groups that operate within specific communities.

Objectives

In the light of this philosophy, community development can be said to be a democratic process for encouraging study of the community and implementing programs designed to make the community a more progressive and wholesome place in which to live. Both its philosophy and its functions are found in the *Rural Community Improvement Guide* developed by the University of Arkansas. This guide lists the following four basic features of the community-development approach: (1) Every community should have a constructive approach to problem solving. (2) Every community should develop leadership. (3) Every community should have a strong sense of community loyalty. (4) Every community should improve its economic base and community activities.[6]

Community development programs are primarily concerned, in both research and practice, with coordination of local activities, leadership development, increased individual participation, and program planning. To many individuals, community development means any step toward general improvement of the place in which one lives. Every state that has a community development or community improvement program has a list of objectives. Most of them are quite similar and are related in some fashion to the nine objectives developed by Sanderson and Polson: (1) to develop consciousness of community identity; (2) to satisfy unmet needs; (3) to stimulate social participation; (4) to maintain social control; (5) to coordinate group activities; (6) to protect the community from the introduction of undesirable influences or conditions; (7) to cooperate with other communities and agencies to satisfy common needs; (8) to provide the mechanism for obtaining agreement; (9) to develop leadership.[7]

Community Study Groups. Several methods of implementing these objectives have been experimented with. Possibly the most successful has been the community-study-group approach. Because communities vary so much in so many respects, the logical first step in any community improvement program is to determine by means of research the significant characteristics of the specific community under study. To this end, many types of social and economic surveys have been made by community research groups. It was not until 1944, however, that experimentation was begun on the type of program which is presently the most

[6] *Rural Community Improvement Guide,* Fayetteville, Ark.: University of Arkansas Extension Service Publication 5727, 1955, pp. 4–5.

[7] Dwight Sanderson and R. A. Polson, *Rural Community Organization,* New York: John Wiley & Sons, Inc., 1939, p. 77.

popular. At this time the so-called "Montana Study" was begun. This was to be a research project in human relations to determine, if possible, how the humanities could contribute to the improvement of life in small communities.[8]

The most significant results of the Montana Study seem to have been the demonstration of the interest that local people manifest in the study of their own community and the effort they are willing to exert to solve the problems revealed by such study. The procedure seems simple enough, as may be seen in the following statement: [9]

They need only to enlist the participation of a true cross section of the citizens in their town, to sit down together once each week around a common table to study and objectively analyze the past, present, and future of their community. And out of this group process they will discover their local problems, the causes and reasons behind them, and the means by which they may be solved. The history, the problems, the causes, and the means of solution will be different in each community, yet the principle of objective study as a community—not as a pressure group or a special clique—will be the same. But the point to start from is study, not action—for intelligent action can come only from long, arduous, and systematic study, which embraces all levels of local society in one unified effort for the common welfare.

If during the process help is needed from outside experts, that help can be obtained from the educational institutions, the extension services, the federal and local agencies in the state concerned. Thus, the people themselves can find a fuller utilization for the public services which they support.

After research projects and various investigations had been conducted in communities scattered over Montana, the leaders of the project developed a community study guide. This guide, containing suggested research problems and other valuable information, has been tested by actual field operations and is a most helpful instrument for communities initiating improvement programs.[10]

The Role of Sociological Research

The sociologist has a definite contribution to make to community development programs. The Southern Committee on Community Study states: [11]

[8] See: Baker Brownell, *The Human Community*, New York: Harper & Brothers, 1950, p. 25.

[9] Richard W. Poston, *Small Town Renaissance*, New York: Harper & Brothers, 1950, pp. 191–192.

[10] For a condensed version of the guide, see: Poston, *op. cit.*, pp. 193–209.

[11] Harold F. Kaufman, et al., *Toward a Delineation of Community Research*, State College, Miss.: Mississippi State College Social Science Research Center, 1954, pp. 6–7.

The major objective of this paper is to point toward a study of community dynamics. The assumption is made that a big step is made in this direction by vigorously pursuing a group, associational, or action-interactional level of analysis. To develop research method and theory, community study must move from its present omnibus and descriptive stage toward more specialized and definitive approaches such as the one suggested.

By "community dynamics" the authors meant the study of specific activities, processes, decisions, or, in a broader sense, patterns of social interaction found in a given society. They divide the action process into the following steps: (1) Goal setting is the process by which a need is recognized and a goal is defined. (2) The small action group functions as a catalyst in analyzing the situation, finding facts, and planning for community action. It should be large enough to be representative and small enough so that each member can participate. (3) Fact finding is the process of gathering and analyzing relevant information regarding the problem situation. (4) Education or promotion is the process of informing the public regarding the need for action and persuading the people to adopt the desired goal. (5) Administration is the process of operating the new facility or service and incorporating it into the community.[12]

The great need at present in community and small-group research is for continued emphasis on methodology. Subjects receiving considerable attention, and deservedly so, are communication, participation, integration, adaptive and integrative changes, leadership development, decision making, and social control. As was indicated previously, it is in research of this type that the professional sociologist or social psychologist may contribute in no small way to community development. The experience of researchers has led one of them to suggest three methodological emphases for community research intended to have broad practical application: (1) a comprehensive statistical study of the locality and its people; (2) a summary of the prevailing issues or social problems current in the locality; and (3) a summary of the prevailing cultural patterns.[18]

Leadership in Community Development

To achieve success, any community development program must have capable leaders. A leader, in very simple language, is a person who directs others in some action, opinion, or movement and who is followed by them. Leaders thus are individuals who exercise a great deal more influence than others.

[12] *Ibid.,* p. 9.
[18] Roy C. Buck, "Practical Applications of Community Research: Some Preliminary Considerations," *Rural Sociology,* 19:296, 1954.

The particular leader who will succeed in a community is the one the community will encourage. Jessie Bernard reveals how this process works: [14]

Historically, institutions grow up which are congenial to one type and not to another. To illustrate: militarism is sometimes greatly exalted. As a set of institutions, militarism fits some people like a glove. They enjoy fighting. They like aggressive behavior. In a time of militarism, soldiers are leaders. In other ages and in other places, on the other hand, priests are leaders. Then a quite different set of institutions is established.

The basis of the authority vested by a community in its leaders varies from one community to another. In some communities the authority may be based on traditional factors such as family background, length of residence, or social position. In other areas it may be based largely on personality factors—the unusual influence of a particular person. In many cases leadership rests on functional authority—the special ability or training of the individual. In some few instances it is associated with certain positions or offices. In such cases authority is based upon law.[15]

SOME EXAMPLES OF COMMUNITY DEVELOPMENT PROGRAMS

A Formal Program

One example of an extensive formal program to build better neighborhoods and communities is the "Texas Rural Neighborhood Progress Contest," sponsored annually by the Texas Agricultural Extension Service in cooperation with the *Farmer Stockman Magazine*. The promotional literature states: [16]

This contest has been set up to stimulate individual family and neighborhood effort toward farm, home, and neighborhood improvement. A group of people who have a feeling that they belong in the locality in which they live, who associate with one another in schools, churches, and other organizations may enter this contest. Scoring will include every farm and family within the designated neighborhood boundaries.

Cash prizes totaling $5,750.00 are distributed to the winners. Each neighborhood plans its goals according to the needs and desires of the people; however, scoring is related to a fourfold improvement program. The four objectives are as follows: to increase and manage more ef-

[14] Jessie Bernard, *American Community Behavior*, New York: The Dryden Press, Inc., 1949, p. 567.

[15] John M. Foskett, "Social Structure and Social Participation," *American Sociological Review*, 20:436–438, 1955.

[16] "Handbook for Progress," Texas Rural Neighborhood Progress Contest, *Farmer Stockman Magazine*, Dallas, Tex.

fectively the family income, to improve health conditions and services, to improve the home and farm, and to encourage social participation.

When a neighborhood or community joins the contest, members begin meeting for regular study in discussion groups. These discussions serve to promote self-analysis or social consciousness on the part of the participants. To develop greater personal and neighborhood consciousness, road signs bearing each farmer's name are erected at the crossroads. Each participant is urged to post a sign bearing his name in front of his home. Experience has indicated that these means of personal identification are soon followed by tangible improvements. In 1956 some 4,507 rural families participated actively in this program. Some 1,809 families helped landscape their church grounds, and 2,335 families helped remodel and repair the church building. Some 2,461 families planned neighborhood recreational activities.[17]

It is significant to note, however, that this program, which began as a neighborhood contest, has now broadened its scope to include communities. As it is now conducted, *neighborhood* and *community* are used in program discussions as synonymous terms.

An Experiment in Informal Community Development

Up to this point, the discussion has centered on formal means of improving communities, which involve considerable time and effort on the part of a group of planners as well as of community members. This fact has pointed up the need for simpler study procedures that can be used as a basis for obtaining more formalized organization of action processes within the community. Dan R. Davis, after observing the results of community self-study by many groups, decided to conduct a research experiment involving simpler procedures and without formal organizational structure.

He conducted two surveys in Community A, a farming community with a village of 2,100 people as its trade center. The first survey was concerned with the social and economic resources of the community trade area. The survey depicted population trends, levels of living, health, education, rural road developments, etc. Data were obtained from the county agent, home demonstration agent, public officials, and the United States census.[18]

The results of the first survey were widely distributed among community members. Each person was sent the results of the first survey along with a questionnaire asking for answers to three simple questions:

[17] Reagan Brown, *Organized Neighborhoods Point the Way,* Texas AES Publication MP-185, 1956, pp. 2–18.

[18] Dan R. Davis, *An Experiment in Informal Community Organization,* Texas AES Progress Report 1323, 1951, p. 1.

(1) What do you consider to be the three greatest assets of Community A? (2) What do you consider to be the three greatest weaknesses of Community A? (3) What in your opinion could and should be done to make Community A a more progressive and wholesome community in which to live? These questions were designed to stimulate study, thought, community consciousness, and, ultimately, action on the part of local leadership. Community leaders who assisted with the two surveys distributed approximately 3,200 copies of the findings to individuals and groups within the community.

The results of this procedure are significant. That community morale was improved is reflected in the fact that more votes were cast in the next election following completion of the surveys than in any year since 1938. Heavy voting as an indicator of community morale is of particular significance in this case, since the population of the community area had declined 29 per cent during the previous ten-year period. After an eighteen-month interval had elapsed, Davis made a final survey of the community to determine what changes and developments had occurred during that period and included these changes in his report. These changes provide ample evidence that this methodology has definite merit.

The Community-council Approach

Community development that is deliberately promoted necessarily has an artificial character and is somewhat alien to the processes that occur in a "folk" type of community. The community council as it now functions in many areas of the nation seeks to overcome this handicap. It is widely used as a means of preparing small groups for intelligent, active participation in local, state, and national affairs.

The exact nature of the community council varies widely, but the following definition contains the basic elements: A community council is a voluntary group made up of representatives of local groups, institutions, and the people at large, who study and plan for the most effective use of the total community resources. Most councils follow the administrative principle of separating planning and policy making from the executive function. The council works with plans and policies and seeks to leave their implementation to various other community groups or organizations.

The functions of the council, as set forth by Hillman, include: (1) Coordinating existing activities and planning for additional facilities or services to meet recognized needs within a local area. The usual practice is that actual operations are delegated to new or existing agencies. (2) Establishing new patterns of social relationships within an area, as a result of contacts and discussion between individuals and group representatives not otherwise in touch with each other, including the possibility of developing social relations between previously hostile groups.

This may be incidental to other functions, but even as a by-product of other purposes it is worthy of note, granted the existence of various conflicts and tensions in communities. (3) Representing local interests within a larger framework of planning in larger cities or metropolitan regions. Conversely, planning bodies on a larger area basis may help to establish local units for decentralized participation in planning.[19]

The community council frequently utilizes the services of professional people to help develop plans or programs. For example, Community A, after the development of considerable antisocial behavior on the part of teenagers, asked their council to take up the problem. The council in turn requested that the State's extension sociologist study the problem and meet with them to help formulate a policy. Interviews with a sample of the adults and a sample of the teenagers revealed the following things: (1) All the acts committed had occurred between June and September. (2) The area was a low-income farm area, the trade center having one small industrial plant. (3) Farmers were not requiring their sons to assist them on the farm, particularly since a large proportion of the farmers had part-time jobs. (4) Except for a few jobs in service stations and grocery stores, no employment was available in the area for teenagers. (5) When school ended, the gymnasium closed and there were no organized recreational opportunities for the youngsters until school opened again.

Although this case is a very simple one, it serves to illustrate the first function of community councils, namely, coordination of activities. The council, after considerable study and discussion, made the following recommendations: (1) The local ministerial council should be asked to take the leadership in the establishment of a softball league. It was suggested that a softball team might be an effective means for recruiting young people into the church program. The ministerial council was asked to study other recreational needs and take whatever action it deemed necessary. (2) The only civic club in the local trade center should be requested to study the problem of summer employment and also consider the feasibility of a club project dealing with handicrafts. The club was asked to study the advisability of asking various groups within the community to sponsor short courses for teenagers in leather tooling, ceramics, photography, and arts and crafts. These recommendations eventually resulted in action by organizations already in existence.

The Virginia Council on Health and Medical Care provides an example of how the resources of the state government may be utilized by a local council. This council, staffed by sociologists and other professional people, works with local groups in outlining the necessary pro-

---

[19] Arthur Hillman, *Community Organization and Planning*, New York: The Macmillan Company, 1950, pp. 161–162.

cedures that must be followed before a doctor's services can be obtained for the community. Once the community is ready, the state council furnishes the group with a list of young doctors who have expressed willingness to serve in rural Virginia.[20] This program, as a result of its accomplishments, has been accorded national recognition.

It should be noted that, regardless of the name by which the group goes or the procedures it follows, the foundation stones of study groups, councils, improvement clubs, and other such organizations are individual participation and responsibility, leadership development, goal establishment or achievement of new levels of aspiration, and the recognition and effective use of resources. It must also be observed that unity within these groups is largely of a functional nature. Councils develop and maintain high morale while delving into areas regarded as significant by the community, but they frequently die out when community opinion indicates that the council is "just another meeting to go to." In other words, a community council must be functional from the standpoint of working toward mutually desirable goals. If it does not function toward accepted objectives, it becomes a sterile structure.

Community Clubs

Because of increasing interest in specialized community activities, interest in community organization in certain areas has focused on special-interest groups rather than on the community as a whole. For example, after an analysis of community organization in the Great Plains area, Kraenzel states: "There is emerging, in the Plains, something new in social organization. There appears to be an emphasis upon formal and legal organization so as to encompass the larger areas that are necessary in order to command the resources and the population base necessary to provide certain services. The functionary (paid official) appears to be essential to the functioning of a program if the organization is to survive and perform a task."[21]

Mississippi State College, in cooperation with the Tennessee Valley Authority, recently conducted a study to evaluate the role of organized community clubs in increasing knowledge and adoption of recommended fertilization and related farm practices. The educational phase consisted of transmitting to farm families knowledge of recommended practices through the club. This phase also included the following community activities: (1) self-analysis, (2) leadership training, and (3) planning of goals. The authors state: "Since the project is not completed, conclusions

[20] *Huddleston Got Its Man: Rural Communities Can Have Doctors*, Charlottesville, Va.: Community Services, Extension Division Bulletin 138, December, 1952, pp. 2–6.

[21] Carl F. Kraenzel, "Sutland and Yonland Setting for Community Organization in the Plains," *Rural Sociology*, 18:357, 1953.

are not final, but it does appear that communities with active clubs have more farmers in the high level of adoption category than do unorganized communities." [22]

Some communities in Texas have organized as one-variety cotton communities in connection with the 7-step cotton program. Concluding a study made to determine how existing social organizations could be most effectively used in gaining the acceptance of a cotton-production and -marketing program, Fred Elliott made the following observations: "The study demonstrated that in a program of this sort the organizational set-up should be very flexible in order to achieve the greatest possible success. The organizational structure should be tailored to the particular situation in each distinct area." [23] This same statement might well be applied to community organization as a whole.

Elliott also observed that "farmers now travel longer distances to attend countywide and area meetings where formerly they thought of attending only meetings in their local community or neighborhood. Neighborhood economy changed to a town-country community and the farmer became a member of a larger unit, thus bringing about a greater degree of specialization on the part of organized groups. In Williamson and Travis counties the county 7-step cotton committees preferred to hold countywide meetings and maintained that the farmers would rather come in from over the county to a well organized meeting than attend smaller meetings. The attendance of 167,055 farmers at 1,001 meetings shows the interest that was maintained." [24]

COMMUNITY DEVELOPMENT IN FOREIGN COUNTRIES

The International Cooperation Administration and various other public and private agencies concerned with technical-assistance programs for foreign countries are turning to community development as a means for carrying out their programs. In reporting on his experiences in Haiti and El Salvador, Daniel Russell states: [25]

All agency directors are anxious to get community cooperation for their programs. Each one going at the community individually, piecemeal, divides the resources and dissipates the energies of the people. The local people are or should be interested in all the programs. To have the force of all the people back of each as well as all of the programs immeasurably strengthens each

---

[22] *Community Clubs and Fertilizer Education,* Knoxville, Tenn.: Mississippi State College in cooperation with the Tennessee Valley Authority, 1956, p. 11.

[23] Fred C. Elliott, "An Analysis of the Development of the Seven Step Cotton Program," unpublished thesis, Texas A. & M. College, May, 1955, p. 13.

[24] *Ibid.,* pp. 133–134.

[25] Daniel Russell, *Manuel de Developpement Communautaire,* Port-au-Prince: U.S. Operations Mission to Haiti, 1955, pp. 2–3.

effort. . . . We all know we must improve all phases of agriculture and local industry in order to raise the economic level of the people. Still, in order to have more intelligent people to understand improved methods of farming and industry we must have better schools and adult education. If people are ill they cannot go to school or work on the farm or in the factory; so we must all be interested in developing better health for all the people. Unless we have roads and transportation we cannot get our products of farm and factory to market, or very well get to our schools.

It should be apparent that the particular approach to community improvement varies according to the cultural development of the area or country. For example, Russell observes: [26]

A casual observation will tell one that the Haitian peasant is in a rut of traditional ways of doing things, i.e., farming with the hoe and machette, building mud *cailles*, transporting goods to market by human head or donkey, going to the witch-doctor when ill, planting seed and coffee trees too thick, etc. . . . These traditional patterns greatly simplify the life of the isolated peasant. He does not have to learn new ways. From the time he is quite young he is educated in traditional methods and ready to follow the ways of his ancestors. The young peasant girl before she is ten years old is skilled in balancing heavy loads on her head and is proudly following her mother in burden carrying. The young peasant boy is as proud of his first machette as the U.S. boy of his first air rifle.

Within each rural community the world over are found vested interests, taboos, customs, and traditions which are powerful forces that must be understood and dealt with in a program of community betterment.[27] Strauss, in his discussion of the status system of Ceylon, points up a problem in community development that exists in many countries. He states: [28]

In a consideration of the implications of the status system, it is important to note that the situation is unlikely to be altered by the issue of directives or instructions to *treat the villager as an equal*. The agent charged with implementing such a directive has been reared in a society which does the opposite and, more important, he must operate in a social system which (whatever the deviations) is fundamentally antagonistic to such an equalitarian pattern. It is therefore emotionally and operationally difficult for Ceylonese to order their relationships with persons of lower status on any other than that of superior-inferior.

[26] *Ibid.*, pp. 25–26.
[27] Additional information on community development programs in India, Egypt, Iran, and Formosa may be obtained from the Community Development Division, FAO, Washington, D.C. These programs were developed by Carl Taylor, Arthur Raper, Daniel Russell, and Ernest Neal.
[28] Murray A. Strauss, "Cultural Factors in the Functioning of Agricultural Extension in Ceylon," *Rural Sociology*, 18:252, 1953.

Aurbach calls attention to another problem in community planning abroad. He states that in 1950 there were 214 collective agricultural settlements (communities) in Israel with a total population of 68,000 inhabitants, or 30 per cent of the rural population of Israel. Although these communities were originally based almost wholly on idealism, particularly the ideas of social justice and equality, it is the general concensus of most of the observers that individualism is making great inroads into the thinking of the collectives.[29] Aurbach notes: [30]

> However, they have made no attempt to return to the mechanical concept of equality which would require all women to participate fully in all the heavy work of the community, for some of which they are not biologically fitted. Similarly, they have tried to bring more and more of the membership into functional responsibility in the community, but they have abandoned the impractical method of short-period rotation of all leadership positions and the practice of leaving all major decisions up to the general membership meetings. The original idealism which was the basis of these communities is not too dissimilar from ideals which were the bases of some of the early American utopian societies.

THE RURAL DEVELOPMENT PROGRAM OF THE UNITED STATES

On January 11, 1954, the special Presidential message on agriculture addressed to the Congress by President Eisenhower called for broad improvements in agricultural programs and placed new emphasis on the need for basic economic changes in certain farm areas. This Presidential message gave impetus to a basic research project and to a broad program of cooperation between Federal and state governmental agencies and private farm, civic, and business groups. The work under the Rural Development Program, as it has come to be known, was, by 1957, being carried on in thirty of the forty-eight States. Since this work is essentially community-development work, a brief description of the Rural Development Program is included in this chapter. Figure 11 shows the location of the first pilot counties in the program.

[29] Herbert A. Aurbach, "Social Stratification in the Collective Agricultural Settlements in Israel," *Rural Sociology*, 18:33, 1953.

[30] For a review of these early communities, see: W. A. Hinds, *American Communities*, Chicago: Charles H. Kerr and Co., 1902. Robert Owen's New Harmony Colony is notable among those that failed partially because of the absence of stratification. For an excellent analysis of cultural values in various areas of the world, see: T. Lynn Smith, "Values Held by People in Latin America," W. A. Anderson, "Oriental Values and Technical Cooperation," and A. I. Tannous, "Technical Exchange and Cultural Values," *Proceedings of the Sixth Conference for Agricultural Services in Foreign Areas*, Washington: USDA-ICA–Land Grant College Association, November, 1955.

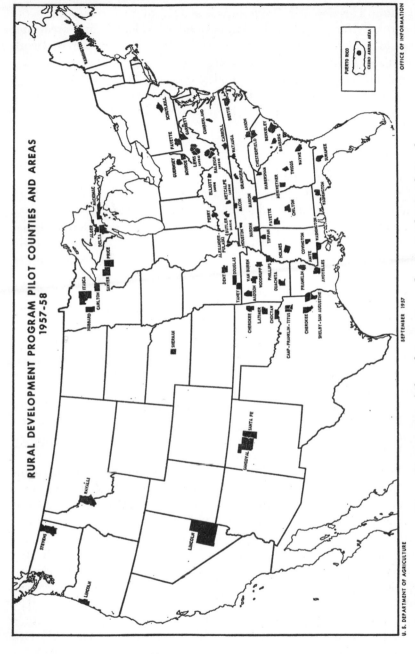

Figure 11. Location of the pilot counties and areas in the Rural Development Program of the United States, 1957–1958.

The Rural Development Program was started to open wider the doors of opportunity for people in the nation's underdeveloped rural areas and communities. State rural development committees tie together the work of the many agencies in the program. These committees select rural counties and areas to participate and give them help in getting their development work under way. The first step in each county is to select a county committee composed of local leaders. The principal activities are:

1. Increased extension work among families on small farms to help them find new sources of income on and off the farm and improve their farm production and homemaking.

2. Credit programs to help small farmers improve their farming and shift to production for newly developed or growing markets in the area.

3. Technical aid especially suited to small farms and underdeveloped rural areas. The aim is to help farmers and community leaders evaluate their soil resources and manage soil, water, and forests for sustained production.

4. A campaign to expand industry, including the promotion of industrial sites in the area and the encouragement of local small industry and business.

5. Help to underemployed farmers and others in finding full or part-time jobs in industry and trades.

6. A review of vocational education to find out whether it is meeting the needs of young people.

7. Surveys to determine and call attention to community health and welfare needs. Information on benefits to older farmers from the expanded social security program is distributed, and projects to improve health services and to attract medical personnel are begun.

The key unit in a local rural development program is the county committee. A typical committee in a county may have representatives from the chamber of commerce, the city planning commission, the county commissioner's office, the Agricultural Extension Service, the Soil Conservation Service, the Farmer's Home Administration, the local health service, the board of education, the various farm organizations, the Indian Service, the ministers' association, the local bank, and the county newspaper among others.

The Rural Development Program includes much more than on-the-farm improvement. It is especially concerned with balancing agriculture with industry and thus creating more job opportunities. The U.S. Departments of Agriculture, Commerce, and Labor are working together to accomplish this phase of the program.

It is the belief of informed persons that the Rural Development Program will help those families on small farms and with limited resources to attain greater opportunities.

Questions for Review and Discussion

1. Why might the Congress of the United States vote an appropriation for a rural development program?

2. What are the major objectives of community development programs?

3. Why are rural sociologists sought to head up programs of community development, both at home and abroad?

4. Explain the significant finding of the Montana Study.

5. Differentiate between formal and informal programs of community development.

6. What contributions can special-interest groups make to community development programs?

7. Look up and outline the objectives and procedures of the Rural Development Program of the U.S. Congress as passed in 1956.

Selected References for Supplementary Reading

Biddle, William W.: *The Cultivation of Community Leaders*, New York: Harper & Brothers, 1953.

Brownell, Baker: *The Human Community*, New York: Harper & Brothers, 1950.

Matthews, Mark S.: *Guide to Community Action*, New York: Harper & Brothers, 1954.

Moore, Harry E.: *Nine Help Themselves*, Austin, Tex.: Southwestern Cooperative Program in Educational Administration, 1955.

Ogden, Jean, and Jess Ogden: *These Things We Tried*, Charlottesville, Va.: University of Virginia Extension Division, 1947.

Poston, Richard W.: *Small Town Renaissance*, New York: Harper & Brothers, 1950.

CHAPTER 8 *The Regional Approach to the Study of Rural Populations*

Rural sociologists are constantly being confronted with problems relating to areas larger than the community, and they have called these larger locality groups *regions*. The importance of the study of regions is made clear by Carl Taylor and his associates: [1]

The concept of the cultural area or region is of basic importance to the social scientist, and to the rural sociologist especially, for it provides a means whereby the spatial aspects of society can be broken down into broadly and relatively homogeneous locality units. This type of delineation makes it possible for scientists to deal with the separate areas as segments of a unified whole— a type of analysis greatly needed to supplement the economic and population analyses that have been done on these same geographic bases, and to supplement and enrich the findings of specific studies that have been made of such subjects as levels of living, leadership, delinquency, family organization, and youth participation in group activities. Studies of cultural areas and of specific subject-matter fields will supplement each other in many important ways. In fact, there is a dawning realization that neither can be done adequately without the other.

At this point, it may be recalled that social groups are recognized as constituting the framework of social life. Regions, as well as communities and neighborhoods, are placed under the heading of territorial or locality groups.[2] The difference between the three is primarily one of size, with neighborhoods generally occupying the smallest space and re-

[1] Carl C. Taylor, et al., *Rural Life in the United States*, New York: Alfred A. Knopf, Inc., 1949, p. 339.
[2] R. M. MacIver and Charles H. Page, *Society, An Introductory Analysis*, New York: Rinehart & Company, Inc., 1949, pp. 213–216.

gions the largest. It is customary to consider regions as including several communities and neighborhoods.[3]

Regional study is a special branch of sociology primarily concerned with (1) the delineation of homogeneous regions and subregions, (2) the study of all forms of human association within a specific regional environment, and (3) the comparative study of regional social systems.[4] This chapter will deal largely with the last two of these areas and will take up only the special types of regions which have a rural setting. However, before describing the rural regions of the United States, we shall first discuss the nature and types of regions and take up the important studies of national rural regions.

A region, from a sociocultural standpoint, is *an area within which historical and environmental factors have combined to create a relatively homogeneous social structure and a consciousness of individuality.* Several conditions are implied in this definition. First, the region exhibits homogeneity in more than one significant aspect. It cannot, like certain subregions or specialized regions, be identified as a unit on the basis of a single characteristic. One region can be distinguished from another in terms of many factors. Each has, in other words, unique characteristics on the basis of several criteria. Second, the people within a region are aware of their uniqueness; they are conscious of having distinctive characteristics of thought and action, and the individual resident readily identifies himself with his region. Finally, a region is necessarily an area with a core, or heart, differing from that of other regions and bounded by broad zones rather than by a sharp line. With few exceptions, it would be highly unrealistic to expect sharp deviations in characteristics from persons living in close proximity. Thus rural regions differ from other regional entities only in that their unifying characteristics are peculiar to the rural environment.

TYPES OF REGIONS

There are, obviously, many ways to divide a large nation into subareas of relative homogeneity. Essentially, however, regions are distinguished according to three major criteria.

The first criterion is the number of indexes used in the delineation of regions. Those regions determined on the basis of a *single factor* are differentiated from *composite* regions, which are delineated on the basis

[3] For a discussion of the region as a sociological group, see: Carle C. Zimmerman and Richard E. DuWors, *Graphic Regional Sociology*, Cambridge, Mass.: The Phillips Book Store, 1952, pp. 138–140.

[4] Alvin L. Bertrand, "Regional Sociology as a Special Discipline," *Social Forces*, 21:132–136, 1952.

of many factors. Specialized regions are not to be confused with the broader concept of the sociocultural region defined above. There are four types of single-factor regions:

1. *Natural regions* are distinguished from one another on the basis of a given geographical characteristic, such as topography, rainfall, or type of soil.

2. *Cultural regions* are set apart on the basis of differences in any material or nonmaterial cultural trait, such as characteristic literature, esthetic expression, architecture, or dress.

3. *Service regions* are distinguished for administrative purposes. There are innumerable examples of such regions in the fields of government and economics, such as Federal Reserve Bank regions and sales regions.

4. *Type-of-farming regions* are based on marked differences in agricultural endeavor. Although these regions might realistically be termed cultural regions, it is advisable to keep them separate for purposes of study. (These are the regions that are of greatest significance to us in this chapter.)

Composite regions, in contrast to single-factor regions, combine a number of these characteristics: geographic, economic, cultural, historical, and social. It can readily be seen that, except for purposes of specialized study, the composite region has greater significance than the single-factor region. As a matter of fact, as noted above, national and world regional delineations are usually of this type.

The second criterion for distinguishing types of regions is the subordinate or superordinate (regional or subregional) relationship of one region to another. In other words, within the larger regional homogeneity there is subregional heterogeneity, which must be recognized and catalogued. The two types distinguished on this basis are the *major region* and the *subregion* (or *minor region*).[5]

A major region is a societal division of the nation delineated and characterized by the greatest possible areal homogeneity. A subregion, or minor region, is a subdivision of a major region representing some variation within the larger framework of the homogeneity of the major region.

The third basis for distinguishing types of regional entities is whether or not political boundaries coincide with the dividing lines between the various regions. The fact that social and economic patterns do not conform to political boundaries has always been a thorn in the regionalist's

---

[5] Odum includes a third term, *district*. However, delineated solely for functional administrative purposes, districts do not appear to constitute a bona fide third type. The subregional classification seems to answer such a purpose fully. See: Howard W. Odum, "Promise of Regionalism," in Merrill Jensen (ed.), *Regionalism in America*, Madison, Wis.: University of Wisconsin Press, 1951, p. 410.

side. He is eternally confronted with the problem of deciding where his own boundaries will be set. On the basis of the patterns that have been followed, two types of regions may be distinguished.

First, there are the so-called group-of-states and group-of-counties regions, which are delineated according to established state and county lines. The advantage in using such boundaries is obvious; analytic data are easy to come by, and administrative functions are easy to establish. In the present state of political thinking, this seems to be the most practical approach to regional divisions.

However, even the uninitiated can see that geographic and societal characteristics do not often coincide with political boundaries. In fact, sociocultural characteristics seldom have distinct boundaries in any society. Rather, there usually exists a relatively broad zone of transition between one culturally homogeneous unit and another. Thus, many authors have chosen to establish their regional boundaries according to these zones, ignoring political lines altogether. Such regions have the advantage of being more realistic than political regions in describing sociocultural wholes; however, they are unrealistic from the point of view of availability of analytical data and the ease with which administrative functions can be established.

BASIC REGION-MAKING FORCES

The region, as we have seen, is a more or less homogeneous entity, a basic configuration of human life. What forces are important in weaving the various threads of a given area into a unified fabric? Three major forces are significant in this process.

Geographic and Physiographic Characteristics. The natural environment, or the elements on the face of the earth which are not man-made, is readily recognized as one of the basic region-making forces. This is true because man's physical setting usually conditions his social adjustment to an observable extent. Thus, differences such as in occupation, dress, architecture, and recreation may often be closely linked to topography, climate, and soils. However, similar natural characteristics do not always bring about similar sociocultural characteristics. Also, the natural environment is not invariably the most potent influence in region making.

History. Accidents of history can become the most powerful region-making force operative among a people, because a strong consciousness of identity is bred through shared experiences and problems. Over and over again, it has been observed that historical factors account in good measure for the regional unity existing in the southern part of the United States. For example, Zimmerman says, "The South was united by the race problem and the resultant Civil War experiences." [6] Odum goes into even more detail in showing the role of historical influences in making a region of this geographic area. He lists among the numerous "crises" that have played a dominant role in developing the personality of the region the following: secession and war, the tragedies of reconstruction, race conflict, turbulent politics, and a cotton-and-plantation economy.[7]

Cultural Experiences. It is inevitable that cultural materials that are invented, discovered, or borrowed in a specific area are shared only unevenly with the rest of the national group. This fact can be accounted for in terms of the rate of acceptance of any given cultural trait and its usefulness in various areas. The extent to which an item of culture will be useful varies directly with such factors as the economic structure and geographic conditions. Rates of diffusion of culture are, of course, dependent on the values, attitudes, opinions, and experiences of the people. Obviously, the amount and kind of cultural material accepted help to determine the sociocultural characteristics of a people and thus constitute a significant region-making force.

In summary, areal entities gradually attain their individuality as regions because of the operation of at least three major types of forces—geographic, historical, and cultural—which condition social development and give it a unique cast in a given place. The exact weight of a given set of forces in developing a particular region cannot be assessed without thorough study and analysis. Research has indicated that in one instance one type of force will be the most important in regional growth, whereas in a second instance another kind of force will determine the course of the development of a region.

STUDIES OF RURAL REGIONS IN THE UNITED STATES

The exploration and study of the geological survey, which led to the early land-classification maps, first directed thought in this country to regional patterns. American geographers, stimulated by such scholars as Fenneman, Bowman, and Barrows, realized that scientific regional study could contribute a great deal to the solution of human problems and to the advancement of human welfare. It was probably the maps showing differences in such factors as soil, rainfall, and temperature over the nation which prompted Spillman to attempt the first delineation of areas on the basis of type of farming. His work was probably the first to deal directly with rural regions of the United States.[8]

[6] Zimmerman and DuWors, *op. cit.*, p. 41.

[7] Howard W. Odum, *Southern Regions*, Chapel Hill, N.C.: University of North Carolina Press, 1936, pp. 11–15.

[8] W. J. Spillman, *Distribution of Types of Farming in the United States*, Washington: USDA Farmers Bulletin 1289, May, 1922.

Although the regional idea did not take hold so early among other social scientists in the United States, their work contributed materially to later delineátions of rural regions. The historian Frederick Jackson Turner was one of the first to give serious thought to areal groupings.[9] As a result of his study of the importance of the frontier in American life, Turner became convinced that the socioeconomic (including the cultural) life of the nation must be described by sections. Sectionalism evolved, according to him, because each section was selfish in its aims and tended to think of itself only and to strive for any advantage it might gain over other sections. Taking a cue from Turner and others, Howard Odum and his associates at the University of North Carolina initiated the era of the "New Regionalism." They took the point of view that "The United States must not, either because of its bigness and complexity or because of conflicting interests, become a federation of conflicting sections but a homogeneity of varying regions." [10] A monumental work delineating and describing six major composite regions of the nation climaxed the researches of Odum and his associates (see Fig. 12).

At the time when Odum and his associates were making their studies of composite regions, Elliott and Baker were working on more refined delineations of rural regions based on type of farming.[11] In the wake of the work of these scholars and others whom they stimulated, practically every state in the nation had produced its own type-of-farming delineations by 1940.

While the state studies were under way, two substantial studies of rural regions in the United States as a whole were being made. A. R. Mangus published his *Rural Regions of the United States* in 1940 [12] and Carl Taylor and his associates brought forth their study, which was quoted at the beginning of this chapter, under essentially the same heading in 1949. A third delineation of regions, subregions, and areas by Donald J. Bogue and Calvin Beale is now in progress.[13]

The Delineation of Rural Regions

The Methodology of Mangus. Unlike earlier scholars, Mangus had a specific reason for delineating the regions of the United States—to con-

[9] *The Significance of Sections in American History,* New York: Henry Holt and Company, Inc., 1932.

[10] Howard W. Odum and Harry E. Moore, *American Regionalism,* New York: Henry Holt and Company, 1938, p. 39.

[11] F. F. Elliott, *Types of Farming Areas in the United States,* Washington: U.S. Department of Commerce Special Bulletin, 1933; and O. E. Baker, *Atlas of American Agriculture,* Washington: Special Report of the Department of Agriculture, 1936.

[12] A. R. Mangus, *Rural Regions of the United States,* Washington: Government Printing Office, 1940.

[13] This is a project sponsored by the Scripps Foundation for Research in Population Problems, the Bureau of the Census, and the U.S. Department of Agriculture.

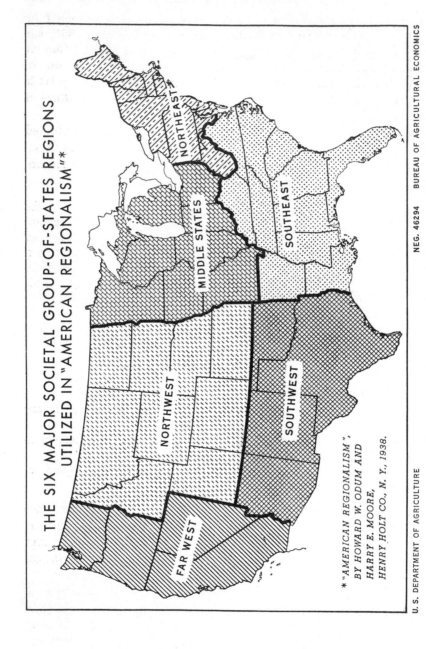

THE SIX MAJOR SOCIETAL GROUP-OF-STATES REGIONS
UTILIZED IN "AMERICAN REGIONALISM"*

NORTHEAST

MIDDLE STATES

SOUTHEAST

NORTHWEST

SOUTHWEST

FAR WEST

*"AMERICAN REGIONALISM",
BY HOWARD W. ODUM AND
HARRY E. MOORE,
HENRY HOLT CO., N. Y., 1938.

U. S. DEPARTMENT OF AGRICULTURE   NEG. 46294   BUREAU OF AGRICULTURAL ECONOMICS

Figure 12. The six major societal group-of-states regions delineated by Howard W. Odum and Harry E. Moore.

tribute to the understanding of the rural relief problem of the 1930s by giving it geographical setting. His approach also differed in another important respect from earlier studies: it was limited to descriptions of carefully selected, empirically determined regional characteristics. In defending this methodology, Mangus contended that quantitative traits or elements, if carefully selected, could be considered valid indicators of the more fundamental, unmeasurable aspects of culture.

On the basis of his study, Mangus selected seven nationally distributed variables and three less widely distributed variables for delineating rural-farm regions and subregions of the United States. The nationally distributed variables were as follows: [14]

1. A rural-farm plane-of-living index combining the average value of the farm dwelling, the per cent of farm homes having automobiles, the per cent of farm homes having electric lights, the per cent having running water piped into the house, the per cent having telephones, and the per cent having radios.

2. A rural-farm population fertility index constructed by computing the ratio of children under 5 years of age to women 20–44 years of age, 1930.

3. Per cent of farms producing less than $1,000 gross income, 1929.

4. Per cent of farm tenancy, 1935.

5. Land value per capita of the rural-farm population, 1930.

6. Per cent of farm produce consumed on farms, 1929.

7. Per cent of rural families residing on farms, 1930.

The variables of more localized concern were:

1. Per cent Negroes constituted of the total rural-farm population in the South, 1930.

2. Per cent "other races" constituted of the total rural-farm population in the Southwest, 1930.

3. Per cent farm-wage workers constituted of all agricultural workers in the West, 1930.

It should be mentioned that Mangus' regional delineations, like those of other scholars, involved careful and complicated mathematical weighting. In addition, he took physiographic and residence features into account where they were important. The regions delineated are shown in Figure 13.

The Methodology of Taylor and His Associates. The procedure of Taylor, Raper, and McKain for delineating regions did not include analysis by means of several factors. Rather, the basis for their delineations was the single factor of type of farming. In defending their approach, the authors make the following case for major type-of-farming areas as modal culture regions: [15]

[14] Mangus, *op. cit.,* pp. 79–80.
[15] Taylor et al., *op. cit.*, p. 329.

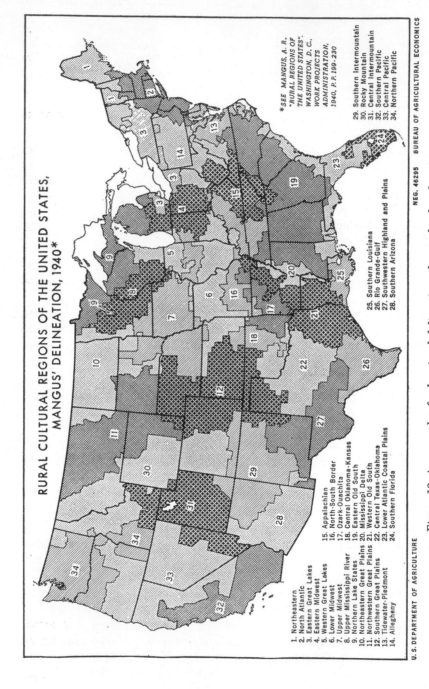

RURAL CULTURAL REGIONS OF THE UNITED STATES,
MANGUS' DELINEATION, 1940*

*SEE MANGUS, A. R.
"RURAL REGIONS OF
THE UNITED STATES".
WASHINGTON, D. C.,
WORK PROJECTS
ADMINISTRATION,
1940, P. P. 199.-230

1. Northeastern
2. North Atlantic
3. Eastern Great Lakes
4. Eastern Midwest
5. Western Great Lakes
6. Lower Midwest
7. Upper Midwest
8. Upper Mississippi River
9. Northern Lake States
10. Northeastern Great Plains
11. Northwestern Great Plains
12. Southern Great Plains
13. Tidewater-Piedmont
14. Allegheny

15. Appalachian
16. North-South Border
17. Ozark-Ouachita
18. Central Oklahoma-Kansas
19. Eastern Old South
20. Mississippi Delta
21. Western Old South
22. Central Texas-Oklahoma
23. Lower Atlantic Coastal Plains
24. Southern Florida

25. Southern Louisiana
26. Rio Grande-Gulf
27. Southwestern Highland and Plains
28. Southern Arizona

29. Southern Intermountain
30. Rocky Mountain
31. Central Intermountain
32. Southern Pacific
33. Central Pacific
34. Northern Pacific

U. S. DEPARTMENT OF AGRICULTURE   NEG. 46295   BUREAU OF AGRICULTURAL ECONOMICS

Figure 13. An example of subregional delineation: the rural cultural regions
of the United States delineated by A. R. Mangus.

These major type-farming areas are used as basis in describing modes of rural life because much significant material has been compiled on the manner, means, and methods of making a living in each of these areas. It is known that there is a general relationship between the way rural people make a living and their levels of living, the range and type of contacts they have with other rural families and with townspeople, the view-points they hold, and the things for which they aspire.

The same authors also make a case for major type-farming areas as rural universes. They point out that in such areas the production of the same crops or combinations of crops results in many common activities among the people and therefore in broadly similar interests, attitudes, and values. In these areas also, marked differences have arisen in response to a combination of physical, economic, and historical factors. The conclusion is that, as basic rural universes, the major type-farming areas are occasionally cut across by significant cultural forces. However, they consider it to be a test of validity that it is possible to keep rural cultural universes in the center of the analytical description despite the fact that warranted attention is given certain locality situations of special cultural importance.

The seven major type-farming regions of the United States delineated by Taylor and his associates are as follows: the cotton belt, the corn belt, the range-livestock region, the wheat region, the dairy region, the Western specialty-crop region, and the general and self-sufficing region (see Fig. 14). Each of these is described briefly in the section that follows.

THE RURAL REGIONS OF THE UNITED STATES

In this section are presented brief descriptions of the rural regions of the United States as delineated by Taylor, Raper, and McKain. The discussion of each region is taken to a large extent from the materials prepared by these scholars. These descriptions are at best only brief summaries; the student should refer to the original work, which has already been cited, for more detailed treatment. Here the major purpose is to identify the rural regions and the major differences between them and to further clarify the "region-making forces" discussed earlier in this chapter.

The Cotton Belt

The cotton belt (see Fig. 14) is a hot-weather region. Cotton is grown in the southern part of the United States and in a few Western states. The history of cotton and cotton culture and the impact it has had on the way of life in the South is so well known as to make elaboration unnecessary.

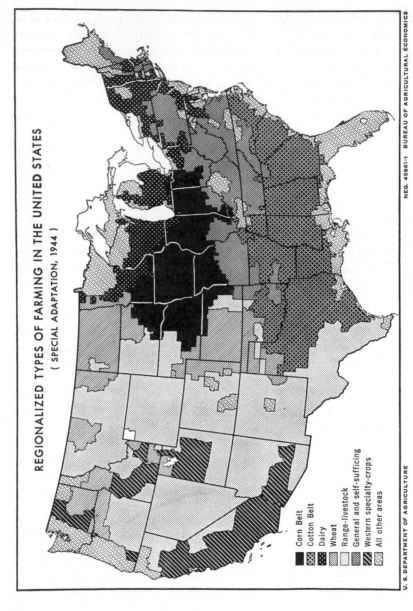

REGIONALIZED TYPES OF FARMING IN THE UNITED STATES
(SPECIAL ADAPTATION, 1944)

Corn Belt
Cotton Belt
Dairy
Wheat
Range-livestock
General and self-sufficing
Western specialty-crops
All other areas

U. S. DEPARTMENT OF AGRICULTURE

NEG. 45861-1   BUREAU OF AGRICULTURAL ECONOMICS

Figure 14. The type-farming areas or regions of the United States delineated by the U.S. Department of Agriculture.

It has been said that almost all the economic and social activities of rural people in the South are attuned to the rhythm of cotton production. Certain times of the year (spring and fall) are busy seasons, whereas other times (late summer and winter) are slack. Churches, recreational groups, and other organizations definitely plan their activities accordingly. Thus, rural schools may not open until the cotton has been harvested, and rural churches hold their revivals after "lay-by," when the crop is in, since the Southerner is a rather faithful church-goer and is inclined to be puritanical in his approach to religion. The traditional "Southern hospitality" may have been the by-product of the periods when there was little pressure of work and people could visit at length with one another.

The cotton belt has a sharply defined class system based on the social distance between the plantation owners and their associates and the sharecroppers, tenants, and operators of family-size farms. This system can be traced back to the early days of settlement, when large tracts of land were granted to or acquired by individuals. The plantation owner-operator is at the top of the social pyramid and has traditionally enjoyed the prestige of the elite. In contrast, the masses of tenants, sharecroppers, and laborers remain in the lower class. Many scholars have associated the high rate of illiteracy and the generally low level of living in the region to the class structure.

The Negro has from the beginning been associated with the cotton culture and has influenced many phases of life in the South, despite his general lack of educational and economic advantages. His contributions are especially notable in the art, literature, music, and humor of this region and give a decided individuality to its culture.

The cotton belt resisted change and long remained a "mule economy," partly because of conservatism and partly because of the difficulty of mechanizing the cotton crop. However, the past two decades have witnessed a technological revolution in this region. Mechanization is advancing at a rapid rate, and the number of "hands" formerly required to produce the crop has been reduced drastically. The Negro especially has moved out of the region in increasing numbers. These trends, coupled with new concepts of work and pay as a result of expanded industrial activity, explain the new look in the region and indicate the direction of further change. However, the region will doubtless continue to be unique in many ways associated with cotton and its culture.

The Corn Belt

Perhaps the richest agricultural region in the United States is what is commonly called the corn belt. The states included in this region can be seen in Figure 14. The deep, fertile soils found here are the product of glacial and dust deposits and, combined with the plentiful and dependable rainfalls, give optimum growing conditions for corn, which in turn is ideally coupled with livestock and poultry production.

The corn-belt farmer as a personality type differs from farmers in other regions in decided ways related to the history of the area as well as to the agricultural enterprises that predominate. First of all, it may be noted that the people who settled in the area, though of diverse origins, came with a common ambition to get ahead. This ambition fostered a democratic atmosphere; and thus the region is generally one of family farms, with few operations of the plantation or estate type. In this regard, it is significant that prestige attaches to successful farming rather than land ownership. Many renters enjoy the same status as or higher status than owners, depending on their success as farmers.

The people of the corn belt turned to mechanized and scientific farming almost as soon as they adopted the corn-livestock combination. It is one of the notable characteristics of the corn-belt farmer that he believes in and uses the latest technological methods in his home and on his farm. In fact, he has little respect for the farmer who uses any but the latest equipment and chemicals. The early settlers in this region fostered a spirit of individualism that persists in the present inhabitants. Another attitude evident among corn-belt people is their tendency to be convinced they are a superior group. They attribute this superiority to the fact that they are hard workers, good managers, and intelligent and moral persons.

Taylor and his associates explain these attitudes as follows: The rich natural resources in the region and the economic period during which its agriculture was developed made progress so easy and so universal that the farmer very naturally came to believe that anyone who worked hard and managed well could succeed. The fact that settlers from various parts of the world had the same success here strengthened his conviction that anyone who did not succeed was "no good."

Travelers through the corn belt are impressed with the great faith its people have in education. No doubt this attitude is closely associated with their belief in and adoption of technology. It accounts for the relatively high level of formal education and the high levels of living in the region.

The corn belt is located in the heart of the great industrial region of the nation. Thus some of the attitudes and values of the farm people can be attributed to their contacts with industry and industrial workers. Nevertheless, for the most part, they have cast their own mold, and the indications are that they will continue to do so in the future.

The Range-Livestock Region

As can be seen in Figure 14, the range-livestock region covers more territory than any other type-farming region of the United States. The topography is the most rugged in the nation, and most of the land is not suited to any other type of agricultural endeavor. Most of the area is arid, although certain sections get ample rainfall.

The farmers in the range-livestock region vary considerably in the type of operation they carry on. At one extreme there are the large ranches of southwest Texas, with holdings running into thousands of acres. At the other extreme are the Indians and Spanish Americans in Arizona and New Mexico, who eke out an existence on subsistence holdings. It is important to understand the many subcultures and cultural islands in the region in order to gain a sense of the region as a whole. However, despite its variety of inhabitants, the range-livestock region is an area of sparse settlement.

All the groups living in the range-livestock region have contributed to its cultural complex. The visitor is struck by the number of words, dishes, and customs of the region that can be traced directly back to the Indians, Spanish Americans, or other groups. There is also a tradition carried over from the days of the old cattle kingdom and seen today in the reverence for good horsemanship and the distinctive cowboy boots and hats in evidence everywhere.

Social institutions must operate under some very real difficulties in the region, and schools and churches are never large. Moreover, they are generally located in the towns, as in the wheat areas, and it is necessary to make special arrangements for attendance. Thus it is not unusual for a "cattle" town to serve a community with a radius of hundreds of miles.

Perhaps the most prominent element in the value system of the range-livestock people is their love for their way of life. They have an appreciation for and a sentimental attachment to the wide-open spaces, and independence is a key factor in their feelings. Managerial ability is the test of the good rancher, and a man who can survive despite the adversities of the climatic conditions is considered successful.

Certain trends in the range-livestock region appear to be of major significance. Mechanization, for one thing, is making a gradual appearance, and the trend toward irrigation will probably do much to improve farming conditions.

The Wheat Region

The wheat region is not, like the cotton and corn regions, one contiguous area. Another distinctive characteristic of wheat as opposed to the other two crops can be seen in Figure 14: wheat is only produced in large quantities where other types of farm production are not possible. Like corn, however, it is grown in relatively small quantities over a large part of the nation.

The wheat country has a very low density of population, with large, widely scattered farms. In describing the wheat farms, Taylor says, "Big farm machines are evident everywhere, either in operation in the vast fields or sitting in the farmyards. In the most extensive wheat areas, there are the largest farm machines in the world; they are operated by men who feel their bigness." [16] The wheat country looks different from other agricultural areas because it is a plains area without many trees. Visitors are always impressed by the sight of the grain elevators, which can be seen from miles away looming on the horizon.

Work and social life in the wheat belt must be adjusted to the seasonal demands of wheat. The work load is heaviest during the relatively short seeding and harvesting periods. Because of the nature of its cultivation, wheat lends itself to the "sidewalk" and "suitcase" operations of the farmer who has a business in town or who moves to the farm for short work seasons but maintains his residence in town. The low density of population accounts for the small number of rural schools and the fact that many children are sent off to boarding schools by farmers who choose not to live in town. It is interesting that, in many instances, the mothers are sent to town with the children in order to see them through school, while the father remains to take care of the farmstead.

Despite the distances between them, wheat-belt farmers pay frequent visits to one another, exchange work, and maintain fairly cohesive neighborhoods. There are many nationality and religious groups in the region which are especially cohesive in their community life. As a matter of fact, individual and family visiting constitutes the major part of what might be termed the recreational activity of the region. The fact that social-class lines are almost nonexistent encourages this type of interaction.

In studying the attitudes and values of wheat farmers, one is impressed by the fact that they have organized one protest after another, usually against market forces that they felt operated to their disadvantage. Such organizations as the Farmers' Alliance, the American Society of Equity, and the Non-Partisan League are almost exclusively wheat-belt organizations.

There is perhaps no other section of the country in which people are so firmly convinced that success depends upon oneself. This attitude is bred in the continuous struggle against the caprices of nature, which de-

[16] *Ibid.*, p. 386.

livers or withholds the precious rain. Efficiency, shrewdness, and endurance are necessary for success.

Changes are apparent in the wheat belt, as in other regions. As the need for institutions such as schools and hospitals is increasingly felt, farmers attempt to remain near the centers, where these services are available. Attention to soil conservation and soil-building practices is increasing the stability of wheat farming and raising productivity. It is doubtful, however, that these changes will have the effect of depriving the region of its individuality.

The Dairy Region

Although milk is produced in almost every farm area of the United States, production is definitely concentrated in one region, the Eastern and Northern states (see Fig. 14). The dairy region is, understandably, close to large population centers, which provide a market for the milk and milk products produced.

Dairy farming differs from other types of farming in many ways. Not only must dairy farmers face the inevitable twice-a-day milkings, but they must maintain sanitary standards requiring special attention to farm buildings and equipment. Because of the milkings, meetings are generally scheduled for the middle of the day, since this is the time when the dairy farmer can best afford to be away from his chores. The arduousness of his tasks tends to make the dairyman a pioneer in the use of new techniques and devices and a practitioner of scientific and mechanized farming. He is usually well informed about the most up-to-date practices in the feeding and care of dairy herds and avails himself of the services of artificial-insemination centers.

Dairy farmers are in close touch with townspeople and perhaps understand them better than most farmers. Their level of living is relatively high, and this is reflected in the stability of their schools and churches. Their economic well-being is further enhanced by the fact that they have a steady income the year round instead of only at harvest time.

The attitudes and values found in the dairy areas include a strong sense of the importance of knowledge and skill in the dairy business and pride in the performance of herds and in the appearance of farmsteads. Home and farm ownership is thought of as a symbol of success. The cooperative approach is encouraged, and many such ventures are undertaken. Education is highly valued, especially vocational education in agriculture and home economics. A high school education is considered to be almost a must.

The growth of dairy areas parallels that of the surrounding urbanized regions. The farmers of the dairy region generally are increasing their productivity through closer attention to scientific farming, and large co-operatives are more and more performing the market services for the farms. These trends, however, tend to accentuate rather than detract from the individuality of the region.

The Western Speciality-crop Region

Figure 14 shows the relatively small areas that make up the western speciality-crop region. A unique feature of this region is that productivity has generally been dependent upon the control of water by human effort. Irrigation has made possible the use of otherwise unproductive lands at the same time that it has promoted an intensive and specialized agriculture. Control of moisture, plus the favorable climatic conditions of the area, makes it possible to grow almost any kind of fruit or vegetable.

People from all over the United States, as well as the Orient, Spanish America, and Europe, settled in the speciality-crop region. Thus a somewhat composite culture and value system exists there. For the most part, farming is carried on as a big business. Commercialization and mechanization are the bywords, and the characteristic type of operation is similar to that of large manufacturing concerns.

This region is doubtless more picturesque than any other rural region of the nation. The well-kept orchards and vineyards and the long, straight rows of vegetables such as lettuce, tomatoes, and carrots give the visitor an unforgettable impression of regularity and perfect symmetry.

A great deal of the uncertainty in farming is absent in the speciality-crop area because of irrigation. At the same time, however, the perishability of the crops makes marketing a critical process. This problem has given rise to huge cooperative organizations with ample facilities for handling, packaging, and shipping the commodities grown. Cooperation is also fostered by the necessity of working with neighbors in the construction and maintenance of dams, canals, and ditches.

Group relationships in this region, as mentioned before, are based on urban patterns. Farm men and women participate with urban men and women in clubs and church activities. In this region, there are few rural neighborhoods as these are known in other parts of the nation. The organizations present are there generally to meet some specific need, such as buying or marketing. The materialistic philosophy evident in the region has in the past been associated with a great deal of speculation.

The future growth of the Western speciality-crop region depends upon new developments in irrigation, the potentialities of which are great. Other trends are in the direction of increased specialization of production and even more use of the factory system in agriculture. The smaller farms seem to be breaking down in the face of these strong forces.

The General and Self-sufficing Region

The last region to be delineated is one which is not concentrated on the production of a particular type of crop or enterprise. As a matter of fact, it is a region of relatively little commercial production of any kind; hence it has been called the general and self-sufficing region. As can be seen in Figure 14, it is located mostly in the Eastern part of the nation and includes, significantly, the most rugged terrain east of the Rockies.

The great number of part-time and subsistence farmers in the general and self-sufficing region is the result of several factors. Above all, however, isolation remains the greatest deterrent to commercial productivity, for poor roads discourage frequent outside marketing trips. The attitudes and values of the inhabitants also seem to promote the subsistence pattern.

Many of the residents in this region are commonly referred to as mountain or hill folk. These individuals still engage in the handicrafts of their forebears and maintain the same simple economy. Family ties are very strong, and there is a great deal of visiting among relatives. The people have a strong attachment to their way of life and to their home localities. They are an independent, resourceful group and are usually suspicious of outsiders. Above all else, the hill people love the freedom of thought and action which their life affords. Most of them trace their ancestry to Northwestern European stock, especially England, Scotland, and Ireland.

Corn is probably the most common crop grown in the general and self-sufficing region, and it is used mostly for meal and for livestock feed. Of course, gardens and orchards are common, and most of the farms produce their own chickens and hogs as well.

A great deal of the land in this region remains in timber, and many of the residents earn some income from working in the sawmills and other forest-products industries. Living standards, as might be expected, are low by comparison to other farm regions. Educational attainment is also low, particularly in the Southern sections of the region. Traditional ways are encouraged throughout the region, with positions of leadership going to the older heads of families.

Modern conveniences and means of communication are encroaching upon the region to some extent, however. Such innovations are sure to bring the residents into closer relationship to the larger society. However, those who are familiar with these areas will hasten to add that the change will not take place overnight.

THE UTILITY OF SOCIAL AREAS OR SUBREGIONS

Within individual states, as well as in the nation as a whole, persons in charge of administering programs and conducting research in rural areas repeatedly face a fundamental problem that is directly related to the cultural diversity of rural populations. It comes to light in two ways. First, it appears in the inability of county agents and others to use successfully the same techniques of disseminating information with all groups. Anyone familiar with the situation in states or areas with many ethnic groups can appreciate how a certain approach might be quite effective in one part of the state but completely ineffective and even objectionable in another area. The second way in which the problem stemming from cultural diversity appears is in the amount of time and effort spent by researchers in the determination of areas suitable for representative sampling. Obviously, studies of marketing practices, attitudes, and other factors lose much of their applicability when they are based on inadequate samples. These problems have prompted rural sociologists to work on the delineation and description of areas of sociocultural homogeneity in several states.[17]

These delineations generally differ somewhat from the state type-of-farming maps of the agricultural economists and the state economic areas of the Bureau of the Census, since additional factors are considered. Figure 15, showing the rural social areas of Louisiana, illustrates such delineations. The ten areas were determined through factor analysis, with seven factors retained as significant measures of homogeneity.[18] These included: (1) school expenditures per parish (county) per student, (2) proportion of land in farms, (3) age index, (4) race index, (5) the level of living of the rural-nonfarm population, (6) the level of living of the rural-farm population, and (7) the fertility ratio of the rural-farm population.

Factors such as these need to be determined for each state before delineations can be made. However, those listed give some indication of the type of variables that are useful in such divisions.

Questions for Review and Discussion

1. Why is regional study a special branch of sociology?
2. Define the term *region* as you understand it and distinguish between major and minor regions.

---

[17] See, for example, C. E. Lively and Cecil L. Gregory, *Rural Social Areas in Missouri*, Missouri AES Research Bulletin 414, 1948; and Alvin L. Bertrand, *The Many Louisianas, Rural Social Areas and Cultural Islands*, Louisiana AES Bulletin 496, 1955.
[18] Bertrand, *op. cit.*, pp. 6–11.

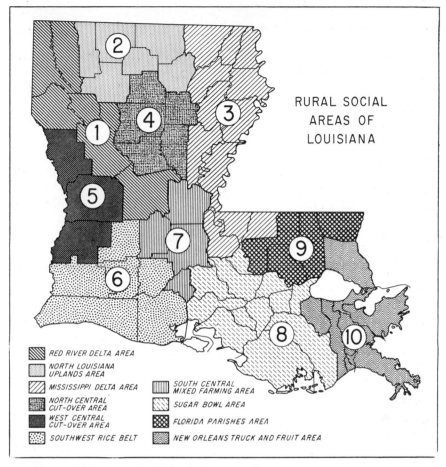

Figure 15. An example of the delineation of areas of sociocultural homogeneity within a state: the location of the ten rural social areas of Louisiana. (From Alvin L. Bertrand, *The Many Louisianas, Rural Social Areas and Cultural Islands,* Louisiana AES Bulletin 496, 1955.)

3. Why is it appropriate to include a discussion of regions in a rural-sociology textbook?

4. What factors primarily account for regional differences?

5. List the more important characteristics of the major type-farming regions in the United States.

6. Why is it important to have a delineation of the social areas or subregions of a state at hand when considering statewide problems?

Selected References for Supplementary Reading

Bertrand, Alvin L.: "Regional Sociology as a Special Discipline," *Social Forces,* 21:132–136, 1952.

Bertrand, Alvin L.: *The Many Louisianas, Rural Social Areas and Cultural Islands,* Louisiana AES Bulletin 496, 1955.

Mangus, A. R.: *Rural Regions of the United States,* Washington, D.C.: Government Printing Office, 1940.

Odum, Howard W., and Harry E. Moore: *American Regionalism,* New York: Henry Holt and Company, Inc., 1938.

Taylor, Carl C., et al.: *Rural Life in the United States,* New York: Alfred A. Knopf, Inc., 1949, part IV.

PART THREE

Social Differentiation and Participation in Rural Areas

The term *social differentiation,* as we saw in Chapter 2, refers to the network of positions that individuals and groups hold in a society along with the differential participation that results from these positions. Part Three has as its major objective the outlining of those structural-functional aspects of rural society which are more or less unique to agriculture as a way of life.

Chapter 9 sets the stage by describing social stratification. In this chapter the peculiar characteristics of social classes and of social mobility in rural areas are treated, as well as the methods used in the study of these phenomena. This discussion is followed, in Chapter 10, by a review of the types and social correlates of social participation. The material presented here draws on several important research works not generally treated in textbooks.

The last three chapters in Part Three are devoted to the specific structural features of farming as an occupation. Chapter 11 takes up the systems of land division and their social significance. Chapter 12 presents the functions of tenure systems and then describes the various tenure statuses and the extent of their occurrence in the United States. Chapter 13 deals with the various social patterns of farming and their advantages and disadvantages and describes the impact of the family-farm ideal on agricultural policy in America.

CHAPTER 9 *Social Stratification in Rural Society*

Many criteria have been used for determining social class. In this chapter we shall discuss some of these ways of looking at social strata and summarize a number of studies illustrating stratification in rural America. The final section of the chapter focuses on changes in the class structure and points out how various public and private programs affect the rank of the several segments of the rural population.

Cultural evaluation is the basis for vertical social differences. Certain individuals are considered superior because their activities, attributes, and possessions are more highly valued than those of others. Similarly, the social positions of greater prestige are those that are considered important in the society and are difficult to attain. Thus the position of the owner of a large farm is considerably above that of the day laborer, and that of mayor of a town carries greater prestige than that of the average citizen.

People who are grouped together because of similar social rank, especially if they associate intimately, are sometimes referred to as a social class, or social stratum. Some of the specific designations are upper class, middle class, lower class, white-collar class, business class, working class, professionals, and farmers.

Such groups often react to the programs formulated by the leaders of business and government in proportion to their tendency to support or to change the existing class structure—the distribution of rights and rewards among the population. The social scientist's concern with social stratification often takes the form of testing the hypothesis that a person's status is closely related to a number of other important characteristics. In other words, if the social status of an individual is known, many other things can be assumed with reasonable accuracy.

The average citizen, whether he is aware of it or not, is deeply involved with the class structure. His self-esteem is determined to no small extent by how well he maintains the status that he and others have defined for him. Many, also, wish to "get ahead," or to gain a higher status. Consequently, most people, especially the socially mobile, have considerable practical knowledge of the class structure.

DETERMINATION OF SOCIAL RANK

A number of criteria have been used to determine social rank. In town and country communities, the following are frequently used: farm tenure (owner, renter, or laborer), income, education, organizational memberships, personal qualities, morals, race, family, religious and political beliefs, years of residence in the area, type of house occupied, and possession of certain items as indicated by style of dress, model of automobile, etc. Two methods employed by researchers in delineating social strata are applying rank-ordering indices or having the individuals themselves, their community associates, or trained analysts rank persons in terms of their prestige and reputation.

Whatever the criteria or method of definition, the class structure in present-day America is much more accurately pictured as a relatively easy-to-climb ladder than as a vertical structure of air-tight compartments into which people are born and must remain. Class structures in American communities have been graphically represented either as diamond-shaped figures or as pyramids (see Fig. 16).[1] The former would indicate a predominantly middle-class society, whereas the latter suggests a relatively large lower class. Agricultural communities with a large proportion of land owners are generally middle class in nature, whereas the class structure in communities in which land is held by a few persons and most of the farmers are either sharecroppers or laborers would more likely approximate the shape of a pyramid.

Although they are everywhere noticeable, social distinctions in town and country communities are not usually so great, nor is rank generally so extreme, as in cities. That is, social and economic distance between persons of the lowest and highest ranks, in whatever way it may be measured, is decidedly greater in cities than in rural areas. This means that in urban society the "height" of the class structure is greater.

Characteristics of the Middle and Lower Classes

A consensus has developed, based on field studies,[2] as to behavior patterns, ideologies, and possessions that characterize the typical persons

[1] W. L. Warner and P. S. Lunt, *The Social Life of a Modern Community*, New Haven: Yale University Press, 1941. Kaufman, in a study of a village-centered rural community, was able to delineate eleven class groupings without difficulty. See *Prestige Classes in a New York Rural Community*, Cornell AES Memoir 260, 1944.

[2] Typical of the studies that have contributed to a picture of the styles of life of given ranks are A. B. Hollingshead, "Selected Characteristics of Classes in a Middle

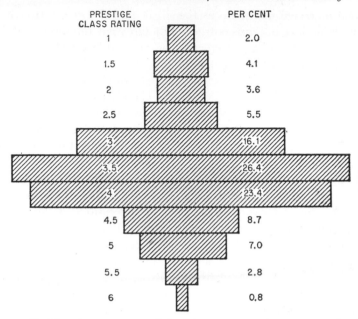

PRESTIGE
CLASS RATING   PER CENT

1	2.0
1.5	4.1
2	3.6
2.5	5.5
3	16.1
3.5	26.4
4	23.4
4.5	8.7
5	7.0
5.5	2.8
6	0.8

Figure 16. The class structure of the Macon community, an example of a diamond-shaped distribution of prestige classes. (From Harold F. Kaufman, *Prestige Classes in a New York Rural Community,* Cornell AES Memoir 260, 1944.)

of middle and lower rank.[3] The middle-class pattern is characterized by relative economic security, emphasizes thrift, and has a goal—the ownership of property. Many middle-class persons may hold little permanent wealth; nevertheless, their concern for property is shown by their great respect for the ownership rights of others. Strong emphasis is placed on personal achievement and self-improvement. The American ideology of "work, virtue, reward" receives its strongest support from this group. Formal education is stressed as a means of getting ahead. The typical occupational groups are the larger and more prosperous farmers (in some regions today this may be the majority) and, in the towns, business and professional people, white-collar workers, and some of the skilled workers.

In the middle-class family, husband and wife share the leadership, the former making the living and the latter directing the home. The child is taught respect for parents, strict sex standards, and cleanliness.

Western Community," *American Sociological Review,* 12:385–95, 1947; W. L. Warner and P. S. Lunt, *The Social Life of a Modern Community,* New Haven: Yale University Press, 1941; and A. Davis, B. D. Gardner, and R. M. Gardner, *Deep South,* Chicago: University of Chicago Press, 1941.

[3] From the standpoint of the mass society, it is doubtful that rural America has a distinct upper-class pattern. Thus the characterization of the "middle-class" given here applies to both the middle and the upper ranks.

A "good marriage" is set up as the ideal, and divorce is frowned upon. The middle-class person controls his aggressive impulses and is not a "rowdy." For commercial recreation he goes to "respectable places." He has some leisure and frequently travels for a vacation.

The major support for community-betterment programs and organized community life comes from middle-class persons. They hold a highly disproportionate share of official positions and organizational memberships. The middle-class pattern stresses support of law and order. Persons with this ideology form the bulwark of organized religion, especially the established churches.

The lower-class pattern offers some definite contrasts to the one just described. Economic insecurity is the rule rather than the exception among persons of lower rank. Getting the necessities of life—food, clothing, and shelter—is a major concern. Little if any property is accumulated. Young men get jobs at an early age. Occupationally, the typical member of the lower class is a farm laborer, a tenant, or an owner with a low-production operation; in the towns, he is a manual worker, customarily unskilled, with a high rate of job mobility.

In contrast to the middle-class family, the mother is dominant in families of lower rank, even in the economic sphere, as she is more likely to be employed than the father. The family unit is not only the nuclear family but may include other relatives as well. There is a relatively high rate of broken homes due to death, desertion, and divorce.

Lower-class persons are frequently criticized by those of higher rank because they lack the desire to "improve themselves." They feel vaguely that some formal education is desirable but that it is not worth too much effort. For this reason middle-class teachers are especially critical of children of lower status. Young people of this rank are not so likely to inhibit their aggressive tendencies as middle-class children and their control over their sexual behavior is less rigid. Drunkenness and gambling are not uncommon, and law and order are tolerated rather than definitely supported.

In contrast to the middle class, persons of this rank seldom participate in organizational activities. If they participate formally, it is likely to be in a church in which they "feel at home" or in a labor union or veterans' organization.

The Basic Characteristic of the American Class System

All relatively complex societies are to some extent stratified. This is necessary because individuals vary in capacity and opportunity for achievement and acquisition and because status-reflecting goods and positions are sometimes limited in amount. Also, it is necessary that a group reward those of its members who exhibit behavior of the highest value. Each society has unique features in this respect, and it is worthwhile to point out the prime distinguishing feature of the class system of the United States.

Getting ahead is the chief characteristic of American society, and there are no rigid class lines to create barriers. Americans are less interested in identifying with their social rank than in rising above it. Rank is so fluid and the notion of class so distasteful to some that they deny a class system exists.

In contrast with, for example, medieval Europe and rural India today, America has a highly fluid class system. The American dream is expressed in such expressions as "from log cabin to White House" and "from farm laborer to farm owner." In periods of economic prosperity, such as the decade following the Second World War, mobility of individuals and groups has been relatively rapid. As we shall see later, however, various public and private programs have had an impact on class structure and social mobility in America.

STUDIES IN STRATIFICATION

The two different approaches characteristically used in the study of rural social classes in this country are socioeconomic scales and indices and ranking procedures. These can best be understood by examining specific studies of stratification.

Socioeconomic Status Scales

The most widely used scale for classifying American rural families was developed by Sewell. In 1937 a survey of 800 Oklahoma farm families was made to determine the distribution of 123 traits related to the home and its furnishings and the family's participation in the community.[4] Analysis showed that there were distinct differences in the distribution of some of the items, and a scale based on 36 traits was constructed. Tests of this scale in Kansas and Louisiana made it possible to reduce the number of items to fourteen: construction of the house, room-person ratio, lighting facilities, water piped into house, power washer, refrigerator, radio, telephone, automobile, daily newspaper, wife's education, husband's education, husband attends Sunday School, and wife attends Sunday School.[5]

Items in scales must be changed as the level of living of a population

[4] William H. Sewell, *The Construction and Standardization of a Scale for the Measurement of the Socio-economic Status of Oklahoma Farm Families*, Oklahoma AES Technical Bulletin 9, 1940. See pages 7–19 of Sewell's report for a survey of earlier attempts at similar scales.

[5] William H. Sewell, "A Short Form of the Family Socio-Economic Status Scale," *Rural Sociology*, 8:161–169, 1943.

changes and new things become commonplace. For example, by 1947 the radio was almost universal and no longer served as an index, while the deep freeze began to appear as an important item.[6] Later, television sets became prevalent. When items become almost universal or are very rare, they are of little or no use on the scale.

Economic scales can be used to rank groups of people as well as individual families. A scale that is widely used in this way at the present time is the level-of-living index developed by Hagood.[7] This index, which applies to farm-operator families, is made up of four items: (1) percentage of farms with electricity, (2) percentage of farms with telephones, (3) percentage of farms with automobiles, and (4) average value of products sold or traded in the year preceding the census.

Hagood's index has been constructed for each county of the United States (see Fig. 17) and for several different census periods. It shows considerable differences from county to county and from one section of the country to another. The highest level of living for farm operators is found in the Middle West and the Far West, and the lowest in the South.

Another index of this type has been used to describe status differentials in four Southern states. It contains the following items: distribution of patterns of income, landholding, size of enterprise, control over labor, and possession of household facilities. It was found that class inequalities were greatest in Mississippi and smallest in North Carolina, with Georgia and South Carolina holding an intermediate position. The extreme inequality in Mississippi is explained in terms of a small class of "elite." [8]

Classes Based on Prestige and Participation

A second way to study stratification is to learn how members of the community rank each other. Such an approach was used in the study of a rural community in New York.[9] Two major measures of status were

[6] John C. Belcher, "Evaluation and Restandardization of Sewell's Socio-Economic Scale," *Rural Sociology*, 16:246–255, 1951.

[7] Margaret Jarman Hagood, "Construction of County Indexes for Measuring Change in Level of Living of Farm-Operator Families, 1940–45," *Rural Sociology*, 12:139–150, 1947; *Farm-Operator Family Level-of-Living Indexes for Counties of the United States, 1930, 1940, 1945, and 1950*, Washington: U.S. Department of Agriculture, Bureau of Agricultural Economics, 1952. See also: Margaret Jarman Hagood, Gladys K. Bowles and Robert R. Mount, *Farm-Operator Family Level-of-Living Indexes for Counties of the United States, 1945, 1950, and 1954*, Washington: U.S. Department of Agriculture, Agricultural Marketing Service Statistical Bulletin 204, 1957.

[8] C. Arnold Anderson, "Economic Status Differentials within Southern Agriculture," *Rural Sociology*, 19:50–67, 1954.

[9] Harold F. Kaufman, *Prestige Classes in a New York Rural Community*, Cornell AES Memoir 260, 1944.

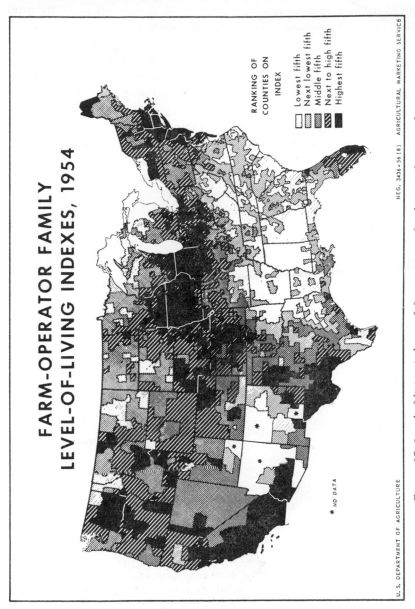

FARM-OPERATOR FAMILY
LEVEL-OF-LIVING INDEXES, 1954

RANKING OF
COUNTIES ON
INDEX

Lowest fifth
Next lowest fifth
Middle fifth
Next to high fifth
Highest fifth

* NO DATA

U. S. DEPARTMENT OF AGRICULTURE

NEG. 3436-56 (8)   AGRICULTURAL MARKETING SERVICE

Figure 17. Level-of-living indexes of farm-operator families in the United States, by counties, 1954.

employed. First, judges were asked to rank the members of the community. The name of each member of the community was written on a card, and each judge sorted the cards into piles indicating relative prestige. The class position of each individual was based on the composite ratings given by the judges. Eleven prestige classes were determined, and the numerical frequency of class membership fell into a diamond-shaped figure (Fig. 16).

Second, the participation pattern of the members of the eleven classes was studied. It was found that most informal associations were limited to members of the same class group. Only 8 per cent of the contacts had a range of more than one class. Similarly, each formal organization—club, lodge, church, and others—tended to draw its membership from one class or from adjacent classes. Organizational, community, and political leadership came from the higher classes, with positions of leadership being held by 89 per cent of the members of the top class and only 3 per cent of the bottom class.

Classes as Cultural Groups

A second study utilizing this methodology is West's investigation of a community in western Missouri, identified as Plainville, U.S.A. Two major class groups were located. About half the people belonged to the "upper class" and the other half to the "lower class." The lower class, however, was not a single homogeneous group but was composed of three subclasses referred to in order of position as "good lower-class people," "lower element," and, at the bottom, "people who live like animals." [10]

By listening to the people of Plainville, West found that the criteria of discrimination seemed to be almost infinite. Nearly every item of human possession and behavior seemed to be involved. In judging another, one Plainviller said, "I add ever'thing I know about him up in my head and strike an average." The most important indices were location (hill or prairie), relation to technology, lineage, wealth, morals, and manners. The upper-class families were identified by such characteristics as living on the prairie, using modern agricultural techniques, coming from "good families," having reasonable financial worth, and being honest and temperate. The lower element was characterized by such traits as coming from the hills, coming from "trashy" families, having poorly run farms, being dishonest, being lazy, getting drunk, and the women "cussing like men." Thus definite styles of life or cultural patterns were seen as characterizing the two classes.

[10] James West, *Plainville, U.S.A.*, New York: Columbia University Press, 1945, pp. 113–141.

CASTES AND FACTIONS IN RURAL SOCIETY

When class lines are relatively rigid and mobility is limited, a caste-like structure is indicated. When the population is small and status differences are horizontal rather than vertical, factions rather than classes may be present. A study by Bailey illustrates both types of stratification.[11]

The Texas Panhandle community of Cotton Center consists of a tiny crossroads village surrounded by large farms. It is located in the belt where "King Cotton meets Queen Wheat" (Fig. 18). At the time of the study, the community nucleus was composed of farm operators and a few businessmen. It was not a uniformly integrated group and was split along

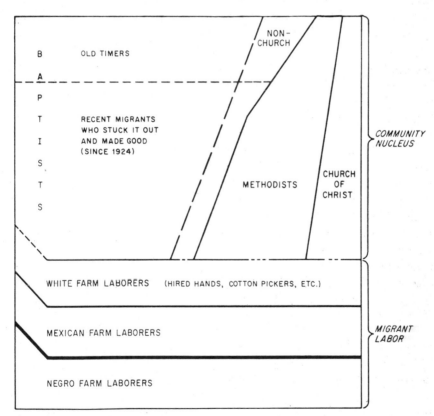

Figure 18. Social stratification in Cotton Center, a diagram of the factions within the community nucleus showing the castelike groups of migrant laborers. (From Wilfrid C. Bailey, "The Status System of a Texas Panhandle Community," *The Texas Journal of Science,* 5:327, 1943.)

[11] Wilfrid C. Bailey, "The Status System of a Texas Panhandle Community," *The Texas Journal of Science,* 5:326–331, 1943.

several cleavage or faction planes. Vertically, the community nucleus was divided into two groups based on time of settlement. The "old-timers" represented the early ranching tradition. Recent migrants were mostly cotton farmers who moved in after 1924, the year marking the climax in the breakup of the big ranches and the building of railroads. The old-timers were the dominant group and exercised their power through control of land.

The second factional division in the core of the community was along church lines. The Baptist, Methodist, and Church of Christ congregations formed distinct groups. The Baptist church was the largest and most powerful. Although the majority of its members were recent arrivals, most of the old-timers belonged to it. Its power was also demonstrated by the fact that all but one of the businessmen, the whole school board, and the officers of all the non-church-affiliated formal associations were Baptists.

The major differentiation in the community nucleus was horizontal rather than vertical. The several factions and clique networks represented much the same status and styles of life. Differences existed among them, however, with respect to access to positions of leadership.[12]

Beneath the permanent community nucleus of Cotton Center was the migrant labor group.[13] Castelike relations existed between the two groups. Although the migrants outnumbered the farm operators at harvest season, the laborers were not considered to be part of the community. Most of them stayed only a few weeks or months and then moved on. This group was itself divided vertically into three divisions: whites, Mexicans, and Negroes. It is interesting that, despite their present social distance from the laborers, the majority of the permanent residents of Cotton Center first arrived as laborers.

Two aspects of class structure are illustrated in Cotton Center. First, when castelike characteristics are present, there are unequal opportunities for upward mobility.[14] The white farm laborers, as indicated, could rise in rank; the Mexicans and Negroes could only rarely move out of their respective groups. Although the Mexicans were usually distinguished by both cultural and physical features, these differences were such that a few were able to lose their Mexican identity and become "whites." However, the distinctive racial features of the Negroes and the strong

[12] For a more detailed description of this type of structure, read the account of the people who left the Cotton Center area for homestead farms in New Mexico. Evon Z. Vogt, *Modern Homesteaders: The Life of a Twentieth-Century Frontier Community*, Cambridge, Mass.: Harvard University Press, 1955.

[13] For a description of California communities in which the community nucleus is distinct from farm labor, see: Walter B. Goldschmidt, *As You Sow*, New York: Harcourt, Brace and Company, Inc., 1947.

[14] A. Davis, B. D. Gardner, and R. M. Gardner, *Deep South*, Chicago: University of Chicago Press, 1941.

feelings toward them made it extremely difficult for them to move out of their group. The differences in opportunity for mobility are indicated in Figure 18.

TRENDS IN RURAL CLASS STRUCTURE

The class system of colonial America was adapted from that of Europe. Feudal remnants did not last long in America, however, because of cheap land and the great scarcity of labor. In this situation, no man with a minimum of ambition would choose serfdom over having his own farm. Other factors which contributed to the "leveling influence" of the frontier were the rapid movement of population, the absence of occupational differences, and the ideology of the people who settled there. These factors served to flatten out the social pyramid and eliminate extreme social classes. In fact, as shown later, the family farm, which developed during the nineteenth century, became the ideal and the cornerstone of rural life. During this period, with the exception of limited areas such as the plantation part of the South, the family farm was the predominant unit in agricultural America. In 1880, 74 per cent of all farms were operated by owners.

Climbing the agricultural ladder—moving from the status of laborer to that of tenant to that of owner—has become much more difficult during the past half century. In 1935, when the number of farms operated by owners had declined to 58 per cent, President Franklin D. Roosevelt stated, "The agricultural ladder has become a treadmill." The proportion of owner operators increased after 1935 to 69 per cent in 1950. This increase, however, was due largely to the decline in the number of tenants rather than to an increase in the number of owners. Major reasons for this trend are that fewer farmers are needed today and that the amount of capital necessary to own a farm has increased tremendously. One aspect of this trend has been the increase in migratory farm labor and in the proportion of laborers not related to the operator.

With shifts in the tenure picture, one might ask if stratification has become greater in the average rural community. It probably has not, because of the shift from agriculture to other occupations of workers who still continue to reside in the community. Full-time and part-time off-farm employment has allowed these families not only to maintain but in many cases to improve their economic status.

The Position of Farmers in the Larger Society

Equally as important as understanding class differences within rural communities and rural life as a whole is awareness of the relative position of farmers in the larger society. Farm families have long been regarded as forming a substantial part of the great American middle class. During the past three or four decades, however, certain demographic and economic forces have tended to make a marginal group—between middle and lower rank—of a sizable segment of the farm population.

Several factors have contributed to this tendency. Technological advancement in engineering and in the techniques of raising plants and animals has increased productivity per worker many times. Meanwhile, the farm population, as we have seen elsewhere in this volume, continues to produce from 50 to 100 per cent more children than are needed to replace the present population.

On the other side of the picture, the demand for agricultural products is relatively inelastic. Thus, except for periods of war and other catastrophes, there is a continuing tendency toward domestic agricultural surpluses, which creates pressure on inefficient farmers to find some other type of employment. These conditions have caused agriculture to be called a perennially distressed industry.

One index of this condition is the relative proportion of the national income which comes to agriculture. In 1954, farmers, comprising slightly over an eighth of the population, received only about one-sixteenth of the income.[15] In the Depression years, they received even less proportionally of the national income. Paralleling the differential in per capita income is one in level of living as measured by the prevalence of certain consumption items. For example, such household items as running water and electricity are found in almost all urban homes; many rural homes lack both, but more have electricity than have running water. Among other consumption items that urban populations use more extensively than rural are the services of physicians and dentists. Although income and level of living of farm people in many sections are still much below the national average, significant increases have occurred since 1940, and the differences between urban and rural styles of living are rapidly diminishing.

A more dynamic picture of agriculture in American society is to be seen in the political and economic activities of farmers' organizations. Historically, the dominant interests of farmers' organizations have been prices, markets, and credit.[16] The central purpose has been to keep agri-

---

[15] National income was estimated at 278 billion dollars, net farm income, including government payments, at 14 billion, and gross income at 34 billion: *The Farm Income Situation,* Washington: U.S. Department of Agriculture, Agricultural Marketing Service, Bulletin 155, 1955. The per capita disposable income of farmers in 1954 was estimated at $840, or 54 per cent of that for the entire population, which amounted to $1,569: Frederick D. Stocker, "Disposable Income of Farm People," *Agricultural Economics Research,* 8:13–17, 1956.

[16] Carl C. Taylor, *The Farmers' Movement, 1620–1920,* New York: American Book Company, 1953.

culture on a par with the rest of the economy. Farm organizations, for the most part, as the public voice of the farmer, have represented the interests of the relatively prosperous, commercial farmer, a segment of the farm population which is solidly middle class.

A majority of the farm population,[17] however, does not have such secure social and economic status. These persons are referred to as the *disadvantaged* rural population; they are, as we have seen, low-income, underemployed farmers on small, low-production farms. The economic and population factors that contribute to this situation were described above. We shall now turn to ways of improving the lot of the lower-income segment of the rural population.

Rural Development Programs and Social Mobility

The term *rural development* has been used increasingly during the past few years because of the growing interest in low-income families at home and technical-assistance programs abroad. Rural development refers to coordinated, multiple-interest programs aimed at raising the level of living of families that fall below the average.[18] The Rural Development Program sponsored by the U.S. Department of Agriculture was discussed in Chapter 7.

In terms of rural social stratification, the major objective of rural development programs is to enable farm families to rise in social and economic rank. Some farm families need assistance in becoming better farmers; others need help in getting into other occupations. In order to do this, the family may need to move to a community that offers greater employment opportunities.

Major channels for vertical social mobility for rural people are (1) schooling, including vocational training, (2) occupational change for those who cannot increase their income in agriculture, (3) larger and more efficient farm operations for those who can acquire the resources, and (4) involvement in community activities and organizations. Inadequate educational facilities and lack of off-farm employment may be regarded as barriers to economic and social mobility. The purpose of a rural development program is to remove such barriers in areas in which they are found.

---

[17] The number of families involved depends upon the criteria of definition used. In 1950 over 60 per cent of the 5.3 million farm-operator families lived on farms where the gross sale of products was less than $2,500. Of the farm-operator families, 53 per cent had a net cash family income from all sources of less than $2,000. See *Development of Agriculture's Human Resources: A Report on Low-Income Farmers*, prepared for the Secretary of Agriculture, Washington: U.S. Department of Agriculture, 1955, p. 1.

[18] See the report cited in footnote 17 for a description of the work recently launched by the U.S. Department of Agriculture.

Certain organizations and agencies facilitate social mobility. The agricultural agencies, for example, give assistance to persons who want to become more prosperous commercial farmers. The recently inaugurated farm-and-home development program of the Agricultural Extension Service has this as an explicit objective. Educational agencies, which provide training and guidance for nonagricultural jobs, and the various employment services offer special assistance to persons who must seek employment outside agriculture. Agencies that promote industrial development also may be regarded as facilitating social mobility in predominantly agricultural communities.[19]

Rural development, of course, concerns other aspects of rural life in addition to economic advancement and technological change. These include the many associations carrying on educational, recreational, religious, welfare, and other activities. This associational life in the small community has a leveling influence that counteracts the stratification process. It makes possible participation that cuts across interest lines, and it brings about the development of common ideologies. For these reasons, as we saw in Chapter 7, rural society—the small community—is perhaps the best seedbed for a social structure with a broad middle class.

Questions for Review and Discussion

1. Define social stratification.
2. What precautions must be observed in describing the social classes in the United States?
3. How is class position related to the socialization of the individual?
4. Is social mobility increasing or decreasing in rural areas of the United States? Defend your answer.
5. How do sociologists go about determining a person's social-class position?
6. Of what use are socioeconomic scales and level-of-living indexes?
7. Differentiate fully between urban and rural class systems.
8. Distinguish between class and caste.

Selected References for Supplementary Reading

Anderson, C. Arnold: "The Need for a Functional Theory of Social Class," *Rural Sociology*, 19:152–160, 1954.
Belcher, John C.: "Evaluation and Restandardization of Sewell's Socio-Economic Scale," *Rural Sociology*, 16:246–255, 1951.
Goldschmidt, Walter: *As You Sow*, New York: Harcourt, Brace and Company, Inc., 1947.

[19] For a more detailed discussion of the implications of rural development programs for facilitating social mobility, see Harold F. Kaufman and Wilfrid C. Bailey, *Rural Sociology and Rural Development Programs*, Mississippi AES, Sociology and Rural Life Series No. 7, 1956.

Hagood, Margaret Jarman, Gladys K. Bowles, and Robert R. Mount: *Farm-Operator Family Level-of-Living Indexes for Counties of the United States, 1945, 1950, and 1954*, Washington: U.S. Department of Agriculture, Agricultural Marketing Service, 1957.

West, James: *Plainville, U.S.A.*, New York: Columbia University Press, 1945.

Loomis, Charles P., and J. Allan Beegle: *Rural Sociology: The Strategy of Change*, Englewood Cliffs, N.J.: Prentice-Hall, Inc., 1957, pp. 167–201.

CHAPTER 10 *Social Participation in Rural Society*

For some years, rural sociologists have noted and studied distinctive features of the social participation of rural people. They have been encouraged in their efforts by professional leaders in such agencies as the Agricultural Extension Service. The concern of agency leaders stems from the fact that the success of action programs depends on the extent to which rural people are willing to participate in organized group activities. As a result of these investigations, a considerable body of literature on the social participation of rural people has developed. Very little of this information has found its way into textbooks, however, and the present chapter is an attempt to fill in this gap for students.

Brief definitions of complex phenomena are always hazardous, but it is sometimes essential to direct attention to the most important aspects. Social participation has been defined as those diverse activities engaged in by a person either with other individuals or with groups.[1] The most significant aspect of this definition is *activities engaged in with others.* Social interaction is not necessarily involved, although the definition suggests it. Social interaction and social participation are easily confused and are sometimes used as synonyms, but care should be exercised to avoid such loose use. Social interaction is the more general term. Operationally, social participation refers to manifestations of social interaction in particular group situations. It does not specify the nature and extent of the interaction; rather it provides a framework for its occurrence. This will become clear in the discussion that follows.

TYPES OF SOCIAL PARTICIPATION

Research interest in social participation has centered primarily on formally organized groups. Churches, farmer organizations, lodges,

[1] A. R. Mangus and Howard R. Cottam, *Levels of Living, Social Participation, and Adjustment of Ohio Farm People,* Ohio AES Bulletin 624, September, 1941.

fraternal associations, service and luncheon clubs, cooperatives, and the various formal groups sponsored or fostered by the Agricultural Extension Service and other agencies provide opportunity for social participation in rural areas. These groups are commonly referred to as special-interest associations (see Chap. 22), since they bring people together on the basis of interests common to the members but not usually common to all persons in the community. Characteristically, they have a special name, formally designated officers, and some form of rules or regulations, such as a charter or constitution and bylaws. Thus they are called formally organized groups to distinguish them from other social groups, which lack these evidences of formalization. Informal social groups are important in their own right, however, and many of the more recent studies of social participation have turned attention to them.

Formal Social Participation

Being a member and taking part in the activities of formal associations is referred to as formal social participation. Obviously, this does not mean that all social interaction within these groups is highly formal in nature. Formal social participation refers to certain interaction situations available to members of specific associations; it is formal organizational participation. The word organizational distinguishes this type of participation from a type which does not require membership in specific formal associations but which arises from a variety of more or less contractual relationships with other individuals or groups.

Semiformal Social Participation

Buying supplies, marketing farm produce, borrowing money, and attending a movie or an athletic event are examples of semiformal social participation. Social interaction is incidental to the activity, and although the activity does not necessarily take place in a recognizable group, it may be sponsored by a formal organization and require a great deal of careful planning. The term *nonorganized* has been applied to this type of social participation. Folkman calls attention to the fact that as agriculture has become increasingly commercialized, such relatively impersonal contacts make up the greater share of the social experience of farm people.[2]

Informal Social Participation

Informal social participation refers to social contact in informal or nonorganized groups. In some studies the term has been used to include the kind of social participation referred to above as semiformal or non-

[2] William S. Folkman, *Membership Relations in Farmer's Purchasing Cooperatives,* Arkansas AES Bulletin 556, 1955.

organized, but, strictly speaking, it should be used to mean membership in and participation in the activities of informal but recognizable groups, such as cliques and friendship groups. These groups are called informal because they are not organized in the formal sense; that is, they do not elect officials, nor do they use formal procedures for selecting leaders and conducting the activities of the group. This does not mean, however, that they do not have group norms and group values that regulate behavior.

MEASURES OF SOCIAL PARTICIPATION

The concept of social participation appears to have developed in response to a desire to measure or at least to estimate the volume of the individual's social interaction. One way to do this is to record the time spent in situations that provide opportunity for face-to-face interaction. Early investigators of social participation used the *social-contact hour,* which was defined as an hour of exposure of a person to an event or situation that has socializing value.[3]

In later studies, emphasis on the time element was dropped in favor of effort to quantify social participation along a very general continuum indicating degrees of intensity of involvement in the group. Intensity is estimated from various manifestations of participation in the activities of the group. Membership, attendance at meetings, financial support, committee membership, and office holding in formal social groups are the more obvious manifestations of social participation or opportunity for social interaction. These are counted and combined to produce participation scores that are descriptive of individuals. The bulk of the research in social participation has included this type of measurement.

Tools for measurement of social participation have had to be developed and refined as knowledge of the subject increased. Most measurement devices have centered on two distinct but related elements of formal social participation, namely, the opportunity for social interaction in formal groups and sympathy with or identification with particular groups or their objectives. The first is a rough, quantitative measure of time, whereas the second measures quality.

Membership

Affiliation with a group is certainly the most overt and easily available evidence of social participation. It is clearly visible and is commonly considered in day-to-day living as prima-facie evidence of social participation. Its major limitation is that it does not account for varying degrees of participation, since mere inclusion on the membership roll of

[3] J. L. Hypes, *Social Participation in a Rural New England Town,* Teachers College Contributions to Education, No. 258, Columbia University Services, 1929.

an organized group may actually tell us very little about the extent of a person's participation in the affairs of the group or his identification with its objectives. Nevertheless, membership is a common denominator of participation and is therefore basic in its measurement. The act of becoming a member of a group at least opens the door to social inter-action and indicates identification with the group or its objective. It is often used when more detailed information is unavailable or difficult to obtain, but other manifestations of participation provide greater accuracy of measurement.

Attendance at Meetings

In time-conscious American society, attending the meeting of a group suggests greater involvement of the individual than mere membership. Physical presence at a group meeting increases the opportunity for social interaction and announces to others, both in the group and outside, that the individual has enough interest in or identification with the group and its objectives to take the time to attend its meetings.

Accurate measurement, however, requires classification of members in terms of the proportion of the group meetings attended over a period of time. A common procedure is to divide members into three attendance categories on the basis of some arbitrary standard. Some define *regular* attendance as presence at one fourth or more of the group's meetings; others set the limit at one half. Those who attend fewer meetings are called *irregular attenders,* and those who attend no meetings are *non-attenders.*

Financial Support

For many formal groups, membership automatically includes financial support. Some, however, do not have compulsory membership fees and are supported by voluntary donations. For this reason financial contribution to the support of an organization has sometimes been used as an additional measure of participation.

Offices and Committee Membership

A trademark of the formal organization is the practice of designating certain leadership positions or offices in the group. These positions do not necessarily encompass all the leadership roles, but they establish a formal framework of statuses. Persons selected to office or committee positions are expected to play specific roles set forth in the group's constitution and bylaws or merely understood and supported by a consensus of the group. Selection to fill a formal leadership position almost inevitably increases personal involvement of the individual. It represents the polar position on the continuum of concrete manifestations of participation.

Office holding generally implies greater responsibility than committee membership. This is recognized in some of the scoring procedures, in which greater weight is assigned to office holding than to membership.

Time Spent in Organizational Activity

Although in recent studies the social-contact hour has not been used as a unit of measure, interest in the measurement of the time dimension of social participation has continued. Estimates of the amount of time a person spends per week or per month in working for the objectives of a group or conducting its activities provide some dramatic evidence of variations in the degree of involvement. Richardson and Bauder found that the ten most active persons (in terms of time spent) in a Kentucky rural community of 2,000 people spent an average of 745 hours per year in organizational activities.[4] One of these ten spent an estimated 1,412 hours per year, or nearly 30 hours per week, in such activities. This person held twelve memberships and eight offices and attended 353 meetings in the year, an average of almost one meeting per day.

Social Participation Scores

One of the most widely used scoring systems for measuring participation in formal groups is the Chapin Social Participation Scale.[5] In the Chapin scale, five of the measures discussed above are weighted as follows: membership, 1; attendance, 2; financial contribution, 3; committee membership, 4; and office holding, 5. The total participation score for a person is obtained simply by summing the weights assigned to each activity category in all organizations in which the person has membership.

A number of modifications of the Chapin scale have also been used. Most modifications involve changes in either the number of items included or the weighing of the items. The item "financial contributions" is sometimes omitted from the list, and a variation to account for the recency of participation is sometimes included in assigning weights. This is done in the following scale used in a Pennsylvania study:[6]

0   Nonmember
1   Past member, now inactive
2   Member only, inactive
3   Member, active (attended within the past year)
4   Past officer, inactive

[4] Paul D. Richardson and Ward W. Bauder, *Participation in Organized Activities in a Kentucky Rural Community*, Kentucky AES Bulletin 598, 1953, p. 18.

[5] F. Stuart Chapin, "Social Participation and Social Intelligence," *American Sociological Review*, 4:157–166, 1939.

[6] Roy C. Buck and Louis A. Ploch, *Factors Related to Changes in Social Participation in a Rural Pennsylvania Community*, Pennsylvania AES Bulletin 582, 1954, p. 32.

5 Past officer, active (attended within the past year)
6 Present officer

Other scales have been developed by other sociologists to meet special needs. Hay developed a scale that combines formal and informal social participation.[7] He added to the Chapin scale weighted data on participation in such semiformal and informal activities as visiting, card games, athletic events, dances, pool, billiards, bowling, movies, drama, group picnics, group parties, exchange of work and equipment, and number of towns to which trips were regularly made.

Being interested in measuring social participation in relation to the community as a whole, Foskett developed a general community participation scale which included, in addition to membership in organizations and associations, such semiformal and informal activities as voting in elections, discussion of community affairs with members of the family, friends, and officials, taking an active part in local governmental and educational issues, attending meetings at which community affairs are the major item for discussion, and associating frequently with community leaders or officials.[8]

There are numerous examples of other classification systems designed to meet the needs of particular studies. Beal has developed a special scale for measuring participation in farmers' cooperatives, which includes such items as using the plant or patronage, participating in decision making, accepting financial responsibility and sharing risks, sharing economic benefits, taking part in educational and informational programs, and accepting organizational maintenance duties.[9] Rohrer and Schmidt used a simple dichotomous classification of people into "actives" and "inactives" in a study of formal organizational participation and family types. "Actives" are persons who attended meetings or held officerships in organizations, and "inactives" are persons who do not belong to any organization or, if they do belong, do not attend any meetings.[10]

SOCIOCULTURAL CORRELATES OF PARTICIPATION

Studies of social participation have been motivated by a very practical interest in determining the characteristics of people who participate

[7] Donald G. Hay, "A Scale for the Measurement of Social Participation of Rural Households," *Rural Sociology,* 13:285–294, 1948.

[8] John M. Foskett, "Social Structure and Social Participation," *American Sociological Review,* 20:431–438, 1955.

[9] George M. Beal, "The Importance of Understanding the Principles of Cooperation," *American Cooperation 1953,* Washington: American Institute of Cooperation, 1953.

[10] W. C. Rohrer and J. F. Schmidt, *Family Type and Social Participation,* Maryland AES Miscellaneous Publication 1960, 1954, p. 11.

most extensively. Even cursory observation reveals wide differences in participation. The question of why these differences exist quite naturally arises. Why do some people "belong to everything" and others "never take part in anything"? Statistical analyses indicate that extent of participation is closely related to certain personal characteristics, but they do not necessarily demonstrate causal relationships.

Age

In the life of the average person, participation in social relationships does not start or stop at any specific age, but the intensity of certain kinds of social relationships does vary with age. For preschool youngsters, social participation is concentrated in informal family and play groups. By school age, the number and variety of groups to which the child is introduced expands greatly. By the age of nine or ten, the average American child has the opportunity to take part in the activities of a number of interest groups, such as the Boy Scouts, the Girl Scouts, the Camp Fire Girls, and the 4-H Club.

From age ten through high school, participation in formal associations increases. But after high school, it apparently decreases rather sharply, especially among rural youth. Mayo, in a North Carolina study, found that the average participation scores for the twenty- to twenty-four-year age group and for the twenty-five- to twenty-nine-year age group was lower than for the ten- to fourteen-year and for the fifteen- to nineteen-year groups.[11] Participation in formal associations appears to increase through middle age. After age sixty, participation drops rapidly to a level comparable to that of the twenty- to twenty-four-year age group and the twenty-four- to twenty-nine-year age group.

Age-related variations in social participation appear to be a function of interest and opportunity. Mayo suggests that the ending of one phase of life activity and the beginning of another, the heavy demands of marriage and early family obligations, and selective rural-urban migration are three factors that may explain the low level of social participation in the twenty- to thirty-year age group.[12] It is in this age group that primary interests are personal, private, and largely unique to the individual. The middle-aged adult turns his attention more and more to broader common interests in contrast to personal interests. Or perhaps a better way to say it is that his personal interests become more and more identified with community interests.

Most studies indicate a precipitous decline in social participation

---

[11] Selz C. Mayo, "Age Profiles of Social Participation in Rural Areas of Wake County, North Carolina," *Rural Sociology*, 15:245, 1950.

[12] *Ibid.*, p. 250.

with the approach of occupational retirement and with the reduction in occupation roles (partial retirement) which is more characteristic in rural areas than full retirement.[13] This suggests that in American society retirement presents the individual with another period of instability having many elements in common with the late adolescent and young-adult periods. Retirement frequently means change of residence. Death removes spouses and thins the ranks of the peer group. High mobility and the American emphasis on the immediate conjugal family tends to isolate the oldsters even from their own children in rural as well as urban environments. Declining physical vigor and higher rates of illness reduce the capacity for taking active roles in groups. These factors combine to reduce social participation sharply even though interest in group activities may remain relatively high.

It is fairly obvious that the core interests that provide rallying points for formal group activities change with the advance of the life cycle. However, a number of studies have revealed a particular pattern of change in interests with the approach of retirement ages. Among rural people, at least, although total participation in organized groups tends to decrease in the later years, participation in church groups tends to increase.[14] Kaufman, for example, found that participation rates in church organizations were highest in the sixty-five- to seventy-four-year age groups, whereas participation rates in nonchurch organizations declined after age fifty.[15]

Sex

Generally speaking, measures of formal social participation indicate that women are more active than men. The exceptions are in certain rural areas where the traditional patriarchal idea that the man should represent the family in extrafamily activities still persists. However, the influence of such traditions is declining fairly rapidly, even in rural areas. Young and Bauder found evidence of decline in the patriarchal tradition in four Kentucky counties that differed only moderately in urbanization. The sex ratio of members of formal organizations exclusive of the church was 156 in the most rural county compared with 122 in the least rural county.[16] Adding church memberships would reduce both ratios as well as the difference between them, since the sex ratio of church

---

[13] John S. Taylor, "How Farm Operators View Retirement," unpublished doctoral thesis, University of Illinois, Urbana, Ill., 1956.

[14] Paul D. Richardson and Ward W. Bauder, *op. cit.*

[15] Harold F. Kaufman, *Participation in Organized Activities in Selected Kentucky Localities,* Kentucky AES Bulletin 528, 1949, p. 29.

[16] James N. Young and Ward W. Bauder, *Membership Characteristics of Special Interest Organizations,* Kentucky AES Bulletin 592, 1953, p. 14.

membership in the United States tends to be low, especially in rural areas.[17]

Status

Participation in social groups may serve a great variety of functions from the standpoint of both the person and the society. One of these has to do with status. The individual may think in terms of gaining or holding a particular status; for society it is a question of social selection or stratification.[18] John Doe and his wife may intensely desire membership in an exclusive organization because it is generally recognized as a mark of high status. They may belong to another organization with little thought of status.

In general, however, extent of social participation, particularly of formal social participation, is associated with status in rural areas. Kaufman found a direct correlation between extent of social participation and high status as determined by prestige ratings obtained within the community.[19] Many other investigators, using socioeconomic status or income levels as indications of social status, have found that social participation is positively associated with these measures.

Occupational Roles

Major occupational categories among farmers are based on tenure or relationship to the land (see Chap. 12). In general, farm owner operators and their families take a more active part in group activities than do tenants and farm laborers. The exceptions to the rule are found in cash-grain, high-land-value areas where tenants and part owners sometimes outrank owner operators in social participation.[20]

In most rural communities in the United States today, agriculture represents only one of a growing number of occupations. Division of labor, manifested in the elaboration and proliferation of occupational roles, is

[17] A series of studies in such widely scattered states as Illinois, Kentucky, Pennsylvania, and New York found ratios varying from 66 to 88. See: John A. Hostetler and William G. Mather, *Participation in the Rural Church*, Pennsylvania AES Journal Series Paper 1762, 1952.

[18] See the discussion of special-interest groups as social selectors in Chapter 22.

[19] Harold F. Kaufman, *Prestige Classes in a New York Rural Community*, Cornell University AES Memoir 260, 1944.

[20] In a recent study in a central Illinois cash-grain county, the present writer found that tenant and part-owner farm operators and their wives had higher social participation scores on the average than did owner operators and their wives. (From unpublished data obtained in connection with a study of the factors associated with the adoption of recommended fertilizer practices.) For a discussion of variations from the usual pattern, see: C. Arnold Anderson and Bryce Ryan, "Social Participation Differences Among Tenure Classes in a Prosperous Commercialized Farming Area," *Rural Sociology*, 8:281–290, 1943.

no doubt an underlying factor in the increase in the number and variety of special-interest associations in our society.

Occupational specialization produces interest specialization. This was evident in a study of four Kentucky counties that represented somewhat different levels of specialization and diversity in division of labor. Although only very crude measures of occupational specialization (census data on occupational groups) were available, the contrast in the number of memberships in special-interest organizations was so great that the suggested relationship could hardly be ignored.[21] In the county with the greatest occupational diversity, 1,318 memberships were found, whereas in the county with the least occupational diversity only 317 memberships were counted.

Education

In American society, formal education is responsive to strong utilitarian and pragmatic considerations, and, as a result, vocational training constitutes a major part of high school and college curricula. It is not surprising, therefore, that educational levels are correlated with specialization in occupational and other interests. Study after study has found education positively correlated with social participation until the weight of the evidence is so great as to leave little doubt of the association.

Residence

Where one lives and how long he has lived there appear to influence social participation. Urban residents generally belong to more organized groups and take a more active part in group affairs than do rural residents. It is a matter, again, of interest and opportunity. Urban society is characterized by a greater diversity of interests, and the greater the density of population, the greater the opportunity for people with very special interests to organize for the promotion of their interests.

Within rural society it also makes a difference where one lives. Residents of small towns participate more extensively than people who live in the open country. Also, organized groups among town residents tend to meet more often and involve more of their members in committee and similar kinds of activities within the group. Even where town and open-country residents share the same interests and belong to the same groups, town residents hold a disproportionately larger share of the leadership positions.[22] Brown found a differential among open-country

[21] Ward W. Bauder, *Objectives and Activities of Special-Interest Organizations in Kentucky*, Kentucky AES Bulletin 639, 1956, p. 8.

[22] Joseph G. Hardee and Ward W. Bauder, *Town-Country Relations in Special-Interest Organizations, Four Selected Kentucky Counties*, Kentucky AES Bulletin 586, 1952.

residents in favor of those who live closer to a town or a city.[23] Whether or not this is generally true we do not know. There is also some evidence that as transportation facilities improve, distance from towns, which are the usual meeting places of organized groups, becomes relatively unimportant.[24]

Length of Residence

How long it takes for a person or a family to be accepted in the organizational life of a rural community varies greatly with the community and with the person or family. Assimilation is slow in the more traditionalistic rural communities.[25] Perhaps the most rapid assimilation of newcomers into the organizational life of a community takes place in urban fringe areas, where social change is extensive and quite rapid. Even in these areas, however, the integration of new residents into the social life of the community is a relatively slow process and often takes the form of a dual development of associational structures, with newcomer- and old-timer-dominated groups existing side by side with imperfect communication and potentially serious conflict.

OTHER FACTORS IMPORTANT IN SOCIAL PARTICIPATION

Suburbanization

The flight to the urban fringe and the open country, so noticeable around the larger towns and cities in the more highly industrialized parts of the United States, has introduced many new elements into the networks of social relationship in erstwhile rural communities. The number of systematic studies of the characteristics of these "new" rural residents and the part they play in the life of the community is still somewhat limited, but enough work has been done to suggest some pertinent facts regarding their social participation.

Urban-fringe and open-country nonfarm people come from both urban and rural backgrounds, but the vast majority are tied to the city by occupation, regardless of their residential history. Interest specialization

[23] Emory J. Brown, *Who Take Part in Rural Organizations?*, Pennsylvania AES Progress Report 103, June, 1953.
[24] Unpublished data obtained in connection with a study of the acceptance of farm practices in a county in central Illinois with virtually no unimproved roads indicate that distance from town is no handicap to participation in group activities.
[25] See the series by W. A. Anderson, *Farm Women in the Home Bureau*, Ithaca: Cornell Rural Sociology Mimeographed Bulletin 5, 1941; *Farm Families in the Grange*, Cornell Rural Sociology Mimeographed Bulletin 7, 1943; and *Farmers in the Farm Bureau*, Ithaca: Cornell Rural Sociology Mimeographed Bulletin 4, 1941; and Emory J. Brown, *Elements Associated with Activity and Inactivity in Rural Organization*, Pennsylvania AES Bulletin 574, 1954.

and diversification tend to follow occupational specialization and diversification; thus it is logical that the over-all effect of the movement of people to the urban fringe and the open country would be to increase the amount of special-interest association at a rate as rapid as or more rapid than the rate of population increase. Whether or not this is true cannot be readily demonstrated, because a large number of other important modifying variables is present. For one thing people moving to the urban fringe come in family units. Very few single persons are involved. Furthermore, the vast majority are members of young families with small children, but with this the homogeneity ends, for people from all economic, occupational, and social levels are represented. The fringe is an area of contrasts in land use, economic enterprises, and levels of living.[26] It has great diversity in nationality and religious and social backgrounds. There is also little evidence of agreement among residents on the reasons for moving to the fringe.[27] It is an area of serious problems in land use, taxation, public or community services, and organizational facilities.[28]

One way to gauge the effect of living in the urban fringe is to compare the participation of persons before and after moving to the fringe. Anderson did this and found that a majority had increased their social participation after moving to the fringe. He also found that it was primarily persons in younger families who increased their social participation, whereas persons in the older (post-child) families tended to decrease their social participation.[29] Other studies have pointed out that the fringe presents a very heterogeneous picture as far as social organization is concerned. On the one hand a "pioneer spirit" sometimes prevails and tends to increase group activities; on the other hand, the newcomer to a rural community, especially if he is from the city, may meet with resistance and even resentment from persons in the established networks of social relationships and experience difficulty finding a position in it.[30] The bulk of opinion favors the position that part-time farmers and rural residents with urban jobs are generally low in social participation, whereas in the more "built-up" areas of the urban fringe

[26] Samuel W. Blizzard and William F. Anderson II, *Problems in Rural-Urban Fringe Research: Conceptualization and Delineation,* Pennsylvania AES Progress Report 89, 1952.

[27] Solon T. Kimball, *The New Social Frontier; The Fringe,* Michigan AES Special Bulletin 360, 1949.

[28] Walter Firey, *Social Aspects of Land Use Planning in the Country-City Fringe: The Case of Flint, Michigan,* Michigan AES Special Bulletin 339, 1946.

[29] W. A. Anderson, *A Summary of Urban Fringe Families and Their Social Participation in Ithaca, New York,* Ithaca: Cornell Rural Sociology Mimeographed Bulletin 43, 1954.

[30] Donald G. Hay, "The Social Participation of Households in Selected Rural Communities of the Northeast," *Rural Sociology,* 15:141–148, 1950.

change is so rapid and so recent that general patterns cannot yet be readily perceived.

Family Life Cycle

Families pass through life cycles that influence interaction patterns among members and their participation in extrafamily group activities. There are a variety of ways to divide the life cycle of a conjugal family into stages or phases, but the following is one of the most descriptive: prechild, young-child (all children under ten), younger-older child (some over and some under ten), older-child (all children over ten) and postchild (all children away from home).[31]

Many studies of social participation have revealed that it is closely associated with the life cycle of the family. The importance of children in determining the social participation of the family is amply illustrated. It is difficult, however, to generalize for all social participation, because there is evidence that different kinds of participation have greater or lesser importance in different phases of the life cycle. In so far as participation in formal organizations is concerned, there is general agreement that its volume is lowest among "prechild" and "young-child" families in rural society, but it is low for different reasons in each of these periods. In the "prechild" phase it is the husband who tends to be most inactive in formal organizational affairs, whereas in the "young-child" phase it is the wife who is most inactive. The reasons for the latter are quite obvious. As the children grow older, there tends to be an increase in formal participation of both husbands and wives, but after the children mature and leave the parental home, formal participation declines.[32]

Informal and semiformal participation follows similar cyclic patterns, with less difference between husbands and wives in the earlier stages, due to the greater number of whole-family types of activities in the informal category.

Attitudes and Values

Differences in social participation are also caused by attitudes and value orientations. Some attitudinal differences are associated with difference in such concrete factors as age, stage in the family cycle, and status, but others are of a more general nature and justify separate treatment.

Attitudes are not measured directly but are inferred from concrete

[31] W. A. Anderson, *Rural Social Participation and the Family Life Cycle, Part I: Formal Participation*, Cornell University AES Memoir 315, 1952.

[32] W. C. Rohrer and J. F. Schmidt, *Family Type and Social Participation*, Maryland AES Miscellaneous Publication 192, 1954.

responses to specific situations, natural or contrived. Thus, we infer a favorable attitude toward a community when a person responds favorably to a series of questions regarding his community as a place to live.

Community Identification. People who are active in organizational affairs express a greater identification with the community in which they live than those who are not.[33] They have a sense of being part of their communities. It is impossible to know, on the basis of our present knowledge, whether people identify with their community because they are active in its organizational life or whether they are active because they identify with the community. Nevertheless, the two things go together.

Satisfaction with the Community. Identifying with a community apparently does not necessarily mean satisfaction with the community. Also, one may have a favorable attitude toward the community as a place to live and still express dissatisfaction with some of its services.

Active participants are inclined to have a more favorable attitude toward the community as a place to live and at the same time express more dissatisfaction with certain community services.[34] Brown found that active participants were more dissatisfied than others with educational, recreational, and health facilities but better satisfied with their communities from the standpoint of friendliness, cooperation, morals, neighboring, and religious facilities.[35]

Satisfaction with Personal Living. Another category of expressions from which attitudes and values can be inferred are expressions of satisfaction with one's everyday, personal life experiences. Satisfaction implies good adjustment of the person to the social situation. People who are active in group affairs are better satisfied with their personal living—with their homes, families, jobs, incomes, and personal-social experience in general.[36] The most active, especially those with leadership positions, are, however, inclined to express a feeling that they are devoting too much time to organization activities and doing more than their share.[37] The evidence previously cited of concentration of leadership responsibility, particularly in formal organizational activities, and the widely repeated saying among people who promote action programs such as those in the Agricultural Extension Service, "If you have a program of action to put into effect in a community, look for some one who is already very busy if you want some one who will do a good job," suggests

[33] Emory J. Brown, *Who Take Part in Rural Organizations?*, Pennsylvania AES Progress Report 103, June, 1953.

[34] Ward W. Bauder, *Characteristics of Families on Small Farms*, Kentucky AES Bulletin 644, 1956.

[35] Brown, *Who Take Part in Rural Organizations?*

[36] *Ibid.*

[37] Mangus and Cottam, *op. cit.*, pp. 44–51.

a very troublesome paradox. Why is it that when a new organizational activity is contemplated, the people who are already the most active are most likely to get the positions of responsibility? Part of the answer may be found in the way people perceive themselves and their roles in social activities.

Self-perceptions and Self-images. The statement that the most interesting subject of conversation to any person is himself is quite true. From early childhood we are concerned with what constitutes the "I" or "me." Our ideas about self are very largely a product of interaction with others. Our self-perceptions or self-images are largely the reflections of self that we see in the behavior of others toward us. Much of the evidence we use in constructing our ideas of self in relation to group activities comes from "cues" we get from others.

Persons who are active in group affairs see themselves as the kind of people who are active in group affairs and at ease in group situations. This may sound redundant, but it is not. Self-perceptions are not only associated with social participation in general but with particular kinds of social participation. For example, Brown [38] reported that certain groups of farmers felt they were expected to be active in certain organizations such as the Grange and the Farmers' Cooperative, but they did not feel they were expected to be active in certain civic organizations or service clubs, although they might belong to them, or to be members of the country club. This was not a part of the role a farmer was expected to play in the communities that Brown studied. In other communities, however, certain farmers might be expected to be active in a country club. Whether a person perceives himself as one who is and is expected to be active in certain group activities or as one who is not and is not expected to be is therefore a crucial factor. The expectations of others regarding one's behavior become "community" expectations which are incorporated into the structure of the self and act as stimuli to conformity to particular patterns or roles.

Self-perceptions are the product of social experience. Social-psychological theory holds that early social experience is especially important in shaping one's self-image. In line with this, Anderson's studies of social participation led him to conclude that early family experience is of paramount importance in determining one's self-image regarding social participation. Families come to accept for themselves a certain status in the community and to participate in group activities in accordance with the roles perceived as appropriate to their position. [39]

[38] Brown, *Elements Associated with Activity and Inactivity in Rural Organizations*, p. 37.
[39] W. A. Anderson, "Family Social Participation and Social Status Self-Ratings," *American Sociological Review*, 11:253–258, 1946.

Participation Patterns

So far, we have viewed the correlates of social participation separately. The introduction of the idea of self-perception and community expectation suggests a model for viewing them collectively in a more meaningful manner. Individual correlates of social participation, such as income, education, and occupation, may be considered as symbols of status or position in the community. Active participants possess more high-status symbols: higher incomes and more education. If community expectations are forces that influence the behavior of the individual, community members will express opinions indicating that the higher income and educational groups are expected to participate more than the lower groups. Brown tested this hypothesis and concluded that various characteristics or qualities do have symbolic meaning to community members and evoke differential patterns of expectancies regarding the social participation of those who possess such characteristics or qualities.[40] For example, education symbolizes certain qualities that are prerequisite to taking part in formal group activities. Therefore, people develop attitudes of expecting people with higher educational attainment to take active roles in formal organizations. Similarly, a family name may symbolize certain qualities of leadership, especially in "old" families, and the community expects members of such families to occupy certain positions.

Since community improvement depends upon increasing the social participation of community members, more systematic analysis of the motivational forces listed above is needed. Further study may suggest ways to break the patterns, produced by self-perception and community expectancies, which cause the concentration of leadership reflected in such comments as "Our community has too few leaders" and "The only people who are willing to take part in group affairs in our community are already overburdened with responsibility."

Questions for Review and Discussion

1. Define social participation.
2. Differentiate between formal, semiformal, and informal participation.
3. Assume you were given the assignment of determining the types of social participation in your community. How would you go about it?
4. How do you account for the fact that different types of leaders are found in different types of social groups?
5. Explain the differences in the social-participation patterns of families as they progress from one stage in their life cycle to another.
6. List several ways in which rural social participation differs from urban social participation.

[40] Brown, *Elements Associated with Activity and Inactivity in Rural Organizations*, pp. 38–39.

Selected References for Supplementary Reading

Anderson, W. A.: "Family Social Participation and Social Status Self-Ratings," *American Sociological Review*, 11:253–258, 1946.

Beal, George M.: *The Roots of Participation in Farmers' Cooperatives*, Ames: The College Bookstore, Iowa State College, 1954.

Brown, Emory J.: *Elements Associated with Activity and Inactivity in Rural Organizations*, Pennsylvania AES Bulletin 574, 1954.

Duncan, Otis Dudley, and Jay W. Artis: *Social Stratification in a Pennsylvania Rural Community*, Pennsylvania AES Bulletin 543, 1951.

Mangus, A. R., and Howard R. Cottam: *Level of Living, Social Participation and Adjustment of Ohio Farm People*, Ohio AES Bulletin 624, 1941.

Mayo, Selz C.: "Age Profiles of Social Participation in Rural Areas of Wake County, North Carolina," *Rural Sociology*, 15:242–251, 1950.

CHAPTER 11 *Land Division and Titles*

The division of the land among its occupants and the establishment of the location and limits of the divisions constitute a series of problems that seldom if ever have been satisfactorily resolved in any part of the world. These problems are widely recognized, but rarely has sustained and concerted effort been made to solve them. Failure to undertake corrective or ameliorative measures is caused not only by the attitudes of the authorities and their supporters but also by the complexities inherent in any system of land division once it has been established and is in operation. Straightening old boundary lines, establishing new base points for reference, and making cadastral surveys involve adjustments permissible only under very special conditions, as well as a level of interpersonal relations and agreements hardly achievable through democratic and peaceful processes. In this chapter we shall discuss the social significance of the major systems of land division.

The havoc wrought by unsatisfactory systems of land division in the rural areas of the United States is still obvious today even though serious attempts to improve the situation were initiated more than 200 years ago. This fact points up the social implications of land division. Faults were inherited from a number of bad systems in Europe. The Spanish system adopted in the Western and Southwestern United States was notoriously faulty, and the English and French systems used elsewhere were scarcely more desirable. To make matters worse, these systems were adopted in areas where boundaries and location were considered to be of little importance because of the abundance of rich, unoccupied, unclaimed land. As a result, problems were created which, even today, have not been resolved satisfactorily. The Court of Land Claims was established in the latter part of the nineteenth century for the specific purpose of settling certain types of disputes over private and public holdings. In the State of New Mexico alone, this court has been asked to settle thousands of cases involving the location of boundaries.

It was not until 1785 that the United States instituted an accurate system of land division and description based on definite points of reference and accompanied by precise surveys. Unfortunately, the system applied only to those areas settled and surveyed subsequent to 1785. Other regions, especially those that were fairly intensely occupied prior to this date, were not greatly affected by the new system. As a result, they are still plagued by faulty deeds that frequently refer to *metes* and *bounds* (measures making use of arbitrarily selected points of reference, such as trees, stones, and streams) that have long since ceased to exist.

In more densely populated parts of the world, existing systems of land division generally are even more unsatisfactory than in the United States. Problems produced by indefinite location, vague boundaries, and faulty titles are especially severe where population density is high and farming methods antiquated. In certain areas of Latin America, conflicts over disputed holdings have flourished for centuries and even today are exploited not only by unscrupulous land barons but by the lawyers who carry their claims through legal channels. A substantial number of lawyers would be left unemployed, or at least seriously underemployed, if a definite system of land surveys and titles were established in Latin America.

The division and legal description of land holdings is a universal phenomenon, and it is not at all surprising that numerous and widely divergent systems have been developed for dealing with it. For our purposes, however, it is possible to classify the operating processes and procedures into four types: the rectangular system, with definitely established reference points on the earth's surface; the river-front pattern of division, with reference points established along rivers or other bodies of water; indiscriminate location, using metes and bounds as points of reference; and a variety of others.

THE RECTANGULAR SYSTEM

This system, as the name implies, involves the division of the land into plots of uniform size which are surveyed and recorded in reference to definite points on the earth's surface—the measurements of latitude and longitude used in all geographic mapping. In the United States these plots are rectangular in shape and six miles square and are called townships. A series of contiguous townships running to the north or to the south is called a *range*, with "the townships counting from the base, either north or south, and the ranges from the principal meridian, either east or west." Each township is subdivided into thirty-six sections one mile square, or of 640 acres, totaling 23,040 acres. The sections may be further divided into rectangular patterns composed of units of 320, 160, or 40 acres each. In other words, sections are reducible to units as small as 40 acres, each of which is readily determinable on location and may be completely and accurately described in titles.

As indicated earlier, the rectangular system of land division was established in the United States in 1785, and all lands patented after that

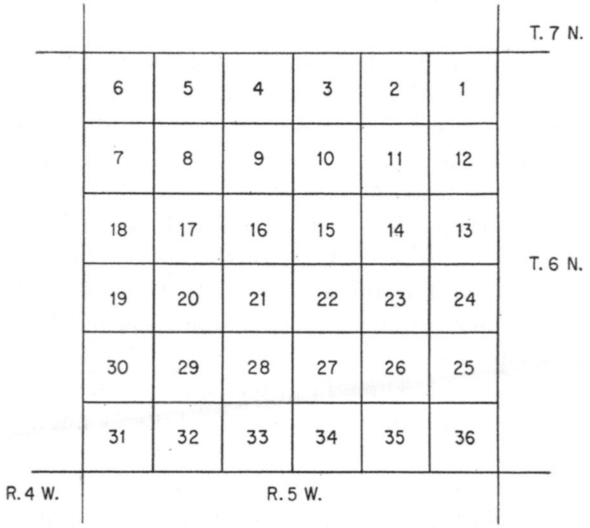

6	5	4	3	2	1
7	8	9	10	11	12
18	17	16	15	14	13
19	20	21	22	23	24
30	29	28	27	26	25
31	32	33	34	35	36

T. 7 N.

T. 6 N.

R. 4 W.   R. 5 W.

Figure 19. Diagram showing the rectangular pattern of the official system of land division in the United States. Note the arrangement and numbering of the thirty-six sections in the township.

date were surveyed in accordance with it. The result is sometimes referred to as the "checker-board" system, because of the pattern of squares it displays on a map (see Fig. 19). It is most prevalent in the Middle West, the Southwest, and the Far West, since other regions of the United States had been fairly well settled before the ordinance establishing the system was passed.

Advantages

Certain advantages of this system of land surveys are obvious. First of all, it provides permanent, astronomically determined points of reference. Its use enables the engineer to fix property limits and boundaries that are easily reestablished with great accuracy for any property as large as or larger than forty acres. Of major importance in avoiding disorganization and litigation is the fact that this system makes possible a simple and accurate deed. Smith calls this system "the ultimate in simplicity of land surveys."[1] The rectangular system also has certain farm-

[1] T. Lynn Smith, *The Sociology of Rural Life*, 3d ed., New York: Harper & Brothers, pp. 260–261.

management advantages in that it provides maximum freedom for the manipulation of farm enterprises.

These features undoubtedly account in part for the adoption of this system in other parts of the New World where new land has been made available to settlers, especially Brazil and Canada.

Disadvantages

The rectangular system of land division has been criticized as erecting barriers to social interaction and imposing economic restrictions on the development of services and facilities. Since the design of farm holdings under this type of land division is a series of squares, the resulting pattern contributes more than any other to the isolation of farm homesteads. T. Lynn Smith, perhaps the outstanding student of the subject in the United States, admits the advantages of the system from the standpoint of surveying and recording but concludes that "from the standpoint of the social and economic welfare of the population on the land it is one of the most vicious modes ever devised for dividing lands. Combined with the scattered or isolated farmsteads mode of settlement, it has greatly handicapped the rural population of the United States of the past century and a half." [2]

Critics claim that the isolation imposed upon farm families by the system may result in the incomplete socialization of individuals, causing personality difficulties and antisocial attitudes and behavior. Unfortunately, little study of an empirical nature has been done to prove or disprove these assumptions. In any case, continuous developments in ways and means of communication and transportation in rural areas are constantly diminishing rural-urban differences.

From a socioeconomic point of view, the rectangular system of land division in the United States obviously has numerous disadvantages. Since it encouraged farmers to live at maximum distances from one another, a condition commonly accepted in much of the rural part of the United States, the cost of rural services, such as roads and telephone lines to individual houses, has been much greater than in areas where both custom and the system of land holding and surveys have served to group the houses closer together. The cost of bringing pavement, for example, to each home in some areas of the Middle West, where the rule is for each farmer to live very nearly in the geographic center of his 160 acres, would achieve proportions unrealistic even in that prosperous area.

Proposed Modification

A scheme has been devised by Smith for modifying the rectangular or checker-board system of land surveys in such a way as to capitalize on

[2] *Ibid.*, p. 267.

its advantages and reduce its disadvantages to a minimum. He suggests that the townships be divided into strips considerably longer than they are wide. If the farmers then placed their houses at the ends of these strips, they would be located relatively close together or at least close enough together to reduce substantially the cost of roads, transportation, electricity, and telephone service and expenses imposed by isolated residence. Moreover, the houses would be so located as to allow ample social interaction among families, thus minimizing the chances, inherent in the system, of producing personal and social problems.

THE RIVER-FRONT PATTERN

In many parts of the world, a common form of land division involves measuring the width of a plot of land along the bank of a river or the shore of a lake or sea. These plots are usually extended back to some topographic feature such as to the foot or top of a hill or a river or stream. This system of land division was used extensively in the United States in colonial times. It was especially well accepted in those parts of the New World which were settled by the French and is much in evidence today in southern Louisiana and in those parts of the Great Lakes region once dominated by the French.

Advantages

The first advantage of the river-front system of land division was evident in colonial days, when water provided the major means of transportation. A second advantage was demonstrated by the Spanish settlers in the Southwest in the division of the irrigated lands along the rivers and streams.

The river-front system of land division is frequently found among the larger estates in Mexico and Central America. Beginning with the river and often continuing back to the ridge of a range of hills or mountains, holdings granted under this system of land division provide the owner with a variety of land and resources, including alluvial or delta land for crops, savannah for pasture and cattle, and timber in the hills for fuel and construction. The variety of land available is a third advantage of this system.

Disadvantages

The major disadvantage in this type of system is the indefiniteness of the points of reference on which the holdings are generally based. In this respect, the rectangular system is undoubtedly superior. In many cases, and especially when the holdings are small, points of reference are finally reduced to the boundaries of other holdings. Property limits obviously present less of a problem for the larger holdings, which may have such definite landmarks as hills and streams. Although these may change, they are at least more permanent and definite than are the memories and impressions of one's neighbors.

In the State of New Mexico today, the tendency to maintain frontage on the river, because of the irrigation advantages, is such that in many areas of the state, holdings along the streams are no more than a few yards in width. The inefficiency and waste of such a division are obvious, not only with respect to the limits placed on efficient operations but in the amount of land that must be set aside for fences or other means of property division.[3]

Present-day Uses

Students of Latin America have observed that modified versions of the river-front system of land holding are being used successfully in several countries with varying degrees of success. Smith reports finding it in areas of new colonization and settlement in Brazil, using new roads running along low ridges as bases for the divisions, which usually extend to a river or stream bed below.[4]

In some of these areas the river-front pattern of land holding has been developed to a very high degree of perfection. The system in use in many of the prosperous rural communities of southern Brazil permits the farmer to reside on the land without sacrificing the social and economic advantages of having neighbors. At the same time the farms and roads are laid out in a pattern that is well adapted to the topographic features of the landscape.

INDISCRIMINATE LOCATION

In new areas of settlement, there is likely to be little interest in how and where individual holdings are divided and recorded in the legal archives. It is not until the population has increased to a certain point that concern over boundaries and locations develops.

The United States in colonial times was a model case for this general rule. For a period of at least two hundred years following the first successful colonization effort in the United States in 1610, families settled much as they chose with little thought of order or system. Throughout the early colonial period of settlement, each colony disposed of its lands

---

[3] For examples of the disadvantageous division of land often found under this system, see: Olen E. Leonard, *The Role of the Land Grant in the Social Processes of a Spanish American Village in New Mexico*, Ann Arbor, Mich.: J. W. Edwards, Publisher, Inc., 1944.

[4] T. Lynn Smith, *Brazil: People and Institutions*, Baton Rouge, La.: Louisiana State University Press, 1946, p. 434.

as it saw fit. The Southern colonies, in particular, where large, widely separated holdings were the rule, allowed almost complete freedom of selection and location. The settler was permitted to claim any unappropriated site. The surveys, according to law, were to be made by public surveyors, but many of these were inexperienced, and there were untold opportunities for error. Furthermore, such records as existed were poorly kept. Individual initiative played a dominant role with respect to location. Anyone could select unappropriated land and have the local surveyor lay it off under the owner's direction. A settler was not required to consider the situation of other properties or their relation to his own. As a result of all this, extensive overlapping of properties and litigation resulted. A few men got a virtual monopoly on the best lands.

There is little to recommend the system of indiscriminate location, and it has definite disadvantages. Under this system, only the best lands are sought, and no thought is given to the marginal ones that lie between. Drastic enough in itself, the system of indiscriminate location in the United States was made worse by the legitimatization of the use of metes and bounds to define the limits of such properties, and these were surveyed and recorded in the same careless way. Trees, rocks, depressions, streams and other existing natural objects were used, many of which were soon altered or moved or could not be identified. Without definite and precise points of reference, rights in land in colonial times were often of little value to the owners even though they had been carefully recorded. Loosely defined property boundaries combined with carelessly executed surveys frequently provided excellent opportunities for fraudulent dealings. Following on the heels of the public land gifts and nominal sales of the late nineteenth century, courts in the Southwestern and Western United States were burdened for years with hundreds of cases involving controversial land claims. Many unscrupulous people took advantage of this confusion to gain enormous concessions of land.

Titles to public lands granted during colonial days in current California and New Mexico territory were very loosely defined. Land records inscribed in local courthouses show that many settlers, learning that lands entered and paid for were already in possession of someone else, merely shifted their title to another district within the same general area. This was referred to as "shifting of titles." Henry George, after studying the Mexican land-grant problem in California, concluded that: [5]

As soon as settlers began to cultivate farms and make improvements, the grants began to float. The grant-holders watched the farmers coming into their neighborhood, much as a robber chief of the Middle Ages might have watched

[5] Henry George, *Our Land and Land Policy*, New York: Doubleday & Company, Inc., 1911, pp. 39–40.

a rich Jew taking up his abode within striking distance of his castle. The settler may have been absolutely certain that he was on Government land and may even have been so assured by the grant-holder himself; but so soon as he had built his house and fenced his land and planted his orchard, he would wake up some morning to find that the grant had been floated upon him, and that his land and improvements were claimed by some land shark who had gouged a native Californian out of his claim to a cattle-run, or wanting an opportunity to do this, had set up a fraudulent grant, supported by forged papers and suborned witnesses. Then he must either pay the blackmailer's price, abandon the results of his hard labour, or fight the claim before surveyor-general, courts, commissioner, secretary, and Congress itself, while his own property, parcelled out into contingent fees, furnished the means for carrying the case from one tribunal to another, for buying witnesses and bribing corrupt officials. And then, frequently, after one set of settlers had been thus robbed, new testimony would be discovered, a new survey would be ordered, and the grant would stretch out in another direction over another body of settlers, who would then suffer in the same way, while in many cases, as soon as one grant had been bought off or beaten away, another grant would come, and there are pieces of land in California for which four or five different titles have been purchased.

In most of the countries of Latin America the problems attached to the indiscriminate location of properties, nonexistent or inadequate surveys, the use of metes and bounds as points of reference, and loosely defined titles have continuously plagued the courts and all too often have served as instruments for graft. To an even greater extent in Latin America than in the United States, extensive acreages of land were available to those asking for it during the colonial period, and little concern was given to any system or order in its distribution. And, once established, the task of undoing the harm done seemed always to be an unsavory if not an impossible one. In the Republic of Bolivia, for example, recorded deeds of property rarely carried points of reference for location other than the limits of the property of others. In the transfer of land it is still not obligatory to establish or to mention the political division in which the property is located, the name of the property, or the names of the vendor and purchaser, although this information frequently is included. The following is a typical contract of property transfer in the State of Cochabamba, Bolivia: [6]

Mr. Notary [name], in the registry of public records, under your responsibility, please insert this contract for the sale of property between [name] and [name], the contract consisting of the following clauses:

    1. I, [name], of legal age, married, property owner, resident of this city

    [6] Olen E. Leonard, *Canton Chullpas, Estudio economico social en el valle de Cochabamba,* La Paz, Bolivia: Ministerio de Agricultura, 1947, pp. 24–25.

and capable of executing this legal document, declare myself to be owner of the farm called [name], located in the County of [name], State of Cochabamba, the rights to which I possess through inheritance from my legal mother, Mrs. [name].

2. For my own interests, and by my own free will, I choose to transfer my rights to said property of [name] to Mr. [name], including all rights for use and possession, rights of access, and without reserving unto myself any rights or actions whatsoever.

3. The price of this property is [price] which I have received in legal tender, and to my complete satisfaction.

4. The property being transferred has the following limits: on the North, foot of the hills of [name], on the South arroyo [name], on the East the property of the heirs of [name], and on the West the properties of Mrs. [name].

5. This property carries no mortgage or lien, and is entirely clear before the law.

6. I, [name], of legal age, lawyer by occupation, resident of this city, and exercising authority vested in me by the authorities, approve, in all its parts, the present contract of sale, and sign in mutual agreement.

Cochabamba, ____ of [month], 18__

Signature_____ Signature_____

It will be noted that in this contract no mention is made of the size of the property, merely of the limits, which are by no means definite. This inattention to areal dimensions is symptomatic of the lack of concern of large landowners in present-day Bolivia for exact acreages in relation to their properties. An international development corporation established in the Santa Cruz area of Bolivia in the early 1940s discovered that owners were frequently in error by as much as 25 per cent in estimating the acreages of their properties. Nelson, in his work on Cuba, found a similar indefinite and cloudy situation with respect to property location and limits. It is his opinion that the indefiniteness of title description gave rise to the Cuban practice of requiring the recording of the names of properties in their transfer.[7]

OTHER FORMS OF LAND DIVISION

Associated with the system of indiscriminate location and the use of metes and bounds to determine limits are a large number of variant systems, only a few of which will be discussed here. One of the more interesting and confusing is the system of circular holdings, which was extremely popular in early colonial Cuba and has been used in other parts of the world. A holding of this type consists of all the property

[7] Lowry Nelson, *Rural Cuba*, Minneapolis, Minn.: The University of Minnesota Press, 1951, p. 109.

lying within a given radius of a certain established point. Its extensive use in Cuba has resulted in an esthetically pleasing map design, but problems growing out of surveys and the later subdivision of circular holdings have been of major proportion. As Nelson points out in his study of Cuba, the division of an area into circular properties creates tremendous surveying problems and leaves awkward interstitial areas that are very difficult to locate and describe with exactness. Considering the absence of competent surveyors and the lack of interest of the owners of the larger holdings in the exact limits of their properties, it is not sur-

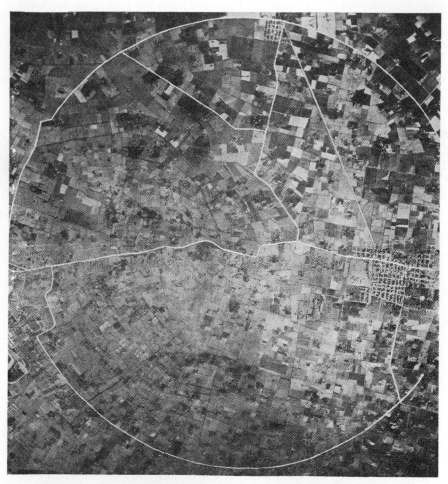

Figure 20. The complex problems resulting from the circular-survey system can be surmised from the layout of this circular land grant in the Municipio of San Antonio de los Banos, Cuba. (Foto—Instituto Cubana de Cartografia y Catastro.)

prising that many of the grants of the colonial period were later found to overlap extensively (see Fig. 20). The settlement of disputes resulting from such errors alone have been extremely burdensome to the Cuban landowner and remains a problem even today.

Serious complications develop when it becomes necessary to divide the circular holding into smaller holdings. How can a circle be divided in order to obtain fairly definite boundaries and descriptions? "Needless to say," Nelson observes, "this could not be done by further use of the circular design."[8] Instead, recourse was had to a series of geometric shapes, especially the trapezoid and prism, none of which were completely satisfactory. In many areas of rural Cuba today, the problem of determining exact property limits has been abandoned, and friendly, neighborly advice and counsel have been substituted in settling disputes. This is a good functional practice but not necessarily a sound legal one.

Another type of division transplanted to the Americas by the Spanish was the "caballo," or the area around which a man could travel on a horse in a given number of days. This type of grant was used extensively in a number of South American countries during colonial days and retained in some of them after their republican status was established. It was a particularly popular method for locating and determining the size of holdings of the crown lands.[9]

The evils that sprang from a system so indefinite as this are easily imaginable. The granting of land by such loose methods produced a situation in which it was difficult for small farmers to acquire their own land. In response to requests for open land, officials sometimes "assumed" that the land was apportioned. It seems likely, too, that often a prospective proprietor hesitated to file claim for land, reasoning that a petition would only invite trouble with some large land baron after improvements had been made. Such problems have been blamed for the slow development of the rich Santa Cruz area of Bolivia.[10]

Another ingenuous method for location of property limits was the "horn blow," determined by the distance a horn could be heard in each direction from an arbitrarily determined point. Fortunately, the Council of the Indies, the governing board of the Spanish Colonies in the New World during much of the colonial period, soon frowned on the use of this system; but in the existing atmosphere, characterized by exploitation and quick profits, little time was lost in discovering other methods that served the same purposes with equal effectiveness.

[8] *Ibid.*
[9] Olen E. Leonard, *Santa Cruz*, La Paz, Bolivia: Ministerio de Agricultura, 1948, p. 27.
[10] Francisco de Viedma, *Descripción de la provincia de Santa Cruz de la Sierra,* Cochabamba, Bolivia, 1889.

Questions for Review and Discussion

1. Explain how the land is divided in the river-front pattern of settlement.

2. When was the rectangular system of land division adopted in the United States? Describe its basic principle.

3. List the advantages and disadvantages of each of the major systems of land division.

4. Should you be assigned the task of recommending a system of land division for an undeveloped country, what principles would govern your recommendations?

5. Look up the official description of a farm in your county or state and see if you can locate it on the basis of the information on record.

Selected References for Supplementary Reading

Donaldson, Thomas: *The Public Domain,* Washington: Government Printing Office, 1884, pp. 575–605.

Leonard, Olen E.: *The Role of the Land Grant in the Social Organization and Social Processes of a Spanish-American Village in New Mexico,* Ann Arbor, Mich.: J. W. Edwards, Publisher, Inc., 1948, chap. 5.

Smith, T. Lynn: *The Sociology of Rural Life,* 3d ed., Harper & Brothers, 1953, chap. 11.

——: *Brazil: People and Institutions,* Baton Rouge, La.: Louisiana State University Press, 1946, chap. 14.

CHAPTER 12 *Land-tenure Systems and Problems*

Throughout the world, wherever there is a shortage of land, there is also a struggle among men for control of this resource. This is inevitable, because land provides the food, fiber, minerals, and timber essential to survival,[1] and in times of crisis, those in possession of the land are less apt to be made homeless or to perish. Thus, in most of the world, land is a precious commodity strongly associated with security and freedom. Furthermore, according to investigators, the social well-being of people on the land is closely related to their rights in the soil. Many bloody revolutions and many less violent social movements can be traced to what has been called "land hunger." Problems of this type are classified as *land-tenure problems* and are of interest to the sociologist because they are involved in social organization.

This chapter is devoted to a review of the functions, types, and problems of land-tenure systems. In addition, a discussion of the origin and character of land-tenure patterns and problems in the United States is included.

Definition of Land Tenure

Land tenure concerns the rights of individuals and groups to the land and the many ramifications of these rights in human relationships. Social scientists have utilized the "bundle-of-rights" concept to explain tenure relationships. According to this concept, rights to the land may be shared with others for a period, by mutual agreement. A tenant, for example, by virtue of the payment of rent, may have the right, according to the stipulation of his contract, to use a parcel of land as he desires. He thus shares in the "bundle," or complex, of rights accompanying the idea of property. Renne's definition of land tenure makes this clear.[2]

[1] Joe R. Motheral, "Comparative Notes on East Asian Land Tenure Systems," mimeographed summary of chapter prepared for the Annual Report of the Philippines Tenancy Commission, July, 1955.

[2] Roland R. Renne, *Land Economics*, New York: Harper & Brothers, 1947, p. 429.

Land tenure is a broad term covering all those relationships established among men which determine their varying rights in the use of land. It deals with the splitting of property rights, for their division among various owners, between owner and occupier, between owner or occupier and creditor, and between private owners and the public. . . .

This is the sense in which the term *land tenure* will be used in this text.

THE FUNCTIONS OF TENURE ARRANGEMENTS

Tenure problems have a long history. The ancients observed that certain tenure arrangements exerted a strong influence upon the way in which agricultural resources were used and upon the level and kind of production achieved. Later observers noted relationships among the type of tenure system, the extent of conservation of natural resources, and the stability of a nation's economy. These and other discoveries have challenged the imagination of social philosophers and social scientists through the ages, and there is now a voluminous literature on tenure topics. Cognizant of these relationships, the leading tenure specialists in the United States recently collaborated in the preparation of a monograph outlining, among other things, the functions of tenure arrangements in a democratic society.[3] A review of these functions provides a basis for appraising the relative merits of specific systems.

1. Tenure Arrangements Should Contribute to Efficient Use of Resources. In the report referred to above, *Agricultural Land Tenure Research,* the authors point out that any elements of a tenure system that hinder or prevent the effective organization of land, labor, and capital employed in agriculture should be changed. Tenure systems involve a host of economic and social factors. For example, a traditional arrangement between landlord and tenant by which the land is to be put to a use that exhausts it is a deterrent to efficient use of resources, as is the employment of less than the optimum amount of long-term capital necessary to maintain the productivity of the land. The ideal tenure arrangement is one which not only allows for maximum use of resources but provides the necessary incentives to fulfill this function.

2. Tenure Arrangements Should Promote Stability of Resource Productivity. History has shown that inadequate tenure systems are contributory to depression cycles. This is explained as follows: When tenure arrangements are rigid, requiring that obligations such as those relating to loan-repayment schedules, taxes, and rents, be met despite a declining price level, there is a tendency to increase production and to further de-

[3] *Agricultural Land Tenure Research, Scope and Nature: Reappraisal, 1955,* a report prepared by the Interregional Land Tenure Research Committee, Chicago: Farm Foundation, 1955, pp. 2–5.

press prices. It is thus a truism that a tenure system that promotes an inverse correlation between production and prices contributes to the instability of an economy. The ideal tenure system makes allowances for a direct correlation between production and prices and thus stabilizes one aspect of the economy.

3. *The Tenure System Should Contribute to Equality of Access to Resources.* The implication of this function is that interested and qualified persons should have equal opportunity to enter farming. Admittedly, this ideal has not been attained in most countries because access to rights in land are usually contingent upon conditions over which the individual has no control, such as inheritance. Nevertheless, the idea of equality of opportunity to acquire land can be maintained as a guiding principle. As the authors of *Agricultural Land Tenure Research* point out, ". . . adherence to this principle would result in the development of a fully competitive system where competitors of equal ability will be on an equal basis in acquiring rights to land."[4] Being on an equal basis, the authors explain, is to be understood in terms of progress toward a reasonable degree of free competition for land resources. This is closely related to social mobility and the concept of the agricultural ladder, as we shall see later in this chapter.

THE AGRICULTURAL LADDER

Tenure systems characterized by relatively high vertical social mobility offer the young farmer opportunity to progress from lower to higher tenure status until he has achieved ownership. Rural social scientists have likened this progress to climbing a ladder. This phenomenon has long been recognized in this country.[5]

Four fundamental steps or rungs are generally identified by rural sociologists and agricultural economists, although others are sometimes added. Each rung represents a definite stage of progress and may be characterized by a letter:[6] The first rung is designated by the letter P to indicate that the individual is on the home farm doing unpaid family labor for his parents. The second rung is labeled H for his succeeding tenure as hired hand or laborer. The third rung is identified with the letter R for renter or T for tenant. The final rung may be designated by the letter O to represent owner status, which is the ultimate goal.

It is possible to add further rungs to the ladder. For example, some

[4] *Ibid.,* p. 4.

[5] W. J. Spillman, "The Agricultural Ladder," *American Economic Research,* Supplement, March, 1919, pp. 29–38.

[6] John F. Timmons and Raleigh Barlowe, *Farm Ownership in the Midwest,* Iowa AES Research Bulletin 361, and North Central Regional Publication 13, 1949, pp. 892–893.

social scientists have included rungs to represent tenure classifications such as farmer with nonfarm employment, mortgaged owner, part owner, and landlord.

In recent years social scientists have recognized what they have termed a "new agricultural ladder." [7] This new ladder differs from the traditional one in the substitution of new statuses for the various rungs, resulting in part from recent innovations in certain farm areas. The first rung of the new ladder is scaled when an interested youngster becomes a member of a 4-H or FFA club. Ostensibly, this is where the first real interest in farming is developed. The next step in the ladder is achieved when the father goes so far as to give his son a monthly wage for his help on the farm. This arrangement is likely to continue for a period sufficient for the son to serve a sort of apprenticeship. The third rung is achieved when a genuine partnership between father and son is decided upon. At this stage all income is shared according to some plan associated with the contribution of each to the total effort. The final rung of the ladder is reached when the father retires and the son assumes full responsibility for the operation of the farm.

Although the agricultural ladder is a useful symbol in gaining an understanding of social mobility and the tenure process, it must be understood as a theoretical construct. The student should be careful to make allowances for its rigidity. For example, certain individuals may move into ownership directly through inheritance or good fortune, whereas others may never scale the heights of the ladder because of lack of opportunity or ambition. Generally speaking, however, there is a high correlation between the age of farmers and their tenure status in family-farm areas, which indicates the validity of the ladder concept.

TYPES OF LAND-TENURE SYSTEMS

A review of history shows that man has been concerned with the use and control of land from the beginning of recorded time. Almost all present-day tenure systems are mere modifications of ancient customs. A great variety of tenure systems is possible, but setting aside differences in detail, five general types can be isolated and listed.

Each of these systems includes numerous subsystems that can be identified because they incorporate the main ideas of the major system. Significantly, all five major systems bear a remarkable similarity to ancient systems and demonstrate marked cultural continuity with regard to land tenure.

[7] John H. Kolb and Edmund deS. Brunner, *A Study of Rural Society*, 4th ed., Boston: Houghton Mifflin Company, 1952, pp. 93–94.

1. Restrictive Right to the Land. The first suggestion of a tenure system is found in certain primitive or preliterate societies. Apparently, as long as it is possible for man to live by fishing and hunting, the appropriation of land is of little importance to him. However, even in societies that have progressed no further than a gathering or collecting economy, exclusive claims are made to special hunting and fishing grounds and to burial sites and other religiously significant places. Although such claims involve no more than a simple restriction of use by others, they represent an elementary tenure system. It is significant that systems of this nature are found the world over, wherever man has not progressed to the settled agricultural stage.

2. Communal Arrangements for Tilling the Soil. The collective or communal type of ownership system dates back at least as far as the beginning of recorded history. Under such systems owners or tenants (if the land belonged to chiefs or kings by virtue of divine right) had only temporary control of a given parcel of land. Generally, there was a periodic redistribution of fallow and cultivated acreage according to some commonly accepted scheme. The "mark" system, characteristic of much of premedieval Europe, consisted of the holding of common territory by a certain number of families or a clan. At one period in the history of the "mark" system, land was allocated annually by lot. Today the best known example of collective farming is found in the Soviet Republic. This system differs quite radically from that of the small communistic societies scattered around the world, however, and there is some question as to whether it fits best under this classification or under the fourth one, described below.

3. Independent Classes of Small-farm Owners. In the second millennium b.c. the Mediterranean basin and the Near East as far as the Indian frontier were conquered and settled by the Assyrians. These conquerors had a social and economic organization based on an Iron Age agricultural civilization, and they replaced the overthrown empires with military communities of free farmer tribes. In Greece the shift to a money economy accounted for the rise of a class of small owners at this time.[8] It is interesting that at such an early date there was, for a time, a widespread abolition of serfdom and an almost complete transition to an independent farmer class in this part of the world. Such holdings also developed over much of Europe during its early history. Today one finds owner-operated family-size farms over much of the United States and in many other parts of the world. Quite frequently, where law and custom permit, such systems are interspersed with other systems. Generally, however, the

[8] Fritz Heinhelheim, "Land Tenure in the Ancient World," *Encyclopedia of the Social Sciences,* New York: The Macmillan Company, 1937, vol. IX, p. 77.

idea of ownership appears to be the ideal of the masses of agriculturists and the goal for which they are struggling.

4. *Large Estates Owned by Church, State, City, or Other Public Bodies.* Another pattern that developed early involved the ownership and control of large domains by certain "public" bodies such as the church, the state, or the nation. Holdings of this type have generally been operated by dependent peasants or serfs. In some instances, these "workers" cannot be separated from the land and thus have certain rights. However, they have little opportunity for advancement.

5. *The Latifundian Type of Private Estate.* Under Roman laws permitting expropriation and gradual enslavement for debt, land was accumulated by private holders in immense estates called *latifundia,* the forerunners of our present-day plantations, haciendas, and other types of large land holdings. The Roman latifundia were usually worked by *colonus,* who paid a fixed rent to cultivate the piece of land to which they were attached. The feudal system which developed in England but failed to flourish in the United States can be traced to this origin. The sharecroppers and peons who operate large private holdings today are reminiscent of the *colonus.* It is significant that large private estates can be found in almost every country.

These are the major types of tenure systems. Each has certain characteristics in so far as the rights of individuals in using the land are concerned, and each contributes to the prevailing rural social organization. The advantages and disadvantages of each can only be assayed in terms of what is considered ideal in the particular society. Nevertheless, it can be stated unequivocably that those systems that give the individual farmer the most freedom tend to encourage initiative and thrift and are generally associated with high levels of living.

LAND TENURE IN THE UNITED STATES

The Major Underlying Tenure Principle

The land-tenure system of the United States evolved for the most part from the feudal system prevalent in medieval Europe.[9] Under this system serfdom was the most common form of servitude, although slavery also existed. Serfs generally had certain rights in the use of the land but were bound to the soil and subject to transfer with the estate. Higher-status tenure groups on the feudal estates were the lesser gentry, the nobility, and the royalty.

In England, until a short time before the colonization of America, it

[9] Charles P. Loomis and J. Allan Beegle, *Rural Social Systems,* Englewood Cliffs, N.J.: Prentice-Hall, Inc., 1950, p. 309.

was customary for the king to allocate land to his faithful followers in return for their military or other services. This practice naturally made the feudal lord beholden to the king, either for military service (known as *knight service*) or for other types of services according to the system known as *socage tenure*. Serfs and tenants on the land also had obligations to their respective lords. Under socage tenure, for example, not only cash rentals but also numerous payments in kind and labor were expected. This type of arrangement was the first to be tried in America by the English and Dutch. From the beginning the English achieved little success in enforcing the payment of rentals demanded of landholders, and the Dutch, although they enjoyed limited success for a time, did not fare better in the long run. It proved impossible to extract payments for the use of feudal lands when a plentiful supply of "free" land was available.

An indication of how strongly the colonists felt about this practice is the fact that the first general legislation by Congress on the subject of real property abolished the principal feudalistic features of the land-tenure system. The ordinance of 1787 decreed that the individual was sole owner of his land, absolutely independent of the state.[10] Since that time, it has been a fundamental principle in this country, both in custom and in actual law, that although the state is the source of title, the individual holder of land has absolute rights over it. Ownership of this type is *fee-simple* ownership. To the state or public body is left only the right of *eminent domain*, the right to use the land in the public interest. Significantly, even under this right, the public must pay a fair price for whatever land it confiscates.

Tenure Classes

The system of tenure classification generally used in this country is that established by the United States Bureau of the Census. Basic to this system of classification is the distinction between operators and laborers; inside each of these groups, a number of different classes are distinguished. The 1954 Census of Agriculture gives the following classifications and definitions:

Full owners own land but do not retain any land rented from others.
Part owners own land and rent land from others.
Managers operate farms for others and are paid a wage or salary for their services. Persons acting merely as caretakers or hired as laborers are not classified as managers.

[10] T. Lynn Smith, *Sociology of Rural Life*, 3d ed., New York: Harper & Brothers, 1953, p. 278.

Tenants rent from others or work on shares for others all the land they operate. Tenants are further classified on the basis of their rental arrangement as follows:

Cash tenants pay cash as rent, such as $10.00 an acre or $1,000 for the use of the farm.

Share-cash tenants pay a part of the rent in cash and a part as a share of the crops or of the livestock or livestock products.

Share tenants pay a share of either the crops or livestock or livestock products, or a share of both.

Livestock-share tenants pay a share of the livestock or livestock products. They may or may not also pay a share of the crops.

Crop-share tenants pay only a share of the crops.

Croppers are crop-share tenants whose landlords furnish all work power. The landlords either furnish all the work animals or furnish tractor power in lieu of work animals. Croppers usually work under the close supervision of the landowners or their agents or other farm operators, and the land assigned them is often merely a part of a larger enterprise operated as a single unit.

Other tenants include those who pay a fixed quantity of any product; those who pay taxes, keep up the land and buildings, or keep the landlord in exchange for the use of the land; those who have the use of the land rentfree; and others who could not be included in one of the other specified subclasses.

Laborers, or those who lack property rights in the land, are listed separately in the census. Three different classes of laborers are recognized: (1) regular laborers, or those working or expecting to work at least 150 days on a given farm; (2) seasonal workers, or those whose period of actual or expected employment is less than 150 days; and (3) unpaid family members working on the particular operator's holdings.

It may be noted that there is some question as to whether or not croppers should be classified as laborers. Smith feels strongly that this group, working under direct supervision and furnishing no capital outlay, is a laboring group.[11] They are distinguished from other laborers chiefly in that they are paid with a share of the crop rather than in cash. Croppers are found primarily in the cotton-plantation areas of the South and customarily receive half of the cotton they produce as their payment.

The census classification outlined above is a basically sound one for the United States. With a few minor exceptions it includes all the types of tenure arrangements found in the nation. The student should, of course, be aware that the customary payments in cash, crop shares, or livestock shares differ from one region to another depending on factors such as custom and type of enterprise.

[11] *Ibid.*, pp. 280–281. It is Smith's contention that the inclusion of cropper units as separate and distinct farms has distorted much of the past census data pertaining to farm units in the Southern region.

The Tenure Situation and Trends

It is significant that in 1950 the proportion of the nation's nearly 2 billion acres of land which was in farms was the greatest in its history. Over three-fifths (60.9 per cent) of the land area of the United States was in agricultural production. It is, perhaps, more important that only 18.1 per cent of the land in farms was operated by tenants. Of course, 36.7 per cent of the farmland was operated by persons who were only part owners, holding some acreage on a tenancy basis. Well over one-third of the farm land (36.1 per cent) was operated by full owners, and a little less than one-tenth (9.1 per cent) was operated by managers.

The percentage of the total number of farms operated by tenants presents a somewhat different picture from the proportion of land in farms operated by them. This proportion shows more impressively the role of the owner operator in agricultural production in this country. Almost three-fourths of the 5⅓ million farms in the nation were owned fully or partly in 1950. By contrast, a little more than one-fourth (26.8 per cent) were rented, and as few as 0.5 per cent were operated by managers.

This tenure picture contrasts sharply with that of a quarter of a century ago. As a matter of fact, the number of tenant farms (including cropper farms) increased steadily from 1880 to 1930, when an all-time high of 42.4 per cent of the total number of farms was reached. Great alarm over the high rate of tenancy was manifested in the early thirties. However, partly as a result of government action programs and partly because of the economic climate beginning with the Second World War, the tenancy rate has declined steadily since 1935. Today there are fewer tenant-operated farms than at any other time since the turn of the century.

While the number of tenants has been decreasing, the number of part owners has been increasing, in some periods phenomenally. For example, the number in this group increased by 34.1 per cent between 1940 and 1950. The number of full owners also increased during this decade, but only slightly, by 0.2 per cent. The tremendous increase in part owners within recent years is explainable by the relatively large number of tenants making an initial move toward full ownership and the number of owners expanding their operations by renting land. In both instances, land which has been vacated by farmers migrating to urban areas is being acquired.

The significant changes in the farm-tenure situation in this country since the end of the Second World War have been concurrent with population shifts. In this period of record-level prices and plentiful nonfarm employment opportunities, the number of people engaged in agriculture has continued to drop steadily. This migration has relieved the pressure on the land and consequently changed the tenure picture for those remaining on the farm (see Chap. 5). The important questions at present seem to be, How long will the trend continue, and what further effects will it have on the tenure situation?

Prevalence and Distribution of Tenure Groups

It is revealing to study the role of each tenant class in the agriculture of the nation. One approach is to determine the amount and type of land operated by the various tenant classes. Although most of the approximately 190 million acres rented in the nation in 1954 were worked according to some form of share arrangement, the largest acreage was controlled by crop-share tenants (see Fig. 21), who accounted for 28.4 per cent of all land in farms operated by tenants. The share-cash tenants follow closely in amount of land operated, accounting for 24.3 per cent of the acreage under tenancy operation. A substantial amount, 19.4 per cent, of the land in tenant farms is rented on a cash basis, and a somewhat smaller acreage, 15.6 per cent, is leased on a livestock-share agree-

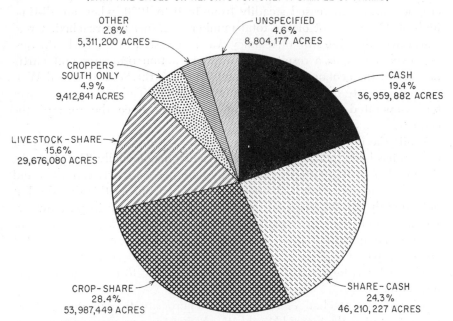

LAND IN FARMS OPERATED BY TENANTS, BY CLASS OF TENANT, FOR THE UNITED STATES: 1954

(DATA ARE BASED ON REPORTS FOR ONLY A SAMPLE OF FARMS)

OTHER
2.8%
5,311,200 ACRES

UNSPECIFIED
4.6%
8,804,177 ACRES

CROPPERS
SOUTH ONLY
4.9%
9,412,841 ACRES

CASH
19.4%
36,959,882 ACRES

LIVESTOCK-SHARE
15.6%
29,676,080 ACRES

CROP-SHARE
28.4%
53,987,449 ACRES

SHARE-CASH
24.3%
46,210,227 ACRES

Figure 21. Proportion of all land in farms operated by tenants in the United States, by class of tenant, 1954. (U.S. Department of Agriculture, Agricultural Research Service, and U.S. Department of Commerce, Bureau of the Census.)

ment. Croppers cultivate 4.9 per cent and miscellaneous and unspecified types of tenants operate the remaining 7.4 per cent of the land controlled by tenants. Figure 22 shows the type of tenure of the operators of all land in farms in the United States according to major uses.

It seems a principle of tenure theory that tenant farms are concentrated in areas of high land productivity. Thus, in the United States, there is a concentration of tenant-operated farms in the cotton and tobacco areas of the Coastal Plains, in the Mississippi Delta, and in the more fertile parts of the Corn Belt. By contrast, full owners, although they are found

PERCENT DISTRIBUTION OF ALL LAND IN FARMS ACCORDING TO MAJOR USES, BY TENURE OF OPERATOR, FOR THE UNITED STATES: 1945-1954

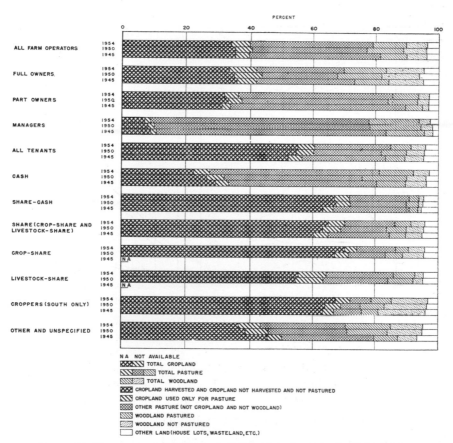

Figure 22. The per cent distribution of all land in farms in the United States according to major uses, by tenure of operator, 1945–1954. (U.S. Department of Agriculture, Agricultural Research Service, and U.S. Department of Commerce, Bureau of the Census.)

everywhere, tend to concentrate in places where productivity and prices of land are low, as in the Southern Appalachian region. However, the data available show full owners to be rather uniformly distributed in the Eastern part of the country and the Eastern part of the North Central

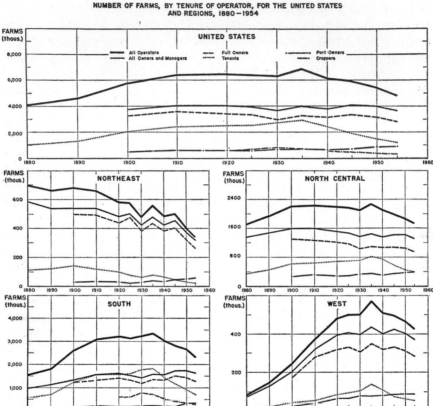

Figure 23. Trend in the number of farms, by tenure of operator, for the United States and regions, 1880–1954. (U.S. Department of Agriculture, Agricultural Research Service, and U.S. Department of Commerce, Bureau of the Census.)

region. Part owners tend to concentrate in the wheat- and corn-producing areas, although like full owners, they have a fairly uniform distribution throughout the United States. Figure 23 shows the number of farms by tenure of operators for the United States and its regions.

Comparative Characteristics of Tenure Groups

As we have seen, there are certain well-defined differences among tenure groups. Generally speaking, owners appear to better advantage than tenants on both the economic and the social level. There are some exceptions to this pattern, however. The comparisons given below are designed to acquaint the student with the major differences between owners and tenants in the United States.

All data cited apply to commercial farms only.[12] Although only two-thirds of the farms of the nation are classed as commercial, these farms account for 98 per cent of the farm products sold in the United States, a figure large enough to justify the omission of noncommercial farms in this discussion. All figures quoted are for 1950, and owners and part owners are considered together for the sake of simplicity.

1. Owners are considerably older than tenants. The data assembled indicate that owners are approximately ten years older on the average than tenants. The average age of owners is approximately fifty-one years as compared with just over forty years for tenants. Age differences are more dramatically seen in the percentage of owners and tenants under thirty-five years of age. Only 12 per cent of all owners of commercial farms are in this age group, whereas approximately 38 per cent of the tenants have not reached their thirty-fifth birthday. Although this differential is generally explainable in terms of respective positions on the agricultural ladder, its implications are significant.

2. Owners have lived on their present farms much longer than tenants. As many as two-thirds of the owners of commercial farms had lived on their farms as long as ten years in 1950. In contrast, slightly less than one-fifth of the tenants had lived this long at their present locations. This difference in length of residence is further highlighted by comparisons based on the percentages of these two groups that have lived less than one year on their present farms. Less than 4 per cent of the owners had moved to their present farms within the year, whereas about 18 per cent of the tenants had. Again, an explanation is found in terms of the agricultural ladder. However, the important conclusion remains that owners are more stable and less mobile.

3. Owner farms, on the average, are worth slightly more than tenant farms. The average owner farm is worth just over $18,000, whereas the average tenant farm is worth slightly more than $15,000. The detailed comparison of the value of land and buildings of owner and tenant farms shows some interesting patterns. For example, part-owner farms are worth approximately twice as much as full-owner farms, and the farms of all classes of tenants, with the exception of crop-share tenants and croppers, are valued more highly than full-owner farms. Share-cash and live-stock-share tenants operate farms of approximately equal value as those of part-owners. Cropper farms, with an average investment of less than

---

[12] The data were assembled by Professor J. Lawrence Charlton, Department of Rural Sociology, University of Arkansas.

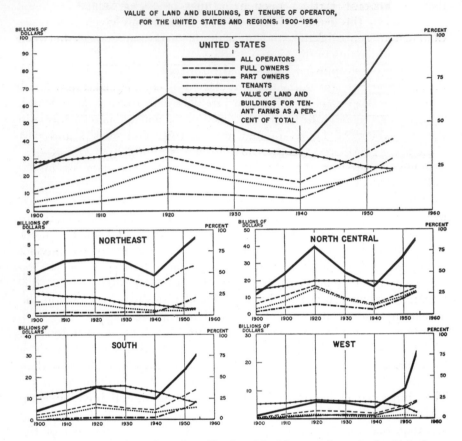

Figure 24. Trends in the value of land and buildings on farms in the United States and regions, by tenure of operator, 1900–1954. (U.S. Department of Agriculture, Agricultural Research Service, and U.S. Department of Commerce, Bureau of the Census.)

$4,000 in land and buildings, are the least capitalized of all. Figure 24 shows the total value of farmland and buildings by tenure for the United States and its regions.

4. Owner farms average larger total acreages than do tenant farms. There are 129 acres more on the average owner (including part-owner) farm, which has 299 acres as compared with 170 acres on the average tenant farm. Full owners' farms, interestingly, are more nearly the size of tenant farms than part-owner farms. The latter, on the average, are about double the size of full-owner and tenant farms. Figure 25 shows the average size of farm by tenure of operator from 1900 through 1954 but does not combine owners and part owners.

5. There is little difference in average acres of cropland on owner and

AVERAGE SIZE OF FARM, BY TENURE OF OPERATOR, FOR
THE UNITED STATES AND REGIONS: 1900-1954

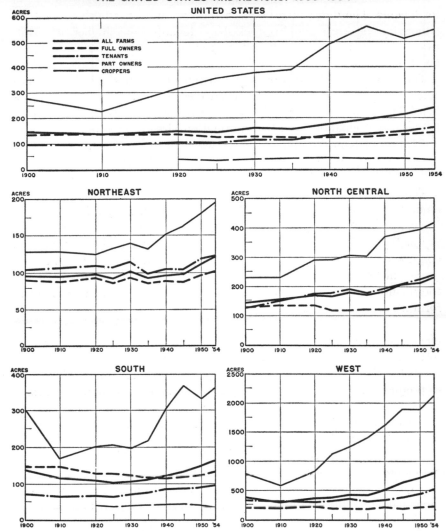

Figure 25. Trends in the average size of farms, by tenure of operator, for
the United States and regions, 1900–1954. (U.S. Department of Agriculture,
Agricultural Research Service, and U.S. Department of Commerce, Bureau
of the Census.)

tenant farms. The former average 93.0 acres, whereas the latter average
about 87.0 acres. Again, however, part owners, share-cash tenants, and
livestock-share tenants stand out above all other tenure groups in size
of operation.

6. Owners generally enjoy higher levels of living than tenants. The average level-of-living index is approximately 150 for owners and 144 for tenants. The differential between the two groups is fairly consistent, although share-cash and livestock-share tenants have higher levels-of-living indexes than both full and part owners. The differences are not great, however.

The differences between owners and tenants in these six major characteristics suggest many of their social characteristics and tenure problems. The student can draw certain conclusions relative to differentials in social participation from the information already presented and from the nature of tenure problems, which we shall discuss next.

The Nature of Land-tenure Problems

Tenure problems, as mentioned in the introduction to this chapter, are among the most serious and persistent in the world. They arise, generally speaking, from inherent characteristics of certain tenure systems and are of two major types. The first type of problem may be identified as conditions that prevent maximum efficiency in production. A given tenure arrangement may affect not only the way in which the land is used but the quantities of labor and capital used in conjunction with the land to form a production unit.

Some farms are clearly more efficient than others. The degree of efficiency in production can, as a rule, be traced to the operator's rights in the land he farms. Under systems that give him relative security and protect his investments of capital and labor, the tenant has incentive to produce efficiently; under systems that allow him no guarantees, he is likely to take an extremely short-time view of production and be governed by the philosophy of getting what he can out of the soil, good conservation practices notwithstanding.

Farm-tenure arrangements affect the lives and well-being of the farm population in other ways than economically, and it is here that the second type of problem becomes manifest. T. Lynn Smith points out, "For the sociologist, one of the most important associations is that between farm tenancy and poor, ill-kept homes and farm buildings." [13] Smith goes on to say that in the United States, where leases have traditionally been of the short-term variety, tenancy has been associated with poorly supported and scantily attended social institutions. In such areas one finds: [14]

1. Poor school attendance with a resulting low level of literacy
2. Weak and poorly supported churches
3. A minimum of participation in civic and governmental affairs
4. A low degree of vertical social mobility

[13] Smith, *op. cit.*, p. 29.
[14] *Ibid.*, pp. 292–293.

By contrast, in those areas where tenancy is relatively low, the tendency is for social institutions to be strong and well supported.

Despite the generally close association of social ills with high rates of tenancy, the records clearly show that it is not tenancy per se that brings about these conditions but the system of leasing or holding the land. For example, protected by a good lease, custom, or law guaranteeing his rights, a tenant will not hesitate to make investments in his operation and in his community.

The ideal tenure system would promote both economic and social efficiency. Most systems fail in one or both of these aims, giving rise to tenure problems. Thus it is clear that each society has a definite stake in solving its tenure problems because its very existence, in the long run, is dependent upon economical food and fiber production and strong communities.

CURRENT TENURE RESEARCH IN THE UNITED STATES

Rural social scientists in the United States have continuously striven to make people cognizant of tenure problems and to discover solutions to them. Recent trends in agricultural technology, plus population shifts and government programs, have tended to produce drastic changes in tenure requirements. These changes have brought about new problems, because of traditions, customs, and laws that have tended to make tenure adjustments lag far behind technical and social adjustments.

The various regional land-tenure research committees sponsored by the Farm Foundation, the State Agricultural Experiment Stations, and the United States Department of Agriculture have been in the forefront of tenure research. The coordinating body of these committees, the Inter-regional Land Tenure Research Committee, has recently published an exhaustive list of twenty-one areas of land tenure in which research is needed or is in progress.[15] In order to acquaint the student with the present need and direction of sociological research on tenure in this nation, ten of the more important research areas are listed here. In some of these areas considerable research has already been done, but in no area has the whole story been told.

1. The Difficulty of Getting Started in Farming and the Land-tenure Processes. The increasing scarcity of land and the high cost of equipment, machinery, livestock, and supplies has made it more and more difficult for the young man to make a successful start in farming. The outlook for the future on this score is not promising, as the quantity of desirable land is limited and the amount of capital required to farm is constantly increasing. These conditions create a serious problem which resolves it-

[15] See *Agricultural Land Tenure Research*, pp. 7–46.

self into the question, How can agriculture acquire and maintain its proportionate share of the best qualified youth of the nation? Quite clearly, ways and means must be found to help young farmers get a start, and this is the direction which research pertinent to this problem is taking.

2. *The Relative Efficiency of Alternative Tenure Arrangements in Agricultural Land Use, Development, and Conservation.* Many studies have shown that there is a positive relationship between rights to the land and the organization and efficient use of resources devoted to agricultural production. Tenure researchers have thus sought to determine what types of arrangements promote optimum efficiency, and they have learned much on this score. However, it has been discovered that the determination of the most efficient arrangement is not enough; there must be an incentive to bring about the necessary changes. This problem, primarily a sociological one, is presently being attacked by researchers in the field.

3. *The Impact of Federal Action Programs on Land Tenure.* Congress is continually passing laws intended to help farmers. However, it is difficult to write a law without inequities, and despite much precaution some of these laws appear to favor certain tenure groups. In the past, owner operators have tended to fare better than tenants, although certain programs were designed especially to help tenants and laborers attain ownership. Rural social scientists are currently working to attain a more complete understanding of the impact of credit, conservation, subsidy, and other such programs on tenure arrangements as well as on tenure groups.

4. *The Effect of Leasing Arrangements on Tenure.* It has long been known that stability as well as social and economic efficiency is associated with certain tenure arrangements. Leasing systems that provide maximum security and protection of the tenant's investment promote a more efficient agriculture as well as more progressive communities. The advantages of the written lease over the oral agreement are obvious, and the lease is now widely used. The need remains for information concerning the types of leases best suited to particular type-farming areas. Such questions as what constitutes an equitable share of crop or livestock production and what arrangements should be made in cash leases for fluctation in market prices remain at least partially unsolved. Gradually, however, data is being accumulated which suggests the best alternatives in specific situations.

5. *The Impact of Migration Patterns on Farm Tenure.* Recent trends in migration, notably the rural to urban movements in this country, have had noticeable repercussions in farm areas. For one thing, large numbers of workers have been brought in from the Caribbean and Central Ameri-

can countries. In view of the fact that both quantity and quality of labor are important to productivity and social life, there is some concern over these new trends. Few studies have been made, however, despite a growing concern over such problems as housing, education, and social participation of immigrant laborers. Perhaps more attention has been given to the Mexican laborer (especially the illegal entrants, or "Wetbacks") than to any other group.

6. *The Impact of Mineral Development on Land Tenure.* Wherever minerals have been discovered in commercial quantities, agricultural production has been affected. For one thing, speculation regarding the presence of additional mineral resources pyramid land prices far beyond their worth for agricultural purposes. In addition, normal tenure processes tend to be disrupted, as landowners generally prefer shifting their land to mineral development. Even when only subsurface rights are concerned, they are less likely to devote their full resources and energies to farming, and there is a corresponding drop in efficiency of production. The problem here is to determine ways and means of maintaining production at a high level despite the presence of supplementary mineral income.

7. *The Tenure Aspects of the Use of Water Resources.* Ever-increasing use of irrigation practices plus greater emphasis on the reclamation of arid lands has pointed up old problems and introduced new ones in the area of tenure research. Questions arise concerning not only control of surface and subsurface water but the responsibilities of owners and renters as well as the rights of urban and rural users. So urgent and so frequent have been the requests for information and guidance on these problems that a major effort is presently under way to learn more about them.

8. *The Impact of Mechanization on Farm-tenure Arrangements.* Agricultural mechanization has proceeded at a fairly rapid pace throughout the nation within recent years. Machines have displaced many hand laborers and have created a need for more skillful workers. As a consequence, persons of all tenure classes have experienced changes in their roles and statuses. Study is being directed to these changes as well as to those elements in certain systems which discourage innovation and retard technology. Researchers are convinced that this particular area represents a real frontier in terms of raising production efficiency and, as a consequence, levels of living.

9. *The Impact of the OASI Amendments on Land Tenure.* In 1954 the Federal social security program was enlarged to bring coverage to several additional groups, including farmers. At the present time it is evident that these programs will have drastic effects on tenure arrangements around the nation. Such practices as changing leases in an effort to obtain

coverage and transferring land ownership because of the income and retirement requirements of the Social Security Act have already been studied to some degree. However, much research remains to be done to determine the full impact of these extended insurance programs on tenure patterns throughout the nation.

10. The Land-tenure Problems of Minority Groups. Minority-group problems exist in connection with land tenure as they do in other areas of social life in the United States and other nations. These problems stem from cultural conditions. Among the groups affected are Negroes, American Indians, Mexicans, and Orientals (especially those of Japanese origin). Although the nature of their tenure problems vary from one group to the other, the problems are all in some degree similar. Usually persons of these groups have to accept lower pay, farm with less capital, use poorer land, and face a certain amount of discrimination of other kinds as well. Social scientists are interested in determining the exact existing differences in order that they may suggest ways of promoting equality of access to land.

Questions for Review and Discussion

1. What do social scientists mean by the term *land tenure?*
2. Name and explain the major functions of tenure arrangements.
3. Describe some of the more common land-tenure systems.
4. Name the important tenure classes in the United States and describe the rights of each.
5. Discuss recent trends in tenancy in the United States.
6. List the problems related to tenancy.
7. Is a high rate of tenancy an evil in itself? Explain your answer.
8. Define, identify, or explain: (1) the agricultural ladder, (2) socage tenure, (3) eminent domain.

Selected References for Supplementary Reading

Agricultural Land Tenure Research, Scope and Nature, Reappraisal, 1955, Chicago: Farm Foundation, report prepared by the Interregional Land Tenure Research Committee, 1955.

Kolb, John H., and Edmund deS. Brunner: *A Study of Rural Society,* 4th ed., Boston: Houghton Mifflin Company, 1952, chap. 7.

Loomis, Charles P., and J. Allan Beegle: *Rural Social Systems,* Englewood Cliffs, N.J.: Prentice-Hall, Inc., 1950, chap. 9.

Smith, T. Lynn: *The Sociology of Rural Life,* 3d ed., New York: Harper & Brothers, 1953, chap. 16.

Taylor, Carl C., et al.: *Rural Life in the United States,* New York: Alfred A. Knopf, Inc., 1949, chap. 15.

CHAPTER 13 *Social Patterns and Systems*
of Farming

Social scientists have long been aware that rural social structure is profoundly affected by the way in which agriculture is organized. T. Lynn Smith, for example, states, "The extent to which ownership and control of the land is concentrated in a few hands or widely distributed among those who live from farming is probably the most important single determinant of the welfare of the people on the land." [1] Awareness of this relationship has led scholars to make comparisons of what they have variously called "size of holdings" and "agricultural systems." It is significant that such terms as commercial farms, hoe culture, part-time farms, large holdings, and family-size farms abound in the literature and have fairly constant meanings.

Despite general agreement on the meanings of terms, there has been little attempt to systematize classifications of what may be called *social patterns* of farming. The census classification of commercial and other farms, for example, does not coincide with the classifications in most texts. Because of this, and because of the way in which census data are reported, it is necessary to present and discuss in this chapter the typologies in general usage. First, however, the world's major systems of agriculture are reviewed. Subsequently, the social patterns of farming as classified by the Columbia University Seminar on Rural Life are presented. The remainder of the chapter is devoted to a discussion of the impact of the family-farm ideal on the political development of the United States and on the development of rural sociology.

[1] T. Lynn Smith, *The Sociology of Rural Life*, 3d ed., New York: Harper & Brothers, 1953, p. 297.

MAJOR SYSTEMS OF AGRICULTURE [2]

A few years ago, T. Lynn Smith discovered that a significant relationship exists between the level of living of a people and the system of agriculture employed by them.[3] In his extensive travels, Smith observed that the simpler and more primitive the methods employed by a people to produce food and fiber, the lower their relative level of living. This fact was later corroborated by extensive study and set forth as a principle of rural sociology.

Smith's discovery makes possible a new understanding of the social patterns of farming. It points up the importance of a knowledge of agricultural systems or patterns for those interested in accounting for differences between the various rural-farm populations of the world. The major agricultural systems of the world are listed and briefly described below.

Riverbank Planting

The simplest of all agricultural systems is riverbank planting. This system is recognized as the first step away from the hunting, collecting, gathering, or appropriating economy toward agricultural technology. The riverbank planting system, however, involves no technology. Members of the tribe or group simply discover that the seeds or tubers of the plants they are accustomed to rely on for food sprout and grow in the moist fertile soil of the bank of a river or stream. This discovery leads to the systematic planting of seeds to produce a food supply. No time is devoted to preparing a seedbed; the seed is simply pressed into the soft earth with the toe or the finger.

Some may question whether riverbank planting should be classed as farming, since it bears little resemblance to agriculture as most people know it. Nevertheless, the fact that it represents a deliberate effort to produce food by planting seeds establishes the practice as a system of agriculture.

It may be surprising to learn that this extremely elementary system of farming is widely used today, with hundreds of thousands of persons obtaining part of their food in this simple manner. For example, large numbers of the inhabitants of the Amazon and Orinoco basins in South America have advanced no further agriculturally than riverbank planting. Accompanying this system of agriculture is a very primitive general

[2] This analysis of the systems of agriculture is drawn almost entirely from Smith, *op. cit.*, chap. 14.

[3] T. Lynn Smith, "Agricultural Systems and Standards of Living," *Inter-American Economic Affairs*, 3:15–28, 1949.

culture. Overland transportation is generally by hand or back, and canoes or dugouts on the rivers or streams suffice for greater distances. Homes and clothes are generally made of materials which are readily available and which do not need a great deal of processing. Tools and utensils are few and simple in nature.

Fire Agriculture

The next step after riverbank planting is to clear larger areas for seed-beds. In a culture lacking advanced tools, burning is the best way to remove bush and trees from a fertile area along the riverbank or delta. This procedure is used in a great many places in Central and South America, Africa, Asia, and Oceania.

The fire-agriculture system, although it represents a second step toward an agricultural technology, is extremely rudimentary. It involves no more than the selection of a likely place for planting seed and the burning off of the growth to make it easier to press the seed into the soil. In some places the burning is not done until the smaller brush has been cut and the larger trees felled or killed. It may be noted that burning rids the soil of weeds as well as brush, and this is another step forward in farming.

Humans are, again, the chief beasts of burden in fire-agriculture economies, although animals are used to a limited extent. Tools, utensils, houses, and other items of material culture are at a very simple level. Societies practicing fire agriculture may generally be classified as rural.

Hoe Culture

The next step in man's endeavor to wrest a living from the soil is the use of sharp sticks or digging implements for stirring or turning the soil. Most of these implements can be identified as hoes of various types. Millions of people live in economies that are no further advanced in agricultural technology than hoe culture, and it is significant that, the world over, the hoe is the most used implement among agriculturists.

The hoe-culture system is generally characterized by the use of the sickle as the principal tool in harvesting grain crops. Scenes depicting large numbers of people hoeing or bending over waving grain with sickles in their hands have symbolized this type of agriculture since pre-Biblical times. Under hoe culture, farm technology begins to show some complexity, although it is still very crude. Threshing, for example, is still done by human or animal labor entirely, but it is handled more efficiently. Transportation continues to be mostly by pack animal or small water craft, but the wheel and sled principles are sometimes applied for moving heavy loads. Homes and utensils show more advanced design and construction. The phenomenon of a maximum use of human effort continues to be the chief characteristic of agricultural production, however.

Rudimentary Plow Culture

The fourth type of agricultural system in order of complexity, and the most prevalent in the world today, is the rudimentary plow culture. This system is characterized by some sort of plow, pulled by animals, for rooting and for turning the soil. Although the hitching is crude and inefficient and the plows are very simple, the fact that the motive power comes from animals rather than humans represents a tremendous advance over the systems already described. It is interesting that in countries characterized by this type of agricultural system, oxen or water buffalo rather than horses are used for power. The horse is usually reserved for riding and for use as a pack animal, and ownership of horses is generally considered to be a mark of social distinction.

Since the wheel is an integral part of the rudimentary plow culture, carts, although heavy and crude, take the place of pack animals and human backs as modes of transportation. Farm and home jobs are time- and energy-consuming, but the stage is set for the development of technology, and the level of living is somewhat higher than under the systems described earlier.

Advanced Plow Culture

When the transition from the crude plow to the well-designed one has been completed and hitching has been made more efficient, the advanced plow culture has been achieved. This system reached its highest efficiency in the United States during the early part of the twentieth century. The major features of agriculture in this country at that time, as listed by Smith, serve to characterize this system: (1) a great deal of horse- or mule-drawn equipment designed so as to be moved with a minimum of power for its size; (2) well-established breeds of draft animals trained to perform farm work of many types; (3) harnesses and hitching equipment designed for making the most efficient use of the power of mules or horses; (4) four-wheel wagons and other equipment especially adapted to the transportation and harvesting of various crops.

The corn belt of the United States from 1910 to 1920 illustrates the advanced plow culture. During this time the typical Middle Western farmer was uniting his labor with that of three or four large draft horses to pull and handle sulky plows, harvesters, combines, and other machinery and equipment. Concomitants of this culture were solid, comfortable homes, large barns, well-kept grounds, and a relatively high standard of living. The culture complex also included pride in good strong animals, well-kept harness, and machinery in good repair. This is probably the least well-represented agricultural system in the world today.

Mechanized Farming

Parts of the United States and Canada and certain other areas of the world have progressed to a still more advanced agricultural system, mechanized farming, which is characterized by the highest technology known in agriculture. The equipment used necessitates a minimum of human labor for even the most detailed job. Associated with mechanized farming systems is scientific methodology applied to such processes as plant propagation, animal breeding, weed control, insecticides, and so on. Under mechanized farming, rural society increasingly resembles urban society in its structure and functioning. This characteristic, more than any other, sets it apart from other agricultural systems.

THE CENSUS CLASSIFICATION OF FARMS

Because of the rapid changes in farm size and organization that have occurred in the past few decades and the growing realization that patterns of farming and social structure are closely related, it has become imperative that a more detailed classification of farms be used in reporting census information. The Bureau of the Census has been working steadily to arrive at a satisfactory classification. Its first major revision of farm classifications appeared in the 1945 Census of Agriculture. Although this classification distinguished broader groups of farms and did a generally better job of outlining the agricultural picture in the United States than the earlier one, an even more detailed system was needed. In 1950 the Bureau of the Census brought out a still more comprehensive classification utilizing the concept of commercial farms subdivided into economic classes. This classification, presented below, is a considerable improvement over previous systems and makes more detailed research possible.

The new census classification differentiates between two major groups of farms, commercial farms and "other" farms.[4] All farms selling farm products valued at $1,200 or more, except abnormal farms, are classed as commercial units. Farms with a value of sales ranging from $250 to $1,199 are also classed as commercial if the operator worked off his farm less than 100 days during the year and the nonfarm income of the operator and members of his family was less than the value of farm products

---

[4] The definitions and data presented here are adapted from the 1950 reports of the Bureau of the Census and R. L. Skrabanek, "Commercial Farming in the United States," *Rural Sociology*, 19:136–137, 1954.

sold. For analytical purposes, commercial farms are subdivided into six groups as shown in the accompanying table.

Economic class of farm	Value of farm products sold
I	$25,000 or more
II	$10,000 to $24,999
III	$ 5,000 to $ 9,999
IV	$ 2,500 to $ 4,999
V	$ 1,200 to $ 2,499
VI	$ 250 to $ 1,199 *

* Within the limits of the provision described above.

The farm units in the second major group, those classified as "other" farms, are subdivided into three classes. *Part-time farms* are those with sales of farm products ranging from $250 to $1,999, meeting one of these two provisions: the operator must work 100 or more days off the farm during the year, or the nonfarm income received by him and members of his family must be greater than the value of farm products sold. *Residential farms* are those with sales of farm products of less than $250, with the exception of abnormal farms. *Abnormal farms* include all exceptions to the general classifications listed above, such as public or private institutional farms, experiment-station farms, and community enterprises.

It can be seen from these definitions that there are two major criteria for distinguishing commercial farms from other farms. The first is whether or not the farm is operated as a business and the second is whether or not farming constitutes the major occupation of the farm family. Although this classification is generally an economic one, it provides a real basis for sociocultural analysis. And since it is the only classification for which census data are presently available, it provides the most objective indexes available for measuring differences between social patterns of farming.

Comparisons of Commercial and Noncommercial Farms

Insofar as commercial and noncommercial farms represent different social patterns of farming,[5] the differences between them are important. At the same time, there are certain major differences among the various economic classes of commercial farms. The more important of these are the following:

1. Commercial farms outnumber residential farms, although the latter are more numerous than any individual economic class of commercial farms. Altogether, over two-thirds (68.9 per cent) of the farms of the

[5] The primary source for the following discussion is Skrabanek, *op. cit.*, pp. 137–142.

nation are classed as commercial. However, there are fewer farms in class I than in any other type of commercial farm.

2. Residential and part-time farms are increasing, while commercial farms are decreasing. Estimates indicate that the number of residential and part-time farms has almost doubled in the past twenty years. During the same time, the number of commercial farms decreased by almost one-third.

3. Commercial farms include almost all the acreage devoted to farming. All other farms made up less than 12 per cent of the total acreage being farmed. The acreage operated becomes progressively smaller for successively lower economic classes of commercial farms. The class of work power of commercial farms by tenure of operator is shown in Figure 26.

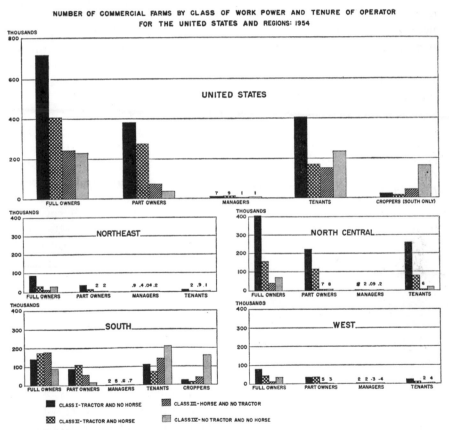

Figure 26. Commercial farms, by class of work power and tenure of operator, in the United States and regions, 1954. (U.S. Department of Agriculture, Agricultural Research Service, and U.S. Department of Commerce, Bureau of the Census.)

4. Commercial farms produce almost all the farm products sold in the United States. The 1950 census data show that 98 per cent of the farm products sold was produced on these farms. It is significant that commercial farms of classes I and II, representing less than one-tenth of the nation's farms, account for more than one-half of all farm products sold.

5. Operators of noncommercial farms are more likely to do off-farm work. Although this would be expected from the nature of the classification, the scale on which this pattern operates is impressive. More than two-thirds of the operators of farms in the "other" group had off-farm jobs, whereas only a little over one-fourth of the commercial farm operators reported nonfarm employment. The proportion of commercial farm operators working off their farms from one to ninety-nine days becomes progressively greater for successively lower economic classes.

6. Commercial farm operators have a longer average period of residence on their farms than noncommercial operators. The difference is not great, however. The fact that class I commercial farm operators include a larger proportion of persons who had been on their farms for as much as ten years is perhaps more significant than the differences in length of residence between commercial and noncommercial farm owners.

7. A higher percentage of commercial than noncommercial farms are tenant-operated. The data indicate that less than one-half of all commercial farms are owner-operated, but more than three-fourths of the noncommercial farms are owner-operated. The percentage of operators who are full owners is lowest in class I farms and progressively higher for each lower income class (see Fig. 27).

8. Commercial farm operators are slightly younger, on the average, than nonoperators. The average age for the former is 47.6 years as compared with 49.8 years for the latter. This differential is not surprising in view of the many part-time and residential farmers who are in semi-retirement.

THE SOCIAL SIGNIFICANCE OF SIZE OF HOLDINGS

As we saw in the introduction to this chapter, patterns of land holding have generally been classified on the basis of relative size of units. Thus terms such as "large holdings" or "large-scale farms" are used to identify what is really a social pattern of farming. The weakness of such designations is that size, as social scientists generally agree, is not easy to determine because of the many variables that affect production. Admitting this difficulty and the individual differences between certain farms that might be classed as large or small, there still remains a fundamental distinction in social characteristics between those farms that

PERCENT DISTRIBUTION OF COMMERCIAL FARMS IN EACH ECONOMIC CLASS,
BY TENURE OF OPERATOR, FOR THE UNITED STATES AND REGIONS: 1954

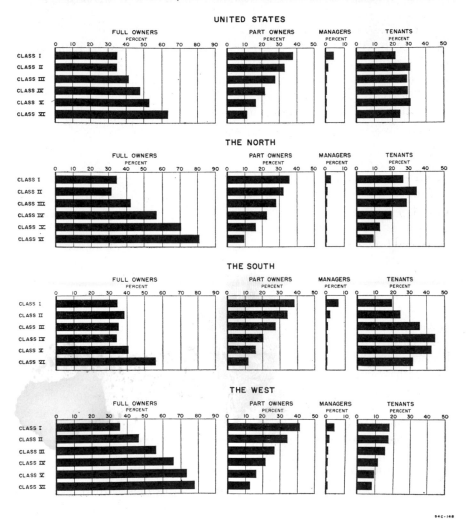

Figure 27. The per cent distribution of full owners, part owners, managers, and tenants, by economic class of farm, for the United States and regions, 1954. (U.S. Department of Agriculture, Agricultural Research Service, and U.S. Department of Commerce, Bureau of the Census.)

carry on large-scale operations and those that maintain family-size operations. These are the distinctions that have been pointed up wherever comparisons have been made. T. Lynn Smith in pointing out sociocultural differences in patterns of farming, includes a third classification which seems worthwhile—farms that are too small to provide an adequate living for the families on them.[6]

In the following detailed descriptions of the generally recognized size-of-holding classes, the student can, in a general way, relate the characteristics of each size group to comparable census classifications.

Large Holdings. The term *large holding* is used to refer to a situation in which control of a large-scale operation is in the hands of a few and many persons are employed as laborers. Examples of such holdings are the plantations of the South, certain Western ranches, and the corporation farms common in California. The large-scale farm has been described as the application of the factory system to agriculture. According to Taylor and Vasey, it is characterized by: (1) intensive agriculture, (2) highly capitalized operation, (3) large-scale farming methods, (4) concentrated ownership, and (5) large payments to labor.[7] Smith adds additional characteristics: ". . . rigid supervision, and specialization by tasks (managers, overseers, foremen, hostlers, blacksmiths, cooks, nurses, plow hands, and more recently, tractor drivers and mechanics). . . ."[8]

Economists usually agree that the large-scale enterprise permits more efficient operation, as labor, capital, and management can be combined most effectively on this scale. There is, however, a definite relationship between size of holding and the organization of rural society itself. Studies to date have indicated that large-scale farming communities have more clearly marked class lines than small-scale farms. In addition, farm workers in these communities have the lowest average levels of living and little chance to develop well-rounded personalities and social institutions. These are the primary reasons why social scientists have concerned themselves with the various social patterns of farming.

In this country, there is a persistent trend towards large farms. As can be seen in Figure 25, the percentage of farms of less than 500 acres has decreased steadily since 1920. In contrast, the percentage of farms of more than 500 acres, and especially those of 1,000 acres or over, has increased rather rapidly in this period. This trend no doubt reflects increased use of technology. Belcher, for one, interprets it as evidence of the increasing industrialization of American agriculture and predicts an

---

[6] Smith, *The Sociology of Rural Life,* p. 300.

[7] Paul S. Taylor and Tom Vasey, "Contemporary Background of California Farm Labor," *Rural Sociology,* 1:419, 1936.

[8] Smith, *The Sociology of Rural Life,* p. 307.

increasing control of the industrialized operations by nonresident farmers.[9] In this sense it portends a new era in terms of social patterns of farming.

The Family Farm. The family farm, more than any other social pattern of farming, has captured the imagination of the American people. Although the question of what constitutes a family farm has been the subject of innumerable debates, a fairly concrete conceptualization is possible. Such a farm has been described as one sufficiently large to provide steady employment for family members but not large enough to require a great deal of supplementary labor. In addition, the family provides its own capital and management. Actual physical size would, of course, vary with such characteristics as type of enterprise and degree of mechanization. As Motheral points out, the family farm has been one of the mainstays of American ideology [10] and the vehicle of three distinctive American traditions: [11] (1) the agrarian tradition, which is associated with the feeling that the relationship between man and the soil is of singular importance; (2) the democratic tradition, which is manifest in the contention that the family farm is especially effective in developing qualities of responsibility and good citizenship in individuals; and (3) the efficiency tradition, which holds that waste is sinful and that any man who does not bend every effort to make the most of his resources is somehow not self-respecting.

Other social scientists have noted that the family-farm system has generally produced strong communities, characterized by stability, relative absence of class distinction, and comparatively high levels of living.[12]

Because of these characteristics, the family farm has been a potent force in the political development of the United States. It has also, in one sense, figured in the development of rural sociology as a discipline. These associations are significant enough to be discussed separately in a later section of this chapter.

Minifundia. Smith borrowed the term *minifundia* from South America to describe extremely small farms. These holdings, never larger than an acre or two, are especially numerous on the mountainsides of Ecuador, Colombia, and Venezuela.[13] They are not of major importance in the United States, although some examples are found in the "hill" sections

[9] John C. Belcher, "The Nonresident Farmer in the New Rural Society," *Rural Sociology*, 19:134, 1954.

[10] Joe R. Motheral, "Land Tenure Policies and the Political Development of the United States," paper read at the International Political Science Association, Geneva, Switzerland, September, 10–16, 1956, p. 1.

[11] Joe R. Motheral, "The Family Farm and the Three Traditions," *Journal of Farm Economics*, 33:514, 1951.

[12] See Lowry Nelson, *Rural Sociology*, 2d ed., New York: American Book Company, 1955, pp. 265–267, and Smith, *The Sociology of Rural Life*, pp. 297–304.

[13] *Ibid.*

of the South and certain other places. Such farms are too small to support even the smallest family at a decent level of living. Because of this, the regions in which they are numerous are problem areas.

A PROPOSED CLASSIFICATION OF SOCIAL PATTERNS OF FARMING

Cognizant of the need (both academic and practical) for a basic and concise classification of farming, the Columbia University Seminar on Rural Life undertook such an assignment during the academic years 1948–1949 and 1949–1950. The result of this study and research was a monograph setting forth a proposed classification for social patterns of farming.[14] The ten patterns delineated are given below, following a brief review of the factors considered in their delineation.

Three major factors were considered in the construction of the typology of social patterns of farming: [15]

1. *The social unit operating the farm.* As a first point of reference for delineation, two basic social units were identified—family units and employer-employee units.

2. *Functions of the enterprise.* Four major functions were used to classify types of farming: (*a*) residence and partial source of income (for farmers); (*b*) retirement (for elder farmers); (*c*) subsistence, including units operated primarily for products to be used by the farm household; and (*d*) commercial farms, or full-time market-oriented enterprises.

3. *Scale of operation.* This measure included gross value of products, with value of land and building as a secondary variable.

Utilizing these factors as criteria, the Seminar distinguished ten social patterns of farming. They are listed and described below.[16]

1. *Employer Farms*—Units which employed more than one and a half man years of labor a year, were market oriented, and had a gross value of products of $8,000 or more.

2. *Large Commercial Family Farms*—Units operated primarily by family labor, market oriented, and with a gross value of products of $8,000 or more.

3. *Medial Commercial Family Farms*—Units operated primarily by family labor, by operators under 65 years of age, market oriented, and with a gross value of products of $3,000 to $7,999.

4. *Residential-Commercial Family Farms*—Units whose operators were 65 and over or who worked off their farms 100 days or more a year, and whose gross value of products ranged from $3,000 to $7,999.

[14] Sloan R. Wayland, *Social Patterns of Farming,* New York: Columbia University Seminar on Rural Life, 1956.
[15] *Ibid.,* pp. 15–16.
[16] *Ibid.,* pp. 18–19.

5. *Part-time Farms*—Units whose operators worked off their farms 100 days or more, utilized family labor primarily, and whose gross value of products ranged from $250 to $2,999.

6. *Elders' Farms*—Units whose operators were 65 and over and who worked off their farms less than 100 days a year, and whose gross value of products ranged from $500 to $2,999.

7. *Subsistence Farms*—Units whose operators were under 65 years of age, worked off their farms less than 100 days a year, whose gross value of products ranged from $500 to $2,999, and the major portion of whose products was used on the farm rather than sold.

8. *Small Commercial Family Farms*—Units whose operators were under 65 years of age, worked off their farms less than 100 days a year, whose gross value of products ranged from $500 to $2,999, and the major portion of whose products was sold rather than used.

9. *Residential Farms*—All units with gross value of products ranging from $1 to $499 except those farms whose operators worked off their farms 100 days or more and had farm products valued at $250–$499.

10. *Nominal Farms*—All units with no farm income reported except those which were placed in other patterns as the result of inspection.

The advantages of this classification, as noted, are in the precision it lends to the analysis and description of social patterns of farming. It is thus an extremely useful tool for sociological research and should be seriously considered in the tabulation of subsequent census reports and in pertinent state and local studies.

THE FAMILY FARM IN THE UNITED STATES

The Family Farm and Political Development

Farm problems are important in every society. Not only are they related to the production of food and fiber, but they are quite frequently identified with national ideological systems. To the extent that these problems represent threats to ideals and ideologies they elicit national concern and action and have a hand in shaping political destiny. In the United States, the family-farm ideal has clearly influenced national policy. The discussion that follows is an attempt to show the nature of the influence of this ideal on political action in the nation.[17]

The conditioning of policy by the family-farm ideal dates back to Thomas Jefferson. As Motheral states,[18]

Jefferson recognized better than most that the young nation faced a two-fold task if it were to endure as a democratic entity. First, feudalistic tradition and

[17] The discussion draws upon Motheral, "Land Tenure Policies and the Political Development of the United States."
[18] *Ibid.*, p. 3.

forms must never be allowed to flower in America. Second, an attitude of citizenship responsibility and participation must be cultivated among the rank and file of the population. Private property rights overlay both problems, and it was natural that Jefferson and others came to espouse the evident practicable distribution of rights in land, the only property of much consequence at the time.

The ideas of Jefferson have received wholehearted acceptance ever since his time and can be recognized in every major legislative and administrative act affecting rights to land. Such laws as those relating to the disposal of the public domain, agricultural research, education, credit, marketing, and production controls are traceable to Jeffersonian principles, which were crystallized in the family-farm ideal.

In its current form, family-farm ideology incorporates definite sentiments and values. According to Motheral,[19]

Almost everyone would agree that a family farm should have enough size to provide a decent livelihood, that the operator should in fact be the manager, that the family should furnish a substantial share of the labor, and that there should be stability of tenure. Further, the income from the farm should be roughly proportionate to its assumed size or value, the operator should not be encumbered with burdensome debt, and farm prices ought to bear some tolerable relationship to the price of things bought by farmers.

Certain corollary "enterprise ethics" are inextricably woven into the fabric of family-farm ideology and contribute to its emotional force. These are the following beliefs: (1) Hard work is a virtue. (2) The "self-made man" is distinctly superior to the person whose career began from a position of advantage. (3) The individual or family is responsible for its own economic security. (4) A man's worth is approximately proportionate to what he receives in the market place.

In very general terms, this is the view of life which conditions legislative action. When the vision is shattered or even marred, the fury of the protest is invariably great. A threat to the family farm is interpreted as far more than a menace to a property right. It is regarded as prejudicial to a way of life and thus intolerable. Such indignation has generated agrarian revolts that have found expression in political action.

The Family Farm and Rural Sociology

In concluding this chapter, it is fitting to point out that the rural sociologist has a closer and more personal interest in the family-farm ideal than most social scientists. In this country, rural sociology as a discipline in large measure owes its existence to a conviction of the nation's past leaders regarding family-farm life. These leaders felt that impor-

---

[19] *Ibid.*, pp. 7–8.

tant intangible agrarian values associated with the family farm were being neglected because of the lure of city life and concern for sheer material production. This fact is made clear in a report of the Country Life Commission appointed by President Theodore Roosevelt to study trends in American Rural Life. This body wrote, "The underlying problem is to develop and maintain on our farms a civilization in full harmony with the best American ideals. The work before us, therefore, is nothing more or less than the gradual rebuilding of a new agriculture and new rural life." [20] It is Taylor's belief that the Commission's report, made after extensive study of the weaknesses of rural life, provided what might be called a charter for rural sociology.[21] It is certain that the research funds available through the U.S. Department of Agriculture would never have been made available without this impetus. The attempt to fill these needs, more than anything else, has spurred the growth of the field of rural sociology to its present state of development.

Questions for Review and Discussion

1. Explain how social patterns of farming can affect rural social structure, illustrating your explanation with examples.
2. List and describe the major systems of agriculture.
3. What criteria does the United States census use for differentiating commercial farms from other types?
4. Distinguish a large holding from a family farm with regard to both physical and social characteristics.
5. What factors did the Columbia University Seminar on Rural Life consider important in the construction of a typology for delineating social patterns of farming?
6. Suppose you were seeking a congressional office from a rural state. List the ideas and values relating to farming and farm life which you would support in your speeches.

Selected References for Supplementary Reading

Ackerman, Joseph, and Marshall Harris (eds.): *Family Farm Policy*, Chicago: University of Chicago Press, 1950, chap. 3.
Motheral, Joe R.: "The Family Farm and the Three Traditions," *Journal of Farm Economics*, 33:14ff., 1951.
Skrabanek, Robert L.: "Commercial Farming in the United States," *Rural Sociology*, 19:136–137, 1954.
Smith, T. Lynn: *The Sociology of Rural Life*, 3d ed., New York: Harper & Brothers, 1953, chaps. 13 and 14.
Wayland, Sloan R.: *Social Patterns of Farming*, New York: Columbia University Seminar on Rural Life, 1956.

[20] Carl C. Taylor et al., *Rural Life in the United States*, New York: Alfred A. Knopf, Inc., 1949, p. 6.
[21] *Ibid.*

The Major Rural Social Institutions

The major institutions provide systems of social relationships for meeting the basic biological and cultural needs of man. The purpose of Part Four is to acquaint the student with the structural-functional aspects of the basic social institutions as they appear in rural society. It may be noted that the various chapters differ somewhat in organization. There are two reasons for this. First, developments within recent years suggest that certain institutions should be approached through the problems connected with them. Second, more research has been done in some areas than in others.

Part Four begins with Chapter 14, which, logically, is a treatise on the characteristics and trends of the family in rural society. It is followed, in Chapter 15, by a consideration of the characteristics and trends of rural education. Chapter 16 is a study of the rural church and its problems. Chapter 17 deals with the characteristics and problems of local government, making direct rural-urban comparisons in several instances. The factors affecting production and marketing, as they impinge on rural society, are presented in Chapter 18, and the many varied social aspects of rural health and welfare are discussed in Chapter 19.

CHAPTER 14

The Family: Characteristics and Trends

Scholars generally agree that the family is the oldest and most fundamental of human institutions. This consensus is based on the fact that in almost every society the family is the most important primary group for the individual. The intimacy which is provided within the family circle makes possible the fulfillment of certain basic needs for each person in what is generally the most satisfactory way possible. The importance of the family makes it logical to consider it first in a discussion of the institutions basic to rural society.

THE FAMILY AS A SOCIAL INSTITUTION

Marriage and the Family Defined

There are a great many differences in marriage patterns and family organization from one society to another. However, these differences are cultural in origin and peripheral to the biological aspect, which is universal. Because of this universality, definitions of marriage and the family have general application.

Marriage, in all societies, is a social affair. In this respect it differs from mere mating, which is a purely biological matter. Because it is a social affair, marriage is characterized by ritual and ceremony which represent social approval. In addition, certain duties and responsibilities are associated with the status of husband and wife, depending upon folkways and mores. Thus Burgess and Locke have formally defined marriage as *a socially sanctioned union of one or more men with one or more women in the relationship of husband and wife.*[1] This definition is understood wherever the term is used in the present discussion.

[1] Ernest W. Burgess and Harvey J. Locke, *The Family*, 2d ed., New York: American Book Company, 1953, p. 6.

Quite obviously, it is necessary for marriage to take place before a family can begin. MacIver and Page acknowledge this in their contention that the family comprises a unity of mates and their offspring, and they maintain that this unity has common characteristics everywhere.[2] The books by MacIver and Page and Burgess and Locke [3] are the sources for the following list of significant characteristics of the family unit, which serves as an introduction to a formal definition of the family.

1. The family is a mating relationship within the bounds of societal approval.

2. The family is composed of persons united by ties of marriage, blood, and adoption in accordance with prevailing custom.

3. The family members typically live together under one roof, although they may not have exclusive use of the premises.

4. The family is a unit of interacting persons, each enacting a role defined by the greater society and strengthened by experience. Much of the interaction is associated with the fulfillment of economic needs, especially those associated with child bearing and rearing.

5. Family members are identified through a system of nomenclature related to the method of reckoning kinship and descent.

In the light of these characteristics, the family may be defined as *a socially sanctioned grouping of persons united by kinship, marriage, or adoption ties, who generally share a common habitat and interact according to well-defined social roles created by a common culture.* It is pertinent to point out that the family can be distinguished from other social institutions in at least four important ways.[4] These differences point up its uniqueness as a social institution and clarify its place in the larger society.

1. Because it is the first institution with which the individual comes into extended contact, the family has a strong influence on the individual. This priority usually gives the family first claim to the individual's loyalty and affection.

2. The family is the smallest of all social institutions. The average family in the United States has less than four members, and many have as few as two members.

3. The family is of central importance to all other social institutions. The support of the family group is almost a necessary prerequisite to the successful functioning of other institutions.

4. The family exercises a profound control over its members. This control is possible because of the strong emotional bonds formed early in life.

---

[2] R. M. MacIver and Charles H. Page, *Society, An Introductory Analysis,* New York: Rinehart & Company, Inc., 1949, p. 238.

[3] *Ibid.,* pp. 238–239; Burgess and Locke, *loc. cit.*

[4] Marion B. Smith, *Survey of Social Science,* 4th ed., Boston: Houghton Mifflin Company, 1956, p. 160.

Selected Cultural Variations in Family Forms

Because of cultural variations, marriage forms and family structure differ quite noticeably the world over. The student should be acquainted with the most important of these differences in order to make comparisons with the American family.

1. *Variations in Forms of Marriage Relationships.* There are three major patterns in marriage, based on the number of men and women who are parties to the marital contract. Under the practice of *monogamy,* which is by far the most common form, marriage involves one husband and one wife. *Polygamous* marriages involve at least one person of one sex and two or more of the other. Two major subtypes of such marriages can be identified. *Polygynous* marriages, quite popular in some societies, exist when one man marries two or more women. The opposite form, in which one woman marries two or more men, is known as *polyandry* and is not widespread. Isolated examples of group marriages—two or more men married to two or more women—have been reported, but it is doubtful if examples could be found today. It is interesting to note that a given society may recognize both monogamous and polygamous marriages.

2. *Variations in Selection Patterns.* The approved way of securing a mate also varies from one culture to another. Perhaps the most common practice is for parents or elders to be responsible for the selection of mates for their children. The logic of this practice is that a choice that affects the welfare of the whole group should not be left to immature and inexperienced persons.

A second rather widely approved method of securing a wife is through purchase. This practice is not as ruthless as it may seem. It is backed by a definite theory that a woman is an economic asset and her family should be recompensed for her loss. Another explanation is that the pay received covers the expense of rearing the girl. The fact that a wife has been purchased does not mean that she can be treated as a piece of property, however; customarily she has rights, even though she was purchased.

In our society it is customary for young people to choose their wives or husbands through what is popularly called *romantic selection*. This custom allows the individual, within the bounds of certain laws and customs, complete freedom in the choice of a mate.

Wife stealing was once practiced to a certain extent by preliterate groups, but it is doubtful whether such a practice exists today, except in symbolic form.

In some instances it is compulsory to marry within the racial, tribal, religious, or national group to which one belongs. This practice is known as *endogamy*. In others, it is necessary to marry outside one's group; this practice is known as *exogamy*.

3. *Variations in the Reckoning of Lines of Descent*. Certain groups insist in reckoning descent solely through one or the other parent. When descent through the male line alone is recognized, the system is called *patrilineal*. In contrast, when descent is counted through the female line, the system is known as *matrilineal*. The more realistic bilateral system is generally found in the more advanced societies, however.

4. *Variations in Place of Residence and Family Circle*. The place of residence of the newly married couple may customarily be with the wife's family, or it may be with the husband's family. The former custom is identified as a *matrilocal* pattern and the latter as *patrilocal*. Both these customs imply a *consanguine* arrangement, in which blood relatives and their spouses live in groups and little stress is placed on husband-wife relationships. Such an arrangement is in contrast to the *conjugal* family, in which each new marital union is a central and more or less independent group.

5. *Variations in Authority Patterns*. Before the advent of the modern family, the *patriarchal* family was almost universal. Such a family vested all or most authority in the husband and father. In some places this power was extended so far as to include the privilege of selling a daughter into servitude or condemning family members to death. In our society the patriarchal family has been gradually superseded by a more democratic system. The ultimate development of this trend, the more or less complete equality of men and women in decision making, is called the *equalitarian* family structure.

One sometimes finds references to *matriarchal* or *filiarchal* families. However, the evidence that either the wife or the children are ever in complete authority, even in primitive societies, is very questionable.

The Functions of the Family

Although forms of marriage and family organization may vary from one society to another, certain basic functions are inevitably relegated to the family. The list of functions presented below are the more or less universal ones. It should be remembered, however, that human interaction and behavior are never static and that the functions of social institutions are subject to change. For this reason the family in certain cultures or subcultures will fulfill the functions listed to a greater extent than the family in neighboring cultures or subcultures. As we shall see later, rural and urban families differ in this respect.

1. *The Perpetuation of the Group*. A basic social need of all societal groups is self-perpetuation. This need has characteristically been met

by the family, which provides an ideal setting for social pressure toward procreation. The importance of this function is seen in the rapid growth of nations and other groups that deliberately promote high birth rates.

2. *The Care and Training of the Young.* The human infant is helpless for an extremely long period, relatively speaking, and must have his every need administered to by adults for several years. It is within the family group that this care is given. Besides feeding, clothing, and sheltering the child, the family also protects him from outside dangers.

3. *The Initial Status Ascription of the Young.* In the beginning, the social position of every individual is fixed by his family. This ascribed status remains with the new family member for a greater or lesser time depending on such factors as the rate of vertical social mobility and individual ability or fortune. Most persons, however, never completely shed the statuses they acquire from their families.

4. *Provision for and Regulation of the Sexual and Parental Drives.* A very definite function of the family in all societies is the regulation of sexual and parental drives. It is usually only within marriages that offspring are legitimatized, and this fact indicates the importance of the function. In addition, such aspects of parental relationships to the young as affection and control cannot be expressed as readily (with social approval) outside the family circle.

5. *The Provision of an Intimate Circle for Affection and Companionship.* All individuals have a fundamental need for love and affection. The family fulfills this function for most persons and in so doing protects the individual from psychosocial isolation. This is an important function because of its connection with feelings of insecurity, which are directly related to instability and disintegration of personality.

6. *The Provision of a Basis for Economic Inheritance of Private Property.* Giving each individual a definite kinship status within the family establishes, in societies characterized by the institution of private property, a definite order of inheritance. This is an important function in a democratic society, as uncertainty as to who should receive the economic substance of the deceased could be a real source of conflict.

7. *The Socialization of the Individual.* Even as it is performing the above functions, the family is introducing the newcomer to his society. This process was referred to earlier as *socialization*. Without the instruction that he receives primarily in the family, the individual could not become a functioning member of his group. In other words, he would not be given the cultural requirements necessary for survival.

INFLUENCES ON RURAL FAMILIES IN THE UNITED STATES

Pioneer Influences

A recognition of the profound influence that recent pioneer experience still exerts is helpful in understanding the present-day family.[5] The following effects of pioneer life, for example, still persist to some extent:

1. The pioneer family lived on its own acreage and was imbued with the idea of private property. This attitude was apparently in part a reaction to the feudal system of Europe, which so many had come to the new world to escape, and in part a result of the vast amount of "free" land available for the taking. A close and powerful association between land, family, and home was developed, carrying a definite sentimental overtone. Both the respect for ownership and the sentimentality associated with farm, family, and home persist in the present rural family.

2. The pioneer family was possessed of a sense of self-sufficiency bred of its relative isolation, which made necessary the production of its own food, clothing, and other requirements. In this respect, the pioneer family was almost completely independent of urban centers. The wife was skilled in spinning, weaving, and sewing, and her husband was his own artisan and repair man. Thus self-reliance and independence were necessary virtues in the pioneer family.

3. The pioneer family was characterized by a sense of solidarity. This characteristic was developed because the joint effort of all family members was necessary in order to survive. First of all, of course, the family was an economic unit, and the efforts and skills of all its members, men and women alike, were necessary for producing what was needed. Beyond this, it was necessary for each family to supply its own protection, not only from the vicissitudes of the frontier but often from Indians and outlaw groups. In addition, it had the responsibility for the care of its aged and incapacitated members. Fulfilling these functions promoted a high degree of family integration. This pattern often extended beyond the immediate family to kinship groups and was encouraged by the practice of kinfolk's settling in close proximity to one another. The rural family of today reflects the strong kinship ties developed at this early date.

Farm Work as an Influence

Although pioneer experiences were the primary early influences on the rural family, the continuing difference between the farm family and families in other areas has to be accounted for in other ways. Despite

[5] Ruth Shonle Cavan, *The American Family,* New York: Thomas Y. Crowell Company, 1953, p. 34.

considerable variation in type of farming from region to region and despite the encroachment of the corporation and other large-scale commercial farms, the majority of farms in the United States are still family enterprises. This fact, primarily, explains the enduring difference between the rural family and any other.

Margaret Jarman Hagood has ably described the potent influence that the family farm has upon its members.[6] In many ways this influence is similar to that of the pioneer family. Hagood points out, first, that the participation of various members of the farm family in the operation of the farm tends to knit the family closely together because a common interest and sense of cooperative effort is developed. The child, particularly, is inculcated with a sense of belonging to his family group, and this is a strong force in his personality development.

Hagood next draws attention to the fact that persons living and working on family farms develop an identification of home with place of work. This identification is seldom equaled in other occupations and has a definite effect on the personality of the individual. This effect is usually manifest in the traits related to stability.

Hagood's third observation is that the farm family tends to be patriarchal in character with a high degree of authority vested in the father. This tendency remains, despite recent trends towards a more "democratic" or "equalitarian" structure over the nation as a whole.

It should be pointed out, however, that the effects of continuous and intimate association on the family farm are not always positive. At least two tendencies fall in the negative category. Although the great majority of family members, as indicated above, come to have deep and abiding affection for the family group, some families develop frictions and conflicts that are quite traumatic. These conflicts can become deep and lasting sources of irritation because of the enforced close association. In addition, the continual close association with family members on family farms has a tendency to produce a narrow outlook in the individual. Children do not have the opportunity to mix with others their own age, and the social contacts of adults are likewise limited in scope.

The following list of the basic characteristics that all farm families, regardless of tenure, type of farming, and other differences, traditionally have produced in the individual will provide a summary of influences on the rural family. These traits go far in explaining the personality of rural folk.[7]

1. An attachment to the land that is deep and abiding
2. A limited background of social participation

[6] Margaret Jarman Hagood, "The Farm Home and Family," in Carl C. Taylor et al., *Rural Life in the United States,* New York: Alfred A. Knopf, Inc., 1949, pp. 44–45.
[7] Cavan, *op. cit.,* pp. 63–64.

3. A routine of life encompassing family members and adjusted to the demands of farming
4. A well-defined attitude toward the roles and statuses of family members, with the father as head and all others having a useful function
5. An attitude of independence, except toward family members and close friends

NUMBER AND SIZE OF RURAL FAMILIES IN THE UNITED STATES

Numerous studies have made it clear that the rural family is more influential than the urban family in molding the personalities of its members. The reason for this, as we have seen, is to be found in the family-centered social life of farm areas. In view of this fact, the rural family has a great potential importance in molding the personality of the nation. For this reason it is important to obtain some knowledge of the numerical importance and size of rural families. The data given below are enlightening in these respects.

According to the latest census releases, there were an estimated 41,020,000 families in the United States in 1953.[8] Of this number, 13.3 per cent, or 5,452,000, were classified as rural-farm. This figure is the smallest ever in the nation and represents a drop of approximately 800,000 families in the past eight years, the number of farm families having been reported as 6,268,577 in 1945. Two facts are evident from these statistics. The first is that farm families make up a rather small proportion of all families. The second is that the number of farm families is declining both relatively and absolutely. Both facts are quite significant in terms of the continuing influence that farm families will have in the nation.

Of the nation's families, 21.4 per cent, or 8,782,000, were classified as rural-nonfarm in 1953. It is reasonable to assume that many of these families are more rural than urban in their characteristics. Thus the influence of the rural family may be greater than the data indicate. At the same time, it is necessary to admit that the data on number of families suggest the influence of the rural family is destined to decline considerably.

The number of families does not tell the whole story of the number of persons influenced by farm families. Differences in the average size of the family are quite important in this respect, as noted. Perusal of the pertinent tabulations shows that, in 1953, the average urban family was still considerably smaller than the average rural-farm family. The

[8] Unless otherwise specified, the data given are from *Statistical Abstract of the United States,* 1954, Washington: U.S. Department of Commerce, Bureau of the Census, 1954.

urban family averaged 3.39 persons, and the rural-nonfarm family averaged 3.64 persons, but the rural-farm family averaged as many as 4.04 persons. For the United States as a whole, the number of persons per family was down to 3.53 persons. The fertility differentials between rural and urban populations were examined in detail in Chapter 5.

RECENT TRENDS IN THE AMERICAN FAMILY

The past half century has witnessed profound changes in the American family, both rural and urban. Until recent years, the urban family led in the acceptance and adoption of innovations. Lately, however, the rural family has quickened its tempo of acceptance of change, and the indications are that it will be more like the urban family in the future.[9] The changes in both urban and rural families have been brought about either by unforeseen cultural developments, such as improvements in transportation and communication, or by deliberate efforts to substitute the new ways for the old, such as women's seeking careers outside the home. It is impossible to distinguish different trends in rural and urban family changes. Hence the trends discussed below are simply listed as changes taking place in the American family.

1. The family has lost or is losing many of its traditional functions. As we have seen, the family of yesteryear, which was more rural than urban, was a self-sufficient one; it provided itself with most of its basic necessities, and in addition cared for its old and ailing members. Moreover, a tremendous number of educational, religious, recreational, and protective functions were performed. Today, only a few rural families, in mountain hollows or other isolated spots, approach this degree of self-sufficiency. The great majority of families in the United States turn to the government or other sources for help in educating their young, caring for their old and infirm, and filling other needs.

2. The roles and statuses of family members are changing. The chief trend seems to be for women to shed their traditional roles and statuses in favor of outside work, professional careers, and other "emancipated" roles. As this takes place, the patriarchally oriented family is giving way to a more democratically oriented one. In their new independence, women have won places alongside men in government, business, and the professions. There is no longer a stigma attached to a woman's remaining unmarried.

3. A third trend is for the family to strive to provide certain psychological values for the individual. Its economic and protective functions are receiving less emphasis, and its function as a source of affection,

[9] Alvin L. Bertrand, *Agricultural Mechanization and Social Change in Rural Louisiana*, Louisiana AES Bulletin 458, 1951, p. 43.

companionship, recognition, and security is receiving greater emphasis. Some sociologists see evidence that the family as an institution is strengthening itself in this trend. The feeling is that such a shift in emphasis is compatible with good adjustment in a complex urbanized society.[10]

4. Another trend which has caused growing concern over the nation is family instability. Statistics plainly show that fewer and fewer marriages are lasting. Prior to 1915 the annual ratio of divorces to marriages did not exceed 1 to 10. However, by 1940 the ratio was 1 to 6, and it increased to an all-time high of 1 to 3 during the war year of 1945. After going down to 1 to 4.33 in 1950, it was back up to 1 to 3.96 in 1953. Indications are that the rate will continue to be high in the near future. The causes of the trend are to be found in certain social forces operative in our society. For example, it is known that factors such as war, mobility, interfaith marriages, and urbanism are related to divorce. The high rate of divorce and the large number of broken homes are due in large part to the fact that our culture leads young persons to expect a great deal of unrealistic erotic, romantic satisfaction from marriage. Perhaps the greater stability of the rural family results from the fact that it does not stress this aspect of marriage so much as the urban family.

RURAL AND URBAN FAMILY STRUCTURE

It is logical to end this discussion with a brief comparison of the rural and urban families in the United States. Considerable differences in family organization and functioning also exist, of course, between the various subcultures and regions of the nation other than those set aside on the basis of residence. Our focus here, however, is on rural-urban differences. Alongside these comparisons, the student will gain an over-all view of the most important structural features of the American family.

The main defining structural features of the family in the United States have been enumerated by many outstanding sociologists. The list below generally follows the one prepared by Robin Williams.[11] To Williams' list have been added rural-urban comparisons based on the findings of numerous studies of family life and functioning throughout the nation. In each case the general structural feature is listed first, then pertinent rural-urban comparisons are made.

1. Marriage is monogamous in the United States. Certain observers

[10] Seba Eldridge and Associates, *Fundamentals of Sociology*, New York: Thomas Y. Crowell Company, 1950, p. 509.

[11] Robin M. Williams, *American Society*, New York: Alfred A. Knopf, Inc., 1951, pp. 46–52.

have pointed out that the practice of divorcing and remarrying is a form of progressive polygamy; nevertheless it is illegal to be married to more than one wife or husband at one time. Rural families, however, have traditionally been characterized by a much lower divorce rate than urban families.

2. Incest taboos in this nation forbid marriage to one's father, mother, child, grandparent, uncle, aunt, niece, or nephew, and in twenty-nine states intermarriage of first cousins is prohibited. With these exceptions, intermarriage of blood relations is seldom objected to. There is little difference between urban and rural families in this regard. Perhaps ruralites tend to marry persons within their neighborhood and community groups more than urbanites do, but this is not a pronounced tendency.

3. Although the name of the family descends through the male line (that is, the children take the father's surname only), little emphasis otherwise is placed on line of descent. In fact, all relatives, maternal and paternal, enjoy equal kinship status. The only generalization that can be made with regard to rural and urban differences concerning this feature is that ruralites tend to stress kinship ties more than urbanites. This characteristic applies more directly to item four below, however.

4. There is an extreme emphasis on the immediate conjugal family (husband, wife, and children) and the solidarity of marital partners is stressed to the exclusion of brothers, sisters, or parents throughout this country. In other words, the bond between wife and husband is closer than that between either of them and their various relatives. Although the immediate family is generally the most important unit from the standpoint of residence, making a living, and consumption, the tendency is for the rural family to include a wider scope of kin in its residence and economic functions. Ruralites feel a greater sense of responsibility for un-attached and dependent kin.

5. The typical family, which in the United States is urban rather than rural, is a consumption unit instead of a producing unit. In other words, the family comes together as a group in the buying rather than in the producing of such commodities as food, furniture, and clothing. Obviously, the rural family differs in being customarily a producing as well as a consuming unit.

6. The family in the United States does not emphasize family tradition and continuity. Occasionally one will find a person who can trace his ancestry to the *Mayflower,* but this is the exception rather than the rule. Most persons cannot trace their ancestry more than two or three generations. Rural families, apparently, are more concerned with lines of descent than urban families. No doubt the importance of kinship ties in rural areas has something to do with this fact.

7. In the United States it is not customary for parents and kin to interfere with the choice of marriage partners of their young. Rural parents, however, are more apt to exert influence of this kind.

8. The rule is more and more for adult children to scatter over the length and breadth of the nation after establishing their independence of the family group. In this connection it is not unusual for a family of four children to be dispersed from Maine to Louisiana and from New York to California. One would expect the close-knit rural family to influence its children to remain near home. However, rural migration patterns are such as to make it doubtful that a differential of this nature exists.

9. American family groups are characterized by patterns of equality among family members. Almost universally, these patterns occur at two levels. To begin with, the family has been classified as equalitarian with respect to authority. This means that in important matters, decisions are reached jointly by the husband, the wife, and the adult children. All are outspoken and exercise little restraint in making their views known. Secondly, all children are granted equal rights to property inherited from their parents and are impartially treated in other ways. In fact, it is considered bad taste for a parent to show partiality to one or the other child. This manifestation of equal treatment extends to the in-laws or the spouses of children and to grandchildren. Some have called this development of the family an extension of the democratic principle of government. The rural family has traditionally been of the patriarchal type, which tends to persist more in present-day rural families than in urban families.

Concluding Observations

At least two general observations can be made in concluding this chapter. The first is that the rural family generally continues to perform the functions of the family more efficiently than the urban family: it is larger, more closely integrated, more stable, more independent, and more responsible for its needy members than the urban family. However, the rural family is in process of change, and this leads to the second observation. The difference between rural and urban families is gradually being narrowed in the United States. Many studies have turned up evidence of this. It is seen in the decreasing size of the rural family, in the weakening of the bonds that have held the rural family together, and in the increasing rural acceptance of urban attitudes and values. This trend is traceable to the urbanization and technological trends that have resulted in decreased isolation. Despite these trends, it is doubtful that rural and urban families will ever completely lose their respective identities. Quite clearly, however, they will come to resemble one another more and more in the years ahead.

Questions for Review and Discussion

1. Define the term family and explain why there are differences in marriage and family patterns the world over.
2. Name the more important variations in family forms.
3. What are the basic functions of the family?
4. Describe the rural family in the United States in general terms and trace the origin of its important characteristics.
5. List the recent trends associated with the American family.
6. Contrast the rural family with the urban family in as many ways as you can.
7. What is your opinion of the statement, "As the family is, so will the society be"?

Selected References for Supplementary Reading

Cavan, Ruth Shonle: *The American Family*, New York: Thomas Y. Crowell Company, 1953, pp. 34–64.

Landis, Paul H.: *Rural Life in Process*, New York: McGraw-Hill Book Company, Inc., 1948, chap. 21.

Smith, Marion B.: *Survey of Social Sciences*, 4th ed., Boston: Houghton Mifflin Company, 1956, chaps. 11 and 12.

Taylor, Carl C., et al.: *Rural Life in the United States*, New York: Alfred A. Knopf, Inc., 1949, chap. 3.

Williams, Robin M.: *American Society*, New York: Alfred A. Knopf, Inc., 1951, pp. 46–52.

CHAPTER 15 *Rural Education: Characteristics and Trends*

The second major rural social institution to be considered here is education. Education, like other social institutions, is a system of social practices oriented primarily around a valued function of the society, in which the persons who participate, the interaction pattern, and the manifest ends and means of the system are culturally specified and approved (see the discussion of social systems in Chapter 2). In this chapter, the institution of education in rural areas is analyzed, and particular attention is given to school and college systems, since they dominate the educational patterns in rural areas. The Cooperative Agricultural Extension Service and several other important adult educational programs will also be examined.

Definition of Education

Although education shares with other institutions certain general elements, as suggested in the definition above, it is distinctive in the specialized characteristics of these elements. Our purpose here is to specify these distinctive characteristics with particular reference to rural life. Education in this formal sense is *a culturally organized system of social relationships in which, as its central function, certain members of a society (teachers) possessing specialized knowledge provide systematized learning experience for other members of that society.* In order that this definition may be clearer, a few illustrations of what is included and excluded will be given. A child learning by himself how to string a bow has extended his knowledge but has not, in this particular act of learning, participated in the institution of education. A child who is taught by his father how to string a bow has extended his knowledge but not, as such experiences are customarily viewed by the father and the son, as a part of a highly systematic set of learning experiences. A child who learns to string a bow as part of an archery program in the Boy Scouts is also engaging in an *ad hoc* learning experience within an organization that provides some education as a means to its own goals, which are not primarily educational goals. On the other hand, a child who learns to string a bow as a part of a systematically organized learning sequence under the continued control of persons defined by the society as competent to teach may be considered to be participating in the institution of education.

In a more general sense, education can be viewed as the "process whereby the socially approved part of the cultural heritage is transmitted from one generation to the next. . . ." [1] In this sense the acquisition of all socially approved knowledge, regardless of the institutional setting, would be classed as education. Since we are primarily concerned with schools in this chapter, however, our first definition is more useful than the second.

THE FUNCTIONS OF EDUCATION

Any large social institution must operate in such a manner as to fit in with the other parts of the social system. Thus a description of the sociological function of education may not necessarily correspond to the stated objectives of educators, who are more concerned with immediate goals.

The central function of education in the sociological sense is the development of certain personal attributes which are prerequisite for the special roles that individuals fill in the society. As a corollary, these personal attributes must be distributed among the population in such a way as to ensure the satisfactory operation of the social system. In a rapidly changing society, adults as well as young people find that they do not possess certain skills and competences that are essential elements in the roles they want or are expected to play. Since new roles for adults are normally extensions or minor modifications of their earlier roles, education is usually a relatively minor phase of the total life of the adult. For young people, on the other hand, the changes from the relatively simple and limited roles of youth to the different, more varied and complex ones of adults are of major significance. Education is thus of central importance in the lives of young people.

Education is not, however, the only means by which young people develop ability to fill the roles that the society demands. The home, peer-group associations, relationships with adults significant to them, the church, and the media of mass communication develop certain attributes

[1] T. Lynn Smith, *The Sociology of Rural Life,* 3d ed., New York: Harper & Brothers, 1953, p. 423.

which to a large degree give meaning to the specialized experiences of the educational system. Several aspects of the central function of education as we have outlined it apply particularly to rural areas.

The Development of Basic Patterns of Social Interaction

Since education is carried on as a group enterprise, the participants inevitably develop basic patterns of social interaction. These patterns change as the student gets older, becoming increasingly like the social-interaction patterns of the adults in the particular community.

Some of the changes are built into the structure of the school. The early grades are usually constant in their composition, so that the transition from the home is not too abrupt. In the upper grades, each child usually has a different teacher and a new set of classmates for each subject. Like the pattern of interaction set by the formal organization of classwork, the pattern of organized extracurricular activities and informal relationships is strongly influenced, although not determined, by the interaction patterns of adults. However, many of the values that lead to prestige positions in the school social system do not fully correspond to those of the adult community. For example, competence in athletics or music or some other fine art, a great deal of academic ability, or organization and leadership skill may lead to high prestige within the school even though the families of the students having these attributes do not hold correspondingly high prestige positions. In communities in which there is tension between town and country residents, it will be reflected in the relationships of students. However, because of the different prestige systems in the school, many individual students will hold prestige positions in spite of their identification with town or country.

The Development of Personal Attributes Adaptable to Diverse Roles

Although some students will learn in school how to function as adults in the role of teachers, most of what is learned there is used in role behavior in noneducational social systems such as the family, occupations, the church, or welfare activities. Since each individual will have a number of different roles, since the combination of particular roles will vary for each individual, and since the content of these roles will vary over a period of time, the problem faced by the educator in determining what to teach to whom is a continuing and perplexing one. With the relatively high birth rate among rural families and the declining opportunities for employment in farming, the large urban migration of the past is likely to be accelerated, particularly in certain regions. Rural schools must therefore contribute to the development of personal attributes for quite diverse roles.

Many specialists in rural education have complained that schools in rural areas follow a curriculum developed for urban youth. This is probably true, but in view of the urban migration of rural youth, the consequences of such a curriculum may have been functionally positive in aiding in the adjustment of the rural migrant to the urban scene. For those who do not migrate, the curriculum may also be functionally positive in that it may have had the effect of diminishing town and country differences.

The Facilitation of Recruitment of Individuals for Special Roles or Jobs

One of the necessary functions for some of the institutions of a technically oriented and changing society is the provision of a channel for recruitment of talent for the various roles required by the society. Only in societies characterized by a rigid caste system does family membership determine the ultimate status of the offspring. In other societies, the family influences the status of its offspring by endowing it through heredity, by teaching basic values, by providing special opportunities as a result of social access to certain segments of the society, and by supporting it financially. The school serves as an institution whereby the human resources of the society are more nearly matched with the requirements of the society than would be the case if status were determined exclusively by family membership. For the reason indicated above, the system works imperfectly. Perhaps half of the potential college students do not have an opportunity or do not value college education enough to continue beyond high school. However, relatively few students of high academic ability fail to finish high school.

As stated earlier, the status-changing function of education is of particular importance to rural young people. For those who move to urban areas, education rather than family status is the significant factor. For those who remain in the country, the rapidly changing character of agriculture, involving skills of a highly technical order, makes education a prerequisite for good farming.

THE IMPLEMENTATION OF EDUCATIONAL FUNCTIONS

The means employed to achieve the results discussed above need not be presented in detail because they are familiar to all. Although public education is locally controlled, the basic framework is established by the state, and the tendency is to operate even the small schools in much the same manner as the large systems.

There is, however, one traditional disadvantage of rural schools. Since urban areas generally pay higher salaries, offer more opportunity for advancement, and provide greater opportunities for continued professional education, rural areas have difficulty in attracting able teachers.

In education, as in the ministry and in other professions bureaucratically organized, work in rural areas may be undertaken as a kind of necessary apprenticeship prior to getting a more desirable job in the city. Because of this, the rural schools historically have not fulfilled the functions of education as successfully as the urban schools. Two developments have done much to erase this differential: the consolidated school, and financial aid from the state and from the Federal government.

The range of the curriculum and extracurricular activities in the large consolidated school is comparable to that of the urban school. As the potentiality of extracurricular activities as a means for achieving broader educational goals has been more fully appreciated, professional supervision and more school time have been made available. In areas where students travel long distances in school buses, rural youth have frequently been deprived of the opportunity for full participation. As a means of meeting this problem, more nonclassroom activities have been scheduled during the regular school hours. For example, in some high schools, the last class is concluded early enough to permit one to two hours of athletics or other nonclass activities.

In order to encourage the provision of adequate vocational training, local schools that meet specified conditions receive financial aid from the state and from the Federal government. Vocational training in agriculture was set up under the Smith-Hughes Act of 1917, and certain other forms of vocational education were provided for under the Smith-Hughes and George-Barden Acts. These programs, integrated into the total education of those who take part in them, prepare rural young people for a wider range of roles.

UNIQUE FEATURES OF THE AMERICAN EDUCATIONAL SYSTEM

Compulsory Attendance

Schooling is unique among the activities in which the American people engage in that all people are required by law to participate in it during a specified period of their lives. There are many activities in which a high percentage of the people do participate voluntarily and many activities which are expressly forbidden to all. This compulsory feature has not been imposed by an act of Congress; rather, the states individually and separately have passed such laws over a period of time ranging from 1640 in Massachusetts to 1918 in Mississippi. The provisions of the laws vary somewhat from state to state. In some states school attendance must begin at six years of age, and for some the leaving age is eighteen. In almost all states the law includes the ages seven to sixteen, although exemption from attendance beyond the age of fourteen is made relatively easy in some states.

Local Control of Schools

Another important and distinctive aspect of the American educational system which should be emphasized in relation to universal compulsory attendance is that control of schools in America rests essentially with the local school district. Although states have the legal power to establish and maintain schools, most of this power has been delegated to local school districts. These districts are usually legally independent of other local legal units, such as towns or counties, although in some places they are coterminous with such units. Since these local districts have the power of decision making with reference to the local schools, there may be significant variations in educational practices within each state.

RURAL-URBAN DIFFERENTIALS IN SCHOOL ATTENDANCE

In spite of compulsory school-attendance laws, there is great variation in school attendance. Rural young people attend school at a substantially lower rate than the school-age population in urban areas.

It is important to distinguish clearly those aspects of the concept of rurality which are significant with regard to education. Two different although interrelated dimensions of rurality in the United States are involved: the style of life associated with farms and sparsely populated areas, and selectivity of residence for subcultural groups in such areas.

Style of Life of Ruralities

The following aspects of the style of life of persons who live in rural areas are important factors with regard to rural-urban differentials in school attendance:

1. The density of population is low, causing the special problem of social organization and transportation created by small numbers of people in large geographical spaces. This is not true in all rural areas, however, since farming in some may be intensive, with small farms prevailing.

2. Since most of America's agriculture is family-operated, involves a high labor input, and may involve a great deal of unskilled or semi-skilled labor, boys and girls at a relatively young age can be productively employed, either as unpaid family laborers or for hire. For those boys who want to drop out of school, productive employment is an alternative.

3. Historically, farming has been carried on by a population with a

\wer level of education than that of the nonfarm population.
nderstood by many as lacking the educational prerequisites
her occupations. Although the level of education of this oc-
.....al group has been rising steadily, it is still lower than that of
any other major occupational group except unskilled laborers.

4. As a familistic system in which social interaction is to a large extent limited to the same occupational group and style of life, access to persons in a variety of occupations is not extensive, and the stimulus to higher education may be less strong.

Selectivity of Certain Groups

High percentages of members of certain cultural groups live on farms and in rural areas.

1. Negroes, many of whom were brought to this country largely to work on farms, are still to be found in that residential-occupational group in large numbers. Two-thirds of the 15 million Negroes in 1950 were living in the South. Whereas 21.1 per cent of the Negroes were in the rural-farm population, only 14.6 per cent of the whites were in this category. Thus any characteristics associated with race are likely to influence the total rural-farm figures. Further, Negroes constituted 13.8 per cent of the rural-farm population, 26.1 per cent of the Southern rural-farm population, and less than 1 per cent of the rural-farm population of the remainder of the nation. Therefore, cultural characteristics associated with color will be found to a great degree in the rural South but to a very small degree in rural areas in other parts of the country.

2. A similar influence of the location of ethnic groups on the cultural characteristics of a region, including its educational patterns, can be observed in other parts of the country. For example, the special combinations of early American stock and certain European stocks in several West North Central states have resulted in a very high record of educational attainment for the rural-farm population. In Nebraska and Kansas the educational attainment rates (grades completed) for rural-farm seventeen-year-old males and females is higher than for the urban seventeen-year-old boys and girls, which are high in their own right. In other states, such as South Dakota, Minnesota, and Iowa, the rural-farm educational rates for males are slightly below the urban male rates, but the female rates are the same for the urban and rural-farm populations at this age. Although other factors may be involved, ethnic background appears to be the decisive factor.

3. Religious cultural systems, although comparable to nationality and rural groupings, deserve special attention. For example, the rural-farm boys and girls at age seventeen in Utah have had almost as good an attainment level as the urban youth of this age and higher than the urban

rate of many states. In the neighboring state to the north, Idaho, rural-farm and urban rates are the same, although they are somewhat lower than the Utah levels. The counties with the highest educational levels, however, are in the southeastern section of Idaho, which is predominantly Mormon. The positive values placed on education by the rural people in these states, because of their religion, has been sufficient to counteract the negative educational influence of rural-farm life.

IMPORTANT CHARACTERISTICS OF RURAL EDUCATION

Rural education in the United States has several striking characteristics that contribute much toward differentiating between rural and urban patterns of schooling. These are as follows:

1. A significant proportion of rural young people of school age is not enrolled in school. Of five-year-olds, one in eight (12.8 per cent) living in rural-farm areas was enrolled in kindergarten in 1955 as compared with over one half (56.1 per cent) of urban five-year-olds. For the age levels six through thirteen, rural and urban enrollments are relatively close. Above thirteen years of age, the differential between rural and urban school enrollment appears again, the urban enrollment for the fourteen- to seventeen-year-old group in 1955 being about seven percentage points higher than rural enrollment rates. Above seventeen, the differentials become substantially greater (see Table 11).

2. The age-grade progress of rural youth in the school system is sharply below that of urban youth. As in any large social system, the schools tend to operate according to well-established rules. Children normally enter schools in the fall closest to their sixth birthday, and at the completion of an academic year they are generally "passed" to the next highest grade. Passing is a function of two factors: capacity of the individual to learn, and exposure to learning experiences. The genetic capacity to learn may be assumed to be distributed randomly in all segments of the population; thus rural young people do not differ in this regard from other young people. The second factor, exposure to learning experience, is a function of social organization and social values. School facilities are not so accessible in some rural areas as in urban areas. In addition, the low value placed on education by the individual or his family as opposed to such competing values as potential labor on the farm or care of younger children results in irregular school attendance and early withdrawal from school. The relative progress of rural children as compared with urban children is shown in Tables 12 and 13.

3. The educational attainment of rural youth is rapidly approaching the national norm. The educational-attainment level of the entire population has advanced greatly during the past half century. The quantity

Table 11. Percentage Enrolled in School by Age and Residence for the United States in October, 1949, and October, 1955

Age levels in years	Urban		Rural-nonfarm		Rural-farm	
	1949 *	1955	1949 *	1955	1949 *	1955
6	96.9	98.6	94.6	98.4	92.0	96.8
7–9	99.5	99.3	99.3	99.1	95.5	98.6
10–13	99.6	99.4	99.4	99.0	96.1	98.6
14–15	96.5	97.5	94.7	96.4	87.1	91.1
16–17	73.3	78.4	68.3	78.5	62.6	73.4
18–19	28.1	33.5	24.3	29.5	17.9	26.7
20–24	10.8	13.7	8.3	6.8	4.2	4.5
25–29	4.1	5.2	4.7	3.1	1.1	0.9

* The 1949 data are subject to some downward adjustment as a result of revision in the estimates of the population base.

SOURCE: Bureau of the Census, Current Population Reports, Series P. 20, no. 30, "School Enrollment of the Civilian Population: October, 1949," April 26, 1950, and no. 66, "School Enrollment: October, 1955," April 6, 1955.

of education measured by per cent of the school-age population in school has increased more rapidly in rural areas than in urban areas. This is seen most clearly in the ten- to fourteen-year-old group, which is least affected by changes in the definitions used by the census at different periods. For the adult population twenty-five and over, the urban increase was greater than the rural increase. Urban males increased from 8.7 to 10.0 in median years of school completed between 1940 and 1950. For rural-farm males, the corresponding figures were 7.7 to 8.6 years. In view of the migration of rural people with more education to urban areas, the rate of increase in educational level of rural people during the 1940-to-1950 period is not a true measure of the advance achieved.

4. The differences in rural and urban educational attainment vary greatly in different regions of the country and among subgroups. As we saw earlier, the degree of difference between rural and urban people in a number of aspects of social life is in part a function of the ethnic composition of the rural population. The West North Central states and certain of the Mountain states have quite favorable educational records in spite of lower density of population. Correspondingly, urban areas with large ethnic groups that place a low value on education rank considerably lower than rural areas in the same region.

Table 12. Per Cent of School Population Eight to Eighteen Years of Age in Expected Grades, by Age, Sex, and Residence, for the United States, April, 1950

Age levels in years	Urban			Rural-nonfarm			Rural-farm		
	Total	Male	Female	Total	Male	Female	Total	Male	Female
8–18	77.9	75.6	80.2	71.8	68.1	75.6	66.2	62.5	70.0
8–13	81.5	79.8	83.2	75.6	72.7	78.7	69.8	66.7	73.1
14–15	70.9	67.5	74.3	63.2	57.8	68.9	58.2	53.4	63.2
16–17	72.7	69.5	75.9	66.7	61.8	71.6	62.5	57.8	67.3
18	74.5	72.4	76.8	66.2	63.7	69.2	59.9	55.0	61.1

SOURCE: Eleanor Sheldon, *Children and Youth*, John Wiley & Sons, Inc., New York, 1956.

Table 13. Per Cent Enrolled in School by Age and Residence for the United States, 1910–1950

Age levels in years	1910		1920		1930		1940		1950	
	Urban	Rural	Urban	Rural	Urban	Rural	Urban	Rural	Urban	Rural
5–9	69.5	56.8	74.3	63.5	78.9	67.6	80.2	68.7	73.0	70.8
10–14	91.7	85.8	94.7	89.6	98.0	94.5	97.1	92.6	96.3	95.1
15–20	27.1	37.6	31.2	36.6	45.5	42.4	52.7	45.1	55.7	49.9

THE MAJOR PROBLEM IN RURAL EDUCATION

The educational system is the largest single social system in most rural communities, as measured by cost of facilities and operations or by the number of persons directly or indirectly involved. More than one person in four in rural areas in 1950 were of school age. It is significant that 22.8 per cent of the rural-nonfarm population and 27.9 per cent of the rural-farm population were in this age group as compared with only 17.8 per cent of the urban population. From 1950 to 1955, the total rural-farm population declined by 13.5 per cent, but the school-age population declined at a less rapid rate. As a matter of fact, the relative size of this group in the rural population increased. In 1955 the per cent of the rural population of school age had risen to 29.0 per cent.

The problem that rural people face in providing education for their young people is similar in character to those they face in other institutional areas, such as health, religion, and cultural activities. In essence, it is the problem of finding a means of social organization which will make accessible institutional services on a level with the standards of more densely populated areas at a cost within the limits of the resources of the rural population. With adequate resources, some of the specific problems of rural schools, such as inadequate plants, underpaid teachers, and outdated programs, could be attacked with good chances of success. The social-organization problem is being solved with some success, even with limited resources, according to the plans described below.

Trends in the Organizational Structure of Rural Schools

The basic unit in the school structure in this country is the school district. This is true for both rural and urban areas. Districts range in size from rural districts operating a one-room, one-teacher system to the large city system. As education has become more complicated and as more specialized services have been introduced, the urban schools have been able to make the structural changes required without modification of the basic unit of administration. This has not been possible in rural areas, however, and changes have had to be made.

Several types of changes have been made in the attempt to streamline rural education. Among the more common plans are: (1) A number of districts have in some places consolidated into one large unit so that the number of pupils served and the tax base are comparable to those of urban centers. This plan often requires elaborate transportation arrangements. (2) Local school districts, as administrative units, have contracted with other districts for the provision of education for all their children together. (3) Local districts have provided their own elementary education and either contracted with other districts for high school education or set up a high school cooperatively with other districts on a regional basis.

The consolidation movement has been proceeding at a fast rate. From 1947 to 1957, for example, the number of school districts declined from 104,074 to 50,403. More evidence of this trend is found in the rapid decline of one-room, one-teacher schools in rural areas. The number of such schools decreased from about 150,000 in 1930 to about 60,000 in 1950. However, it is significant that in 1950, nearly two out of five rural schools (39.0 per cent) were one-teacher, one-room schools.

The process of determining which districts should join together has been of particular interest to rural sociologists. In the South, where the county is a very important administrative and legal unit, it naturally became the administrative unit for educational purposes. In New England, where the county is of minor importance in the life of the people and the town of central importance, cooperative arrangements between towns have been developed. Normally, there has been no consolidation of districts, because of the significance of towns in the social fabric.

In other areas, and in particular in New York State, an effort has been made to ensure that the enlarged districts encompass a sociological community. Thus the following has been reported: [2]

Experience indicates that when the boundaries of a newly reorganized school district coincide closely to the boundaries of the natural or sociological community—a village, town or city, together with the tributary trade and service areas of smaller population centers and open country—the district is almost always successful. Because patterns for association and lines of communication are already established, the school district established on the natural community basis has the advantage of benefits from all the existing factors contributing to social cohesion.

An additional structural element designed to provide specialized services and supervision to the school district that is not able to finance such services alone is the *intermediate unit*. This is a unit which serves several districts and has no authority, or at most limited authority, and which facilitates access to specialized services, leaving the major responsibility for education in the hands of the local district. An arrangement of this kind is in operation in about three-fourths of the states.

EDUCATION FOR RURAL ADULTS

Relatively early in American history, the public gave expression to its belief that any important aspect of life was a legitimate area for advanced and continued study. In 1862, land-grant colleges were made possible through Federal legislation and financial support. These colleges have served as major instruments for the development of new knowledge, for the training of a large body of expert personnel, and for the extension of knowledge to the general public.

Education of rural adults has been extended through several quite different means: the Cooperative Agricultural Extension Service, adult education programs sponsored by local schools, farm organizations such as the Farm Bureau, commodity organizations such as breeder associations, producer and consumer cooperatives, agents of commercial enterprises who sell supplies and equipment to farmers and who purchase farm produce, and commercial journals and magazines. The first two of these are primarily educational in character, and the others are multipurpose associations with education as one phase of their total operation.

[2] *The Community School and the Intermediate Unit*, 1954 Yearbook, Department of Rural Education, National Education Association, Washington.

Since the educational activities and benefits of farm organizations, newspapers and journals, and salesmen are discussed elsewhere (see Chapters 24 and 25), they will not be elaborated at this point. The programs of schools will be briefly touched upon, but the importance of the Agricultural Extension Service deserves rather extended treatment.

Adult Education through Schools

Public schools in general have been increasingly serving adults through formal educational activities. Rural schools have shared in this movement in two ways. In the large centralized or consolidated schools, special evening classes have been set up for adults, covering the subjects in which the people in the school districts are interested. Since these schools may serve as community centers for a wide range of activities, members of the community come to view the school as an institution that serves adults as well as young people.

In more depressed agricultural areas, the vocational agricultural personnel in the schools frequently work with the families of their students, and home economics teachers also work in the community. This may occur on the initiative of the individual teacher or as a part of a general community development program.

The Agricultural Extension Service

In 1914 Congress passed the Smith-Lever Act, which formally brought the Agricultural Extension Service into existence. This action was the culmination of a long series of developments, beginning with the Morrill Act, passed in 1862, which provided for the establishment of Colleges of Agriculture in the various states of the Union. Figure 28 is a diagram showing the organization of the Agricultural Extension Service. The second major link in the chain of events leading to the Smith-Lever Act was the Hatch Act, passed in 1887, which provided for the establishment of agricultural experiment stations to be attached to the land-grant or agricultural colleges. With the experiment stations formed to discover new ways of doing things, it was logical that the Extension Service was designed to carry the information obtained to farm people.

The man most often credited with fathering the Extension Service is Seaman A. Knapp. Knapp was successful in getting a demonstration farm started in Texas, and his results, plus the boll weevil crisis, moved the United States Department of Agriculture to employ a county agent in 1906. The idea caught on and culminated in a full-fledged agricultural extension service within a few years.

In the original act establishing this agency, the Cooperative Agricultural Extension Service was designed to emphasize the more technical aspects of farming and homemaking. This has been broadened over the

THE COUNTY EXTENSION OFFICE
How People Use It

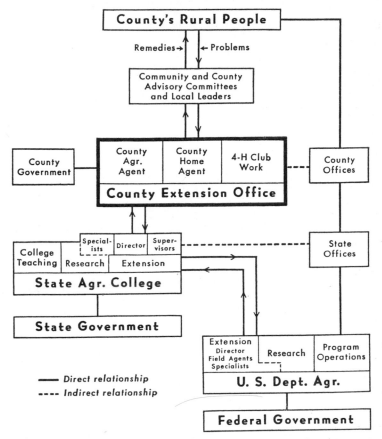

Figure 28. Diagram showing the organization of the Agricultural Extension Service. (From Arthur F. Raper and Martha J. Raper, *Guide to Agriculture, U.S.A.*, Washington: Agriculture Information Bulletin 30, U.S. Department of Agriculture, 1955.)

years to include any phase of the life of rural people and their communities, such as community organization, health, child rearing, and human relations.

The Extension Service has made several important adjustments in its structure and program. Except for a very few states, it has organizationally severed its tie with the Farm Bureau. It is increasingly serving rural-nonfarm and even urban people through certain phases of its program. In several states, the program for women is predominantly serving nonfarm women. Planning with individual farm families to cover all phases of farm and home management on a coordinated basis is becoming increasingly characteristic. The presently emphasized rural development program gives promise of a new era of activity. Personnel in both the youth and adult phases of the program are more highly trained professionally now than earlier. A more efficiently organized interstate (regional) program for training the professional staff has been developed.

The extent of its operations has led some scholars to identify the Agricultural Extension Service as the largest rural education agency in the world. Be that as it may, it is certainly a potent influence among rural people, youths as well as adults.

Questions for Review and Discussion

1. Why can education be called a major social institution?
2. What has been the trend in rural education in your state?
3. Do you believe there should be Federal aid to schools? Why?
4. Define education in its fullest sense.
5. What are the major functions of education as a social institution?
6. In what ways do urban schools usually differ from rural schools?
7. Do you think present trends will erase the relative educational disadvantage of rural young people? Why?
8. In your opinion, do adult education programs serve a useful purpose? Explain.

Selected References for Supplementary Reading

Butterworth, Julian E., and Howard H. Dawson: *The Modern Rural School,* New York: Thomas Y. Crowell Company, 1957, pp. 48–65.

Kolb, John H., and Edmund deS. Brunner: *A Study of Rural Society,* 4th ed., Boston: Houghton Mifflin Company, 1952, pp. 313–360.

Kreitlow, Burton W.: *Rural Education: Community Backgrounds,* New York: Harper & Brothers, 1954, pp. 21–45, 110–143.

Loomis, Charles P., and J. Allan Beegle: *Rural Sociology: The Strategy of Change,* Englewood Cliffs, N.J.: Prentice-Hall, Inc., 1957, pp. 237–266.

Rodehaver, Myles W., William B. Axtell, and Richard E. Gross: *The Sociology of the School,* New York: Thomas Y. Crowell Company, 1957, pp. 48–65.

CHAPTER 16

The Rural Church:

Characteristics and Problems

Religion, the third social institution to be discussed in Part Four, has always played a significant role in the lives of rural Americans. The functions and problems of rural religious organizations are discussed in this chapter. A brief review of religious patterns and trends in the United States is included as an introduction to the discussions of the church and religion in the rural United States.

RELIGIOUS PATTERNS AND TRENDS IN THE UNITED STATES

The early migrants to the United States included many groups seeking religious freedom. This fact, plus the complete religious freedom that has characterized the nation, accounts in the main for the multiplicity of denominations and sects found in both rural and urban areas of the nation today. The *Yearbook of American Churches* listed 254 different religious bodies in the continental United States in 1954. In this same year the total membership of all religious groups was estimated to be 97,482,611 persons.[1]

In general, there has been a vigorous postwar growth in church membership in the United States. Not only do more persons belong to churches today than ever before in the nation's history (see Table 14 and Fig. 29), but church membership is growing at a faster rate than is the population. The increase in church members was 2.8 per cent from 1952 to 1953, whereas the total population increased only 1.7 per cent in the same period. The same pattern holds true for Sunday or Sabbath schools. Some 37,623,530 were enrolled in these schools in 1954, and this represented an increase of almost 8 million persons since 1950.[2]

[1] Benson Y. Landis (ed.), *Yearbook of American Churches for 1956*, New York: National Council of the Churches of Christ in the U.S.A., 1956.
[2] *Ibid.*

Table 14. Total Number of Church Members for All Religious Bodies in the United States, for Selected Years

Year	Number of members
1926	54,576,346
1940	64,501,594
1950	86,830,490
1953	94,842,845

SOURCE: Benson Y. Landis (ed.), *Yearbook of American Churches for 1955*, National Council of the Churches of Christ in the U.S.A., New York, 1955.

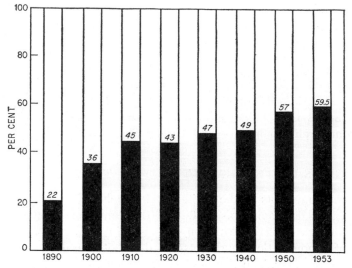

Figure 29. The trend in church membership in the United States from 1890 to 1953. (From Benson Y. Landis (ed.), *Yearbook of American Churches for 1956*, New York: National Council of the Churches of Christ in the United States of America, 1956.)

These facts indicate the growing interest of Americans in the church and religion.

It is interesting to compare the membership estimates of the various major religious groups in the nation. The ratio of relative size has apparently changed little for these groups within recent years. As can be seen in Table 15 and Figure 30, Protestants make up about 59 per cent, Roman Catholics 33 per cent, Jews about 5 per cent, and others about 3 per cent of the total church membership.

In summary, it can be said that the United States is both a religious and a Christian nation. With this in mind, it is easier to understand the characteristics and problems of the rural churches in the nation.

Table 15. Church Membership in the United States, by Major Religious Groups, 1953

Religious body	Members	
	Number	Per cent of total
Protestant..............	55,837,325	58.9
Roman Catholic..........	31,476,261	33.2
Jewish..................	5,000,000	5.3
Eastern Orthodox.........	2,100,171	2.2
Old Catholic and Polish National Catholic........	366,088	0.3
Buddhist................	63,000	0.1
Total....................	94,842,845	100.0

SOURCE: Benson Y. Landis (ed.), *Yearbook of American Churches for 1955*, National Council of the Churches of Christ in the U.S.A., New York, 1955.

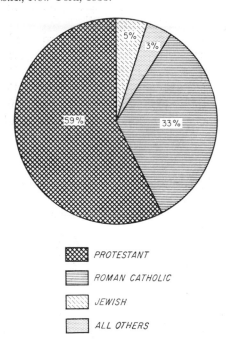

Figure 30. Church membership in the United States, by major religious groups, 1953. (From Benson Y. Landis (ed.), *Yearbook of American Churches for 1956*, New York: National Council of the Churches of Christ in the United States of America, 1956.)

The Functions of the Church

As a social institution, the church has a definite sphere of activity. Its special concerns are matters pertaining to the moral, religious, and spiritual life of the community and its individuals. Lowry Nelson has listed the functions of the church as follows: to teach religious doctrines, to exhort its members to obedience to and practice of its precepts, to provide the physical facilities for religious activities, to carry on welfare and recreational activities, to counsel members on personal problems, and to serve as an agency of social control.[3]

The importance of the functions of the rural church is indicated by the fact that recent studies in several states have shown that the activities of religious groups provide one of the most important forms of participation of the rural population.[4] A survey made by Selz Mayo in North Carolina indicated that 78 per cent of the social participation of a sample of rural people was through their churches, whereas only 22 per cent was through all other community agencies combined[5] (see Fig. 31). These figures reveal the potential for influencing behavior which religious institutions may have in farm areas.

THE RURAL CHURCH AND ITS MEMBERS

The rural churches in the United States are predominantly Protestant. This fact is important in understanding the characteristics of these churches and their members.

Hostetler and Mather abstracted pertinent information concerning the factors associated with participation and nonparticipation in the rural church from a number of studies made in the United States. As a result of their readings, these authors listed the following characteristics of the rural church and its members.[6]

1. Women generally show more active interest in the rural church, both by attendance and membership, than men. Of the white Sunday

[3] Lowry Nelson, *Rural Sociology*, 2d ed., New York: The American Book Company, 1955, p. 343.

[4] Raymond Payne and Harold F. Kaufman, *Organizational Activities of Rural People in Mississippi*, Mississippi AES Circular 189, 1953; Donald G. Hay and Robert A. Polson, *Rural Organization in Oneida County, New York*, Cornell AES Bulletin 871, 1951; R. L. Skrabanek and Vernon J. Parenton, "Social Life in a Czech-American Rural Community," *Rural Sociology*, 15 (3), 1950; Harold F. Kaufman, *Rural Churches in Kentucky*, Kentucky AES Bulletin 530, 1949; and S. Earl Grigsby and Harold Hoffsommer, *Rural Social Organization of Frederick County, Maryland*, Maryland AES Bulletin A51, 1949.

[5] Selz C. Mayo, "The Country Church—Number 1 Rural Influence," Raleigh, N.C.: *Research and Training*, 8:3, 1949.

[6] John A. Hostetler and William G. Mather, *Participation in the Rural Church*, Pennsylvania State College School of Agriculture AES Paper 1762, Journal Series, 1952.

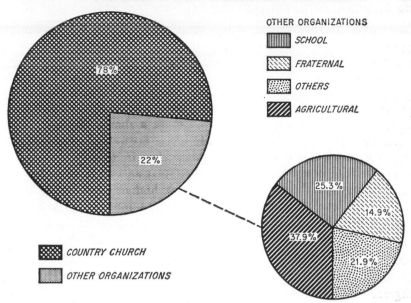

Figure 31. Participation by the rural population in the church and other formal organizations. (From Selz C. Mayo, "The Country Church—Number 1 Rural Influence," *Research and Farming*, 8, 1949.)

School teachers in rural areas, approximately 60 per cent are women. Men, however, are more likely to be selected as leaders in the rural church than women. This pattern is related to the traditions and attitudes of rural people, which tend to prevent women from holding particular church offices.[7]

2. Participation in the rural church is more common among older rural residents than among younger ones. In a Kentucky study, for example, it was found that persons fifty-five years of age or older made up 34 per cent of the church membership. By contrast, only 23 per cent of the persons who were not church members were fifty-five or older. At the other extreme, the younger ages (thirty-five years or less) made up only 19 per cent of all church members but accounted for as many as 33 per cent of the nonmembers.[8]

3. Geographical factors and place of residence affect church membership. In areas where households are great distances apart or where churches are far from households, church attendance is low. The importance of distance is indicated by a survey in New York, which showed that 58 per cent of the people living in a village had attended church there the Sunday previous to the survey. However, only 17 per cent of

[7] Harold F. Kaufman, *Religious Organizations in Kentucky*, Kentucky AES Bulletin 524, 1948.
[8] *Ibid.*

the persons living as much as four miles from the village had attended the church.[9] In this context, it has been observed that a larger proportion of families living on paved roads attend churches than of those living on unimproved roads.

4. Participation in the rural church is related to length of residence. People who have lived in a given community longer, as a general rule, participate in rural church activities more frequently and more diligently than families who have resided there a shorter time.

5. Farm ownership is, in general, more favorably associated with church membership than farm tenancy. That is, tenants do not as a rule participate in church activities to as great an extent as do owners.[10]

6. Persons with higher incomes and of higher class status show a more active interest in the rural church than persons with lower incomes and of lower class status. This general observation, however, also holds true for other types of organizational activities.[11]

7. In the local community, persons belonging to the dominant ethnic group participate more in church activities than persons from minority groups. As our nation was settled, immigrants tended to locate in areas where there were people of their national origin. Consequently, churches of a particular ethnic group tended to become firmly established in certain communities. As long as such a group remains the dominant one in the community, persons of the majority group participate more actively in church affairs than persons of minority groups.

8. Church members in rural areas usually have more formal education than do nonmembers. Furthermore, the more highly educated persons are more likely to hold church offices and positions of leadership.[12]

9. As a rule, persons who participate in rural church activities also participate in other community organizations. This phenomenon indicates a relationship between community leadership and church leadership.

Rural Church Trends

The data relating specifically to religion and the church in rural areas today are unsatisfactory. The most recent census figures available are from the 1936 Census of Religious Bodies.[13] These data are so out of date as to be useless except for historical comparisons. As a consequence, in determining recent rural church trends, we must rely on local studies.

[9] William G. Mather, *The Rural Churches of Allegany County,* Cornell AES Bulletin 587, 1934.

[10] W. A. Anderson, *The Membership of Farmers in New York Organizations,* Cornell AES Bulletin 695, 1938.

[11] Kaufman, *op. cit.*

[12] *Ibid.*

[13] Congress failed to authorize a census of religious bodies in 1946 and 1956.

Almost without exception, studies conducted within the past several years indicate that the number of these churches, as well as the number of their members, has been declining. For example, as early as 1949, 16 per cent of the previously existing village churches and 36 per cent of the previously established open-country churches in one Missouri county had been disbanded.[14] In Pennsylvania, the closing of rural churches occurred with such frequency as to attract widespread attention and study.[15] All in all the evidence is so clear as to leave little doubt of the general decline of rural churches.

The basic factor in the decline of the rural church is the decrease in the rural population. However, other factors that bear on this trend will become evident in the discussion that follows.

THE RURAL CHURCH IN AN ERA OF CHANGE

At mid-century, the rural church in the United States is in the midst of a technological revolution. Its survival is closely related to the effective solution of certain serious problems that either arise from the changing times or are accentuated by contemporary changes. These problems are reviewed below.

Slow Adaptation to Change

Despite the important part it played in our early history and continues to play today, the rural church has not been able to adjust to recent changes as rapidly as other institutions. Several explanations for this have been offered. One of these is summarized by Calvin Schnucker as follows: [16]

The roots of the American rural church problems are not to be found in the United States. Rather are they to be found in the spires, the great organs, the stained-glass windows, and the heavy rock walls of the European cathedrals. Christianity, as it developed after the Roman Empire made it the official State religion, has always been urban-centered. The masses of population were town- and city-centered. It seemed most appropriate to build the cathedral type of church where the densest population was located. Consequently, urban concepts of church work always prevailed in Europe. . . .

With immigration to the United States came the same church concepts that were long held by the European nationals, with one exception: the idea of separation of Church and State early took root here. More and more immi-

[14] Lawrence M. Hepple and Margaret L. Bright, *Social Changes in Shelby County, Missouri,* Missouri AES Bulletin 456, 1950, p. 34.

[15] T. C. Scheifele and William G. Mather, *Closed Rural Pennsylvania Churches,* Pennsylvania AES Bulletin 512, 1949.

[16] Calvin Schnucker, *How to Plan the Rural Church Program,* Philadelphia: The Westminster Press, 1954, pp. 11–13. By permission.

grants arrived on our shores; they pressed ever farther inland. Land was plentiful; it seemed inexhaustible. So long as expansion of population continued, the European concept of church seemed adequate. Each group of immigrants brought its particular brand of sectarian Christianity along and organized a church on that basis. If our country had developed the same density of population that plagued central Europe, a rural church problem would not have developed. However, as small numbers of Lutherans, Reformed, Roman Catholics, and Methodists moved into the same approximate neighborhood, each group sought to develop its own denominationalism. By the end of the nineteenth century it became apparent that the rural population would soon reach its greatest extension, and that the population density per square mile would fall far short of that in Europe. The result of this stabilization of population immediately reflected itself in church life and activity. Quite different from in Europe, there were not sufficient people in any given rural area to support all the denominations represented in the population. This was not so apparent at first while the population was growing and goods rather than money were the medium of exchange.

With the adoption of the principle of separation of Church and State, Government support of churches did not long exist in the United States. Thus by 1915, without an adequate population density and without government support, the churches serving the rural areas were in deep trouble. It has been exceedingly difficult to understand just why this trouble has developed and just how to overcome it. Because we have been unable to shake ourselves loose from the old European concepts of church, serious decay has struck deeply at the heart of the church.

Too Many Churches for a Declining Rural Population

In the early days of settlement a mere handful of people was considered enough to organize a local church. The hope was that new migrants into the community would increase the numbers of the established congregations. This pattern, encouraged by denominational zealousness, resulted in what has been called *overchurching*. For example, in Virginia it was found that there was ". . . an average of 37 rural churches per 225 square miles." Elaborating on their findings, the authors of the Virginia study stated, "Were these churches distributed evenly all over the state, there would be 13 churches within five miles and 52 churches within ten miles of any one farm home."[17] Gee cites sixteen rural field studies of churches made in the 1940s, largely in the Northeast and Middle West. The conclusion reached was summarily put: ". . . assuming the long-standing Home Mission Council's standard of 1,000 population per church as normal, the area surveyed had as a whole more than twice too many churches."[18]

[17] C. H. Hamilton and W. E. Garnett, *The Role of the Church in Rural Community Life in Virginia*, Virginia AES Bulletin 267, 1929, pp. 38–39.

[18] Wilson Gee, *The Social Economics of Agriculture*, 3d ed., New York: The Macmillan Company, 1954, p. 558. By permission.

The distribution of country churches has caused some writers to raise the question as to whether or not some denominations should continue their expansion plans in rural areas. One writer on this subject points out that: [19]

Our tragic heritage of *overchurched communities* results in many hundreds of areas of *underchurched people*. Too many churches with too few people, all struggling with an inadequate program, all merely trying to keep alive. . . . In numerous places there are too many weak, struggling churches, almost apologetic for their existence. . . . Look at that little village of 562 people in Florida, about half white and half nonwhite. The whites are trying to support four churches; one Methodist, one Presbyterian, and two Baptist. . . . Or that little crossroads in Virginia with four churches for a dwindling white population. Or consider that little town in Mississippi with two Presbyterian churches, one U.S. with 79 members and one U.S.A. with 18 members, both of them home mission churches. Are these isolated instances? . . . Such is the picture in literally hundreds of local scenes.

Inadequate Programs

A major problem of rural churches is maintaining a well-defined program. The greater part of the responsibility for the program is left in the hands of the local minister. Yet, with fewer than one open-country church out of ten and only two out of five village churches having a full-time minister, it is evident that a vast majority of rural churches in the United States have little choice but to settle for an inadequate program.[20]

By what criteria should the adequacy of the rural church program be judged? Although denominations may vary as to emphasis, most of them accept the main points of the criteria prepared by Rockwell Smith in the form of a list of questions: [21]

1. Does the program provide some emphasis on all the elements of the Christian gospel? Evangelism, Christian nurture, stewardship, missions, Christian fellowship and fun, worship and Christian service should all find expression in the program. If any of these elements are missing or slighted, to that extent the entire program of the church is one-sided and incomplete.

2. Does the program reflect the environment of the people? Here geography, climate, and work patterns are all-important in determining participation in a town and country church program.

[19] James M. Carr, *Bright Future: A New Day for the Town and Country Church,* Richmond, Va.: John Knox Press, 1956, pp. 32–33.

[20] T. Lynn Smith, *The Sociology of Rural Life,* 3d ed., New York: Harper & Brothers, 1953, p. 471.

[21] Rockwell C. Smith, *Rural Church Administration,* Nashville, Tenn.: Abingdon Press, 1953, pp. 49–50. By permission. For another approach, see: Dan R. Davis, "A Rural Challenge to the Protestant Church," *The Christian Rural Fellowship Bulletin,* No. 51, The Christian Rural Fellowship, New York, April, 1940.

3. Is the program integrated with the general life of the community? There are other churches; are they recognized as we plan what we intend to do? What of the other organizations of the community? Do we recognize the high school and its youth program and gear ours to it?

4. Does the program take into account the special emphases of the denomination to which the church is related? . . . There is a strength that comes in doing things together; a certain impetus and enthusiasm are generated when all churches of a denomination are carrying on the same program at the same time. Then local churches are shaken out of their lethargy and challenged by outside stimulation to do things they have not thought possible.

5. Is the program as adopted and carried out arrived at cooperatively and democratically? That is really to ask: "Is this the program of the church?" . . . a truly significant and Christian program always comes from the people who are the church, and belongs to them.

The number of members is a second important factor in determining church programs, and open-country churches are known for their small congregations. Studies have indicated that the larger a church congregation is, the more programs it can support. Comparing rural churches with less than 50 members to those having 300 or more members, Kaufman concluded that ". . . of the former group 35 per cent had women's societies, 17 per cent youth organizations, and only 2 per cent men's organizations, while the respective percentages for the larger churches were 100, 90, and 44." [22] Thus, until such time as open-country churches have larger congregations, most of them cannot hope to develop strong programs.

Inadequate Finances

One of the most important reasons for the ineffectiveness of rural churches is inadequate finances. Since the church is a voluntary organization and is not tax-supported, it must depend on the donations of its membership for operating funds. Several denominations have developed progressive programs for aiding their needy churches. For the most part, however, rural churches are forced to operate on collections from their members.

In general, the problem of inadequate finances of rural churches stems from two conditions: the relatively small number of families per church, and the farmer's inability to make his contributions with any degree of consistency because of crop and price uncertainties.

With regard to the first condition, there is no question about the farmer's willingness to provide for the support of his church. The basic factor is that the relatively low income of farm families has to be spread too thin. In 1955 the realized net farm income averaged only $2,268 per

[22] Kaufman, *op. cit.,* pp. 33–35.

farm in the United States (Fig. 32). This income is shared by more than four people per farm, on the average, and such items as taxes, social security, food, clothing, home furnishings, transportation and formal education must usually be paid for before the church can enter the picture.[23]

The Shortage of Ministers

In every church the minister is the key figure, but in the rural church he assumes a position of special importance, because the institutional framework in which he works is generally so limited. A minister who serves rural residents must first understand the people and the motives that impel them before he can influence their behavior.

Several Protestant denominations, particularly in the South, "farm out" their rural churches to part-time student supply pastors. Consequently open-country churches are frequently referred to as training grounds for future urban ministers. This situation is analogous to that of the young doctor in a country practice or the young schoolteacher in a one-room school. The circumstance chiefly responsible for this situation is the meager salaries that small open-country churches can afford to pay. A quotation from the writings of a young pastor brings out this point: [24]

One of the problems of the town and country field grows out of the salary situation . . . that of keeping men in the field to serve the "smaller churches." None of us are in the Lord's work for what we can get, but the economic pinch is most often in evidence in the smaller church. Of ten men in my graduating class (1950) who fully intended to dedicate their talents to the town and country field, only three are still serving churches in this category. In discussions with them these facts come out: minimum salary to start, increasing family responsibility, salary not keeping pace with family responsibilities, and increased living costs, and finally, the move to a church field where the salary will pay grocery, doctor, and clothing bills. At the present time I am fortunate to be in a town and country church which allows me to meet my expenses. However, the first four years of my ministry cost me $2,000 of my savings accumulated while in military service. Don't misunderstand me . . . it was money well spent. However, many have no savings to use.

The low salary scale for the rural clergy is in turn reflected in a number of other problems connected with obtaining and keeping well-qualified rural ministers. For one thing, there is a relatively high degree of mobility in this group. Some ministers go to higher-salaried city churches;

[23] For a discussion of the relationship between family farms and strong rural churches, see Marshall Harris and Joseph Ackerman, *Town and Country Churches and Family Farming*, New York: National Council of the Churches of Christ in the U.S.A., 1956.
[24] Carr, *op. cit.*, pp. 34–35.

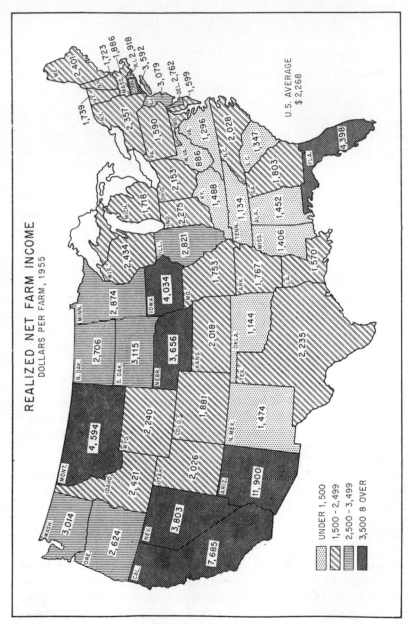

REALIZED NET FARM INCOME
DOLLARS PER FARM, 1955

U.S. AVERAGE
$ 2,268

Legend:
UNDER 1,500
1,500 - 2,499
2,500 - 3,499
3,500 & OVER

Figure 32. Realized net farm income per farm in the United States, by states, 1955. (U.S. Department of Agriculture, Agricultural Marketing Service.)

others change their profession for closely allied work, whereas others still return for additional schooling to prepare themselves for more lucrative employment.

Another consequence of a relatively low salary scale is the sharing of one minister by congregations of the same denomination, often miles apart. The number of churches served by one minister varies with different denominations and the distance between churches. The following is quoted to give the student some idea of how thinly some pastors must spread their talents in ministering to the needs of a number of rural churches at the same time: [25]

The congregation is too small and the number of pastors too few for the [church] to have a resident minister. The minister is presently (25 miles distant) in a home which is furnished him by the Unity. He serves a large circuit of 12 different churches which are located within a radius of 130 miles of his home. He conducts an average of 24 or more worship services and over 8 funeral services in these communities each month. Every Sunday he has to conduct at least 3 worship services and occasionally 4, sometimes having to travel 75 to 100 miles between two consecutive communities he serves. Such being the case, the pastor is usually in the community only a part of each day that he holds services. On the Sunday that they are held, he arrives a few minutes before the hour of beginning. After the services he finds a few minutes in which to greet a few of the members and to chat with them, but he must hurry to the home of one of the members for his noon meal. Usually as soon as he has eaten he must hurry to the next community where his congregation is awaiting him.

Another consequence of a low salary scale for rural ministers is that most ministers serving rural churches have to supplement their incomes with part-time "public" jobs. This cuts down on the amount of time available for them to devote to their church duties.

MEETING THE PROBLEMS OF THE RURAL CHURCH

A review of the problems facing the rural church may leave the student wondering about its future. It would not be accurate, however, to create the impression that the rural church is beset with problems too difficult to solve. Although it is true that country churches have been neglected by a few parent denominations, it is encouraging to note several developments that show promise of a better future for the rural church.

[25] R. L. Skrabanek, *Social Organization and Change in a Czech-American Rural Community,* unpublished doctoral thesis, Department of Sociology, Louisiana State University, Baton Rouge, 1949, pp. 196–197.

Denominations Organizing for Action

Most of the larger denominations have now formed country-church departments in their national headquarters. These departments are designed to improve rural church situations by organizing and implementing action programs for that purpose. Among the more active organizations that are concerned with the problems of the rural church are the Federal Council of Churches of Christ in America, the Home Missions Council of the International Council of Religious Education, and the Christian Rural Fellowship of Southern Churchmen. The National Convocation of the Church in Town and Country is an interdenominational body, including both Catholic and Protestant rural leaders, working toward the betterment of rural churches. Since 1920, when the National Catholic Rural Life Conference was formed, this body has developed one of the most positive programs for rural church improvement in operation at the present time.

Some concrete results of the work of the numerous country-church departments and larger councils have already been demonstrated. As a result of working together more closely, denominational leaders are becoming convinced of the wisdom of cooperation, and the spirit of rivalry is slackening at the higher levels.

Consolidation of Services and Churches

Since so many rural churches do not have an adequate membership and can provide neither a full-time minister nor a vigorous program, denominational leaders are beginning to accept the idea of consolidating either churches or certain types of services. The advantages of consolidation would be essentially the same as those realized by consolidating school systems. For one thing, the services of a full-time minister would become available in a church-consolidated community. This, in itself, is a great advantage, since a full-time minister is able to devote more time to the planning and implementation of the church program.[26]

Training Ministers for Rural Work

Since the minister plays such an important role in the rural church, he should be properly trained for his work. Hunter lists the following as desirable qualities for a rural minister.[27]

---

[26] For a description of several successful church-consolidation plans, see: Garland A. Bricker, *Solving the Country Church Problem,* New York: Jennings and Graham, 1913, pp. 83–87. For a listing of numerous successful larger parish plans in the United States, see: Carr, *op. cit.,* pp. 114–115.

[27] Edwin A. Hunter, *The Small Town and Country Church,* Nashville, Tenn.: Abingdon Press, 1947, p. 97. By permission.

1. He should love rural people because they are people and believe they are entitled to the best ministry within his power to render.

2. He should love the open spaces and the out-of-doors and be so acquainted with the interests and customs of rural people as to feel at home among them and to make them feel at ease in his presence.

3. He should be able to interpret and apply religion in terms of the needs for the whole life of the people he serves.

4. He should have a wife who sees eye to eye with him in these matters and lends her fullest cooperation.

5. He should study his problems as diligently as any city pastor studies his and seek solutions of them for his people's sake, just as he might elsewhere for his reputation's sake.

A movement aiming at specialized training for rural ministers has been gaining considerable headway since about 1940. A number of agricultural colleges, in conjunction with their departments of rural sociology, are now offering a pretheological major for ministerial students. This training has been accredited for admission by the majority of American theological institutions. In their pretheological training, students concentrate upon agriculture and rural problems rather than on liberal arts courses.

A number of state colleges are also cooperating in various ways in providing agricultural training for ministers. Annual conferences are conducted specifically for rural pastors, usually during the summer, and various rural and agricultural problems are studied.

In addition to those described above, other types of schools, institutes, coaching conferences, internships, work camps and travel seminars are being used to train pastors for working with rural churches and people. Through these media, these churches and their programs stand to be strengthened.

Financing the Rural Church

Although some larger denominations have instituted subsidies for needy rural churches, such aid does not solve the basic financial difficulties of these churches. If rural churches are to be successful, a progressive program of financing must be developed locally. Many plans have been evolved for raising funds for financing local church operations. Three fund-raising techniques that have been successfully used by rural churches are presented below.

The Every-member Canvass. The most effective fund-raising technique for rural churches in general has been the every-member-canvass system. This is accomplished by the simple expedient of soliciting pledged contributions from all members.

The Lord's Acre Plan. The Lord's Acre plan, sometimes also referred to as the Lord's Portion plan, was begun in rural churches in North Carolina around 1930. Since that time it has been estimated that approximately three thousand churches in the United States use this plan every year. Under this system, each member of the church and, also, all who receive benefits from the church set aside some portion of their crop or livestock and donate the profits derived from these sources to the church. Nonfarmers also pledge a certain portion of their profits to the church, usually setting aside certain days out of the year on which a certain percentage of their total sales will be given to the church.

The Church Farm. Occasionally farm land is willed to the church, and the members donate their labor and time to produce profits from the land for the church. More commonly, however, the church board may rent farm land. Such farms are operated on a cooperative basis, the farmers lending their machinery and the village and farm residents supplying the labor. Seed and fertilizer may be donated by local merchants. After the crop is harvested and sold and the rent and any other miscellaneous expenses are paid, the proceeds are turned over to the church.

Questions for Review and Discussion

1. List the functions performed by the church.
2. Why can the United States be called a religious and Christian nation?
3. What do you think the future holds for the rural church? Explain your answer.
4. On the basis of your own experience or of an interview with someone acquainted with a rural church, outline the program of such a church.
5. Why is it difficult to recruit ministers for rural churches?
6. List several ideological "foundations" of our nation which can be traced to the rural church.
7. How can you account for the large number of denominations found in the United States?

Selected References for Supplementary Reading

Buie, T. S.: "The Land and the Rural Church," *Rural Sociology,* 9, 251–257, 1944.

Hostetler, John A., and William G. Mather: *Participation in the Rural Church,* Pennsylvania AES Paper 1762, 1952.

Hunter, Edwin A.: *The Small Town and Country Church,* Nashville, Tenn.: Abingdon Press, 1947.

Kaufman, Harold F.: *Rural Churches in Kentucky,* Kentucky AES Bulletin 530, 1949.

Schnucker, Calvin: *How to Plan the Rural Church Program,* Philadelphia: The Westminster Press, 1954.

Smith, Rockwell C.: *Rural Church Administration,* Nashville, Tenn.: Abingdon Press, 1953.

CHAPTER 17 *Local Government:*
Characteristics and Problems *

All societies have governmental institutions, although their organization, structure, and forms vary widely. This chapter is primarily concerned with the unique features of rural local government and the ways in which it contrasts with urban local government.

Obviously, *government exists when a group of people establish means and methods, through political arrangements, for the attainment of their goals and for the adjustment and control of their relationships.* Systems of social control characterize all known societies. It follows, therefore, that there are governments in all societies, as social control is maintained chiefly through government.

Making and enforcing laws is not, however, the only function of government. Public service is one of its important functions, and promoting social change is another. Other characteristics of government as a social institution are brought out in the discussion that follows.

Government and Society

The folkways and mores of a society mature into governmental systems, and most legal systems and law-enforcement patterns can be traced directly to the accepted customs of a people. In democracies, government is a mechanism for expressing the desires and interests of the people and for fulfilling their needs and purposes. Political institutions, therefore, derive their organization from society. In other words, government exists to serve the community, which must share in selecting officials and in policy determination if government is to achieve its purpose. In a

* The author wishes to express his indebtedness to Mrs. Ruth Lawrence, Dr. Raymond D. Thomas, Dr. Guy R. Donnell, Dr. O. D. Duncan, and Dr. Joseph S. Vandiver for their assistance and criticism in the preparation of this chapter. Financial assistance was furnished by the Research Foundation of Oklahoma State University.

democracy or a locally autonomous society, governmental machinery expresses the community life itself, since it furthers the ends and serves the purposes of the people in that society. In this sense, political organization reflects the social organization of a group, although social organization is the more basic, since it determines what type of political institution will be maintained. This is the important point to remember.

The Number of Local Units

There are over 102,000 local governments in the United States (see Table 16 and Fig. 33), employing 3.7 million workers and having a

Table 16. Number of Local Governmental Units, Employees, and Amount of Monthly Payroll by Type of Government, United States

Type of local government	Number of units (1957)	Total employees, Oct., 1954 (in thousands)	Per cent of total	Payrolls, Oct., 1954 (in millions)	Per cent of total
Municipalities.......	17,167	1,420	38.8	396.2	39.5
Counties...........	3,047	579	15.8	138.2	13.8
School districts......	50,453	1,365	37.3	409.5	40.8
Townships..........	17,214	184	5.0	28.5	2.8
Special districts.....	14,423	113	3.1	31.2	3.1
Total local government.......	102,353	3,661	100.0	1,003.6	100.0

SOURCE: Department of Commerce, Bureau of the Census, *State Distribution of Public Employment in 1954*, and *Governments in the U.S. in 1957*.

monthly payroll of over 1 billion dollars. In addition, local units spend over 10 billion dollars annually for general governmental purposes.[1] This figure does not include debt retirement, contributions to the unemployment compensation trust fund, and aid received from other governments. From these figures it is clear that local government is a vast enterprise.

TYPES OF LOCAL GOVERNMENTS

There are five basic types of local governmental units in the United States, serving both rural and urban inhabitants: counties, municipali-

[1] The Tax Foundation, *Facts and Figures on Government Finance, 1952–53*, New York: The Tax Foundation, 1952, p. 53.

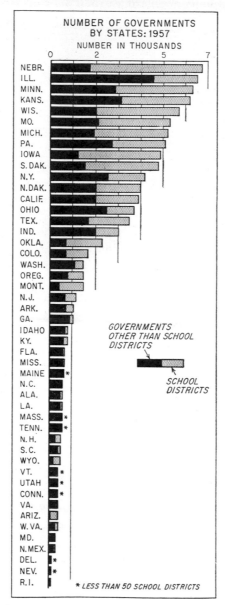

Figure 33. Local governments in the United States, by states, with school districts shown separately, 1957. (From *Governments in the United States in 1957,* Washington: Bureau of the Census Release G-CGA-No. 2, 1957.)

ties, townships, school districts, and special districts. However, rural local governmental units differ from urban ones in two ways: they have a smaller scope of action, and officials more often lack training and specialization.

Counties

The most widespread unit of local government in the United States is the county. All persons, except those who reside in fifty-four scattered geographical areas, live in counties with organized governments. In the New England states, counties are relatively unimportant because towns, townships, and cities are the principal local governmental units. In general, counties serve rural areas and provide certain services for residents of municipalities. The county serves as an agent of the state for law enforcement, judicial administration, the conducting of elections, highway provision and maintenance, educational administration, and other important functions. Certain counties have acquired functions and powers of a municipal character, some of them transferred from municipalities of limited size and resources. These new functions, such as the ownership and maintenance of airport facilities, are proprietary in nature.

The responsibilities of counties have increased in importance within recent years because the national government has found the county more convenient than the municipality as a local unit for a number of grant-aided programs. In three fields—welfare, health, and agriculture—in which Federal grants-in-aid programs affect large numbers of people, the county seat is the local headquarters for the officials administering the programs.

It is significant that nearly 45 per cent of all county-seat towns have fewer than 2,500 inhabitants and that about half of all counties are distinctly rural.

Municipalities

There are approximately 17,000 incorporated places that have powers of general government. Nearly 65 per cent of the inhabitants of the United States live under municipal government. Significantly, over 75 per cent of all municipalities have less than 2,500 inhabitants and are therefore classed as rural-nonfarm. More than 9.5 million persons live in the 13,000 municipalities falling in this category. However, these rural residents account for less than 10 per cent of the total population of municipalities.

A municipality may be a city, a village, a borough, or—except in New England, New York, and Wisconsin—a town. In these places, a town is an area subdivision of the county or state and includes residents living outside incorporated places. The number of municipalities is increasing slightly as a result of new incorporations.

Townships

Organized township governments are found in twenty-two states. These governments include units locally called "towns" in the six New England states, New York, and Wisconsin, as well as governments called townships in other areas. Over 85 per cent of the 17,214 townships are rural local governments performing a limited range of services for nearly 11 million people.

In New England, the town or township is the chief local governing unit. There and in a few other states where townships include densely populated areas, they provide a range of services almost as varied as those of most municipalities. In New England the town is functionally analogous to the county in other sections of the nation. The old-fashioned town meeting is a traditional institution, although some towns have become so large that they have adopted a limited, or representative, form of town meeting.

School Districts

There is a long-standing tradition in this country that public schools belong directly to the local people and that they should be free from external political influence and interference. These attitudes resulted in the creation of separate governmental units called school districts, operated by local boards with their own taxing powers, and subject to statutory and constitutional limitations.

In 1957 there were 50,453 school districts that had status as independent units of local government rather than as administrative segments of state, county, city, or township governments. In addition, more than 2,400 other public school systems in twenty states were operated as part of state, county, municipal, or township governments rather than by independent school districts.

The types of school services provided vary with the size and resources of the districts. Some offer not only elementary and secondary education but also junior college facilities. Others do not operate schools but furnish transportation to schools in nearby districts. Most of the districts cover small rural areas and offer only elementary instruction. In fact, two-thirds of the independent districts have fewer than 50 pupils. These districts had a total of 625,000 pupils, which is only 3 per cent of the total independent school-district enrollment.

Recently, the number of school districts has declined markedly, chiefly as a result of consolidation, annexation, and abolition in rural areas. The

NUMBER OF LOCAL GOVERNMENTS
IN THE UNITED STATES, BY TYPE:
1942, 1952, AND 1957

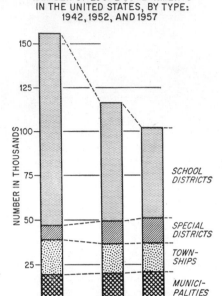

Figure 34. Trends in the number of local government units in the United States, by types, 1942, 1952, and 1957. (From *Governments in the United States in 1957,* Washington: Bureau of the Census Release G-CGA-No. 2, 1957.)

number of school districts decreased almost 40 per cent between 1942 and 1952 and 25 per cent between 1952 and 1957 (see Fig. 34).

Special Districts

There are well over a hundred different types of special districts, with more of the various types located in urban than in rural areas. Most of the 14,423 special districts were established to perform a single function, although some have authority by their enabling legislation to provide a variety of services.

Two-thirds of all districts function as fire, drainage, soil-conservation, or cemetery districts or as housing authorities. In rural America the most important special district governments are the soil-conservation, drainage, and irrigation and water-conservation districts.

These separate governmental units have been organized because the functions they fill may involve the areas of many local governmental units. A drainage district, for example, may be organized around a watershed in parts of three or four counties; or several states may be affected, as in the Delaware Port Authority, which involves Delaware and Pennsylvania in a joint port development. These special districts are nonpolitical to the extent that partisanship does not enter into their elections.

Increasingly, states and local governments are creating "authorities" to undertake the construction and operation of toll roads and bridges, port and airport facilities, public buildings, and other revenue-producing facilities. Therefore, special districts are increasing numerically. Between 1942 and 1952, the number increased by almost 50 per cent, and between 1952 and 1957 by 17 per cent. As noted, when citizens demand a new service or function, there is a tendency to set up a new unit for that particular purpose rather than to see whether some existing unit can perform the new function.

FINANCING LOCAL GOVERNMENT

Local governmental services in this country are provided through a complex structure made up of a multiplicity of agencies and units with power to levy taxes. The cost of all public services demanded of local governments far exceeds the amount of taxes the public is willing to pay. Hence, all levels of local government face the difficult task of keeping spending within the limits of available revenues. The importance of money in government necessitates an acquaintance with government financing at the local, state, and national levels.

The two important questions about the financing of local government are: (1) Where does it get money? and (2) For what does it spend its money?

During the past quarter century, the combined Federal, state, and local taxes increased from about 11 per cent of the national income to over 27 per cent. The national government's taxes climbed from 4 per cent of the national income in 1929 to almost 21 per cent in 1953, whereas state and local taxes remained around 7 per cent. This development is evidence of the American trend toward centralization of government.

The national government now takes about three-fourths of all governmental revenues. Federal internal revenue collections in 1953 amounted to 68.7 billion dollars, mostly from individual income, corporation income, and excise taxes.

Local governments do not themselves raise all the revenue they spend, nor do they spend directly all they collect. Grants-in-aid, shared revenues, and reimbursements from the states, the Federal government, and other local governments provide part of their revenue. In turn, local governments distribute to state and to other local governments portions of their revenues. In 1952, local governments throughout the United States collected 9.4 billion dollars in tax receipts.

Property taxes yield over 70 per cent of the total general revenue of local governmental units from their own sources, or nearly 90 per cent of all tax collections. Because local units rely so heavily upon property taxes for their locally collected revenues, they are placed at a decided disadvantage fiscally, compared to the state and Federal governments. For one thing, the lack of uniform practices in appraisal and assessment results in inadequate valuations of large amounts of private personal and real property. Then, too, homestead exemptions take billions of dollars of real estate from the tax rolls. The local property taxes collected in 1953 probably represent only about 1 per cent of the cash value of privately owned land, buildings, and equipment, which comprise the bulk of locally assessed property. In addition to assessment inequities, billions of dollars in personal property have not been assessed. A further drawback of the property tax is that property is a relatively diminishing proportion of the total national wealth. This means simply that local governments, with limited revenue sources (because of constitutional and statutory regulations) are restricted to inadequate tax revenues, which are very difficult to administer equitably.

Only a few municipalities and school districts levy income taxes. Where they are used, they are generally important sources of revenue. However, they account for less than 1 per cent of all locally collected tax receipts.

An increasing number of local governments, chiefly cities, obtain substantial revenues from sales and gross receipt taxes. Death and gift taxes, all collected by cities, are minor sources of revenue. Around 500 million dollars in tax revenues comes annually from miscellaneous sources, including licenses of various types.

Nontax general revenue, which is derived chiefly from charges for governmental services and sale of products such as water, electricity, and natural gas, provided 2.3 billion dollars of the total general revenue in 1953. However, this is a minor source of local governmental revenue compared to real and personal property taxes.

Special districts derive their revenues largely from charges for their services and utilities—transit, electric-power, water-supply, and gas-supply systems.

Most local governments have been hard pressed to meet their fiscal needs. Their total income has risen, but so have costs. It is, of course, a matter for each state to develop its own particular arrangements for enabling local governments to discharge their obligations adequately. Some have placed payroll, income, sales, and other nonproperty taxes at the disposal of their local governments.

Although some cities do not levy property taxes, many large municipalities have almost reached their limit. The solution of the revenue problems of local governments appears to lie largely in strengthening the property tax, broadening the tax base to include nonproperty revenue, and providing greater assistance from state revenues. Usually, states can help by promoting better assessment practices and more effective equalization of assessments.

These revenue problems of local governments have prompted the recommendation that the Federal government serve as the sole collecting agency for all taxes. Since it already gets about 75 per cent of all general revenue, or tax receipts, the additional burden would not be great. The Federal government then would make disbursements to states and local governments. The proponents of this measure state that the Federal government is the only governmental agency that can equalize the quantity and quality of public services among all people in this country. As might be expected, the champions of local home rule oppose this proposal.

The solution to inadequate local revenues apparently lies in only two alternative courses of action. Either the suggestion described above can be followed, or local governments must be permitted a more balanced and diversified tax structure with authority to raise a large part of their revenue from nonproperty sources.

Local Government Expenditures

In 1927, local governmental expenditures accounted for more than half the total cost of government; one quarter was expended by the Federal government and less than a fifth by state governments. Since then the total cost of our national government has increased tremendously as a result of its entering the welfare field on a large scale and because of war expenditures. The great increase in the cost of Federal government has changed the distribution so that nearly three-fourths of the expenditure is now Federal. In contrast to its spending position a quarter century ago, local governments expend the least money of all at the present time. The actual net amount spent for goods and services by the local government totaled 10.8 billion dollars in 1952.[2]

The major functional expenses of the five types of local governmental units vary somewhat. For example, the largest single expenditure of special districts is for public housing and community redevelopment. The most costly item for counties is for highway provision and maintenance. For school districts, cities, and townships, education is the largest single item of expense.

For all governmental units combined, education is by far the largest single item of expense. The provision and maintenance of highway facilities ranks second; public welfare ranks third; local police protection is

[2] *Ibid.*

fourth; then, in order, are sanitation, general control, hospitals, housing and community redevelopment, local fire protection, and miscellaneous categories.

THE IMPLICATIONS OF RECENT TRENDS IN GOVERNMENT

Traditionally, it has been the responsibility of local governments in this country to furnish public services in the field of human welfare. States began accepting responsibility of this type only recently. As these needs have increased, state and local governments have been hard pressed to meet their responsibilities from their own resources. The Federal government has been very slow indeed to accept responsibility in financing programs in the fields of health, education, and welfare. Until the great depression of the 1930s, the national government steadfastly maintained that charities, through voluntary contributions and local governments, should accept the sole financial responsibility for poor relief.

The Federal Emergency Relief Act of May 12, 1933, the first major legislation during the presidency of Franklin D. Roosevelt, represented a radical change in Federal relief policy. It abolished the principle of short loans to the states, adopted in the administration of Herbert Hoover, and substituted for it a new concept of Federal responsibility for human welfare. Federal grants to the states were provided to assist them in meeting the urgent needs of their citizens.

The Social Security Act of 1935 embodied the first permanent organization of a welfare system in this country, with the Federal government sharing in its expenditures, and marked a very important milestone in the acceptance of Federal responsibility for human welfare. It comprises three main programs: (1) social insurance, consisting of a Federal old-age insurance system and a Federal-state system of unemployment compensation; (2) public categorical assistance, including old-age assistance, aid to the needy blind, and aid to dependent children; and (3) a program of health and welfare services.

Since 1935 the Federal government has assumed partial responsibility for other welfare services. Many requests have come during recent years for additional Federal aid to schools, library service in rural areas, and a greatly expanded highway construction program. It seems safe to predict that the Federal government will take increasing responsibility for supporting such programs.

Significantly, the Federal government returned 2.9 billion dollars, 4.2 per cent of its 68.7 billion dollars in general collections, in 1953 to territories, states, and local governments for all grants-in-aid programs. By comparison, this is less than the annual cost of operating the postal service.

If the Federal government does not continue to assume increasing responsibility for the growing needs in health, welfare, and education, it must strengthen state and local finances adequately so that these units can provide needed services and functions.

Since the formation of the United States, the two major persistent intergovernmental problems have been (1) reducing the fiscal imbalances among the Federal, state, and local governments and (2) readjusting the functions and services that the three levels provide. These two problems will continue to confront each successive generation as it seeks for adequate solutions to meet changing conditions.

RURAL LOCAL GOVERNMENTAL PROBLEMS

In addition to the financial problems that plague all local governments, there are many other important problems that need to be emphasized at both the rural and urban levels. The former are listed first, although the problems are not mutually exclusive. Since the county is the most important and most common type of rural local government, its particular problems are listed below. These problems apply to other governments to a greater or lesser degree.

1. *Lack of Central Authority.* An unfortunate ill of the county system is the lack of a central authority to take responsibility for progressive action and legislation.

2. *The Long Ballot.* The people of a county traditionally are faced with a long ballot on election day. There is a bewildering list of candidates, most of whom are unknown to the voter. Political machines find the long ballot a very effective way of confusing the voters and keeping their slates in office.

3. *Small Size.* In earlier days, horse-and-buggy transportation greatly influenced the size of counties. County seats were so located that the round trip from any point in the county would not take more than one day. Although conditions today are vastly different, county boundaries have changed very little since then. Counties should provide public service with maximum effectiveness and minimum cost; this, according to Millspaugh, requires a minimum of 25,000 people each.[3] Only about 35 per cent of our counties meet this requirement. Texas, for example, has 195 counties with less than 25,000 inhabitants.

4. *Inadequate Revenue.* Most county commissioner districts have insufficient capital to own and operate the heavy road machinery needed today. Most county areas are not only too small in area and in population, but their taxable wealth is also too scant to provide adequate social

[3] Arthur C. Millspaugh, *Local Democracy and Crime Control*, Washington: The Brookings Institution, 1936, pp. 80–86.

services. Some students of local finance believe counties must have a minimum taxable wealth of at least 10 to 20 million dollars if they are to furnish public services from their own resources.[4] Some counties actually have less than $500,000 of taxable wealth.

5. *Business Mismanagement.* Backward office practices are a drain on the taxpayer's pocketbook, but often rural people consider the initial outlay for modern methods as inappropriate. There is a great lack of centralized purchasing, budgeting, and other streamlined methods in financial matters.

6. *The Parochial Attitude.* Perhaps the greatest weakness of local government is that it is too local. Most people vote for the candidate who they feel will protect their rights and interests and who believes as they do. In respect to representative government, a man's social compatibility does not qualify him to run public business effectively and efficiently. Rural people in general do not take into account the necessity for trained administrators. The farmer performs a multitude of tasks without specialized training, and he is inclined to believe that men with "practical common sense" can administer government. City people are much better acquainted with specialization of labor and come much closer to an understanding of the need for qualified administrators. The attitude of distrust and disdain of professionalism is one of the largest hindrances to rural government.

7. *Attitude toward Public Service.* Farmers, as a rule, are strong believers in democratic principles and do not like the idea of a firmly entrenched local government. They feel that administrative offices are rather easy jobs that should be passed around. This attitude accounts for the fact that public service is not looked upon as a career at the local level.

8. *Low Salaries.* Local governments frequently are forced to employ unqualified, incompetent office holders because salaries are exceedingly low. The low salaries mean that an official must have another source of income to live decently. It is not surprising that graft and corruption have been greatest in local government because of this.

9. *Clouding the Issues.* Although presumably officials are elected on the basis of their qualifications and their ability to serve the public, in actual practice elections too often are determined by irrelevant, even frivolous factors. Election to public office has not uncommonly resulted from the success of the candidate in strumming a guitar, singing mountain music, hog calling, or other such aptitudes unrelated to the requirements of the office. Sometimes, especially in local elections, the wounded veteran, the blind man, or the victim of some other tragedy is given a

[4] Lowry Nelson, *Rural Sociology*, New York: American Book Company, 1948, pp. 447–448.

vote based upon sympathy alone. In some elections, the skill of campaign managers, catchy slogans, a picture of the candidate with an honest twinkle in his eye and a firm jaw, posing with his lovely wife and children, or an impressive list of memberships in civic and social organizations appears to be responsible for a candidate's success. Sometimes military achievement results in election. Indeed, one can surmise that the less informed or astute voters sometimes consider almost everything except the candidate's qualifications to represent the public.

Rural-urban Differentials in Local Governmental Problems

In the 168 standard metropolitan areas (counties with a central city of at least 50,000 population) of the United States reside nearly 85 million people, or 56 per cent of our nation's population. The local governmental problems in these areas are, therefore, very significant in terms of people alone. However, they are included in this discussion to point up the differences in types of problems faced by rural and urban local government.

1. *Multiplicity of Governments.* Sociologically, the large metropolitan areas are integrated, complex communities. However, they are not organized as integrated governmental units because the sociological community goes far beyond the corporate boundaries of the cities and includes many local political units, all of which are independent, with responsibilities limited to their own areas. The greatest obstacle to the full development of an integrated metropolitan-area government is the great number of conflicting and overlapping political and administrative units into which each area is divided. Cook County, Illinois, alone has no less than 422 different units of local government, and there are 960 separate, independent local governments in the Chicago metropolitan area. This multiplicity of governments serves the interests of preying politicians and confuses the general issues.

2. *Political Corruption and Inefficiency.* Political machines have been much more important in urban than in rural areas in local governmental affairs. Both major political parties have vigorously opposed major reforms in city governments which would eliminate patronage offices. The merit system for the selection of non-policy-making governmental employees helps to remove government jobs from boss patronage and to make merit rather than political subservience the basis for selection and promotion.

3. *Centralization and Specialization.* Direct participation of citizens in local governmental affairs was possible when small, stable, isolated communities characterized this country. As mobility increased, as cities grew in size and complexity, local government became more specialized, and representatives became further removed from their constituents.

People today generally know little about local affairs and their participation in government is almost nil.

4. Inadequate Tax Base. As we have observed, most local governmental units have too few people and too little taxable wealth to provide adequate services. It would seem that the large metropolitan cities should have enough of both to operate efficiently. However, they, too, are too small to finance their activities from their own resources. An added factor is that the tax base of the metropolitan cities is slipping because people and businesses are moving to the suburbs to escape high taxes and congestion.

An advisory committee report on local government describes the problems of metropolitan areas as follows: [5]

The people and the governments of the metropolitan areas cannot solve their problems with the governmental and private devices now available. The central city usually guarantees services such as hospitals, transportation, fire protection, and utility services for the entire area but it (the central city) lacks the authority to collect for its services and sometimes is forced to serve without compensation. In other cases the metropolitan counties have taken over a function, such as health or welfare, and relieved the central city of the financing and administration. No one has yet been able to develop a method to establish area-wide policies on matters affecting a metropolitan area. The area itself does not exist as a legal entity which can act. The very size of the metropolitan areas makes their cities and sometimes their counties more inclined to look to the national than the state governments. The situation is further intensified where the state government and the government of its large cities are not in harmony. The metropolitan governments must surely be a major concern in any reshaping of the relations between the federal, state, and local governments.

THE NEED FOR STRENGTHENING LOCAL GOVERNMENT

The theory of political democracy as a system of government is deeply imbedded in American culture. The idea or ideal of local community self-determination and extensive citizen participation in the affairs of local government is an inseparable part of this theory. The old-fashioned New England town meeting was the nearest American approach to this ideal.

The perpetuation of weak, ineffective local governmental units, unable to satisfy modern public-service standards from their own resources, has weakened the effectiveness of local government. In the name of local control, these units have held tenaciously to their inefficient boundaries, refusing to consolidate, and have been forced to go to the state and Federal

[5] *An Advisory Committee Report on Local Government,* submitted to the Commission on Intergovernmental Relations, June, 1955, p. 26.

government for subsidies. Instead of retaining local control they have lost it to a central government. The central government did not reach out and steal control from the local units; rather, the local units could not meet the requirements of the people. The inadequate local governmental unit is one of the greatest threats to local autonomy, and the unwillingness of citizens of such units to reorganize is one of the most important obstacles to be overcome. As a consequence, we are getting farther and farther away from the ideal of political democracy at the local level and becoming more and more centralized. One of the most important political questions of the day is: How can we achieve decentralization and strengthen local government?

The strengthening of local governments requires that those local functions and services that can be most effectively performed by these units be allocated to them, together with the financial resources necessary for their support. Facilitating legislation and fiscal inducements have sharply reduced the number of school districts. However, reduction in the number of other units of local government has proceeded very slowly. In fact, the number of special districts continues to mushroom within the present chaotic pattern of overlapping local governments.

States can do four things to create local units that are efficient in providing governmental services. First, they can reduce the number of local units by using their powers over the incorporation, annexation, elimination, and consolidation of units. This should promote both efficiency and citizen participation in local affairs. Second, states can advance the cause of local self-government by giving all counties the opportunity to obtain modern charters, to use modern methods of administration, and to exercise more home-rule powers. The strengthening of rural counties especially would take some of the load off states and simplify the task of administering Federal programs based upon counties. Also, they can encourage county governments to set up an administrative head or executive officer for each county. Third, states can promote more local home rule to units other than counties. Small existing local units can more effectively provide locally needed services if states constitutionally grant home rule, flexible optional charter systems, and liberal legislative grants of municipal powers. Fourth, the states can strengthen the local governments by providing more leadership and guidance to local fiscal officials and technical assistance and consultation in local planning, zoning, and community development.

The Federal government can also help the states promote stronger, more effective local governments by withholding its grants-in-aid from small, weak, inadequate, and overlapping local units that duplicate and confuse functions. The present system of state and Federal grants-in-aid only prolongs the lives of these outmoded local units.

The Outlook for Needed Political Reforms

Every student of government knows that much of our local governmental machinery is antiquated. Political machinery changes very slowly, and only after the needs have become too intense to ignore.

It is a well-established fact that most reforms concern trivial governmental matters. For instance, citizens grow restive and demand longer terms for elected officials, ignoring the basic problems. Although everyone knows that there are too many weak, inefficient counties and that the hodgepodge of overlapping units and boards creates confusion, vested local interests shackle change and improvement under the guise of preserving local autonomy and the status quo.

More attention should be given to the education of citizens with respect to their responsibilities to their local communities. Local government cannot be improved and strengthened without special effort to maintain adequate sources of information, channels of communication, and forums for discussing local issues.

Questions for Review and Discussion

1. Explain why government is a universal social institution.
2. List and describe the different types of local governmental units found in the United States.
3. Are you in favor of centralization of government? Defend your answer.
4. List some of the special problems of rural local governmental units.
5. What reforms would you suggest to strengthen local governments in this country?

Selected References for Supplementary Reading

An Advisory Committee Report on Local Government, submitted to the Commission on Intergovernmental Relations, Washington: Government Printing Office, 1955.

Anderson, William, and Edward W. Weidner: *State and Local Government in the United States,* New York: Henry Holt and Company, Inc., 1951.

Gosnell, Cullen B., and Lynwood M. Holland: *State and Local Government in the United States,* Englewood Cliffs, N.J.: Prentice-Hall, Inc., 1951.

Lancaster, Lane W.: *Government in Rural America,* 2d ed., Princeton, N.J.: D. Van Nostrand Company, Inc., 1952.

Nelson, Lowry: *Rural Sociology,* 2d ed., New York: American Book Company, 1955, chap. 22.

Wager, Paul W. (ed.): *County Government Across the Nation,* Chapel Hill, N.C.: University of North Carolina Press, 1950.

CHAPTER 18   *Social Aspects of Production*
and Marketing in Rural Areas

Patterned behavior relating to the satisfaction of the material needs of man can be observed in every society. This type of behavior is recognized as both economic and institutional in nature. Economic institutions are among the most important in any society; they relate especially to the production, distribution, and consumption of food and other commodities. In this chapter the social aspects of economic activity in rural areas is discussed, and special emphasis is put on the production and distribution processes, since these are the processes that have undergone and are undergoing most change.

Historical Perspective

There was a time when almost any man could get a piece of land at a price he could afford to pay—namely, his labor. Having acquired land, he was secure in the knowledge that his family would have a place to live, food to eat, and clothes to keep them warm. The land was a guarantee of independence, freedom, and security, for if he owned the land free and clear, he was king and ruler of his domain. He was his own boss and had little need for money.

Today land is capital and acquires value through use. The farmer lives in a money economy, and land represents a decreasing proportion of the total capital required for the operation of the farm. As American agriculture has been transformed from a self-sufficing economy to a money economy—from production primarily for use to production primarily for the market—the farmer has become increasingly dependent upon others. The farmer's decisions as to production and marketing practices are being steadily circumscribed by group decisions of the farm community, the government, and the marketing agencies.

This trend has created problems for the farmer. The nature of these problems and the alternatives available in terms of freedom and security are brought out in the following discussions.

THE EFFECT OF LOCAL GROUP CONTROLS ON PRODUCTION

The Frontier: Freedom from Control

On the frontier, the farmer was almost completely free of group controls in determining his use of the land. The various homestead laws made land available to anyone who would settle on it and begin some form of agricultural operation. One could stake out his claim and register it with the land office, or he could simply move in and begin to work the land. If the land had not already been claimed, or if no one challenged the squatter, the land became his after he had lived on it the required number of years. The details of the homestead laws changed from time to time, but throughout the history of the frontier, use of the land for agricultural purposes was a primary criterion in determining ownership.

The nature of the agricultural enterprise was determined by the conditions of frontier life. The frontier family needed a cow, some pigs and chickens, and perhaps some sheep. The farm had to produce feed for the animals, food for the family, and possibly a small surplus that could be sold for cash to supply the meager money requirements of the family.

The American frontier economy emphasized production for use on the farm. In the early history of our nation, it took nineteen people on farms to produce enough surplus to feed one person not living on a farm. With such meager surpluses, money only rarely found its way into the farm home. Such community services as were essential—schools, churches, and even medical care—had to be paid for in part by the labor and products available on the farm.

In the frontier economy the farmer depends primarily on his own and his family's labor to produce the crops and livestock products needed by the family. Farming is one way, frequently the only way in a frontier society, in which land and labor can be combined to produce the minimum requirements of living for the farmer and his family.

Under conditions such as these, the farmer is free to select from a limited range of alternative uses for the land. His decisions are limited by the needs of his family but are affected by the decisions of other farmers in the community or in other areas of the nation or the world. As the farmer moves into a commercial economy and produces more and more for the market, his choices are limited or expanded by the decisions of other farmers and by commodity buyers.

Increase in Group Controls with Specialization

As the frontier became settled, each area developed its specialty—a crop or livestock product which it could produce and market competitively. Depending upon the area, the specialty might be tobacco, cotton, corn, wheat, livestock and livestock products, or some other product. Nevertheless, some parts of the country remain largely undifferentiated today, with general and self-sufficing farming persisting.

Once specialization set in and the community had discovered the crop or crop-and-livestock combination that would yield the highest return, the individual farmer found himself under pressure to conform. These pressures became formalized in rental agreements and, to a lesser extent, in mortgage and loan contracts. Today, the tenant who contracts for the use of a piece of land is expected to conform to the dominant land-use pattern of the area, even though this expectation may not be formally stated.

The limitation imposed by custom is more stringent in cash-crop areas than in the diversified-farming areas. The tenant in the Cotton Belt, whether he is a share cropper or a renter, has only a very limited entrepreneurial function. The managerial decisions left to him refer only to the time sequence of operations, the amount and kinds of fertilizer, insecticides, and weed control. Frequently, even these practices are imposed by the owner at the time the rental agreement is made.

How Group Controls Affect Production

Prior to 1920 it would have been difficult to rent land in Mississippi even on a cash-rental basis for any other purpose than to grow cotton. Even as late as 1950, capital for the purpose of developing livestock production was so scarce in Mississippi that a state fund was established by the legislature for the sole purpose of making development loans to farmers who were interested in going into livestock production on a commercial basis.

Although the loan fund was used sparingly, it served the purpose of breaking down an institutional barrier to change, namely, the aversion of local bankers to livestock loans. This aversion was the basis for the colloquial comment, "After all, cows and mules can die!" Drought, excessive rain, or weevils may cause failure of the cotton crop, but this is a known risk, and the banker was willing to gamble on the ability of a given farmer, whereas the same farmer would be refused a livestock loan.

In contrast, during the same period, an enterprising farmer in Colorado could procure with little or no security the money to buy an entire herd of range cattle. He could then obtain feed on credit, neither the feed dealer nor the banker giving a second thought to the death rate among cows. In this case, the mortality of cows was a known risk, and the ability of range cattle to put on weight under proper feeding was also known. The only remaining gamble was the future relationship of the price of feed to that of beef. To the Colorado banker the gamble was worth taking.

These examples show that in a commercial agricultural economy the farmer's freedom to select alternative uses of land and capital is limited. Land and operating capital are available to him only if he is willing to follow the established crop and livestock practices of his area.

THE EFFECT OF INTERNATIONAL INTERDEPENDENCE ON PRODUCTION

Once the farmer has embarked upon production for a market, he also finds himself limited by other and more remote influences. His decisions as to alternative uses of land can no longer be made solely in terms of the immediate needs of his family, since his success or failure may be determined by the performance of farmers and governments that in earlier days had no influence upon his farming procedures.

The cotton farmer in the South finds himself in competition with the new producers in the Southwest and Far West, where irrigation is bringing into production lands not previously cultivated. Each year the congressional battle for a bigger slice of the allotted acreage is waged anew, and each year up to 1950 found the West steadily gaining ground. The cotton farmers of the South and West find themselves united in their alarm over the threat of new producers across the border in Mexico, the expanding potential of the forerunner of both along the Nile River in Egypt, and the ever greater threat of man-made fibers such as rayon and nylon.

The dairy farmers in Denmark have in the course of a century developed a quite outstanding production and marketing system for standardized dairy products, yet they are finding their markets curtailed by the internal politics of their major customers. The governments of Britain and Germany, which are the two primary markets for Danish dairy products, are subsidizing agriculture in their respective countries in an effort to become self-sustaining and thereby guard against the repetition of the critical food shortages experienced in both countries during the Second World War. The current subsidy for British agriculture is equal to the net profit, thus putting the British farmer in a position to compete with the Danish farmer for the first time in more than fifty years.

The American rancher and livestock feeder looks askance at the importation of meat from Argentina, Mexico, and Canada. Each session of Congress brings renewed demands for outright embargoes or for maintaining tariffs on a whole range of farm products. These demands have been complemented by the parity-price program, which has finally reverted from a constantly expanding program to one that covers only the five basic crops.

The farmer finds it increasingly necessary to look beyond the fence line for the answer to the problem of what to do with his "south 40" or his "northeast quarter." There is no longer simply "cotton land," "wheat land," and "corn land." Even in those sections of the country where cropping systems have been established by long tradition the farmers are finding themselves forced to look for alternative uses for the land.

THE EFFECT OF GOVERNMENT CONTROLS OF PRODUCTION

In the early 1930s farmers in nearly every part of the nation found themselves with large surpluses. Already in 1925 they had begun to feel the pinch of declining prices for products sold and rising prices for commodities purchased. The farmer responded to this declining income by doing the only thing he knew to do: he worked harder to put in a bigger crop in order to have more to sell and thus bring his income up to the required level.

But the bigger crop resulted in a larger surplus, the surplus resulted in lower prices, and the farmer found himself deeper in debt. Then came farm foreclosures and the big depression. Finally, with the advent of a new administration in 1933 came a many-pronged farm program.

Early Control Programs: A Gain in Security, a Loss in Freedom

The many phases of this farm program had one thing in common: the final responsibility for their administration rested with the local group.

The acreage-control program was administered by county committees composed of operating farmers. Soil-conservation districts were composed of groups of farmers who had agreed to work together to solve an erosion problem or a drainage problem that required cooperation in following a master plan. The Resettlement Administration and later the Farm Security Administration were operated on the local level under the watchful eye of a county committee.

Farmers throughout the nation began attending community and neighborhood meetings to discuss their mutual problems. Farmers have been discussing problems of production and marketing for years in the church-yard after services on Sunday and on the courthouse lawn on Saturday afternoon or when the fields were too wet to work. The difference was that heretofore the farmer knew full well that when he returned home the decision as to what to do with the "south 40" was still his to make; but when he returned from the community meeting this decision had already been made. At the community meeting the farmer had sacrificed some of his entrepreneurial freedom and in return had received a greater degree of security in terms of a fixed minimum price for his commodities.

Later Control Programs: More Security, Less Freedom

Subsequent government programs have further limited the farmer's freedom in his entrepreneurial function. Under the soil-bank program the farmer agrees to set aside a certain portion of his land and not use it for crop production for two or more years. Under the conservation aspects of the program he even commits himself to make certain expenditures in labor and money during the period of the contract. In return for this he receives a fixed rent on the land involved. Under the social security program he has agreed to set aside a certain portion of his income annually in order to be assured of a minimum retirement income after he has reached the age of sixty-five.

In making these decisions pertaining to government programs, the farmer has been forced to choose between basic cultural values. The choice, however, has been between relative rather than absolute values. In the social security program, the farmer retains control over 97 per cent of his net income but makes a lifetime commitment for the remaining 3 per cent. Under the soil-bank program, he limits his control over a certain part of his land for a specified period only and retains control of the remainder of the farm. He makes these concessions because experience has taught him that under the present price structure he cannot be assured of security in his old age or of a reasonable return for his commodities. No doubt there is a point at which the price of security in terms of freedom will come too high, just as the price of freedom can be too high in terms of security.

THE IMPACT OF MARKET LIMITATIONS ON THE FARMER

The farmer of today finds his alternatives further limited by the organization of the marketing system. As the various regions developed crop specializations, they also developed the unique facilities for processing, storing, and marketing the dominant crop in the area. Hence the cotton gin is the landmark of the South, the tobacco warehouse is prevalent in the Appalachian Highlands, the cheese factory and the creamery dominate the Great Lakes region, and the grain elevator breaks the otherwise unbroken horizon in the Plains states. Each of these physical symbols of the marketing process represents a matrix of human interaction as varied as the symbols themselves.

The Farmer's Dependence upon the Market

It is understandable that the great advances in marketing were made for the major crops in each area. These marketing channels have been capable of handling the dominant crop of a specific area even in years of high production. The deviant or innovator in any area is frequently stymied by the lack of market channels for his experimental crops. This became an increasingly important factor under the acreage-control program. In areas specializing in crops that are in surplus supply, the farmer is limited in alternative uses for the land because there are no marketing facilities.

The soils in the cotton belt are well adapted to growing pastures, but a decade ago there were few marketing channels for the livestock that could be grazed on these pastures. There were no livestock-loading ramps at the railroads and very few truckers with experience in hauling livestock. In fact, there were few opportunities to market any crop except cotton. In many cases the production and marketing techniques had to be developed simultaneously. This is costly because not all experimental programs prove successful.

As we shall see in Chapter 25, farmers, like everyone else, learn new methods through demonstration, or by seeing other people using them. Very few try out something new merely because they have heard about it. For example, if there is only one dairy farmer in a county, he can expect to answer untold numbers of questions about his farming operation. The farmer who is the first one to produce chickens or turkeys on a large scale will find that his neighbors have occasion to stop by with greater frequency than before, will cast a critical eye over the dairy barn, chicken lot, or turkey range, and possibly drop a caustic comment or two about the "experiment." If the operation succeeds visibly, the visitors will begin to assess its possibilities on their own farms and ask critical questions about how he got started in this "crazy" thing. If the venture fails, no alibi or rational explanation can erase the black mark scored against the experiment in the minds of the observers. The reason it failed may be that transportation costs to market absorbed the profits or that inexperienced handlers caused excessive damage to the product en route. The primary impression made on those who observed the experiment, however, is that it "didn't work."

The Complexity of Specialized Marketing Procedures

In the Cotton Belt, the production and marketing system is built around a complex of advance credit which, in the small-farm areas, frequently centers around the country store and sifts down from the farm owner to the tenant and laborer. In the plantation area, the credit structure begins with the banker or the cotton broker and sifts down through the plantation owner to the share cropper.

The plantation owner secures a short-term loan to put in the crop, and he, in turn, advances money to the tenant families for living expenses. The "advance" begins in March and carries through to the middle of August, after which the tenant can expect to draw on his returns from the crop. Through this credit structure the cotton crop is funneled into the market channels. The amount of cotton marketed through cotton brokers was changed only slightly by the system of government-sponsored commodity loans and support prices characterizing the period following the Second World War.

In the North Central dairy areas, farmers found their incomes sharply curtailed during the first quarter of the twentieth century by a hit-and-miss marketing system that resulted in rancid butter and cheese of poor quality. Partly as an outgrowth of their Scandinavian origin, the early settlers in this region embarked upon the development of cooperative creameries. It soon became apparent that the real boon to the farmer would come through improvement and standardization of the products marketed. The farmers discovered that by working together, not only in the local community but throughout the region, they could increase their profits. The Land O'Lakes brand name and regional organization, with approximately 400 member cooperatives, is but one example of cooperative marketing of dairy products. Not only is the farmer finding it desirable to work with his neighbor down the road, but he is learning to work with farmers throughout the nation who are engaged in producing the same products.

Strengthening Communities through Well-developed Markets

The importance of marketing and processing facilities in disposing of commodities locally is pointed up in a study of the impact of industrial development upon farmers in the surrounding areas. The study was made in four areas with varying levels of industrial development. In the two areas where there were well-established industries with histories of twenty-five years of operation, the facilities for processing local products were well developed. Both areas had milk-processing plants, broiler processors, egg distributors, slaughterhouses, canneries, and other facilities. The processors also had adequate sales and distribution personnel to get and hold the major portion of the local retail business. They had even been able to break into the mass buying practices of the chain-store outlets in the town and to negotiate contracts with local producers to deliver farm commodities in quantity on a year-round basis rather than on a random, hit-or-miss schedule. In general, the local commodities were considered to be equal to or better than the products from more remote producers.

In contrast, the two areas in which industry had been established during the preceding ten years had none or only selected processing plants. In these areas only small quantities of local products reached the retailer. Milk and eggs accounted for the major portion of the local commodities marketed. Milk was marketed through local processors and eggs were generally marketed with the retail merchants, who took upon themselves the responsibility for standardizing and grading. Both the producer and the consumer had many complaints about the marketing process and about the quality of the product.

The comparative analysis of the four centers leads to the conclusion that the development and exploitation of markets for local products is a complex and time-consuming operation. The income of farmers does not rise immediately when industrial payrolls are brought into the local economy, for food marketing is a highly competitive business in which processing and packaging play a very prominent part. For some commodities the farmer is able to do his own processing and packaging. In general, though, the real boost to farm incomes must await the establishment of specialized processing and distribution agencies to handle each of the commodities for which an increased demand has developed.

Questions for Review and Discussion

1. By what reasoning can economic activity be called institutional in nature?
2. What recent economic trends have created problems for the farmer?
3. Is it necessary to have group control over agriculture? Explain your answer.
4. What is the present economic outlook for farmers in your county or type-farming area?

Selected References for Supplementary Reading

Dickens, Dorothy, and others: *Industrialization and a Market for Food Products in the Kosciusko Trade Area*, Mississippi AES Bulletin 534, 1955.

Griswold, A. Whitney: *Farming and Democracy,* New York: Harcourt, Brace and Company, Inc., 1948.

Hathaway, Dale E.: "Agricultural Policy and Farmer's Freedom: A Suggested Framework," *Journal of Farm Economics,* 35:497–498, 1953.

Pedersen, Harald A., and Arthur F. Raper: *The Cotton Plantation in Transition,* Mississippi AES Bulletin 508, 1954.

Ruble, Kenneth D.: *Men to Remember,* Chicago: The Lakeside Press, 1947.

CHAPTER 19

Social Aspects of Health and Welfare in Rural Areas

Good health is a basic social value of great importance to individuals and to society. When ill health prevails, most of the other ills of society also flourish, since poor health takes a heavy toll in economic productivity, loss of earnings, and cost of treatment. To date, advances in medical science, nutrition, and sanitation have reduced to a remarkable extent the losses caused by many types of diseases. A great amount of work remains to be done, however, for there are still people suffering from preventable illnesses.

Although facilities for treating ill health and attitudes toward disease and sickness vary considerably in urban and rural communities, health care and practice is institutionalized to a large extent. In the first part of this chapter, the structural-functional aspects of this institutionalization in the rural setting are described. The second part of the chapter is devoted to a relatively new institution in rural areas: formally organized welfare programs.

HEALTH IN ITS RURAL SETTING

The rural population, like the urban, has definite health problems. In some respects conditions have been more favorable for the rural population, but in other ways they have been less favorable. It has been customary to refer to the obvious advantages of outdoor work, fresh air, and lack of crowded conditions in rural areas as health advantages. On the other hand, medical and hospital facilities in most rural areas are inadequate, and unsanitary conditions sometimes exist. Low cash incomes make it difficult for a great many rural families to pay for medical care when it is available. These and additional factors bearing on rural health care are discussed in detail in this chapter.

The death rate is one of the best indicators of health conditions. Table 17 shows the death rate for the urban and rural populations of

Table 17. Death Rates for Urban and Rural Areas of the United States, 1940 and 1949, by Place of Residence, Exclusive of Fetal Deaths and Deaths among Armed Forces Overseas

Rates per 1,000 Population

Area	1949	1940	Percentage of difference, 1940–1949
Urban.......	10.8	11.5	−6.1
Rural *	8.9	9.8	−9.2

* Places 2,500 or less in population.

SOURCE: Federal Security Agency, Public Health Service, 36 (11), February 7, 1952, Vital Statistics Special Reports, Death by Race and Urban and Rural Areas.

the United States from 1940 to 1949. These data show a decline for both groups, though the decrease is somewhat greater in the rural population. This decline was caused by the recent improvement of health facilities and services throughout the nation and the development of new techniques and drugs. The significant fact for this discussion is that the death rate for the rural population is lower than for the urban.

Census reports point out that certain characteristics of the population and discrepancies in reporting deaths may account in part for this difference in death rates. For example, the rural population has a proportionally higher percentage of young people than the urban population, a difference which is not offset by the relatively greater number of older people. Also, there is still the likelihood that the reporting of death is not so complete for the rural population as for the urban. A third factor is the practice in some areas of assigning deaths to place of occurrence rather than to place of permanent residence. It is highly unlikely, however, that these factors account for more than a fraction of death-rate differentials.

With the gradual improvement of health conditions in rural areas, the difference in death rates between rural and urban areas for specific diseases has decreased. Detailed studies of mortality rates in two states in different regions of the United States, Michigan and Louisiana, support this statement. In the Michigan study the following comments are relevant: "The more urbanized the county, the lower the crude death rate tends to be. This is true for both the rural and urban segments of such counties." [1] The data in this study showed that small cities were less healthful than large cities and rural areas. Chronic diseases, especially heart disease, cancer, intracranial lesions of vascular origin (apoplexy), and nephritis were more prevalent in the rural population, but there were proportionally more older people in that population classification. In the Louisiana study, the research warranted the following conclusion: "These data indicate that the causes of death vary somewhat in importance between the rural and urban classifications. However, insofar as rank order of importance is concerned there is little difference among the various residence categories." [2]

The Need for Medical Care

Another indication of health conditions is need for medical care. There is obviously a difference between need for care and care received, because not all persons needing medical care receive it, as a result of factors that will be indicated presently. Moreover, the definition of need itself may vary. It is conceivable that a person may believe that he is very healthy, when a medical examination would reveal that he is in serious need of medical care.

Determination of Need. The fact that the individual's judgment as to the condition of his health is not a dependable criterion has led to a consideration of ways to establish a reasonably objective standard for determining on a statistical basis the extent of unmet need for medical attention. One solution to this problem is the "symptoms approach" developed by E. A. Schuler and his associates in their work for the U.S. Department of Agriculture and tested by clinical examination of individuals in a Michigan study. [3]

When the twenty-six symptoms were used in a statewide survey of a sample of households in both rural and urban areas of Michigan, the results showed clearly that approximately one person in each four in the rural areas and one person in each five in urban areas needed medical attention. The detailed data are presented in Table 18.

[1] Paul M. Houser and J. Allan Beegle, *Mortality Differentials in Michigan,* Michigan AES Special Bulletin 367, 1951.

[2] Homer L. Hitt and Paul H. Price, *Health in Rural Louisiana at Mid-Century,* Louisiana AES Bulletin 492, June, 1954.

[3] Charles R. Hoffer and Edgar A. Schuler, in cooperation with Rosalie Neligh, M.D., Michigan State College, and Thomas Robinson, M.S., University of Michigan, "Determination of Unmet Need for Medical Attention among Michigan Farm Families," *Journal of the Michigan State Medical Society,* 46:443–446, 1947.

Table 18. Percentage Distribution of Individuals Classified according to Individual Levels of Health Care and Designated Sample Areas of Michigan, 1948

Sample area	Total rural	Metro-politan	Urban	All areas
Number of individuals in sample..........	1,738	548	1,500	3,786
Per cent..............................	100.0	100.0	100.0	100.0
Higher level				
No positive symptoms.................	56.3	64.8	61.7	59.8
All positive symptoms treated by M.D.*.	16.5	15.9	19.1	17.4
All positive symptoms treated by non-M.D...........................	1.1	0.4	0.5	0.7
Lower level				
One or more untreated positive symptoms †	26.1	18.9	18.7	22.1
Some positive symptoms treated by M.D., others untreated..............	7.1	4.7	6.7	6.6
Some positive symptoms treated by M.D. or by non-M.D. and others untreated.........................	1.0	0.7	0.9	0.9
All positive symptoms untreated.......	18.0	13.5	11.1	14.6

* In this table dentists who were consulted about dental problems were included in the same category as M.D.s.

† The percentages for this category represent the total of the three following classifications.

SOURCE: Charles R. Hoffer et al., *Health Needs and Health Care in Michigan*, Michigan AES Special Bulletin 365, 1950.

The symptoms approach has been used in a number of other states, where it has again revealed need for medical care. In Green County, North Carolina, for example, a survey of 266 rural families indicated that about half (48.4 per cent) of the population of the county had medical needs that were not being met. In this county the percentage of persons with unmet needs was higher among females than among males, and as in other similar surveys, the need for medical attention increased as age of the population increased.

In a survey in two counties in Mississippi which involved 423 white families and 109 Negro families, the need for more medical care was evident. The informants were asked two questions: (1) As you see it, what should your family do to improve its health? and (2) Was there any time within the past year when a member of your family should have seen a doctor or dentist or should have gone to the hospital and

Table 19. Percentage of Families in Two Mississippi Counties Reported as Needing Specific Types of Medical Care

Type of need	White (314 families)	Negro (109 families)
Needing		
1. Medical care to improve health.................	19.0	25.0
2. Dental care to improve health.................	4.0	7.0
Some member		
1. Should have gone to a doctor and did not go........	33.0	39.0
2. Should have had a doctor at home and did not do so..	12.0	23.0
3. Should have gone to a dentist and did not go	52.0	66.0
4. Should have gone to a hospital and did not go........	8.0	11.0

SOURCE: Marion T. Loftin and Robert E. Galloway, *The Use of Health Services by Rural People in Four Mississippi Counties*, Mississippi AES, Sociology and Rural Life Series 5, 1954, p. 103.

failed to do so? [4] The results of this study are presented in Table 19.

Reasons for Neglect. Why do unmet medical needs exist? Although the unavailability of doctors may sometimes be a cause, it is not the principal explanation. In the Michigan Health Survey, for example, there were some individuals with unmet needs in communities well supplied with doctors and other facilities for medical care. The informants in this survey gave the following reasons for not consulting a doctor: (1) expense (26.2 per cent); (2) "Too far, distance too great" (24.3 per cent); (3) lack of time (17.4 per cent); (4) symptoms not thought serious (12.3 per cent); (5) neglect ("Just haven't gotten around to seeing a doctor") (7.5 per cent); and other reasons (10.8 per cent).[5] It is clear that most of these reasons are socioeconomic or psychosocial in nature. Therefore, in planning programs to prevent neglect of health, attention

[4] Marion T. Loftin and Robert E. Galloway, *The Use of Health Services by Rural People in Four Mississippi Counties*, Mississippi AES, Sociology and Rural Life Series, no. 5, 1954, p. 103.

[5] Hoffer et al., *op. cit.*, p. 28.

must be given to both the cost of medical care and existing attitudes toward it.

Differential Use of Health Services. Another indication of need for medical attention, though not a direct measure of it, is the extent of use of medical and other health services by families in various socio-economic groups. A study of this type in four Mississippi counties reveals some interesting facts.[6] A total of 909 families, including 3,443 individuals, were involved. It is observed in this study that two patterns of health-care practices exist—one in which health status is regarded highly and hence health facilities are used, the other characterized by neglect of health. Families following the second pattern seldom go to a doctor unless an emergency exists and go to dentists mainly for extractions. There can be little doubt that unmet needs for medical care exist among these families.

A study of the use of health services in two northern Pennsylvania communities, involving a total of 1,071 families, showed that illnesses and accidents occurred at about the same rates in the two communities with no significant differences between residence classes. However, doctors made fewer home calls per illness in the rural areas and fewer persons were hospitalized. Little use was made of dental services. It was found that rural parents were less likely to have their children's physical defects corrected than were the borough (town) parents, even though rural children were in greater need of correction.[7]

The Influence of Change. In earlier years a medical practitioner would locate in a community if he decided that it would be possible to make a satisfactory living at that location. It was tacitly assumed that the law of supply and demand would operate. Hence if the need for a doctor existed in the community, a doctor would be forthcoming. When a doctor did establish a practice in the community his professional status and close contact with his patients often made him their friend and counsellor. Thus the idea became generally accepted that each local community should have a doctor. With his services at hand the people felt secure so far as medical care was concerned.

Social change has affected this aspect of rural life, however, just as it has many others. The rural population, especially the farm population, has declined in many areas. Consequently, the population is so small in many communities that a doctor would not have enough patients for a practice, though the people remaining there still need a doctor.

At the same time, changes in the nature and organization of medical practice have not been favorable to the traditional pattern of having one

[6] Loftin and Galloway, *op. cit.*, p. 124.

[7] Ruth M. Connor and William G. Mather, *The Use of Health Services in Two Northern Pennsylvania Communities*, Pennsylvania AES Bulletin 517, 1949.

doctor in each community. In modern times the doctor needs the facilities of a hospital and a laboratory for diagnosis and treatment. Most small towns cannot supply these facilities; hence doctors tend to locate where such facilities are present. The result is that many towns that formerly had a physican no longer have one.

Availability of Physicians. The foregoing considerations lead to the question of the availability of physicians. There have been numerous attempts to measure the adequacy of supply of physicians. The measure most often used is the ratio of population per active physician within a designated area. The area most frequently used is the county, because the population of counties is readily available from United States census reports. It has been customary to regard 1,000 population per physician as a reasonable ratio, and as a matter of fact the ratio computed on a statewide basis does come close to this figure for many states.[8] Some rural states, however, have ratios that exceed this number by several hundred. As the percentage of the rural population increases, the ratio tends to be higher. In Louisiana, for example, a calculation for 1950 shows some parishes with 2,000 to 3,000 or more persons per doctor,[9] and in Missouri sixteen counties had an average of 2,175 persons per physician and twenty-six counties an average of 3,360 persons per doctor.[10] Again, in Mississippi, where a person-physician ratio of 1,512 is obtained, sixty-four of the eighty-two counties contained larger proportions of the state's population than of its physicians and consequently had person-physician ratios that were higher than the ratio for the state as a whole.[11]

These examples of uneven distribution of doctors are not intended to convey the idea that a redistribution of doctors should be made so that the person-physician ratio would be fairly even in all parts of a state. Studies have shown that, where medical service is available, people follow approximately the same pattern for health services as for trade.[12] Moreover, one county might have a high ratio of people per doctor because a large city in another county is located near its border and provides medical services for the population of both counties.

The problem of distribution raises the question of the distance people will go, or can go, for the services of a doctor. The research findings per-

[8] Frederick D. Mott and Milton Y. Roemer, *Rural Health and Medical Care,* New York: McGraw-Hill Book Company, Inc., 1948, pp. 158–160.

[9] Paul H. Price, *The Availability of Medical Personnel in Rural Louisiana,* Louisiana AES Bulletin 459, June, 1951.

[10] John H. Land, *What Has Happened to the Country Doctor?* Missouri AES Bulletin 594, 1953.

[11] Loftin and Galloway, *op. cit.,* p. 7.

[12] Linwood Hodgdon, "An Operational Method for Measuring Medical Needs and Resources in Rural Communities," unpublished doctoral thesis, Michigan State College. See also Frank G. Dixon, Bureau of Medical Economics, American Medical Association Bulletin 94B, 1954.

taining to this factor are not entirely consistent. In the Mississippi study previously referred to, it was observed that persons living greater distances from the several types of medical services and facilities were less likely to use them than persons living closer. Also, the data in the Michigan health survey showed that the population living eleven or more miles from a physician had more unmet medical needs than persons living less than eleven miles away. However, when the informants were asked why the person with unmet medical needs had not seen a doctor, the reason "Too far; distance too great" was mentioned in only 24 per cent of the cases. It was exceeded by "too expensive" (26 per cent of the cases). On the other hand, a Missouri study found that the average distance was eight miles to a physician and that distance to a physician appeared not to make any difference in the use of physicians.[13] It is concluded from data in another Missouri study, however, that as the distance farm families resided from a physician increases, the incidence of bed illnesses at home increases. Of course, other factors besides distance were also involved.[14]

It is probable that distance becomes a definite consideration in the use of medical service whenever the family must travel to a place other than the customary trade center in order to see a doctor. If the doctor is at the trade center to which the family customarily goes, travel to seek medical service appears to be regarded as a routine matter. With the use of the automobile it is not difficult for a family to go fifteen or twenty miles to see a doctor or to obtain other goods and services. Small towns of less than 1,000 population which formerly had a doctor may not even need one now if the people can conveniently go elsewhere to see a doctor. If they cannot, then it is clear that a doctor is needed.

Thus it becomes evident that the important question is, How well are communities—that is, communities in the ecological sense—provided with doctors? One study from this point of view has been made recently in Michigan. A total of 297 communities (outside Wayne County, in which Detroit is located) were delineated.[15] The results of the research are shown in Table 20. These figures clearly demonstrate that there is an uneven distribution of doctors among communities in Michigan, and it seems likely, judging by the person-physician ratio based on county population data, that similar variations exist in other states. Some communities, then, are well provided with physicians, whereas others are not.

---

[13] Harold F. Kaufman and Warren H. Morse, *Illness in Missouri*, Missouri AES Bulletin 391, 1945.

[14] Paul J. Jehlik and Robert L. McNamara, "The Relation of Distance to the Differential Use of Certain Health Personnel and Facilities to the Extent of Bed Illness," *Rural Sociology*, 17:264, 1952.

[15] John F. Thaden, *Distribution of Doctors of Medicine and Osteopaths in Michigan Communities*, Michigan AES Special Bulletin 370, 1951.

Availability of Dental Services. Dentists and dental service have not received so much attention in research as physicians, although it is generally recognized that dental service is essential to the maintenance of good health. People have been advised to see a dentist twice a year; however, it is a well-known fact that this is a standard which a very small percentage of people attain. Many individuals do not seek dental services at all unless they have a toothache. In the Michigan Health Survey it was found that 80 per cent of the rural population had not visited a dentist in the six months preceding the interview. The corresponding percentage of the urban population was 73.[16] Likewise, in the Mississippi survey it was found that only 20 per cent of the population in the survey used the services of a dentist during the survey year.[17] The location of dentists tends to be like that of doctors, the persons-per-dentist ratio in-

Table 20. Number of Communities in Each of Seven Persons-per-physician Categories, Michigan, 1951

Persons per medical doctor	Number of communities
No doctor	15
Less than 1,000	16
1,000 to 1,500	65
1,500 to 2,000	67
2,000 to 2,500	51
2,500 to 3,000	34
3,000 or more	49

SOURCE: John F. Thaden, *Distribution of Doctors of Medicine and Osteopaths in Michigan Communities,* Michigan AES Special Bulletin 370, 1951.

creasing as the population of a county or community decreases. Assuming that a dentist is as near the rural family as the store where dresses, suits, and coats are purchased, it seems clear that the problem of increasing the use of dental service is a matter of education and the cultivation of favorable attitudes. This was brought out in two recent Louisiana studies.[18]

Availability of Hospital Services. The hospital has become an essential element in health care in rural as well as in urban areas. It is needed for both diagnostic services and for the treatment of illness. Distance from

[16] Hoffer et al., *op. cit.,* p. 27.
[17] Loftin and Galloway, *op. cit.,* p. 20.
[18] Alvin L. Bertrand and Homer L. Hitt, *Parental Attitudes and Dental Care for Children in Selected Rural Areas of Louisiana,* Baton Rouge: Louisiana AES in cooperation with Louisiana State Health Department, 1948; and Paul H. Price, *Modifying Dental Attitudes Through Community Programs,* Baton Rouge: Louisiana AES in cooperation with Louisiana State Department of Health, 1952.

a hospital is usually not a major problem for urban dwellers, as most hospitals are in cities. Rural people are not so fortunate in this respect; hence ways of making hospital services available to them need to be devised. One response to this need was the passage by Congress of the Hill-Burton Act, which provides financial assistance for qualified communities needing hospital facilities.

Certain practical matters concerning cost and type of service must be considered in providing hospital services. Hospitals are very expensive to build and to operate; hence it is obvious that not every rural community can finance the construction of a hospital or provide funds for its operation. There must be a balance between distance, size of hospital, and population per hospital bed.

The provision of hospital service is further complicated by the fact that it is not feasible for all hospitals to offer all types of services. Four types are designated in connection with the 1955 Michigan State Hospital Survey and Construction Act. They are (1) teaching-center hospitals, (2) regional-center hospitals, (3) area-center hospitals, and (4) community hospitals. The variety and types of service increase from the community hospital to the teaching center. The community hospital would offer the following types of service: internal medicine; obstetrics; eye, ear, nose, and throat medicine; dentistry; selective surgery; laboratory; X ray; and bacteriology. It might also provide administrative public-health offices. These four types of hospitals bear a certain relationship to one another; thus, considered together, they constitute a system of hospital services for rural people beginning at the community hospital nearest the farm home and extending to the largest and most specialized hospital, the teaching-center hospital. Figure 35, based on the system that exists in the state of Michigan, illustrates the pattern. The principle is the same in all parts of the United States.[19]

The smallest unit in the system is the community hospital, which in many instances is not a community hospital in the ecological sense but a county hospital. As a matter of fact, the most popular hospital jurisdictional unit for 218 Hill-Burton hospital projects which were included in a recent research study was the county.[20]

The fact that rural people do use hospitals is fairly well demonstrated by research. In the Mississippi study quoted earlier, it was found, for

[19] See, for example: Homer L. Hitt and Alvin L. Bertrand, *The Social Aspects of Hospital Planning*, Baton Rouge: Louisiana AES in cooperation with the Health and Hospital Division, Office of the Governor, 1947; and Elsie S. Manny and Charles E. Rogers, *Hospitals for Rural People*, Washington: Farmers Bulletin 2110, USDA, 1957.

[20] Paul A. Miller, *Community Health Action*, East Lansing: Michigan State College Press, 1953, p. 156.

Figure 35. The Michigan plan for hospital areas, showing the proposed locations of the different types of hospitals designated in connection with the Hospital Survey and Construction Act. (From *Michigan State Hospital Plan,* rev. 1955, State of Michigan, Office of Hospital Survey and Construction.)

example, that one fourth of the families surveyed, involving 6 per cent of the individuals, used general hospitals during the survey year. The Michigan study showed that 4 per cent of the rural population used hospital service in a six-month period. Similarly, a survey in New York showed that 8 per cent of the individuals involved utilized hospital services during the survey year.[21]

[21] Olaf F. Larson and Donald G. Hay, "Rural Health in New York," *Rural Sociology,* 16:228, 1951.

Availability of Public-health Services. The services of a public-health department are a valuable aid in the health care of the population. Their activities include such programs as: (1) preventive disease control, (2) health education, (3) sanitation, (4) examination of school children, (5) maternity and child care, and (6) examination of food handlers and others. In rural areas the unit of administration is the county or district.

Funds for such a service are provided cooperatively by the county, the state, and the U.S. Public Health Service. It has been estimated that at least one dollar per capita would be necessary to carry on a reasonably complete public-health program in a county. Some counties make no appropriation at all for this service, and others provide for a complete program. Since public-health activities emphasize prevention and prevention is more economical than treatment, the failure of counties to provide funds for this service is an important problem.

Reports from the studies that have been made indicate that rural people use the services offered by county public-health units. In the Mississippi survey 72 per cent of the families and 36 per cent of the individuals used one or more services of the county health department.[22] In Michigan, 25 per cent of the rural population gave an affirmative answer to the question "Have you (or any member of your family) been personally examined or advised by a public-health nurse or officer within the past year?" It seems probable, however, that the majority of the people do not understand very clearly the organization and purpose of their county public-health departments. When a sample of families in two Michigan communities was asked, "Would you say that you are acquainted with the work of your county (or district) health department?" 44 per cent of the informants answered "yes" in Pellston, a community located in a district that had had an active public-health department for several years. In the other community, Tecumseh, which is in a county where the health unit had been recently established, 26 per cent of the families in the survey sample made an affirmative reply.[23]

Cost as a Deterrent to Health Care

When asked why they do not seek medical care when it is needed, many people reply that it is too expensive. What they actually mean is that in consideration of their income and the ways in which they are forced to spend their money or would like to spend it, the cost of health care is likely to be more than they feel they can pay. The value of the service to the patient or the expenditures which were made by the doctor

[22] Loftin, *op. cit.*, p. 19.
[23] Charles R. Hoffer and Clarence Jane, *Health Needs and Health Care in Two Selected Communities,* Michigan AES Special Bulletin 377, 1952.

or hospital to provide the service is quite a different matter. A cash expenditure for health care is usually an expense in addition to routine ones and hence is likely to seem especially high and burdensome, regardless of what it may have cost to provide it.

Expenditures for Health. Several surveys of rural families have included an estimate of their expenditure for health care. A survey of 306 rural families in Michigan showed that the average expenditure per family in 1946 was $99.21.[24] This amount was distributed as follows: doctor bills, $50.46; hospital beds, $28.48; dental bills, $20.29. A later Michigan study (1949) in two selected Michigan communities showed that the average expense for doctor's care, including fees for surgery, was $47.67 in a community lacking doctors in the immediate vicinity and $65.59 in a community well provided with doctors and hospital facilities. In Green County, North Carolina, the cost of a professional physician's care plus drugs was about $37.00 per family.[25] In two southern Pennsylvania communities, the average cost per family for medical, hospital, dental, and nursing services was $72.61.[26] The corresponding amount in two northern Pennsylvania communities was $125.00.[27]

These average expenditures may not seem unduly large, but it should be remembered that they are average expenses and that some families paid nothing at all, whereas others had to pay very large sums. Hence the figures do not constitute a norm or a standard. In the Michigan study of 306 families just mentioned, 24 per cent of the families spent nothing during the year for doctors' fees; 78 per cent had no hospital expenses, and 45 per cent had no dental bills. On the other hand, 25 families spent $100 to $200 for doctors' bills and 14 families paid over $200 for this service.

Prepayment Plans. The difficulty of paying for health care has led to the idea that some kind of prepayment plan is desirable. In fact, most people now believe that such a plan is a good idea. In the Michigan health survey a majority of the informants stated that they favored insurance to pay hospital and doctors' bills. In a survey of 595 representative rural families in the state of Washington, nearly two out of every three persons stated that they wanted comprehensive coverage in their medical-care program—all services, including home calls, office calls,

[24] Charles R. Hoffer, *Health and Health Services for Michigan Farm Families*, Michigan AES Special Bulletin 352, 1948.

[25] Selz C. Mayo and Kie Sebastian Fullerton, *Medical Care in Green County*, North Carolina AES Bulletin 363, 1948.

[26] W. G. Mather, *The Use of Health Services in Two Southern Pennsylvania Communities*, Pennsylvania AES Bulletin 504, 1948.

[27] Ruth M. Connor and William G. Mather, *The Use of Health Services in Two Northern Pennsylvania Communities*, Pennsylvania AES Bulletin 517, 1949.

hospital service, surgical service, nursing service, and dental service.[28] It appears, in fact, that no group in the United States has any major objection to prepayment plans. The only point of debate is how such plans can best be organized and supervised. Some people believe supervision of a prepayment plan for doctor and hospital bills is a necessary and practical function of government, like education or social security. Others maintain that supervision of prepayment plans by the government is unwise. It would lead, they claim, to bureaucracy and bureaucratic control, and it might become too expensive.

This is not the place to present a discussion of the arguments for and against government-sponsored prepayment plans. However, the advantages of prepayment plans are so great that people will probably demand them eventually. If non-government-sponsored agencies cannot or do not meet the demand, then it seems likely that the people will insist that government meet it.

At the present time, only a very small percentage of the rural population is participating in prepayment plans other than payments for surgery and hospitalization. Even for these services the percentage participating in prepayment plans is not large. A survey sponsored by the Health Information Foundation revealed that in a sample of 252 farmers, 35 per cent had some coverage.[29] "Some" in this connection means that at least one person in the family is to some extent covered by a hospital, surgical, medical, major-medical-expense, or dread-disease (or polio) policy. For hospital expenses the percentage of persons with some coverage was 38 for persons classified as rural-farm, 52 for rural-nonfarm, and 63 for urban. The research in Mississippi found that of the 545 farm families included in the survey, only 12.1 per cent, or 229, had one or more members covered by voluntary prepayment medical and hospital-insurance plans.[30] In the Michigan health survey, 46.1 per cent of the families living in the open country had at least one member partially or wholly insured for hospital bills. For surgical expenses the percentage was 41.6.[31] It thus seems clear that many rural families do not have the advantage of prepayment plans for health care. In view of the fact that the proportion believing such plans are a good idea is much larger than the percentage having them, it seems likely that prepayment plans for rural people will be extended and improved in the near future.

[28] R. W. Roskelly, *The Rural Citizen and Medical Care*, Washington AES Bulletin 495, 1947.
[29] Odin W. Anderson, "National Family Survey of Medical Costs and Voluntary Health Insurance," New York: Health Information Foundation, p. 18.
[30] Loftin and Galloway, *op. cit.*, p. 97.
[31] Hoffer et al., *op. cit.*, p. 55.

WELFARE AND SOCIAL SECURITY IN RURAL AREAS

The term *welfare* has a variety of meanings. In one sense welfare may be regarded as any activity or program that enhances the well-being of the people. It may be an educational program, a plan to prevent unemployment, or a law that foods must meet certain standards of quality. The term *welfare state* is used to refer to the government which, as the agency of the state, is actively engaged in promoting the welfare of the people.

A more restricted meaning of the term welfare will be adhered to in this discussion. In this restricted sense the term implies programs and activities designed to help individuals who are unable to provide themselves with a living at the level judged by the state to be minimum. Thus, destitute persons or families, old people, widows, orphans, handicapped persons, and delinquents qualify as welfare cases—persons who, in the judgment of the state, should be helped to make the best possible adjustment to life.

The Traditional Approach in Social Welfare

The traditional approach in social welfare was based on the assumption that the individual himself was mainly to blame for his plight. Exceptions were the handicapped, widows, and orphans, who were regarded as victims of unfortunate circumstance and who should be grateful for whatever charity they received. If these individuals could not stay in their own homes or in the homes of relatives or friends, they were sent to the county "poor house" or "poor farm." The "poor house" was an institution supported by county funds which tended to become a haven for a variety of human beings who had little hope of improving their situation. In many instances the "poor house" was overcrowded and badly managed, and far too frequently it served as a catchall for individuals who should have been cared for in other ways.

Gradually, through the application of scientific and humanitarian principles, changes were made in the administration and financing of welfare programs. Eventually it was recognized that keeping an elderly person in his own home is more desirable than having him live at the "poor house." Similarly, it is surely wiser to provide financial aid to a widow with children so she can maintain a home for them than to have the children cared for in a boarding home or in an orphanage. It is logical to believe that physically and mentally normal children should be placed in homes for adoption; those who require special care should be put in a state institution equipped to treat and care for them. Thus, during the decades immediately preceding passage of the Social Security Act in 1935, most states had developed plans for public assistance in such areas as aid to mothers, old-age assistance, and aid to the blind. In a majority of counties, county agencies were established to administer the fund, at least in some categories.[32]

The Depression as a Turning Point in Welfare Programs. The depression years of the early 1930s made evident the inadequacy of the existing legal and financial means for filling welfare needs, means devised at a time when the United States was predominantly rural and welfare problems were few, or, at any rate, when welfare expenses were comparatively low. In an industrial economy the traditional system was inadequate. Consequently, a series of emergency measures was enacted by Congress. The FERA, CWA, WPA, and other special Federal agencies and programs were designed to provide relief or work or a combination of work and relief for the unemployed.

Rural Rehabilitation Programs

The Rural Rehabilitation Corporation was one of the series of economic programs organized in the early thirties by the Federal government. Since then it has evolved through a series of legislative acts until at the present time its successor is the Farmers' Home Administration. The central purpose of this agency was and still is to provide credit for qualified farmers so that they may continue farming. However, a farmer is eligible for FHA assistance only if he is financially unable to obtain credit at a bank or some other commercial source. The credit received from FHA may be used to carry on farm operations, make improvements in the home, or start the purchase of a farm. If the farmer qualifies and the loan is made, the use of the credit is carefully supervised.

Actually, the FHA is not a welfare activity in the restricted meaning of that term but rather a special supervised credit program that helps to establish and to keep the farm family on the land, a goal that has been central in our national agricultural policies. The results of the FHA program have amply proved that it is a sound procedure. Payments on loans have been made on schedule, and losses have been very low. Even though the opportunities for industrial employment have been especially good since 1940, a great majority of the borrowers have stayed in farming. One intensive study of the effectiveness of the program over a period of years has demonstrated that the FHA borrowers achieved success in farming comparable to that which non-FHA farmers in the same community achieved and that they participated as much as nonbor-

[32] Campbell G. Murphy, *Community Organization Practice*, Boston: Houghton Mifflin Company, 1954, pp. 40–41.

rowers in community organizations. Leaders in the community or county had a high regard for the FHA borrowers or former borrowers.[33]

The Social Security Act

The Social Security Act, passed by Congress in 1935, may be considered as a landmark in welfare activities in both rural and urban districts. It represented the relinquishment of some of the concepts of laissez-faire philosophy and the acceptance of governmental responsibility for assisting the people in meeting certain needs. It provided a comprehensive program of welfare, involving the establishment of an old-age and survivors' insurance system and Federal-state programs for specific groups— older people in need, dependent children, and the needy blind. Later, in 1950, the act was amended and a fourth category, persons who are permanently and totally disabled because of physical or mental handicaps, were included. No distinction is made between urban and rural residences with reference to these services and benefits. Hence it is not possible to find statistical tabulations for the rural population only.

In some respects, the old-age and survivors' insurance system is the most far-reaching because most employed persons must participate through a payroll contribution amounting to $2\frac{1}{4}$ per cent of their income up to $4,200.00. Then, beginning at the age of sixty-five, the person receives monthly payment as long as he lives. His wife also may receive full benefits when she reaches the age of sixty-five, and she may receive payments at a reduced rate from age sixty-two to age sixty-five. However, if the insured worker dies, the widow can get return benefits at any age if the children are under eighteen years of age. Thus, as workers reach retirement age they will be assured of a minimum income, which, it is hoped, will be supplemented by pensions or in other ways. As this program expands, the need for direct relief will obviously be greatly reduced. Farmers and farm workers were not included in the Social Security Act when it was passed in 1935. However, by 1950 regularly employed farm workers were insured, and in 1954 the act was amended to include farm operators also.

A superficial examination of the income of farmers may lead to the conclusion that such protection is not greatly needed, but this conclusion is not justified. Tables 21 and 22 obviously give a much clearer idea of the income and financial resources of farmers and of the nonfarm self-employed in the rural population than do averages. It is evident from the data in these tables that many farmers will need some kind of assistance when they reach retirement age.

[33] Walter E. Boek, "An Examination of a Social Action Program with Ex Post Facto Methods as Exhibited in an Evaluation of the Farmers' Home Administration," unpublished doctoral dissertation, Michigan State College, 1953.

Table 21. Amount of Net Worth of Household Spending Units, by Occupation of Head of Unit, Early 1950.

Occupation of head of spending unit *	Percentage distribution of spending units by amount of net worth †						
	Total per cent	Nega-tive	Amount of net worth, in dollars				
			1–999	1,000–4,999	5,000–24,999	25,000 and over	Not ascer-tained
All spending units...	100	8	27	23	32	8	2
Nonfarm self-employed ‡	100	2	3	11	47	24	12
Farm operator.......	100	3	12	20	41	22	2
Owner operator......	100	0	2	18	43	35	1
Nonowner operator..	100	9	29	21	36	1	4

* The term "spending unit" is defined as all persons living in the same dwelling and related by blood, marriage, or adoption, who pool their income for their major items of expense.

† Difference between total selected reported assets and total reported liabilities.

‡ Excludes managerial employees and professional self-employed persons.

SOURCE: Alfred M. Skolnik, *Social Security Bulletin*, 15(5):8, May, 1952.

The manner in which the social security system operates for the farmer may be illustrated with a hypothetical case of Bill Brown, who was thirty-five years of age in 1957; his wife was thirty-three, and their three children were aged twelve, eight, and five. Bill's annual income is $3,600, or $300 per month, and his social security tax is $117 per year. By mid-1959, Bill Brown's family will have financial protection in the event of his death, and a monthly income would be paid the widow and the children as long as there are children under eighteen.[34] For three children under eighteen, the mother would receive $200 per month; for two, $197 per month; and for one, $150 per month.

If Bill Brown lives to be sixty-five and his net farm profit for the next thirty years averages $3,600 a year, he will have paid less than $5,500 into the social security system, taking into account increases in the tax

[34] *Michigan Farm Economics*, No. 142, November, 1954, Cooperative Extension Service, Michigan State College, East Lansing, Michigan.

Table 22. Amount of Income Saved or Dissaved by Household Spending Units, by Occupation of Head of Unit, 1950

Type of saver and amount saved	Percentage distribution of spending units, by occupation of head of unit, 1950		
	All spending units	Farm operators	Managerial and self-employed
Total per cent..........	100	100	100
Positive savers.........	61	62	72
Amount saved:			
$ 1–199..........	20	16	10
200–499.........	14	10	10
500–999..........	12	12	13
1,000 and over......	15	24	39
Zero savers............	7	6	2
Negative savers........	32	32	26
Amount dissaved:			
$ 1–99............	6	4	5
100–499...........	14	12	9
500 and over........	12	16	12

SOURCE: Alfred M. Skolnik, *Social Security Bulletin*, 15(5):7, May, 1952.

rate. In return, he can expect to receive a retirement benefit of $98.50 a month. Within two years his wife also will receive monthly checks for half that amount. Together they will receive a total of $147.80 a month.

At age sixty-five, Bill has a life expectancy of at least 12 years, and his wife will have a life expectancy of fifteen years when she reaches sixty-five. This means that Bill would receive $98.50 a month for two years; then for the next ten years, he and his wife would receive $147.80 a month. Mrs. Brown would receive a widow's pension of $73.90 for five years after Bill's death. Thus, during the seventeen-year period after Bill Brown reaches sixty-five, the old-age and survivors' insurance program would provide a total of $24,534 for his and his wife's later years. The value of social security can thus scarcely be questioned. Not only does it provide the certainty of income beyond the age of sixty-five for a farmer and his family, but it also provides him with a measure of security that makes it possible for him to plan farm expenditures and improvements with more confidence during his younger years.

The Administration of Welfare

The principal governmental unit for the organization of welfare activities in the rural or semirural areas of the United States is the county. This pattern has developed because the county is a reasonably convenient administrative area, and both custom and fortuitous circumstance favored it as an administrative unit. At one time the township was the political subdivision that provided poor relief, but in most parts of the United States this function has been allocated to the county, as has been the case in road-building and public-health activities.

The Social Security Act also utilized the county unit, for it required that county committees or bureaus be established to administer aid to persons qualifying under the Act, namely, the aged, dependent children, the blind, and the handicapped. Moreover, it is necessary that these funds be supervised by persons selected for their position on some kind of a merit principle, such as a civil-service examination. Thus the elements of an organized program of social welfare now exist in most parts of the United States.

Persons presenting behavior problems, chiefly juveniles, are handled by the probate court, which in rural and semirural areas acts in the capacity of a juvenile court. A probation officer will represent the court, but he may not have professional training. Moreover, clinics for diagnosis and treatment of children with deviant-behavior problems or emotional and mental illnesses do not exist in most rural and semirural counties. To obtain these services the child must be taken to a district clinic, usually sponsored by a city in cooperation with a state agency for health.

Nonpublic Welfare Agencies

Volunteer, or non-tax-supported, welfare agencies exist in many rural and semirural areas. An example is the American National Red Cross. A number of other organizations, especially in the field of health, are also active in rural areas. The American Society for the Control of Cancer, the National Infantile Paralysis Foundation, the National Tuberculosis Association, and the American Heart Association are representatives of this group. Rural people know about these and other similar organizations and generally approve and support them. Like social security programs, they are gradually bringing rural dwellers into relationship with other segments of society, and as a result they share with them in responsibilities and benefits.

At the local community level there are a number of organizations, such as churches, lodges, and luncheon clubs, which engage in charity work. These activities are traditional and spring from humanitarian motives that merit approval and commendation. They can be encouraged and expanded with great benefit to the people, for they supplement the social security programs and those carried on by state organizations.

Questions for Review and Discussion

1. List some important consequences of poor health to a society or nation.
2. How do rural areas compare with urban areas in terms of health? In terms of availability of medical care?
3. What procedure is used by research workers to determine unmet health needs?
4. Why is it hard to attract doctors, dentists, and nurses to rural areas? What solution would you offer for this problem?
5. Comment briefly on the trend toward increasing government responsibility for health and welfare.
6. Distinguish between rural and urban welfare problems.
7. What, in your opinion, will be the impact of the revised Social Security Act on rural life?

Selected References for Supplementary Reading

Hitt, Homer L., and Paul H. Price: *Health in Rural Louisiana at Mid-Century,* Louisiana AES Bulletin 492, 1954.

Hoffer, Charles R., Duane L. Gibson, Charles P. Loomis, Paul A. Miller, Edgar A. Schuler, and John F. Thaden: *Health Needs and Health Care in Michigan,* Michigan AES Special Bulletin 365, 1950.

Landis, Benson Y.: *Rural Welfare Services,* New York: Columbia University Press, 1949.

Lane, John H., Jr.: *What Has Happened to the Country Doctor?* Missouri AES Bulletin 594, 1953.

Loftin, Marion T., and Robert Galloway: *Uses of Medical Services by Rural People in Four Mississippi Counties,* Mississippi AES, Sociology and Rural Life Series, no. 5, 1954.

Miller, Paul A.: *Community Health Action,* East Lansing: The Michigan State College Press, 1953.

Mott, Frederick D., and Milton I. Roemer: *Rural Health and Medical Care,* New York: McGraw-Hill Book Company, Inc., 1948.

Sewell, William H., Charles E. Ramsey, and Louis J. Ducoff: *Farmer's Conceptions and Plans for Economic Security in Old Age,* Wisconsin AES Bulletin 182, 1953.

PART FIVE

Social Processes and Special-interest Groups in Rural Areas

It was pointed out in Chapter 2 that the social processes comprise the dynamic element of society. These processes have already been identified as special forms of interaction that occur with great regularity and uniformity. Part Five is devoted to a detailed discussion of the major social processes.

Chapter 20 deals with the processes of cooperation and opposition, with special emphasis on agricultural cooperatives as the prime example of cooperation in rural areas. The social processes of acculturation and assimilation are taken up in Chapter 21 and compared to the cultural process of acculturation.

The last chapter in Part Five, Chapter 22, is an attempt to provide new understanding of special-interest groups. Although these groups do not represent social processes, they involve a specific kind of social interaction and for this reason can logically be included in this part of the text.

In Part Five, the understanding of concepts and terms is emphasized rather than descriptive examples. Although this approach was dictated in part by considerations of space, it is nevertheless true that once the theory is mastered, there will be no difficulty in drawing numerous examples from rural society.

CHAPTER 20 *Cooperation and Opposition*
in Rural Society

If we were to observe people meeting together in their homes, at a Farm Bureau meeting, or in the local crossroads store, their behavior might appear infinitely varied, without pattern or consistency. More careful and prolonged observation, however, would reveal that the behavior of people in interaction tends to fall into regular patterns that can be classified as belonging to a relatively few basic types. In our everyday experience we have all recognized some of these patterns, and the terms for them are a part of our common language.[1] Cooperation and opposition (in the form of competition or conflict) are basic, familiar forms of these interaction patterns.

From our culture we have received certain beliefs and understandings of cooperation and opposition, as well as rather strong attitudes regarding their "goodness" or "badness," "appropriateness" or "inappropriateness." However, in spite of direct experience with these basic forms of behavior, the conceptions of them we have inherited from our folk wisdom contain serious misunderstandings. In spite of our traditional evaluations, cooperation in itself is neither good nor evil. It is only in relation to the situation in which it occurs, as appraised in the light of some set of subjective, culturally determined values or norms, that such an evaluative label can be attached to it. Similarly, competition and conflict cannot be adjudged good or bad in themselves.

Let us now proceed to a more detailed examination of these forms of social interaction as they are expressed among rural people.

---

[1] For classifications of these forms of behavior, see: R. E. Park and E. W. Burgess, *Introduction to the Science of Sociology,* Chicago: University of Chicago Press, 1921; E. E. Eubank, *The Concepts of Sociology,* Boston: D. C. Heath and Company, 1932; H. P. Fairchild, *Dictionary of Sociology,* New York: Philosophical Library, Inc., 1944; Lowry Nelson, *Rural Sociology,* 2d ed., New York: American Book Company, 1955; T. Lynn Smith, *The Sociology of Rural Life,* 3d ed., New York: Harper & Brothers, 1953.

COOPERATION AS A SOCIAL PROCESS

If a formal definition is necessary for such a common term, we might say that *cooperation* is any form of social interaction involving two or more persons or groups working together to accomplish a common end or ends.

Because of the nature of the world in which we live, the satisfaction of our wishes and interests is sometimes difficult. As a result of this, and of the self-centeredness of human beings, some have been led to believe that cooperation is contrary to "human nature." However, cooperation is not necessarily incompatible with self-interest. An important element often overlooked is that among the most important limiting factors in the situation of any individual are his own limitations as to time, energy, special knowledge, and other needs. This being so, the most effective method of overcoming these limitations is some form of cooperation. Thus a person can further the purposes of self-interest through cooperative as well as through competitive activities. Frequently, some combination of the two can be used at the same time as the solution to a specific problem. What one regards as appropriate in a given situation is largely a matter of cultural definition. As Margaret Mead has pointed out, some cultures place great stress upon competitive behavior, whereas others stress cooperative measures.[2] In no instance is one emphasized to the total exclusion of the other, however.

Competitive striving for "success" is a conspicuous aspect of our culture. This is particularly apparent in, but not confined to, the business and sports fields. On the other hand, in spite of our rather strong cultural bias in favor of competition, cooperative behavior is generally considered more appropriate than competition within family and neighborhood groups as well as within most religious and fraternal organizations. Considering the American farmer's tradition of individualism, it is perhaps surprising to what extent cooperative activities are commonplace in our rural life.

Types of Cooperation

Symbiosis. Ecologists have found symbiosis to be a common phenomenon in the natural world. Plants and animals of different species sometimes adjust to an unfriendly environment by developing mutually dependent and mutually advantageous arrangements in their life pattern. Certain species of ants, for example, offer protection and solicitous care to some types of plant lice. In return, these creatures excrete liquids that

---

[2] Margaret Mead (ed.), *Cooperation and Competition Among Primitive Peoples,* New York: McGraw-Hill Book Company, Inc., 1937, p. 460.

constitute an important part of, if not all, the food of the ants. The lichens that abound on rocks and tree trunks also provide an example of symbiosis. This widespread group of plants actually consists of an alga in intimate association with a fungus. The chlorophyll of the algal cells carries on photosynthesis, and the tissues of the fungus protect the delicate algal cells and collect and store water and minerals for their needs. Both the alga and the fungus are maintained by the profits of the partnership. Such symbiotic relations may be found among individuals of the same or widely different species.

Human beings, as a part of nature, are frequently involved in this type of mutual dependence, and on the social level, also, we find human behavior quite analogous to the symbiosis of nature. For example, the essentially unconscious development, over a period of time, of some system of division of labor may be seen in this light.[3]

Informal Cooperation. Informal cooperation is common within families, neighborhoods, and other groups that have close affiliative contacts among members. This type of cooperation is further up the scale from symbiosis in terms of the conscious, deliberative character of the type of behavior involved, but it is still quite spontaneous and noncontractual in nature. Farm neighbors have always found it advantageous to work together in this manner for their mutual benefit. Examples of informal types of cooperation are particularly prevalent in historical accounts of frontier life in this country. Barn raisings and husking bees are examples from early community life in this country of the forms that informal cooperation may take.

Even with mechanization, informal cooperation is still relatively common in many agricultural areas. In a recent study in Arkansas, it was found that almost three-fourths of the farmers interviewed had engaged in some form of such cooperation within the previous year.[4] Although we have evidences of "neighboring" (in the sense of mutual aid) still being practiced, there is little documentary evidence for comparison with earlier times. The nostalgic reminiscences of old-timers are apt to be exaggerated. There seems little doubt that neighboring is not what it used to be, however, and that informal cooperation between farm families has decreased considerably in recent years.

Formal Cooperation. Although, as was indicated above, rural areas still operate on a fairly informal basis in carrying out many of their

[3] See Adaptation No. 3, "Negro-Pygmy Relations" in Leonard Broom and Philip Selznick, *Sociology*, Evanston, Ill.: Row, Peterson & Company, 1955, pp. 36–39. This is from an account by Patrick Putnam in Carleton S. Coon, *A Reader in General Anthropology*.

[4] William S. Folkman, *Membership Relations in Farmers' Purchasing Cooperatives*, Arkansas AES Bulletin 556, 1955.

activities, formal and special-interest organizations are steadily increasing. A third type of cooperation is most prevalent in such situations. This type, which we might call *formal* cooperation, is of a deliberate, contractual nature. In contrast to other types, the reciprocal rights and obligations of the cooperators are more or less specifically spelled out. Beyond those obligations prescribed for the achievement of the explicit purposes of the organization, the members have no claim on one another. Participants in a situation involving formal cooperation need not even be acquainted with one another, although acquaintance may facilitate cooperation.

Farmers' cooperatives are apt to come to mind when we think of examples of this type of cooperation. They have become very common and have absorbed a significant portion of certain economic functions in most agricultural areas of this country. Because of the attention they have attracted, there is some tendency to think of "cooperation" only in terms of such organizations. The type of adaptive behavior displayed in farmers' cooperatives demonstrates the frequently close relationship of cooperative and competitive interaction. Through formal cooperative organizations, farmers have consciously agreed to work together in order to compete more successfully with others or control impersonal economic or natural forces. Despite their name, the cooperative aspect of these farmers' organizations is not their truly distinguishing characteristic. Cooperative interaction among the members for the purpose of improving their competitive position does play an important part in these enterprises, but probably no more important a part than it plays in the activities of many of their "noncooperative" competitors.[5] The characteristics that set them apart most distinctly are found in the somewhat nebulous ideology under which they operate. Nevertheless, since they occupy such a conspicuous place in the organizational life of rural communities, they are treated extensively in the discussion that follows.

Farmers' Cooperatives

The cooperative movement is largely rural in this country. It has mainly developed around the marketing, purchasing, and service functions of agricultural production. Consumers' cooperatives are less popular in urban areas in this country than in certain other countries. In Great Britain and Sweden, for example, cooperatives are an important urban phenomenon.

Taylor sees the development of cooperatives in this country as a part of a larger movement which he has called the "American farmers' move-

[5] C. P. Loomis and J. A. Beegle, *Rural Social Systems,* Englewood Cliffs, N.J.: Prentice-Hall, Inc., 1950, p. 641.

ment" [6] (see Chapter 23). Cooperative organizations represent a relatively nonviolent manifestation in a long series of attempted adjustments by farmers to what they have interpreted as recurrent economic and social maladjustments. In a still larger context, the cooperative movement in the United States is a part of a world-wide movement. The pattern represents one of a number of different attempted adjustments to problems arising from the industrial revolution. Although there has never been much concern within the movement for an explicit basic philosophy, it is apparent that certain ideals concerning human relationships (such as universality, democracy, liberty, fraternity, and unity, as well as self-help) were adopted from the rationalist and romantic philosophies current at the time the movement was taking form.

The Principles of Cooperative Organization. In the main, the functional structure of American cooperatives represents a limited number of variations on a set of principles developed by a small, humble group of weavers from the flannel mills of Rochdale, England, in 1844. This guide, which has been quite generally accepted by cooperatives around the world, makes these provisions:

1. Membership open to all
2. Democratic control—one member, one vote
3. Limited interest on share capital
4. Refunds to patrons in proportion to their patronage
5. Sell at the market price, for cash
6. Constant education

The two major assumptions underlying this set of principles are that a cooperative should operate for the benefit of its members as users, not as investors, and that the members as owner-users should control the organization.

Historical Background. The development of agricultural cooperatives in the United States has been separated by historians of the movement into rather distinct stages or periods.[7]

The first period has been called one of experimentation. Dairy cooperatives are reported to have been organized as early as 1810 in New York and Connecticut. From this time till about 1870, there were isolated attempts to organize enterprises for the cooperative production of dairy products and for the marketing of grains, fruits, and vegetables. A pattern of organization that would provide a stable, efficient basis of

[6] Carl C. Taylor, *The Farmers' Movement, 1620–1920*, New York: American Book Company, 1953, chap. 19.

[7] R. H. Ellsworth, *The Story of Farmers' Cooperatives*, Washington: Farmer Cooperative Service Educational Circular 1, rev. June, 1954. See also Henry H. Bakken and Marvin A. Schaars, *The Economics of Cooperative Marketing*, New York: McGraw-Hill Book Company, Inc., 1937, pp. 46–77.

operation was lacking in the culture, and in general these early ventures were short lived.

The second recognizable period occurred during the decade following 1870. The National Grange of the Order of Patrons of Husbandry was organized in 1867 for social and fraternal purposes (see Chapter 23). Agriculture was in a depressed condition as a result of the post-Civil War situation. The Grange began to concern itself more and more with these economic problems. The members were encouraged to purchase and market cooperatively. A delegation was sent to Europe to study cooperatives there firsthand.[8] As the country recovered from the depression of the 1870s, many of these cooperative activities were discontinued, and the Grange withdrew its support.

The next period was one of relative inactivity. During this period, extending from about 1880 to 1895, agriculture continued to be depressed. Few new organizations were formed, but some farmers continued their experiments in this new type of enterprise. They were slowly evolving techniques for operating their own facilities.

From 1895 to 1915, there was a period of gradual expansion. Agricultural cooperation began gaining national recognition and the support of political and educational leaders. The Country Life Commission, appointed by President Theodore Roosevelt in 1908, started a train of events that greatly stimulated the development of agricultural cooperatives. The Farmers' Union and the American Society of Equity, both organized around the turn of the century, were concerned with promoting cooperatives. In 1913, President Woodrow Wilson appointed a commission to study agricultural cooperation in Europe and report on its findings.[9]

During this period, local cooperatives first began to join together into federations. In 1914 the Clayton Act, which was a forerunner of the Capper-Volstead Act, was passed. This act strengthened the legal status of farmers' cooperatives.

The years 1915–1920 marked a short period of very rapid expansion influenced by the war and high agricultural prices. The American Farm Bureau Federation, which was to become important during the next decade in encouraging agricultural cooperatives, was developing an interest in this method of meeting marketing problems.

The next decade saw a decided change in emphasis. Up to this time local associations were the predominating type of organization. But along with a disastrous fall in farm prices came a popular proposal for large-

[8] Charles M. Gardner, *The Grange—Friend of the Farmer,* Washington: The National Grange, 1949, p. 57.
[9] *Report of the Inquiry on Cooperative Enterprise in Europe,* Washington: U.S. Government Printing Office, 1937.

scale associations created to handle the entire output of specified crops and thus provide monopoly control. This idea caught on quickly, and there was a rapid expansion in membership for a few years. The "iron-clad" contracts used to ensure that the farmers delivered their crops to the cooperative proved unenforceable in the face of widespread defection from the organizations, and the plan for monopoly control collapsed.

More lasting developments also took place during this period. Such currently successful organizations as the Minnesota Cooperative Creameries Association (now the Land O'Lakes Creameries, Inc.) and the GLF (Grange League Federation) were begun at this time. Cooperatives continued to extend their services more and more toward the terminal markets. The National Cooperative Council and the American Institute of Cooperation were formed during the 1920s, and the Capper-Volstead Act of 1922 was an important governmental contribution to the legal side of cooperative marketing. As a result of the Sherman Antitrust Act, cooperatives had been placed in a precarious position, but the 1922 act remedied the situation by definitely authorizing the association of agricultural producers and permitting them to engage in interstate commerce. Four years later, Congress provided for a Division of Cooperative Marketing in the United States Department of Agriculture.

The Federal Farm Board was set up in the summer of 1929 under the authority of the Agricultural Marketing Act. Among other things, a half-billion-dollar revolving fund was authorized to assist cooperatives.

In 1933 the Farm Credit Administration was formed, and the lending features of the Federal Farm Board were taken over by this organization. In addition to other farm credit functions, it provided for banks for cooperatives which extend credit to farmers' marketing and purchasing associations.

The period since 1933 has been characterized as a period of adjustment. The interest in monopoly control has quite disappeared. There has been a shift from independent local enterprises to large-scale consolidated businesses with federated or centralized organization. Purchasing cooperatives have carried their activities further toward the ultimate source of supply, whereas, to a considerably lesser extent, marketing organizations have carried their functions toward the ultimate consumer.

Farmers' Cooperatives Today. In spite of very humble beginnings and numerous setbacks, cooperative business in the United States today has achieved a secure position. Cooperative enterprises have become widespread and complex. They have proved adaptable and efficient in providing various economic functions under a wide range of conditions. They continue to expand, but probably at no greater rate than business generally. There is a trend away from small, independent, local enterprises toward large, federated or centralized associations. This trend, along with the advantages of large-scale operation, has brought new problems of membership relations. Reciprocal communication between members and management in a large, complex organization is difficult to maintain but is still essential if the organization is to function cooperatively. Such a cooperative faces the danger of becoming impersonal and remote, its members viewing it as just another commercial firm.

The standing of cooperatives in the United States today is indicated by a recent survey made by the Farmer Cooperative Service of the U.S. Department of Agriculture.[10] This survey shows that the total membership in marketing, farm supply, and related service cooperatives reached a new high of almost 7.6 million in 1954 and 1955. The present system of reporting does not permit adjustment for duplication, but it is estimated that this figure represents some 3 million different farmers who are members of at least one farm cooperative. During the 1930s, membership fluctuated somewhat, with no observable trend up or down; since that time there has been a constant growth in membership (Fig. 36).

The value of farm products marketed and farm supplies handled by cooperatives increased greatly in the period following the Second World War. The gross dollar volume for 1953–1954 totaled $12.5 billion. After duplication for business cooperatives was eliminated, the total net business amounted to $9.7 billion.[11]

Figure 37 indicates the proportion of all farm production that is marketed through cooperatives in the various states. It should be pointed out that the net marketing business of farmer cooperatives is not entirely comparable with cash receipts from farm marketings, inasmuch as the cooperative figures on net business include, in addition to farm values, such things as the value of containers, processing costs, and some transportation expense incurred at the local level. These are all components of the f.o.b. plant or packing-house value. This does not, of course, affect significantly the picture of the relative importance of cooperative marketing in the different parts of the country. For a fuller understanding of the total role of farmers' cooperatives it should also be observed that these organizations may perform a number of the many services required in the marketing of farm products. Cooperative marketing varies greatly from region to region. In general, the states in the

[10] Anne L. Gessner, *Statistics of Farmer Cooperatives, 1954–1955*, Washington: Farmer Cooperative Service, U.S. Department of Agriculture, General Report 31, 1957.
[11] *Ibid.*, p. 16.

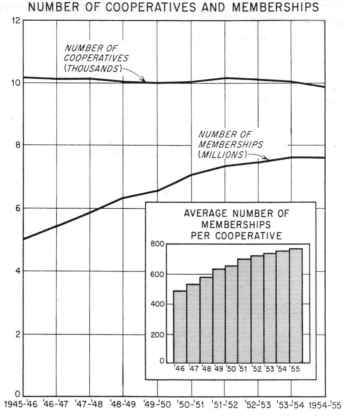

Figure 36. Membership in farmer cooperatives, 1945–1946 to 1954–1955. (From *Statistics of Farmer Cooperatives, 1954–1955,* Washington: Farmer Cooperative Service, U.S. Department of Agriculture, General Report No. 31, 1955.)

North Central region, which grow such a large part of our farm production, market a high proportion of these products cooperatively. On the other hand, most of the Southern states market only a small proportion of their products cooperatively. Changes are taking place, however. The Southern areas have increased their cooperative activity in recent years, and the West North Central area has lost in relative importance.

Supply-purchasing associations also play an important part in the current cooperative picture. Forty years ago, purchasing constituted less than 2 per cent of the total cooperative business. Today it represents one-fifth of the total.[12]

[12] Ellsworth, *op. cit.,* p. 27.

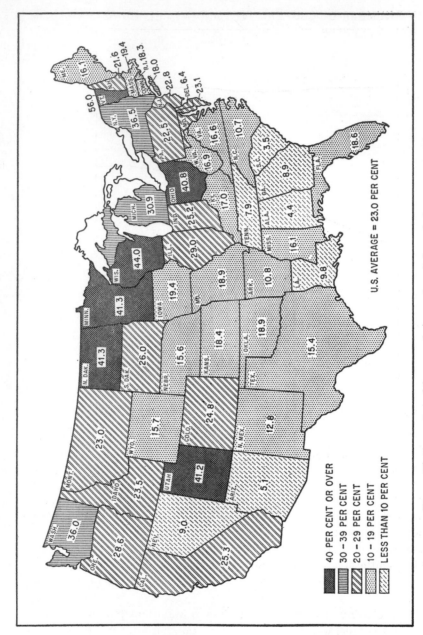

Figure 37. Proportion of farm products marketed through farm cooperatives, 1952–1953. (Data from the Farmer Cooperative Service, U.S. Department of Agriculture.)

U.S. AVERAGE = 23.0 PER CENT

■ 40 PER CENT OR OVER
▤ 30 – 39 PER CENT
▨ 20 – 29 PER CENT
▦ 10 – 19 PER CENT
▧ LESS THAN 10 PER CENT

It is somewhat more difficult to assess the importance of some of the other types of cooperatives. Their contributions cannot be readily converted into monetary values. It can be seen from Table 23, however,

Table 23. Major Types, Number, and Membership of Farmer Cooperatives in the United States

Type	Year of data	Associations	Estimated membership or participants
Marketing and farm supply:			
Marketing................	1954–1955	6,316	4,212,890
Farm supply..............	1954–1955	3,344	3,322,360
Miscellaneous services.......	1954–1955	227	67,880
Services:			
National farm loan associations..................	1957	1,064	362,582
Production credit associations	1957	498	477,063
Banks for cooperatives......	1957	13	3,157,425
Rural Federal credit unions..	1956	125	40,000
Rural electric cooperatives...	1957	905	4,109,636
Rural health cooperatives....	1956	17	179,694
Farmers' mutual fire insurance companies..............	1955	1,700	3,000,000
Production:			
Mutual irrigation companies.	1950	9,374	137,880
Dairy-herd improvement associations................	1957	1,700	41,638
Dairy-cattle artificial-breeding associations..............	1957	56	480,000

SOURCE: Anne L. Gessner, *Statistics of Farmer Cooperatives, 1954–1955*, Washington: Farmer Cooperative Service, U.S. Department of Agriculture, General Report 31, 1957, p. 73.

that in terms of numbers of organizations and members involved, such associations as mutual irrigation companies, artificial-breeding associations, credit organizations of various types, mutual fire insurance companies, and rural electric cooperatives do constitute a significant part of our cooperative activity.[13]

13 See: William S. Folkman, *Implications for American Cooperatives from Danish Membership Experience*, Ithaca, N.Y.: Cornell University, Department of Rural Sociology Mimeographed Bulletin 41, 1953, for an account of how important a part cooperatives can play in rural social life.

OPPOSITION AS A SOCIAL PROCESS

Because of our cultural predilection, we are apt to be more conscious of the oppositional forms of social interaction in our society than of those that are cooperative in nature. We have mentioned earlier the prominent place we have accorded to competitive strivings for success in our business-oriented society. The conspicuous nature of conflict, whether among toddlers in the sandpile or among world powers on the international level, draws considerable attention to it.

It is in the nature of the world in which we live that the interests of one group are often inconsistent with those of another. For example, two farmers' organizations may seek to recruit the same people as members. Industrial organizations find communities bidding against one another for a new plant to be located in their area. In every four-year period the Democratic and Republican parties expend vast amounts of time, energy, and money in a struggle for public offices.

The multiplication of many types of special-purpose groups has been one of the distinguishing characteristics of our contemporary urban society, and it is rapidly becoming characteristic of our rural society as well. This proliferation of diverse associations pursuing their own ends is accompanied by an increased competition for the limited funds, energy, time, and attention of the members of the society. *Opposition* is mutually opposed effort to obtain the same scarce commodity or reach an objective that can be reached by only a limited number of persons. The Darwinian theory of the "struggle for existence" and the related "survival of the fittest" attributes the evolution of the innumerable forms of life on our planet to this oppositional interaction. From the lowest form to the highest, they strive for their place in the sun (literally and figuratively), for the satisfaction of their fundamental drives, wants, and needs in a universe in which the means for satisfaction are generally scarce. Much of this striving is oppositional in nature, but as we have seen, mutually dependent and mutually advantageous arrangements are not uncommon in the plant and animal worlds.

In rural society, agricultural land is the focal point of much oppositional interaction. In southern Italy, the Luzon Valley of the Philippines, Egypt, India, China, and many other areas of the world, tensions that developed over the control of limited land resources have brought about or are threatening to bring about radical and even violent attempts at readjustment. Even in this country, where through much of its history land has been comparatively abundant, we have also had competition and at times conflict over this basic resource.

In more arid sections of our country, the scarcity of water has been the factor responsible for much of this type of behavior. In almost every community in the irrigated areas of the West there have been incidents in which one farmer has bloodily contested another's control of this resource.

Types of Opposition

Although differences in types of behavior are readily apparent, the types tend to merge imperceptibly into one another, and it is difficult to determine where one form begins and another ends. For analytic purposes, however, it is necessary to attempt some sort of classification. Most authorities recognize two general types of oppositional behavior—*competition* and *conflict*. A third type, *rivalry*, intermediate between the other two, might also be distinguished.

Competition. Of the forms of oppositional interaction, competition tends to be the more continuous in its duration. In contrast to the others, it is also characterized by the impersonal or even unconscious nature of the behavior involved. In competition, the goal is the thing; the other competitors for the goal are secondary. In rural society, this form of opposition is perhaps most apparent in economic activities. However, the seeming omnipresence of competition may be as much due to our particular cultural orientation as it is to an actual differential incidence of competitive behavior in various segments of our social life. Our society stresses the economic function, and we are taught to expect competition in this area as a "normal" concomitant of it. Perhaps we are, therefore, more apt to look for, and consequently find, competitive behavior in the business world than in intrafamily relations, for example.

A cotton farmer is in competition with all other cotton farmers in the marketing of his products. Together with all these farmers he is also competing with other producers of natural or synthetic fibers. At the same time, all these farmers and manufacturers are in competition with the producers of such things as television sets and refrigerators for a part of the consuming family's budget. In each instance the farmer, as an individual or as a member of a unit, is seeking to gain what others at the same time are endeavoring to gain. The nature of the situation prevents them from achieving this goal in equal amounts; the success of one individual or unit reduces by that amount the success of the others. However, even while engaged in this activity, this competing farmer is apt to be only vaguely, if at all, aware of his competitors as competitors.

In our society, the virtue of competition is highly extolled. It is especially regarded as the basis of our economic life and an essential aspect of the "American way." To one who has more than a superficial understanding of the economic sphere, it is readily apparent that the real pattern departs very radically from this ideal. Despite the often-expressed cliché to the effect that "competition is the lifeblood of trade," we have many extra- as well as intragovernmental restrictions on the free play of competition in our society. "Gentlemen's agreements" and other techniques of avoiding competition are frequently used. Competition in a free market has been partly, if not largely, replaced by a highly tangible web of financial and organizational controls.[14] Each society formulates and enforces more or less recognized rules for competition. Those for one segment of the society, such as the economy, may sometimes be at variance with those for other segments, but in no society is perfect competition found. Although competitive behavior in our society is most often expected as a part of our economic activities, it is by no means confined to them. Within families we have siblings—and parents as well—competing for response and recognition from the other members of the family. The same may also be said for the interaction involved in religious, recreational, and other types of activities.

Rivalry. As awareness of being in competition with others for the same goal increases, the original goal may lose some of its importance and the defeating of the rivals may become the primary goal. Thus rivalry might be seen as personalized competition, but it has enough distinctive characteristics to be recognized as a separate form of oppositional interaction.

As contrasted to competition, rivalrous interaction is personal and conscious. Its expression tends to be more intermittent than competition, which is by nature more or less continuous. Like competition, it may take place between individuals, groups, or individuals and groups. It may be organized or unorganized. Rivalry, perhaps as much as competition, is subject to rules designed to prevent, or at least lessen, the possibilities of the activity deteriorating into conflict. These rules may consist of laws enforceable by the courts or of mores and codes of conduct (rules of the game) with social or group sanction behind them.

Young boys at summer camp may engage in very intense rivalry over a shiny harness brooch adorned with a hank of red horse hair. This may be regarded as childish or irrational behavior by their elders, but when these same boys are playing a team from the neighboring community for the school-district basketball championship, these same staid adults may develop a very high state of emotional involvement.

The besting of the rival is the objective of rivalrous behavior. Status or prestige are the rewards to the successful, although sustenance needs are also at times involved.

[14] See: "Imperfect Competition," in Robin M. Williams, Jr., *American Society*, New York: Alfred A. Knopf, Inc., 1951, pp. 160–163.

It is obvious that rivalry quite frequently has an element of fun or "sport" about it. Because of this, it often adds spice to rural life. Farmers strive to be the first to get their crops planted in the spring, to have the best stand of corn, or the highest yield per acre, or whatever is defined by the group as being a worthwhile adult equivalent of the boys' shiny harness ornament. The competition between rural trade centers frequently develops into intense rivalry in which all phases of community life may be involved, the sports contest referred to earlier being only one among many manifestations of it.

Is rivalry "good" or "bad"? As we have seen, rivalry may have a rather wholesome effect in lightening what would otherwise be a monotonous round of existence in the rural community. It should also be recognized, however, that many intense forms of rivalry require an inordinate expenditure of time and energy in comparison to the resulting amount of collective or individual social good. How many farms are overcapitalized because machinery was bought for the purpose of keeping up with Farmer Jones rather than because it could be efficiently utilized in the farming enterprise? Physical and mental health as well as economic well-being are also sometimes affected by intense rivalries. In terms of other values held by the society, it is apparent that a more satisfactory balance would be attained if some of the less socially beneficial forms of rivalry were less emphasized.

Conflict. The competitive or rivalrous interaction we have been examining takes place within quite well-defined and recognized channels. When these channels, or accepted "rules" for behavior, are ignored or evaded, conflict occurs. In addition to the relative absence of established regulations, conflict, like rivalry, is also characterized by its intermittent nature. Even more than in the case of rivalry, the goal in conflict becomes the impeding, thwarting, or destruction of another. To accomplish this end, the opponent must be effectively eliminated, if necessary by annihilation. Physical violence, however, is not necessarily characteristic of this form of opposition. Some of the most important present-day conflicts are not fought on the level of overt violence. We have seen ample evidence of this in our recent exposure to psychological or "cold" warfare with its propaganda, economic reprisals, espionage, fifth columns, and other manifestations of nonviolent conflict. On the other hand, the rivalrous behavior of contact sports such as football, boxing, and hockey permits intense physical struggle which only occasionally gets "out of hand" and shifts from rivalry to conflict.

It should be emphasized again that there is not a sharp distinction between the various types of opposition. There are usually elements of competition and rivalry in any example of conflict we might select from actual social behavior. And such examples may even demonstrate some form of cooperative behavior. Even war, which one might regard as the ultimate in conflict, is not entirely unregulated. Certain conventions are more or less subscribed to by the participants. One may recall the great wave of moral indignation that arose in this country during the Second World War and again during the Korean struggle because the enemy did not adhere to some of the regulations we felt should apply in combat. Even though this was war, it was felt that the enemy should fight "fairly." In spite of such instances of violation of the regulation of warfare, certain other conventions were followed by both sides because of fear of retaliation if not for moral or ethical reasons.

Social conflict, like the other forms of interaction, finds expression in practically all avenues of social life. In rural areas, however, some aspects have been more important than others. Taylor points out that there have been few decades within the past 300 years in which some American farmers have not been moved to protest vigorously, and sometimes violently, against economic and social conditions affecting their lives.[15] Conflicts over the control of land (and in some areas, water) have been persistent and widespread.[16] Our mythology of the Old West as it has been preserved—or, more accurately, developed—in the Western film and novel abounds in conflict situations. There are depicted (in highly stylized form, to be sure) the perpetual conflict of the ranchers versus the homesteaders or squatters, the cowboys versus the Indians, the cattlemen versus the sheepmen, and the "good guys" versus the "bad guys." These sagas are usually exaggerated parodies of our history; nevertheless, these periods were in actuality characterized by strife, and this representation influences the development of our attitudes regarding conflict today.

Although only vestiges of antagonism exist in most of our rural communities today, the opposition of town and farm people has been expressed by conflict at various times in the past. Real or imagined discriminatory treatment, school consolidation, taxation, and other problems have bred misunderstanding and hostility. With increased contacts resulting from improved transportation and communication, much of this misunderstanding and attendant antagonism has dissipated. However, all the difficulty between the two sides cannot be attributed to lack of understanding. In spite of a great deal of mutual interdependence, some of their interests are not complementary, and we may again see strife develop between town and country.

Relations between races in this country have resulted in conflict, especially in the South, although, as Smith points out, since the period

---

[15] Taylor, *op. cit.*
[16] See Chapter 12 of the present work. See also Howard Kester, *Revolt Among the Share-croppers,* New York: Crown Publishers, Inc., 1936.

of reconstruction they have been stabilized by a castelike form of organization.[17] In rural areas particularly, this has kept overt conflict to a low level. Race riots have been essentially an urban phenomenon. However, the recent Supreme Court decision concerning racial integration in public schools has disturbed this equilibrium, and adjustments to the decision have already precipitated a number of conflicts. Continued conflict might well be expected for some time before a new level of adjustment is firmly established.

Questions for Review and Discussion

1. Why are cooperation and opposition called social processes?
2. Define cooperation and differentiate between the various types of cooperation.
3. List and explain the Rochdale principles of cooperative organization.
4. In what regions of the United States are farmers' cooperatives concentrated?
5. Why is it said that conflict is a universal phenomenon?
6. Differentiate between competition, conflict, and rivalry.
7. List some examples of conflict and competition which are typical of rural areas.

Selected References for Supplementary Reading

Bakken, Henry H., and Marvin A. Schaars: *The Economics of Cooperative Marketing*, New York: McGraw-Hill Book Company, Inc., 1937, pp. 46–77.

Beal, George M.: *The Roots of Participation in Farmer Cooperatives*, Ames, Iowa: The College Book Store, Iowa State College, 1954.

Casselman, Paul H.: *The Cooperative Movement and Some of Its Problems*, New York: Philosophical Library, Inc., 1952.

Deutsch, Morton: "A Theory of Cooperation and Competition," *Human Relations*, 2:129–132, 1949.

Ellsworth, R. H.: *The Story of Farmers' Cooperatives*, Washington: Farmer Cooperative Service Educational Circular 1, 1954.

Folkman, William S.: *Membership Relations in Farmers' Purchasing Cooperatives*, Arkansas AES Bulletin 556, 1955.

May, Mark A., and Leonard W. Doob: *Competition and Cooperation*, Social Science Research Council Bulletin 25, 1937.

[17] Smith, *op. cit.*, pp. 506–507.

CHAPTER 21 *Accommodation, Assimilation, and Acculturation*

In the preceding chapter the social processes of cooperation and opposition and the manifestations of these processes typically found in the rural environment were described. In this chapter, two additional social processes, accommodation and assimilation, and one cultural process, acculturation, will be described. Although specific reference to the rural setting is not always made, the student should have no difficulty in recognizing examples of these processes in rural society.

ACCOMMODATION

Battles among men may be waged with words, fists, lawsuits, guns, or atomic bombs and may range in seriousness from minor spats between lovers to bloody world wars. However, conflict, no matter what form it takes, cannot continue indefinitely. Lovers kiss and make up; a small boy yells "uncle" to acknowledge his successful opponent; belligerent nations seek an armistice. Conflict is a stop-and-go form of interaction, for men not only fight, they also make peace. This process of peacemaking, of halting or avoiding conflict, is called *accommodation* by the sociologist. Hornell Hart has defined accommodation in greater detail as follows: [1]

. . . any social process, whether conscious or unconscious, which consists in the alteration of functional relations between personalities and groups so as to avoid, reduce or eliminate conflict and to promote reciprocal adjustment, provided that the altered behavior pattern is transmitted by social learning rather than by biological heredity; and the social relationships which result from this process.

[1] Henry Pratt Fairchild (ed.), *Dictionary of Sociology*, New York: Philosophical Library, Inc., 1944, p. 2.

Several points in this fairly lengthy definition should be emphasized. Accommodation is, above all, reciprocal adjustment—adjustment between the two or more parties to conflict. In part, this consists of nothing more than the alteration of plans and activities by each participant in response to the cessation of conflict. Nations, for example, may immediately cancel some of their arms contracts. Ordinarily, however, adjustment by the parties to conflict includes a recasting of their roles in relation to their erstwhile opponents. As we shall see, such adjustments between opponents may assume a variety of forms and may be lasting or only momentary.

Accommodation as a Means of Preventing Conflict

Accommodation is typically described, as in the preceding paragraph, as the process of adjustment to the ending of an actual conflict. Our definition, however, specifies that accommodation consists of any "alteration of . . . relations . . . so as to avoid, reduce or eliminate conflict." Accommodation as a process applies as fully to adjustments that prevent or minimize conflict as to those that end existing conflicts. To be sure, the process is more evident and more easily described when it ends overt conflict, and for this reason, probably, most studies of accommodation emphasize such instances. It is, however, probable that the process more often prevents than ends conflict. Even when the parties to a potential conflict are such highly organized groups as nations, they often find it desirable to adjust the points at issue and thus avoid the disruptive aspects of war. Certainly, in intimate, personal relationships, accommodation to prevent conflict is far more common than accommodation following conflict. If the student will examine his own behavior with his family, friends, and roommates during the past week, he will probably recall far more instances in which he altered his relationships with others and thus avoided a threatened argument than he will actual rows in which he participated.

Accommodation instead of conflict is particularly likely when the potential conflict situation involves an individual, on the one hand, versus established authority or highly organized groups, on the other. In such situations the individual may well feel that he has little choice but to adjust to conditions, however unpleasant, in order to avoid a conflict in which he would be crushed. In the totalitarian dictatorships of modern times, for example, persons may accept and adjust to governmental abuses out of simple inability to engage in effective opposition; there are many potential rebellions for each rebellion that actually occurs. Less grim but more familiar instances may be found in our own society. The individual of limited financial resources often accepts and adjusts to what he considers abuse because of his inability to enter into expensive legal proceedings. The small farmer, for example, may accept treatment that he considers unjust from a bank, a buyer, a shipper, or some other agent with whom he necessarily comes in contact.

Similarly, accommodation instead of conflict often occurs when large numbers of unorganized or loosely organized individuals are confronted by more highly united groups. For example, farmers have avoided many potential rural-urban conflicts by accepting, grumblingly, actions initiated by the better organized municipal authorities or business groups of the town. This does not imply that farmers themselves are necessarily unorganized or unable to exert collective pressure. Through political action and especially through their own organizations, American farmers often vigorously oppose actions of other segments of our society; indeed, both the development of the major farm organizations and the periodic political movements of American farmers owe much of their support to the widespread desire of farmers for greater strength in potential conflict situations (see Chapter 23). Even so, many farm communities in our nation have little or no effective organization for fights in the collective interest, and a lack of such organization may leave an individual farmer little choice other than to accept even those actions of others which are detrimental to his welfare.

Accommodation as a Process and a Condition

Another significant part of our definition of accommodation extends the usage of the term to the social relationships that result from the process. In other words, the term accommodation refers both to a process of adjustment and to an attained state, or condition, of adjustment. Accommodation as a state of adjustment is analogous to a state of balance: although it may continue indefinitely as long as the elements involved remain undisturbed, any rearrangement of elements or addition of new ones is likely to upset it. It permits cooperation between former antagonists, at least to the extent that they are able to interact without renewal of conflict. Once achieved, a state of accommodation provides a pattern within which further relationships may safely take place. Thus, whereas the process of accommodation develops from actual or threatened conflict, the condition of accommodation becomes the safeguard against the renewal of conflict. The disruption of an established accommodative pattern thus creates an immediate possibility of struggle. However, new adjustments may occur, and there may be frequent alteration from process to condition to process, and so on. When the process of adjustment produces a state of balance, this state of balance then provides the basis from which new demands for adjustment must be made. Otherwise, accommodation could only be short-lived, for no specific adjustments could provide a pattern of interaction capable of governing all possible future situations.

To illustrate these points, let us assume that the members of a family have frequent disputes over the handling of the family's income. To reduce disharmony within the family circle, its members undertake the creation of a detailed, comprehensive budget. Such a task, if it is to succeed at all, involves setting aside funds for all the necessary group purposes and, more difficult, allocation of funds to the various members of the family for individual purposes. The task of drawing up such a budget exemplifies accommodation as a process. If our family succeeds in creating an inclusive budget, its acceptance exemplifies the attainment of accommodation as a state. As long as the members of the family adhere scrupulously to the adopted budget, conflict over money is avoided; but as soon as any member of the family yields to temptation and knowingly exceeds his allocated expenditures, a renewal of conflict threatens. A change in the elements that influenced the making of the budget—for example, a handsome raise in the father's salary—likewise alters the state of accommodation, posing the threat of renewed conflict unless accommodation as a process is revived in the form of altering the budget so that it allows more leeway for the economic desires of the members of the family.

Conscious and Unconscious Aspects of Accommodation. The process of accommodation may, as noted in Hart's definition, be either conscious or unconscious. Since overt conflict is highly conscious, the process of achieving a working relationship between antagonists also involves a high degree of awareness. However, particularly in interpersonal relationships, subtle behavioral alterations designed to reduce the likelihood of conflict may occur quite without conscious awareness of accommodation. Likewise, a condition or state of accommodation, once thoroughly established, may become so habitual that those abiding by it have little conscious realization of its accommodation function.

Forms of Accommodation

Domination. Ordinarily, each party to conflict desires to win the points of contention and to end the conflict by mastering the situation. Similarly, each party fears most that his opponent or opponents may gain the victory. The form of accommodation that results when one party to a conflict gains a decisive victory is *domination,* or, as it is often called in sociological literature, *superordination.* The loser is in a position of submission or subordination. Domination, with the acceptance by the loser of the victor's right to dominate, is a form of accommodation unlikely to last unless definite inequality of strength between the contestants continues to be very manifest.

Compromise. Often, however, a clear-cut victory seems unlikely, or at least seems to be worth less than the cost of attaining it, and the parties to conflict may seek some other means of ending the struggle. They may engage in compromise, which is that form of accommodation consisting of mutual concessions by the opponents. Compromise often involves a "splitting of the difference" between the participants: a strike may be settled when management offers a wage distinctly higher than that which has been paid though lower than that initially sought by the union. In somewhat more complex situations, compromise may involve accepting submission in some respects as the means of gaining domination in others: a nation may cede disputed territory to its enemy in return for preferential trade rights.

Complete domination by the victor implies that he has made no concessions whatever to the vanquished opponent. Similarly, compromise involves complete equality in the net balance of relationships between the contenders. In actual situations of accommodation, elements of both domination and compromise are present. The winner in a conflict usually will make some concessions to his antagonist, if for no other reason than to increase the latter's willingness to surrender. Similarly, examples of compromise so complete that neither party gains any net advantage are far less frequent than partial compromises. In evaluating the conflict situation, the parties involved are likely to weigh very carefully their possible gains against their threatened losses and thus will often settle for some particular blend between domination-submission and compromise. If the winning side asks too much, the resistance of the losing group will be strengthened, and they may fight on, less in hope of victory for themselves than in hope of gaining greater concessions.

Many factors, of course, determine the precise conditions that the participants to a conflict will accept. The issue may be more important to one party than the other. For example, the running argument over the Civil War which sometimes occurs between soldiers in training camps is, to most Northern boys, an idle diversion, something to "kid" about. Southerners sometimes react to this argument with a much deeper emotional involvement, a fact which at first amazes, then amuses, their Northern comrades. The degree of solidarity within conflicting groups is another important factor affecting the willingness of the groups to continue conflict; thus, nations at war attempt, through propaganda, to attack the morale of the enemy. Cultural values likewise affect the willingness of individuals and groups to accept compromise. Conceptions of honor that must be maintained, even at the risk of life, and feelings of intense shame at loss of face, to use the Oriental phrase, exemplify cultural values which, when literally followed, make compromise difficult and prompt the continuation of struggle until clear-cut domination by one party can be established. These and many other factors, including a lack of information or possession of actual misinformation concerning the strength and intentions of the enemy, enter into the willingness of the participants to compromise.

Toleration. Occasionally compromise may be out of the question. This is sometimes true when strong loyalties are involved; it is especially likely concerning matters of belief, as when points of disagreement cannot be minimized or conceded without undermining the integrity of entire systems of values by which the contending groups function. As an example, it is characteristically difficult to effect compromise between religious groups in conflict over theological interpretations. At the same time, it may be that no party to a conflict of loyalties or values can achieve domination; indeed, complete domination may not even be desired. In such situations another form of accommodation, toleration, often provides an adequate solution to conflict. Toleration consists of the adoption by actual or potential disputants of a "live-and-let-live" policy with regard to certain specified aspects of their relationships. It consists of an agreement to exclude from the interaction of the participants those areas of activity that are recognized as potentially productive of conflict, thus permitting peaceful interaction in other respects. Two farmers who have known each other for years may, for example, become active participants in rival farm organizations. Each may develop strong loyalties to his own organization and become convinced that it is the only proper spokesman for farmers. At the same time, they may wish to continue friendly interaction. They may, in effect, agree, "We get along O.K. except for one thing. You think the Grange is the answer to the farmers' needs; I think the Farmers' Union is better. Let's not argue the point any more; let's avoid this matter altogether in our conversations. That way we can continue to be friends."

Truce. Although toleration settles no point of contention, it does provide a means for permitting cooperation and peaceful interaction between the parties involved. In this sense it differs from another accommodative device, that of simply stopping conflict because of the exhaustion of the participants. This form of accommodation is often called truce. Truce in itself settles nothing, provides no course of action between contenders. It may, of course, create an opportunity for the contenders to get together and achieve a more adequate type of accommodation—perhaps compromise or toleration. In such instances, truce becomes merely a transition phase between conflict and effective accommodation. Otherwise, truce offers hope for little more than a temporary respite from conflict.

In summary, the process of accommodation covers any adjustment of their interaction made by the participants in an actual or threatened conflict. The process includes a variety of forms. The cooperation it produces may be harmonious or begrudged, and the duration of the accommodative condition which grows out of the process may be long-lasting or momentary.

ASSIMILATION

Another social process that leads individuals and groups into closer, more harmonious relationships is called assimilation, "the process whereby individuals or groups once dissimilar become similar, that is, become identified in their interests and outlook." [2] It is a process, then, of blending, of fusion, of disappearance of differences. Like accommodation, assimilation is both a process and a condition that results from the process; the process of assimilation is complete, and the condition achieved, when the differences that initially distinguished the individuals or groups from each other have vanished. Furthermore, it is common usage to refer to degrees of assimilation, as in the statement, "The assimilation of the Irish is advanced in this country; they are much closer to complete assimilation than are the Spanish-speaking groups of the Southwest."

Americanization as an Example of Assimilation

The example of assimilation which most readily occurs to Americans is that of the Americanization of immigrants. In this instance, the process is heavily one-sided—the immigrants must change in order to become like other Americans. This example signifies the individual nature of the process of assimilation, for even when fusion between groups occurs, the necessary adjustments are actually made by the individuals concerned. The process of Americanization also illustrates the continuous and long-lasting nature of assimilation in its most characteristic forms. A newcomer does not learn to be "American," nor is he accepted as such, in a day. On the contrary, he and his sons and daughters are in the process of becoming American for many years, perhaps for their entire lifetimes. To be sure, instances of assimilation can be cited which do not require long, continuous, and difficult adjustments. The fusion of two groups similar in nature—two civic clubs, for example—fits the terms of our definition. A blending of such groups may be a relatively easy task, quickly accomplished. Major sociological interest in assimilation, however, has been focused on the gradual growth toward each other of originally disparate individuals and groups.

[2] William F. Ogburn and Meyer F. Nimkoff, *Sociology*, 2d ed., Boston: Houghton Mifflin Company, 1950, p. 185.

Conscious and Unconscious Aspects of Assimilation. In part, Americanization consists of the learning by the immigrant of American customs, techniques, viewpoints, etc. This aspect of the social process of assimilation is related to the cultural process of acculturation, as we shall see later in this chapter, and consists of both conscious and unconscious behavior. The immigrant engages in a deliberate effort to learn our language and customs, but he also acquires "American" habits of thought and behavior as the indirect product of all his associations with Americans over the years.

Acceptance of the Newcomer. For assimilation as a process to be complete, and thus for assimilation as a condition to be attained, it is not only necessary for the immigrant to model himself after Americans; there must also be a willingness on the part of American society to accept the newcomer as an in-group member, as a "plain" rather than a "hyphenated" American. Otherwise, one finds two groups, no longer particularly distinguishable in culture or behavior, but nonetheless separate. The most emphatic example from our own society, of course, is that of the Negro in the rural South, who, although he has lived in the South since early colonial days and his African culture has long since vanished, has still not been accepted into full and equal participation in the life of the region. Lacking such acceptance, complete disappearance of group differences and complete identification of the interests of the two races—in short, assimilation as an achieved condition—is manifestly impossible.

Physical Differences and Group Identification. In popular usage, the word assimilation often refers to the blending of groups, or to the absorption of a smaller by a larger group, in a biological sense as a result of intermarriage. Most sociologists prefer to restrict the concept of assimilation and designate biological fusion of groups by the term *amalgamation*. It is true, however, that, when applied to populations of different racial, national, religious, or ethnic origins, the concepts of assimilation and amalgamation are closely related. In the instance of racial groups visibly distinguishable from one another, the process of assimilation might be completed and the condition of assimilation attained long before a sufficient number of generations had passed to permit a complete fusing of the different physical strains. The achievement of the social condition of assimilation, however, implies that any remaining physical differences are no longer significant as a basis of group identification, and if this is true, no barrier remains to prevent eventual amalgamation.

Although the American melting-pot tradition emphasizes assimilation as a goal, it has been only partially achieved. One reason lies in the importance of other, contradictory values in American life. As mentioned above, our racial attitudes have blocked the full assimilation of Negroes into American life. To a somewhat lesser degree, other nonwhite groups have also been denied complete assimilation. Even within the white race, natives of Southern and Eastern Europe have found slower acceptance in America than have persons of Northwestern European origin.

Other Factors Influencing Assimilation. A number of other factors influence the degree to which the process of assimilation approaches completeness. One of the most important of these is the size of the immigrant group in a community. The individual immigrant who locates in a community containing few others of his own background must perforce become acquainted rapidly with Americans and American ways. His quick acceptance of American customs and his acceptance by Americans as one of them are obviously far more likely in such a community than in a ghetto composed of his own countrymen in a large city. Even the latter setting is likely to bring the immigrant, or at least his children, into closer and more constant contact with the mainstream of American life than is the compact agricultural community composed of a single nationality. Especially in the Middle West one finds a number of such communities—of German, Czech, Dutch, Scandinavian, Polish, Finnish, or other origin—in which third-, fourth-, and even fifth-generation Americans follow, to some degree, European customs. When intense devotion to a distinctive religion is added to compact rural settlement there is strong resistance to assimilation.

It is important to note that resistance to assimilation may come from "foreign" groups as well as from the rest of the American population. Indeed, in many instances of partial assimilation, it is the reluctance of the nonassimilated group to lose its distinctiveness that perpetuates its separateness; the young man from an Old Order Amish community in Pennsylvania, for example, may, if he wishes, leave his community, drop its distinctive practices, and be fully accepted as just another American with a Germanic surname. To do so, however, would involve for him the loss of the faith and the way of life in which he was reared. The widespread American assumption that assimilation is possible only if the immigrant divests himself of everything that makes him different from other Americans is countered by a continuing devotion within ethnic and religious communities to precisely these differences. The sociological concept of the marginal man (an individual torn between two ways of life) is aptly demonstrated by persons who are drawn toward the greater American society of which they are a part but at the same time are tied by strong bonds to the traditions of their origin.

Cultural Pluralism in America. Many persons have questioned the wisdom of our expectation of complete conformity to a standard American type. They point out that, among the major nations of the world, ours has a unique diversity of origins. They maintain that this very diversity is a source of rich variety and stimulation in our national life. Adherents to this approach, known as cultural pluralism, consider ideal only that degree of assimilation necessary to achieve a unity based on strong common bonds (such as loyalty to nation, democratic ideals, and common participation in national educational, economic, and cultural opportunities); they acknowledge and respect the cultural differences of all groups that maintain such differences. Whether this goal is desirable or not, it seems certain that the powerful pressures toward assimilation which exist in American life will continue to present a strong inducement to young people to identify, as much as they can, with the dominant American prototype.

Language as a Measure of Assimilation. That such pressures toward assimilation are strong can hardly be doubted, although means of measuring degrees of assimilation are difficult to devise, and, as a result, data on a national scale are extremely limited. Perhaps one of the most revealing indications of assimilation in America is the rapid adoption of the English language by groups that were originally not English-speaking. To be sure, adoption of English proves neither that the adopters have relinquished other distinctive traits nor that they have been fully accepted by other Americans. So important, however, is language as a cultural phenomenon in itself and as a means of transmitting culture that habitual use of a language other than English by native-born Americans of native parentage may be presumed to indicate quite definitely that full assimilation has not occurred.

The census of 1940 presented data on the "mother tongue" of the American white population. The strong tendency to drop other languages before the third generation is indicated by the fact that 96 per cent of all such Americans spoke English as their mother tongue (see Table 24). There was a very slight tendency for the rural population to show a lesser usage of English than the total population. In rural America, three languages—German, Spanish, and French—accounted for four-fifths of all non-English mother tongues reported among people whose families had been in America for three or more generations. The largest such enclave in any state, numerically, was the French (Acadian, or "Cajun") population of Louisiana, but the Spanish-speaking segment of New Mexico represented a much larger proportion of the population of the state. In these instances, and in that of the "Dutch" (German) group in Pennsylvania, the presence of these populations from colonial times indicates long-standing resistance to loss of group identity, comparative isolation, or both. Texas and other Southwestern states likewise had sizable Span-

Table 24. Mother Tongues of Americans of the Third and Subsequent Generations

	Total population	Rural population	Rural-farm population
English............	78,352,180	40,774,620	20,213,400
Per cent of total...	96.4	95.9	95.3
German...........	925,040	644,340	440,140
Pennsylvania.....	140,500	88,980	38,600
Wisconsin........	128,080	84,420	60,000
Spanish...........	718,980	387,180	189,440
Texas...........	272,080	149,060	87,800
New Mexico......	192,820	146,240	71,820
French............	518,780	316,220	170,780
Louisiana........	289,760	225,420	138,140

SOURCE: *Sixteenth Census of the United States, 1940.* "Nativity and Parentage of the White Population."

ish-speaking groups of long residence, whereas Wisconsin and neighboring Middle Western states recorded significant numbers speaking German.

Assimilation in Its Broader Setting. This discussion of assimilation has been limited almost entirely to the American setting, where there has been striking absorption of diverse elements by a larger group. Assimilation may occur, however, in a much less one-sided way as the result of the thorough blending of two or more originally distinct groups. The classic historical example of assimilation in this form is that of England in the two or three centuries following the Norman Conquest of 1066, when the Norman-French aristocracy and the Germanic masses fused into a unified people and developed a language and a culture which, neither French nor German, was distinctively new.

ACCULTURATION

The concept of acculturation, borrowed by sociologists from cultural anthropology, is closely related to the sociological concepts of assimilation and accommodation. In the course of its development, this concept has had a wide range of usages, but as we shall use it here, it refers to the results of culture contact. More specifically, *acculturation* refers to the changes in culture that result from the continued contact of individuals, groups, or entire societies with the bearers of or the content of other cultures.

Perhaps an example will clarify the concept. A few centuries ago, the Amharic area of the Ethiopian highlands was successfully invaded by a nomadic but numerous African people, the Galla. Many Galla settled in the highlands; others established themselves at lower elevations to the south, where they continued their traditional pastoral way of life. Today the outsider finds it difficult to distinguish at first glance between the highland Galla and the earlier Amharic inhabitants of the area. Amhara and Galla alike depend on farming rather than herds for their livelihood; their houses and clothing are similar, and they have similar loyalties to provincial and national authorities. Some of these Galla have joined the Coptic Christian church of the Amhara; more of them, perhaps, have been converted to Islam. At any rate, relatively few maintain their former religion. Thus, in many important respects, these Galla resemble neighboring highland people more than they do their nomadic kinsmen to the south.

These changes in Galla culture, then, exemplify their acculturation by contact with Amharic and other Ethiopic cultures. In significant respects, however, the Galla remain distinct. In language, for example, and in much of their social organization they continue to resemble the southern Galla groups that have changed little in recent centuries. Even in the highlands the Galla remain, in their own minds and in those of their neighbors, a distinct, separate people.

Acculturation as Distinguished from Accommodation and Assimilation

In part the distinction between acculturation and the social processes of accommodation and assimilation is parallel to the basic distinction between culture and society. The social processes refer specifically to relationships between persons; acculturation, a cultural process, refers specifically to changes in culture—that is, in behavior and knowledge. In this sense the concepts refer to a different order of phenomena. It is true that the theoretical distinction between the social and the cultural may be overemphasized and that, in actual situations, the same relationship may be both social and cultural.[3] Even so, the different implications of acculturation and assimilation are significant. To illustrate: two visitors to South Louisiana might note the pronounced impact of urbanization in the area, the presence and influence of the oil industry there, the easy access into formerly remote areas on today's roads, the increasing attendance of young people at secondary schools and colleges, and the impact on these same young people of motion pictures, radio, and television. One visitor might comment on the rapid acculturation underway

[3] For a discussion of the manner in which these concepts are interwoven, see: A. L. Kroeber, *Anthropology*, 1948 ed., New York: Harcourt, Brace and Company, Inc., 1948, pp. 267–269.

in Louisiana; in a precise sense, he would refer to the alterations that all these influences are producing in the indigenous French way of life. The second visitor might announce that assimilation is increasingly apparent in Louisiana; his comment would imply that, accompanying these alterations in the French way of life, old cleavages between Acadian and non-French Louisianians are yielding to an increasing unity in interaction. To be sure, before assimilation between groups of different cultures can occur, the process of becoming alike in behavior—acculturation—must be under way. In such instances, acculturation may be considered a necessary phase of assimilation, but acculturation does not necessarily lead to assimilation. Acculturation on the part of German and French cultures in relation to one another, for example, has been under way for centuries, but certainly assimilation of the German and French societies has not occurred.

The concept of acculturation does not carry the implication, present in assimilation, of moving toward a completed state or condition; nor does it imply, as does assimilation, that the individuals affected by the process necessarily move in the direction of personal acceptance of one another. Groups in conflict and societies at war may be undergoing acculturation—that is, they may be learning from one another and altering their cultures in response to one another. Indeed, cultural changes often produce, instead of assimilation, a need for readjustment of relationships between the affected groups or societies—in short, accommodation.

The Types of Acculturation

As Gillin has pointed out, there are two quite different types of acculturation, the relatively balanced and the unbalanced types.[4] These in a sense are analogous to the two types of assimilation (the fusion of groups and the absorption of a smaller by a larger group). In the balanced type of acculturation, the societies whose cultures are changing stand in a relatively equal relationship to one another. Their contrasting ways of life influence one another and lead to changes within each culture, but the relationship is reciprocal. The example of the French and German cultures epitomizes this type of acculturation. Alterations in the cultures of the remnants of Southeastern, Middle Western, and Plains Indian tribes when placed in close contact in what is now Oklahoma represent another such example. In this instance, however, the balanced type of acculturation was far overshadowed by acculturation of the unbalanced type, in which the representatives of one way of life are in a position to impose their practices on other groups. The cultural adjust-

[4] John Gillin, *The Ways of Men,* New York: Appleton-Century-Crofts, Inc., 1948, pp. 557–558.

ments which Oklahoma's Indians made in respect to each other were minor compared to the alteration of their old ways of life necessitated by the ever-encroaching demands of the general American culture. Unbalanced acculturation has been more thoroughly described in the literature than has balanced acculturation, because the unbalanced situation is that usually encountered in anthropological field studies. Another example of unbalanced acculturation is afforded by the cultural changes made by an immigrant group as it undergoes the process of Americanization.

Balanced and unbalanced acculturation contrast in the degree of reciprocity in cultural change. In balanced acculturation, the exchange of cultural traits is two-way, whereas in unbalanced acculturation, most of the alterations perforce must occur in the culture of the subordinant group. Even so, the process is not entirely one-directional. The dominant group does learn from the subordinant one; the more complex culture does adopt some aspects of the less complex one. A case in point is the variety of agricultural products, with the appropriate means of tillage, which Europeans adopted from the American Indians. The acceptance of traits into the culture of the dominant society obviously can be highly selective, for only the products and usages that appeal to its members are incorporated into its way of life.

Although unbalanced acculturation may lead to assimilation into the dominant society, it often results instead in the members of the weaker group facing the necessity of accommodation to inferior status. As in the case of American Negroes, such inferior status may become a castelike position. It may consist of a separate but dependent existence in territory controlled by the dominant group, as in the example of the reservation Indian. If the territory of the weaker society is distinct from that of the dominant one, colonial status may result.

Although the process of acculturation does not necessarily imply moving toward a completed state, the term is nonetheless used to refer to degrees of familiarity with, and acceptance of, the culture of the dominant society. Thus, we may say that Negroes in America are "acculturated"; that is, their African cultural heritage has been supplanted by the American culture. Similarly, we may state that the Cherokee Indians of Cherokee County, Oklahoma, are "more acculturated" than those of adjacent Delaware County, meaning that more of the Indians in Cherokee County speak English, go to high school, watch television, register as Democrats, and otherwise act like their white neighbors.

Questions for Review and Discussion

1. Define accommodation.
2. List examples of accommodative behavior at the national, international, and individual level.
3. List and define the major forms of accommodation.
4. Differentiate fully between acculturation and assimilation, giving examples of each.
5. Is it possible to be assimilated without being acculturated?
6. Explain what is meant by the statement, "The acceptance of culture traits can be highly selective."

Selected References for Supplementary Reading

Bossard, James H. S., Walter A. Lunden, Lloyd V. Ballard, and Lawrence Foster (eds.): *Introduction to Sociology*, Harrisburg, Pa.: The Stackpole Company, 1952, chap. 14.

Landis, Paul H.: *Rural Life in Process*, New York: McGraw-Hill Book Company, Inc., 1948, chaps. 16 and 17.

Nelson, Lowry: *Rural Sociology*, New York: American Book Company, 1955, chap. 10.

Cuber, John F.: *Sociology: A Synopsis of Principles*, 3d ed., New York: Appleton-Century-Crofts, Inc., 1955, chap. 33.

CHAPTER 22 *The Characteristics and Functions of Special-interest Groups*

American society has long been characterized by the large numbers of groups of which it is made up. As early as 1835, the American penchant for forming groups moved the Frenchman Alexis de Tocqueville to write: [1]

> Americans of all ages, all conditions, and all dispositions constantly form associations. They have not only commercial and manufacturing companies in which all take part, but they have associations of a thousand other kinds— religious, moral, serious, futile, general or restricted, enormous or diminutive. . . . Wherever, at the head of some undertaking you see government in France, or a man of rank in England, in the United States you will be sure to find an association.

One type of "association," the locality group, was discussed in Part Two of this volume. In this chapter we shall study the nature and functions of special-interest groups, some of which have already been described. We have seen that locality groups are based on physical proximity. Other types of groups exist because of special needs or interests— for example, the Parent-Teachers Association; the 4-H Club; home-demonstration clubs; women's home missionary societies; the Lions, the Kiwanis, and other service and luncheon clubs; the Women's Club; the Masons; the Elks; the Veterans of Foreign Wars; the American Legion; farmers' cooperatives; and a host of others.

Locality groups develop because of a geographic factor; people living in close proximity come to associate their day-to-day interaction with a particular geographic area. In contrast, special-interest groups, although space-bound like all human groups, exist because of interests or needs

---

[1] Alexis de Tocqueville, *Democracy in America* (1835). From a translation by Henry Reeves, 1876, p. 242.

shared by their members. They are not necessarily limited by geographic space, and their membership often cuts across locality-group boundaries.

THE FUNCTIONS OF SPECIAL-INTEREST GROUPS

A wide variety of specific functions are performed by special-interest groups, as any survey of their objectives and activities will reveal. However, some of the general functions performed by these groups are not usually made explicit in statements of objectives. In the description of these functions which follows, it will be seen that many special-interest groups are closely related to the major institutions.

Support of Institutions

The process of specialization and differentiation in modern society has resulted not only in the compartmentalization of social activity into institutional areas but also in rather extensive specialization within institutional areas. For example, we have elaborated a complex set of norms regarding formal instruction of the younger members of the society. Most of this instruction takes place within the organizational framework of the public school, but it is not limited to the school. We also have parochial schools, colleges, vocational schools, on-the-job training programs, veterans' farm classes, night classes, art institutes, and a host of other associations for giving specialized types of instruction. Even within the public school, formal instruction is both provided and supplemented by such organizations as school bands, science clubs, athletic teams, and glee clubs, whose objectives supplement or support the activities of the school. There are numerous other examples of institutions that support special-interest groups.

Liaison between Institutions

One of the products of specialization and differentiation in society is an increase in conflict potential and the consequent need for liaison mechanisms. The situation in education will serve as an illustration. In a simple and relatively undifferentiated society, responsibility for instructing the young rests largely with the family. A highly complex society such as ours, with an elaborate technology, cannot rely on informal instruction within the family and other informal groups. Therefore, we delegate a major share of this responsibility to the school, and in so doing we have infringed upon the prerogatives of the family. When most schools were one-room, neighborhood schools, this infringement and the resulting conflict potential did not produce any need for organized group action, but when rural schools were consolidated and pupils were concentrated in larger village and town schools, instruction was so far removed from the surveillance of the family that the possibilities of misunderstanding and conflict were greatly magnified. It was at this point in our history that the Parent-Teachers Association emerged as the liaison group between the family and the school. Parent-teachers associations may have a great variety of objectives and engage in numerous different activities, but basically all of them exist because they perform this liaison function.

Integration of Institutional Groups with the Community

Generally, special-interest groups cluster around the central institutions of a community. They stand between the institutional organization and the community as a whole, and many of their activities are integrative or conciliatory in nature. The typical businessmen's luncheon or service club illustrates this integrative or conciliatory function.

The norms that blueprint economic activities in American society emphasize interindividual and interfirm competition. The effects of such competition on the community tend to be divisive: the actions of individual business firms are influenced by the short-run need to compete successfully with other firms, even though success for one firm may mean failure for another. Luncheon and service clubs draw their membership primarily from business personnel. These clubs make extensive use of the symbols of brotherhood, and the word "Brother" is often used as a form of address among members at club meetings. Furthermore, the major activities of these groups are oriented to the community at large, even when they are not concerned with increasing commerce or industry in the community. The frequency with which these groups undertake such projects as providing for the handicapped and underprivileged and supporting community centers illustrates the orientation to community goals and the conciliatory nature of their activities.

The Development of Institutions

All societies develop along two related and functionally dependent routes, cultural and social. Cultural change is manifest in the elaboration of rules or norms regulating the means to the goals of the society. Social change is manifest in the elaboration of networks of association which come into existence to facilitate the achievement of goals.

Some norms are obligatory and differ from other cultural norms primarily in the intensity of social sanction and in the unanimity of the support they receive.[2] They are relatively permanent, and their enforcement is accomplished through definitive social organization. For example, the prohibition of murder is an institutional norm. It is based on a

[2] Robin M. Williams, Jr., *American Society*, New York: Alfred A. Knopf, Inc., 1951, p. 29.

general consensus that no one has the right to take the life of another. Its enforcement and the punishment for infractions are vested in units of local government generally and in the police and the courts specifically. There was a time, as the frontier moved Westward, when governmental organization lagged. Voluntary associations, often in the form of vigilante committees, emerged to enforce the prohibition against murder; they punished its infractors, sometimes by death without trial. Significantly, the voluntary *ad hoc* association of the vigilante committee often provided the initial basis for stable local government. This is an example of a special-interest group serving in an intermediate capacity in the development of a formal institution.

Completion of the Socialization Process

Reference groups are important determinants of behavior, especially in multiple-group situations. In the simpler rural society of the past, the number of groups with which a person was identified was relatively small. He was a member of a particular family or kinship group by virtue of birth or adoption; he was identified with a particular neighborhood or locality group because of residence in it; and he was likely to belong to the church of his parents and to be identified as a member of a status group by the same token. These groups provided the basis for his orientation to the life of the community and to the larger society. They were the groups that influenced his behavior and shaped his personality, and he had relatively little choice in the matter.

With the shift to the multiple-group condition that exists today in both urban and rural communities, the situation for the individual has changed. Family and neighborhood groups are still important determinants of basic behavior patterns, but the individual is now conditioned in large part by membership in or identification with a variety of special-interest groups that serve as points of reference.

Social Selection

Students of social stratification have observed the role played by special-interest associations in sorting people into social strata. Informal groups such as cliques are of major importance in performing this function. Clique relationships begin early in life. Grade-school children express preference for the companionship of certain other children and spend more time with them than with others, but their selections of "friends" are usually not very permanent and are not necessarily crucial in determining behavior. By high-school age, with the advent of adolescence and an awakening interest in persons of the opposite sex, these friendship cliques take on a new importance. They consume much of the time and interest and encompass most of the activities of the adolescent youngster; from the testimony of the adolescents, these groups are often more important in determining behavior than are parents.

Clique groups are small. Among adolescents, they include from two to five or six persons of the same sex,[3] and among older youth and young adults, from two to four or five couples. They are informal, and membership is voluntary; and although there are no explicit rules, the clique has a common set of values that determines the choice of members and how members who do not live up to these values will be censured.

Not all cliques have social-status significance, but many do, especially among adolescents and young adults. Hollingshead found that approximately two-thirds of the clique groups among Elmtown's youth were composed of persons in the same prestige class, and only 4 per cent were composed of persons representing three prestige classes.[4] Kaufman also found that the prestige range of intimate association was very narrow. A person and his intimate associates are very likely to have the same prestige rank. Of 467 mutual choices or bonds observed in a New York rural community, only 8 per cent had a range of more than one class.[5]

Many formal associations are widely recognized as symbols of class position. Nearly every community of any size has its country clubs, its high-prestige and its lower-prestige associations. That this is general knowledge and constitutes a concrete basis for behavior is substantiated by the fact that individual citizens can readily rank associations in terms of the "standing" or "rank" of the groups in the community.[6]

CHARACTERISTICS OF SPECIAL-INTEREST GROUPS

Two general categories of special-interest groups can be distinguished. The first, formal associations, includes most of the groups usually subsumed under the heading of special-interest groups. In addition to being voluntary and organized around a special interest, these groups have formally chosen (elected, appointed, or employed) leaders or officials and have definite written rules to guide their activities (constitutions, bylaws, procedure manuals, charters, or organization charts). The second type includes the informal groups—cliques, friendship groups, gangs, and coteries. Although the rules that guide their activities may be quite specific, they are not formalized in written regulations. Similarly, they may have recognized leaders, but their leaders are not referred to as

[3] A. B. Hollingshead, *Elmtown's Youth*, New York: John Wiley & Sons, Inc., 1949, pp. 207–208.

[4] *Ibid.*

[5] Harold F. Kaufman, *Prestige Classes in a New York Rural Community*, Cornell University AES Memoir 260, March, 1944.

[6] Raymond Payne, "Community Standing of Rural Organization in Four Kentucky Counties," unpublished master's thesis, University of Kentucky, 1950.

officials, and the selection of leaders is not guided by formal procedures.

Because of their number and formal nature, research on rural special-interest groups has been concentrated largely on formal associations. As a result, there is a substantial body of knowledge about these groups. Aside from the fact that they are based on interests rather than locality, they have several other distinctive characteristics, which we shall list and discuss here.

Dependence on Leadership and Promotion

The mere awareness of an interest is not sufficient to ensure the formation of an association. Although neighborhood groups may develop willy-nilly as the result of interaction occasioned by geographic proximity, formal special-interest groups will not develop except through purposive action on the part of one or more persons.

Frequently, the original motivation or the driving force for the organization of the group comes from an outside source.[7] This is especially true of such agency-sponsored groups as the Red Cross, 4-H clubs, and Extension-sponsored farm organizations. Promotion is carried out either by representatives of state and national agencies or organizations or by leaders from local organizations in neighboring communities.

Promotion by outsiders is especially important in communities in the earlier stages of urbanization. In the study referred to above, the more rural counties, representing an early stage of urbanization, had less specialization and diversification of interests and as a consequence had fewer formally organized groups than the less rural counties. However, among the formal groups present, a higher proportion reported that the original motivation for their formation had come from outside the county.[8]

Not only is the organization of formal special-interest groups dependent on promotional activities, but their continued functioning is highly dependent upon the leadership of a small number of the members. The responsibility for keeping the organization going falls largely on the elected officers and committees. Many larger groups even employ specially trained personnel to shoulder part of the responsibility for a program.

Importance of a Formal Program of Activities

Formal special-interest groups must have a program of activities to survive, even though the connection between the program and the objectives

---

[7] Ward W. Bauder, *Objectives and Activities of Special-interest Organizations in Kentucky*, Kentucky AES Bulletin 639, 1956.

[8] *Ibid.*

is not always clear to the casual observer. Sometimes deviation from formally stated objectives is due to an actual departure from original objectives—some organizations change their objectives without formal acknowledgment. More often it is because the objectives are not clearly stated, whereas activities are concrete events that can serve a variety of objectives depending on one's point of view.

The more highly specialized the interest or objective involved, the closer the correspondence between objectives and the program of activities. A bridge club, for example, may limit its activities to playing bridge, whereas a Parent-Teachers Association may engage in a wide variety of activities, some of which do not seem to be very closely related to its principal objective. In both instances, the lack of a program would destroy the organization's reason for existing.

Self-perpetuation

The discrepancy between objectives and activities is in part a product of another general characteristic of special-interest associations, namely, their tendency to continue to function after their original objectives have been accomplished or are no longer timely. The tenacity with which such groups hang on after they have served their stated purpose is truly remarkable. It has been suggested that there is great need for an acceptable burial ceremony for organizations that have outlived their usefulness. Even those organizations that are for all practical purposes dead frequently refuse to be buried and steadfastly conjure reasons for postponing their demise. Sometimes, of course, new objectives are successfully introduced without reorganization.

Centralization

Large-scale, centralized, formal organizations increasingly occupy a strategic position in rural society and in the total society. Such groups as the American Farm Bureau Federation, the Farmers' Educational and Cooperative Union of America, and the Grange have developed into rural pressure groups and serve as spokesmen for the rural and, especially, the rural-farm segment of the population. The role of such organizations is discussed in greater detail in another chapter, but they are mentioned here to illustrate the importance of centralization.

An important consequence of centralization is the increased permeability of rural communities to chains of interaction and influence initiated in regional, state, and national centers of organization. In spite of conscious efforts to retain a familistic type of structure in local units of nationwide farmers' organizations and in spite of supposedly grassroots programs for developing policy, it is no secret that in most of these associations the central organization exerts a disproportionate influence on actual policy. The exigencies of legislative programs at the state and national levels of these organizations make this inevitable.

Bureaucratic Structure

Many large-scale special-interest associations have very complex internal structures with numerous specialized statuses arranged in intricate systems sometimes referred to, partly in jest, as "wheels within wheels." They share with "big" business and "big" government the centralization and bureaucratization of organized controls. Although the vast majority of rural special-interest groups are too small to be complex, the presence in rural communities of local units of state or national organizations and agencies exposes rural people to a milieu of tensions for which their past experience provides inadequate preparation.

The impersonality of large-scale organization produces the possibility of conflicting norms and expectations at the points of contact between the organization and the public. Thus the well-known need for public-relations programs. The individual facing the organization at its contact edge has his own unique needs and circumstances, which to him are of great importance, whereas the representative of the organization sees the individual as a case, often identified solely by a number, to be dealt with in terms of explicit general rules.[9] Any college freshman who has been through the registration process in one of our major state universities knows the personal frustrations and threats to ego security that such a situation can bring. The tendency of rural people to project patterns of expectations learned in primary-group interaction on to new situations further increases the likelihood of misunderstanding and frustration when they are brought into contact with a bureaucratic organization.

Membership-relations Problems

Within the bureaucratic structure there are certain safeguards that operate to protect the individual to some extent from the impersonality of the organization. Inevitably, informal groups develop within or alongside the formal structure. These perform a variety of functions, including that of providing sources of affective support to their members. Nevertheless, the very complexity and impersonality of the large formal organization has produced a number of troublesome and persistent membership-relations problems. Farmers' cooperatives have sponsored or encouraged systematic study in an attempt to find solutions to these problems.[10] State units of the larger farmers' organizations employ organ-

9 Williams, *op. cit.*, pp. 473–476.
10 For good examples of such studies, see: William S. Folkman, *Membership Relations in Farmers' Purchasing Cooperatives*, Arkansas AES Bulletin 556, 1955;

ization specialists with responsibility of maintaining good membership relations.

SELECTED ECOLOGICAL ASPECTS OF RURAL
SPECIAL-INTEREST GROUPS

From an ecological point of view, human activities may be classified as *field* and *center* activities.[11] Field activities are concerned with processing and distribution. They involve primarily rural locality groupings —rural communities, neighborhoods, and type-farming regions—whereas center activities involve urban locality groups such as trade areas, metropolitan districts, and industrial areas.

A large amount of special-interest association in rural communities takes place in areas of activities that represent a merging of the interests of town and country. Farmers' marketing cooperatives, for example, bring together people involved primarily in field activities who are interested in extending their control over their product into the area of processing and distribution. Farmers' purchasing cooperatives, on the other hand, extend the activities of the farmer into the area of processing and distribution from the other end of the cycle.

Although special-interest groups can be distinguished from locality groups in terms of the space factor, special-interest groups are nevertheless responsive to geography. Studies of formal rural special-interest groups indicate that the headquarters of such groups are usually located in the larger towns and urban centers. The more specialized and limited the interest, the greater the tendency to gravitate to the larger centers. In a Kentucky study, for example, the majority of the formal organizations were centered at or had headquarters in the towns. Furthermore, they tended to be concentrated in the county-seat towns, which in this particular study were the largest towns.[12] This is a response to the same ecological forces that produce patterns of concentration of population in specific areas.

George M. Beal, Donald R. Fessler, and Ray E. Wakely, *Agricultural Cooperatives in Iowa; Farmers Opinions and Community Relations*, Iowa AES Research Bulletin 379, 1951; W. A. Anderson and Dwight Sanderson, *Membership Relations in Co-operative Organizations*, Ithaca, N.Y.: Cornell University Department of Rural Sociology, Mimeographed Bulletin 9, 1943; George F. Henning and Earl B. Poling, *Attitudes of Farmers Toward Cooperative Marketing*, Ohio AES Bulletin 606, 1939. For a more complete listing, see: *Bibliography on Cooperation in Agriculture*, Washington: USDA Library List 41, 1948 and more recent supplements.

[11] C. P. Loomis and J. A. Beegle, *Rural Sociology, The Strategy of Change*, Englewood Cliffs, N.J : Prentice-Hall, Inc., 1957, p. 39.

[12] Joseph G. Hardee and Ward W. Bauder, *Town-Country Relations in Special-Interest Organizations, Four Selected Kentucky Counties*, Kentucky AES Bulletin 586, June, 1952.

Concentration of Membership and Leadership

Concentration in the ecological sense refers to the tendency for in-creasing numbers of people to settle in a given area.[13] It is both a pat-tern and a process, and it applies to associations as well as to people, though in a somewhat different manner. It is generally true that special-interest association increases with urbanization. At the same time, the proportion of the population with multiple memberships in special-in-terest groups increases more rapidly with urbanization than the propor-tion with single memberships.[14]

This tendency toward concentration of memberships in the hands of a few is also noticeable in many rural communities. In a Kentucky com-munity of 2,000 people, 10 persons held one-tenth of all the organiza-tional memberships in the community, an average of over 11 member-ships per person.[15] Not only is there a concentration of memberships, but there is also a concentration of leadership positions in the hands of a few. In the study cited above, 11 persons held 15 per cent of all the offices in formal organizations. These same 11 persons spent an estimated average of over thirteen hours a week in organizing and carrying out the activities of the formal associations to which they belong.

Although the concentration of leadership positions bespeaks the con-centration of power in the community, it also reflects a space factor in that the incidence of membership and office-holding among rural peo-ple tends to decrease with distance from centers of population that serve as meeting places.

Regional Variations

When we consider these two factors together—the interstitial position of special-interest associations between field and center activities, and the concentration of special-interest associations in response to a gen-eral space factor—we have a logical explanation for certain regional vari-ations. They help to explain why there are more special-interest groups in the dairy regions or in the Corn Belt, for example, than in the gen-eral and self-sufficing farming areas of the Appalachian Ozark region (see Chapter 8).[16]

[13] R. O. McKenzie, "The Scope of Human Ecology," *American Sociological Society Publications*, 20 (14), 1925.

[14] Harold F. Kaufman, *Participation in Organized Activities in Selected Kentucky Localities*, Kentucky AES Bulletin 528, 1953.

[15] Paul D. Richardson and Ward W. Bauder, *Participation in Organized Activities in a Kentucky Rural Community*, Kentucky AES Bulletin 598, June, 1953.

[16] Carl Taylor et al., *Rural Life in the United States*, New York: Alfred A. Knopf, Inc., 1948, part 4.

Questions for Review and Discussion

1. What is meant by the term *special-interest group?*
2. What are the functions of special-interest groups?
3. Distinguish between formal and informal special-interest groups.
4. Why are there regional differences in special-interest groups?
5. Explain how an organized group might revive a rural community showing signs of disorganization.

Selected References for Supplementary Reading

Barber, Bernard: "Participation and Mass Apathy in Associations," in Alvin W. Gouldner (ed.), *Studies in Leadership,* New York: Harper & Brothers, 1950, pp. 477–504.

Hollingshead, August B.: *Elmtown's Youth,* New York: John Wiley & Sons, Inc., 1949.

Kaufman, Harold F.: *Prestige Classes in a New York Rural Community,* Cornell University AES Memoir 260, 1944.

Kolb, John H., and Edmund deS. Brunner: *A Study of Rural Society,* Boston: Houghton Mifflin Company, 1952, chap. 15.

Komarovsky, Mirra: "The Voluntary Associations of Urban Dwellers," *American Sociological Review,* 11:686–698, 1946.

Social Movements and Social Change in Rural Areas

Rural society in the United States is, as we have seen, in process of rapid change. Part Six focuses attention on some of the more important movements, processes, and results of this change.

Chapter 23 is concerned with the major farmers' movements and their characteristics as social movements. Chapter 24 explores the role of communication in bringing about rural social change, and in Chapter 25 acceptance of innovations by farmers is discussed as a rural social process. The major changes resulting from technological innovations in farm areas are listed in Chapter 26, and rural-urban interaction and rural social change are discussed in Chapter 27.

CHAPTER 23   *The Farmers' Movement*

In every complex society, some persons, over a period of time, become deeply dissatisfied with their lot. This dissatisfaction is related to social change, which in certain periods creates many inequalities, insecurities, or frustrations. When people make a collective attempt to change unsatisfactory conditions, then a social movement is in the making.

By definition, then, a social movement is a conscious striving by a relatively large group of persons to bring about societal change or a new order of life. In Taylor's words, it is ". . . a type of collective behavior by means of which some large segment of a society attempts to accomplish adjustment of conditions in its economy or culture which it thinks are in maladjustment." [1] One of the main criteria of a social movement, as Heberle points out, is the aim to bring about fundamental changes, especially in the basic institutions of property and labor relationships. [2] This criterion indicates the distinction between social trends, such as urbanization and mechanization of agriculture, and social movements.

CHARACTERISTICS OF SOCIAL MOVEMENTS

A great many types of social movements have been identified and classified according to their peculiar characteristics. Some, for example, are secular in nature, whereas others have a religious orientation; some are inclusive of whole national groups, others appeal only to smaller special-interest groups or certain classes. However, three conditions appear to characterize social movements. Green has outlined these conditions as follows: [3]

[1] Carl C. Taylor, *The Farmers' Movement, 1620–1920*, New York: American Book Company, 1953, p. 1.

[2] Rudolf Heberle, *Social Movements*, New York: Appleton-Century-Crofts, Inc., 1951, pp. 6–10.

[3] Arnold W. Green, *Sociology*, 2d ed., New York: McGraw-Hill Book Company, Inc., 1956, pp. 530–538.

First, mass dissatisfaction must be focused upon some group or institution, or some other symbol of a menace. Second, the greater society must be structured in such a way as to permit separative organization within it. In other words, nonconformity must be tolerated. Third, strong, dynamic leadership, along with an efficient organization, must emerge early in the history of the movement. When all these conditions are met, there is some likelihood that the movement will have a measure of success.

Green has described the stages in social movements as follows: [4]

1. Social Unrest. This is the period when discontent and dissatisfaction are first in evidence. It usually follows rather drastic social change, when roles and goals have been changed or destroyed. Not all unrest crystallizes into movements, but it is a necessary element for their development.

2. The Popular Stage. At this stage an enemy is identified and the people decide that the cause of the trouble must be eliminated. It is now that a champion with a plan guaranteed to succeed begins to be heard above all others. Slogans are coined, and a great deal of enthusiasm is generated.

3. Formalized Organization. The third stage, if the movement is not arrested, is achieved when a definite organization is formed. This includes a hierarchy of command, definite goals, and a network of dedicated local leaders. Propaganda organs are enlisted, and the cause is proclaimed far and wide. However, if the movement is to survive, some success in attaining its goals must be achieved. Quite frequently this does not happen, and the movement fizzles out.

4. Institutionalization. This is the final aim of all movements and involves general acceptance of the change sought. In actual practice, very few movements succeed in this objective.

This explanation of the conditions that characterize social movements and the stages of their development provides the essential background for the discussion of farmers' movements in the United States, which is the subject of this chapter.

Social Movements in Rural America

The rapidity with which the United States was transformed from a comparatively simple agricultural community into a complex and modern industrial community helps one understand the social unrest that has at times prevailed in rural areas of the nation. In the process of economic adjustment, the agricultural classes have felt exploited, and the result has been a series of revolts. Taylor chooses to think of these

[4] *Ibid.*

revolts as indicators of a more inclusive Farmers' Movement. In his words, "The tide of American farmers' discontent has ebbed and flowed with economic conditions . . . and the various farmers' revolts have been only the high tides of a Farmers' Movement which is as persistent as the Labor Movement."[5] This view appears to be a valid one, and it helps to explain the farmers' uprisings through the years. However, it does not preclude the identification of each specific revolt as an individual movement in and of itself. The discussion of farmers' movements in this chapter is organized to show the developmental stages of certain important earlier movements—the Grange, the Greenbackers, and the Populists. Other movements are briefly taken up in chronological order to acquaint the student with their number and variety.

THE EARLIER REVOLTS AND UPRISINGS

No nationwide farmers' movements appeared in the United States before the Civil War. However, several local revolts and uprisings wielded considerable influence on the course of events in the nation. For example, as early as 1634 discontented farmers in the Massachusetts Bay Colony protested certain special privileges of the leaders of the Colony.[6] Bacon's Rebellion in colonial Virginia was more violent, developing into the first organized struggle of the frontiersmen against the planters, although it had its inception in Indian troubles. There is no doubt that this "rebellion" foretold much that was to come, since the frontiersmen were dissatisfied because of high taxes and inadequate shipping facilities.

The early years of American independence saw at least three more armed protests on the part of organized groups of farmers. The first of these occurred in western Massachusetts in 1786 and is known as Shays' Rebellion. On this occasion the farmers prevented courts from meeting, refused to pay taxes, and in general behaved much as farmers of the early 1930s behaved during the period of the "Farmers' Holiday." A somewhat similar situation arose a few years later, after the Constitution had been adopted and the new republic was struggling to establish its authority. This was the "Whiskey Rebellion," which spread along the entire frontier from Georgia to New York in protest against a tax on distilled liquors enacted as part of Hamilton's revenue program. Apparently, the frontiersmen depended on the sale of whiskey for cash to purchase what they could not produce (its keeping qualities made it easy to transport over long distances). Thus the tax threatened them

[5] Taylor, *op. cit.*, p. 1.
[6] W. B. Bizzell, *The Green Rising*, New York: The Macmillan Company, 1926, pp. 102–104.

at their most vulnerable point, and mass meetings were organized to plan resistance to it.[7] Fries' Rebellion in eastern Pennsylvania was a more localized revolt against taxes which came as an aftermath of the Whiskey Rebellion.[8]

These instances of organized agrarian "revolts," localized as they were and usually concerned only with immediate issues, are nevertheless interesting in their basic similarity to later movements. Such movements and "rebellions" were obviously not new things that developed spontaneously for the first time in America. Rather, they grew out of the experience of the peasantry in Europe. Most of the European peasant movements, however, were concerned with tenure problems—i.e., establishing the rights of the peasant to the land. In America, such problems were not an important feature of the earlier movements because the vast amounts of free land in the West prevented the social stratification and the accumulation of lands in the hands of certain owners which were common in Europe.

The passing of the free lands apparently heralded the farmers' movement. Bizzell maintains that psychological adjustment to the end of unlimited expansion was basically responsible for the numerous depressions and business crises of the last thirty years of the nineteenth century. These "hard times" were directly related to attempts by dissatisfied elements in rural society to bring about change, and thus the first large-scale farmers' movement got under way.[9]

THE GRANGE

The first of the major farmers' movements in the United States was the Patrons of Husbandry, ordinarily known as the Grange. Although founded in 1868, this movement did not make much headway until the hard times of the 1870s. It grew very rapidly from 1873 to 1875, claiming at this time a membership of 750,000. At its peak it boasted members in every state except Rhode Island.[10]

The Grange owes its conception and initial organization to Oliver Hudson Kelley. Kelley, a clerk in the government service at Washington, was sent by the Agricultural Bureau to the South to gather information for the Department. In his travels he was struck by the lack of progressive spirit among the agricultural classes and came to the conclusion that a national secret order of farmers was needed to further

[7] *Ibid.*, pp. 246–247.
[8] Taylor, *op. cit.*, pp. 53–56.
[9] Bizzell, *op. cit.*, pp. 126–128.
[10] Newell L. Sims, *Elements of Rural Sociology*, New York: Thomas Y. Crowell Company, 2d ed., 1934, p. 189.

the industrial reconstruction of the South and the advancement of the agricultural class throughout the country.

Eventually Kelley moved to the Post Office Department. Here, in 1867, he began planning with a fellow clerk the rituals to be incorporated into the society he envisioned. Later in the year they enlisted William Saunders, a clerk in the Agricultural Bureau who was about to attend a meeting of the U.S. Pomological Society at St. Louis. Kelley gave him a written outline of the proposed fraternal order to circulate among the farmers with whom he came in contact.

As a result of circulation of his outline, several people wrote to Kelley and manifested an interest in his scheme. The work of getting the order under way and preparing an elaborate ritual was now taken up in earnest. Seven men are usually recognized by the Grange as the "founders" of the order. These included one fruit grower and six government clerks, equally distributed among the Post Office, Treasury, and Agriculture Departments. From the standpoint of sociological analysis it is very significant that this movement did not originate with farmers.[11]

After a slow beginning, the Grange by 1875 included 750,000 dues-paying members. It attained its greatest influence in the Middle West, especially in Iowa, Illinois, Wisconsin, and Minnesota. It was an important influence in Indiana, Missouri, Kansas, Michigan, Nebraska, and the two West Coast states of the time, Oregon and California.

The Grange was distinctly not a political movement in its original intent. As a matter of fact, the Grange constitution quite distinctly forbade any political activities and stressed fraternal, social, and economic aims. However, the Grange did have political effects, the chapters avoiding the constitutional injunction forbidding political activity by the simple expedient of declaring the formal meeting adjourned and then holding an unofficial political discussion.

The principal political issue in which the Grange became involved was the fight against the railroads. The farmers, seeking someone to blame for their ills, seized on the corporations or monopolies, particularly the railroads. Although many of the problems of the Western farmer arose from other factors than railroads, the presence of the railroad as a scapegoat was of great psychological importance in rallying followers around the Grange banner. The farmers' objections to the railroads can be summarized as follows: (1) Freight rates from the Western prairies to Eastern markets ate up the farmers' profits; (2) farmers resented the practice of rebates to certain shippers; (3) farmers, realiz-

---

[11] For a detailed account of the early history of the Grange, see: Solon J. Buck, *The Granger Movement*, Cambridge, Mass.: Harvard University Press, 1933, pp. 40–43.

ing that the end of free land was in sight, resented the railroads' possession of vast amounts of good land obtained from the government.

Although the regulation of the railroads was the most spectacular of the Grangers' political attempts, they were concerned about a number of other issues as well. According to Edwards, they favored the following: the provision of government credit for farmers, the increased printing of currency, regulation of the charges of grain elevators, control of speculation in farm crops, and abolition of tariffs.[12] Taylor adds still other objectives, such as the establishment of state boards of agriculture, compulsory education, appropriations for state land-grant colleges, water transportation, improvement of the Weather Bureau, regulation of weights and measures, and the establishment of a Federal Bureau of Agriculture.[13]

The second major concern of the Grangers, following their political objectives, was the introduction of a number of schemes for cooperation in such matters as the purchase of supplies, the marketing of farm products, and insurance. Thus, the popular watchwords of the day were "Cooperation" and "Down with monopolies," both of which doubtless provided the intended appeal to farmers.

Granger support at the polls was given to candidates friendly to Granger ideas. The organization sought first of all to see that only those candidates who could be counted on to fight against the railroads were elected from the local districts. Often they used questionnaires to force the candidates to state their positions in black and white and then withheld support from all who seemed doubtful with regard to regulation of the railroads. Individual Grangers of influence in each district followed closely the legislative records of all elected candidates and visited the candidates in the state capital to tell them of the wishes of the Granger constituents. More directly, in several cases, Granger conventions took place in the state capitals at the same time that the legislatures were considering railroad bills, and large numbers of the Grangers would attend the debates, making their wishes plainly known by their gallery reactions and by their visits to the legislators. It took a reckless politician to ignore the wishes of the Grange when representatives of the organization watched his every move.

The Grange declined after 1875 almost as fast as it had risen. By 1880 it had become a relatively minor organization. A second cycle of growth has begun, however, and in 1957 the organization had a membership virtually as large as in its peak days. Its greatest strength today

[12] Everett E. Edwards, "American Agriculture, The First 300 Years," in *Farmers in a Changing World*, The Yearbook of Agriculture, 1940, Washington: Government Printing Office, p. 259.

[13] Carl C. Taylor, *Rural Sociology*, New York: Harper & Brothers, 1926, p. 443.

is to be found among the conservative farmers of the Northeast, an area in which the organization was weak in its early days.

Buck explains the rapid decline of the Grange after 1875 as follows: (1) Any organization that grows too rapidly is prone to decay with equal rapidity; many farmers joined only for the sake of novelty or vogue and soon dropped out. (2) The method of organization contributed to its decline, because each chapter was established by an outside organizer without provision for follow-up work. (3) Organizers and deputies, in their ignorance, allowed enemies of farmers, such as commission men and persons only incidentally interested in farming, to join the organization. (4) Demands for reduction of the power of the national organization led to frequent revisions of the constitution, which only impaired the power of the national structure without satisfying the discontented. (5) The unfortunate experiences of the farmers in their attempts at business cooperation alienated many of the members.[14]

THE GREENBACKERS

During the period of the Grange's activities, numerous other farmers' clubs were organized, especially in the Corn Belt states. Many of these organizations were purely local, and none of them grew into a large organization of lasting significance. They served the purpose, however, of aiding the Grange in the support of the interests that all farmers shared. The movement of greatest size, the Greenbackers, was not exclusively a farmers' movement, but for the sake of continuity we are justified in considering it briefly at this point.

The Greenbackers were a political party designed especially to exploit the unrest expressed through the Grange organization. Many of the leaders of the Grange, as it began to decline, became active in the Greenback party, and when it in turn became insignificant, many of these same leaders went into subsequent farmers' movements. This development, which began with the Grange, has been continuous down to the present time.

The Greenback party was officially organized at Indianapolis in 1874. Currency reform was the chief prescription of this party, as the regulation of railroads was the main concern of the Grangers. Not content with working through a major party that necessarily contained conservative interests, some agrarians had looked about for allies to form a separate party. They found that laborers suffering from widespread unemployment, accompanying if not caused by contraction of the currency,

[14] Solon J. Buck, *The Agrarian Crusade, A Chronicle of the Farmer in Politics,* New Haven, Conn.: Yale University Press, The Chronicles of America Series, 45: 60–63, 1920.

had formed the National Labor party. This party had adopted a green-back platform in 1872. Thus, as a result of the panic of 1873 and the failure of the Granger movement to relieve the agricultural depression, farmers and workers joined in the Independent National party, known as the Greenback Labor party, to correct these evils.[15]

The party gained little headway until after 1877, which was a year of great hardship for farmers and of considerable labor unrest as well. In the elections of 1876, the party had had local successes, particularly in Illinois. The year 1878, however, marked the high point of the movement. In polling a million votes and sending fifteen men to Congress, this party indicated what success an agrarian political party might conceivably achieve. Because most of its support came from rural sections and most of its outstanding leaders carried the agrarian stamp, it is not too far-fetched to call it the forerunner of the great Populist "revolt."

It is of interest to note that, as Fine points out, three of the Greenback Congressmen were from the South. This marks the Greenback party as the first agrarian political campaign to have any notable success in this area.[16] The party was destined to be short-lived, however, and never again repeated the limited victories of 1878.

THE FARMERS' ALLIANCES

Throughout the two decades from 1880 to 1900, difficult conditions continued. The first of these decades was marked by the development of the Farmers' Alliances. As we have seen, in spite of the decline of the popularity of the Grange, the idea persisted that farmers' clubs could serve not only social and fraternal needs but could work for the economic advancement of the group as well. So many men had seen the potentialities of these movements that the idea could not remain dormant. The Grange itself continued to have a considerable membership, although it retained little of its zest for reform and its prestige. The various farmers' independent clubs also continued to exist. Many of the more enthusiastic of the farm leaders had entered the Greenback movement and placed their hopes in it, but it was never to amount to more than a weak third political party, and when it declined, no outlet for political expression was left. It is not surprising, therefore, that another movement arose to fill this need.

The Farmers' Alliances were of multiple origin. Farmers' organizations that had sprung up more or less independently of each other, in various states, were gradually merged under this name. Eventually, two

[15] Edwards, *op. cit.*, pp. 260–262.

[16] Nathan Fine, *Labor and Farmer Parties in the United States, 1828–1928*, New York: Rand School of Social Science, 1928, p. 64.

great Alliances, the Southern and the Northwestern, absorbed all the other good-sized movements. Although these two organizations long toyed with the possibility of a union, they never accomplished it, although they did cooperate in many ways.

Of the two organizations, the Alliance of the Southern states became the larger and probably the more influential. The Farmers' Alliance of Texas, founded in 1875, is generally considered to have been the parent stem of the organization.[17] At the same time, in Louisiana there had developed a strong organization, with similar concentrations of interests, known as the Louisiana Farmers' Union. The Texas Alliance was ready to spread and become nationwide, and the first step it took in this direction was to combine with the Louisiana Union in 1887. The combined organization was officially known as the National Farmers' Alliance and Cooperative Union of America.

Meanwhile, an even larger organization than the Louisiana Union had been formed in Arkansas and had spread throughout that state and into other states. This was the Agricultural Wheel, first organized in 1882. In 1885 the Wheel absorbed still another agrarian movement, the Brothers of Freedom. In 1888 the two major organizations combined under the new name of National Farmers' Alliance and Industrial Union, to comprise the largest agrarian organization, from the standpoint of number of members, that had ever been known before in the nation, although the organization was still virtually confined to the South.[18]

But the great number of its members by no means represented the full extent of the influence of the organization. In 1889, the organization entered a "confederation" with the Knights of Labor, a labor organization of considerable power, which meant that the two organizations were united on matters of general policy but maintained separate rituals and separate rights of membership. In 1890 a similar relationship was entered into with the National Colored Farmers' Alliance and Cooperative Union. This organization was modeled after the white Alliance but tended to be more conservative politically and stressed above all things the necessity of living on good terms with the white South. At the same time, the Alliance federated with the Farmers' Mutual Benefit Association, a farmers' organization which originated in Johnson County, Illinois, and which had considerable strength in southern Illinois and adjacent areas.[19]

In the meantime, the Northwestern Alliance was also flourishing. This

---

[17] Robert Lee Hunt, *A History of Farmers' Movements in the Southwest, 1873–1925*, College Station, Tex., Texas A & M Bulletin, 1935, pp. 29–30.

[18] Edward Wiest, *Agricultural Organization in the United States*, Lexington, Ky.: The University of Kentucky Press, 1923, p. 457.

[19] *Ibid.*, pp. 457–460.

organization was founded in Chicago as a result of the meeting of some local Alliances established in New York State and other organizations of the Middle West. This group never became strongly established in the Northeast or even in the more eastern parts of the Corn Belt, but it became quite strong in the Northern Plains states and territories.

The first two Farmers' Alliances in Texas and Louisiana were at the outset primarily concerned with the problems of the cotton farmer. They were opposed especially to the credit system under which cotton production in the South was organized.

With regard to labor, the Southern Alliance never made much distinction between the economic interests of farmers and those of laborers. In part, this was due to the fact that both had certain common interests at that particular point in history. In part, this attitude was due to the influence of the Wheel membership, for the Agricultural Wheel had started out to be a farmer-laborer organization.

With regard to Negro-white relations, the organization was probably the most liberal that has ever gained wide influence in the Southern states. Although Negroes were excluded from membership, the Alliance sponsored a separate Negro organization. When it confederated with this organization, it permitted individual states to determine whether or not Negroes were eligible for membership in the Alliance proper.

In general, the political aims of the Southern and Northwestern Alliance were the same, although the latter may have been a bit more radical. The Southern Alliance, according to Buck, emphasized higher taxation of lands held for speculative purposes, prohibition of alien ownership of land, prohibition of dealing in futures of farm products, full taxation of railroad property, effective interstate-commerce legislation, abolition of the national debt, and the issue of legal tender notes on a per-capita basis.[20]

According to its aims as outlined by Wiest, the Northwestern Alliance went a little further politically than the Southern Alliance. It sought the more liberal circulation of money, but it hoped to attain this by free, unlimited coinage of silver as well as by increasing the amount of paper in circulation. It proposed national banks and insisted upon government ownership of railroads. It agreed with the Southern Alliance on all its other aims and added the adoption of amendments authorizing the election of the President, Vice President, and senators by direct vote, the adoption of the Australian ballot, and an income tax.[21]

The Alliance program achieved instantaneous success in the elections of 1890. Buck felt that "The election of 1890 constituted not only political revolt, but social upheaval, in the West. In Kansas especially . . .

[20] Buck, *The Agrarian Crusade,* p. 114.
[21] Wiest, *op. cit.,* p. 448.

it was like a religious revival." [22] The two most colorful campaigners, perhaps, were "Sockless" Jerry Simpson and Mrs. Mary Elizabeth Lease of Kansas, who gained fame by telling Kansas farmers to "raise less corn and more hell." [23]

The results of the election in Kansas gave Alliance men control of the lower house of the state legislature and sent five congressmen and one senator to Washington. In Nebraska, the farmers also gained control of the legislature and so split the vote that a Democrat was elected governor. In South Dakota the Alliance men did not have a majority, but controlled the state legislature by prudent use of their balance of power. Other states also had several Alliance men in their capitals and sent others to Washington. In short, there was no doubt that a major political movement was stirring.

In the South, the Alliance men did not attempt to put up separate candidates, but took the far easier method of fighting it out within the Democratic Party. Alliance men gained control of the Democratic machine in several states, thus taking over the governments at one stroke.

The sensational success of the Alliance movement brought about the decision to form a political party, an action that can only be considered as anticlimactic, since the organization was already that. For this purpose, a convention was held in 1891 with all confederated groups in attendance. The party itself, named the People's Party and called the Populist party, was officially organized in time for the presidential election in 1892. As the efforts of its leaders were focused on the political party, the Alliance began to decline. By the time the Populist bubble burst, the Alliance was already dead.

THE POPULIST PARTY

The first definite step toward the formation of a large-scale third party was taken by a minority of Southern Alliance members without waiting for official action by the parent group. These men issued a call for a political convention to meet on Washington's Birthday, 1891, at Cincinnati. They invited all farmers' organizations, independent state parties, soldiers' organizations, and some labor organizations. However, the convention was postponed until May when the Northern Alliance agreed to participate.

Actually, the Cincinnati convention took the first definite steps in organizing the national People's Party. The 1,400 delegates who assembled there on May 19, 1891, represented thirty-three states and territories.[24]

[22] Buck, *The Agrarian Crusade*, pp. 134–135.
[23] Anna Rochester, *The Populist Movement in the United States*, New York: International Publishers, 1943, pp. 52–58.
[24] *Ibid.*, pp. 61–63.

A skillful compromise enlisted the delegates who felt that a party should be organized but were not ready to do it at this time, and the party was launched on its colorful way.

Nine months after the Cincinnati convention another larger group met in Saint Louis to organize the party formally. This group included not only representatives of all the farm organizations and the Citizens' Alliances, but of the Knights of Labor, the United Mine Workers of Ohio, and scattered delegates from several other labor-union bodies as well as from some reform movements.

The Saint Louis meeting was a lively gathering. A platform with an eloquent preamble was presented and both were adopted. A committee was chosen to confer with the already organized People's Party for the purpose of setting a time and place for the nomination of candidates. They decided to meet in Omaha on July 4, 1892.

Meanwhile, the preamble and platform just adopted by the Saint Louis convention were to serve as the basis of a campaign which would reach into every state and county and bring to the nominating convention delegates elected by the people, eight from each congressional district and eight at large from each state.

The Omaha convention, like the Saint Louis meeting, was spontaneously enthusiastic. The delegates were imbued with a deep sense of their patriotic responsibility and felt that the great masses of the people were behind them. According to Rochester, they recognized the kinship of all those who toil, and they were certain that only by seizing monopoly privileges could the masses profit. When the delegates nominated a Union general, James Baird Weaver of Iowa, for president and a Confederate general, James G. Field of Virginia, for vice president, there was weeping and applauding. Apparently, the North and the South had reunited.[25]

Eventually, such organizations as the Ancient Order of Anti-Monopolists, the National Reform Press Association, and the Women's Christian Temperance Union joined the ranks of the Populists. However, although it included a part of the discontented of the towns and cities, McVey believed that the People's Party could best be defined as a class movement chiefly involving men engaged in agriculture.[26]

The program upon which the Populists finally agreed has been described by Edwards as follows: "A national currency, safe, sound and flexible, issued by the general Government only, free coinage of silver, the subtreasury system, a graduated income tax, postal savings bonds,

---

[25] *Ibid.,* pp. 61–68.
[26] Frank L. McVey, *The Populist Movement,* New York: Published for the American Economic Association by The Macmillan Company, Economic Studies, I (3): 133, 1896.

Government ownership and control of railroads and telegraph lines, and abolition of land monopolies. To attract the labor vote, resolutions were adopted favoring the 8-hour day and the abolition of the Pinkerton labor-spy system." [27] As Bizzell points out, these political pronouncements clearly indicate that the farmers throughout a great section of the country had been transformed from the most conservative to the most radical element in the population. [28]

One finds repeated reference to the mass appeal of the Populist conventions. There were always many good speakers and spontaneous mass singing to entertain the delegates and the audience. Some of the most colorful politicians ever to enter the American scene were in the Populist group. Such men as Judge William V. Allen of Nebraska, Tom Watson of Georgia, and Ben Tillman of South Carolina were characteristic leaders. The charismatic quality of their leadership played an important part in bringing the Populists together under one banner.

Women also played a great part in the Populist movement. Rochester maintains that the reason for this was that on farms in predominantly agricultural areas the wife is always the working partner of her husband. [29]

The party leaders carried on a vigorous campaign with speakers, parades, leaflets, and press notices. They made it a point to say the things the masses wanted to hear. The following song is one of many composed for campaign purposes: [30]

> I was once a tool of oppression,
> And as green as a sucker could be
> And monopolies banded together
> To beat a poor hayseed like me.
>
> The railroads and old party bosses
> Together did sweetly agree;
> And they thought there would be little trouble
> In working a hayseed like me.
>
> But now I've roused up a little,
> And their greed and corruption I see,
> And the ticket we vote next November
> Will be made up of hayseeds like me.

Although the campaign tactics differed from one state to another, all were designed to appeal to the masses. The most spectacular, perhaps, was the mass demonstration staged by Coxey's Army. Realizing the political importance of mass demonstrations, Carl Browne of Berkeley,

[27] Edwards, *op. cit.*, p. 263.
[28] Bizzell, *op. cit.*, p. 172.
[29] Rochester, *op. cit.*, p. 53.
[30] *Ibid.*, on back of title page.

California, and Jacob S. Coxey, a wealthy Populist of Massillon, Ohio, developed the plans under which seventeen different columns of unemployed workers converged upon Washington in the summer of 1894. Although this demonstration was more or less in vain, it has been the model of others that have had greater success.

In the election of 1892, with General Weaver of Greenback fame as its presidential candidate, the party cast a bombshell by polling more than a million popular votes and winning twenty-two electoral votes—the first time since 1860 that a third party had achieved electoral recognition. This was partially due to the strategy of combining forces with the Republicans in the South and the Democrats in the West. In the congressional election of 1894, the Populists further increased their vote to a million and a half, electing seven congressmen and six Senators.

The decisive year was 1896, when agrarianism, with labor as an ally, made its supreme bid to power. All the bitterness and unrest of thirty years of economic and political exploitation were compressed in that presidential campaign. The leaders chose free silver as the one issue on which to wage the battle, but they made thereby a fatal error. The Western Populists were determined that the party, having swallowed the silver issue, should endorse Bryan. In opposition stood the majority of the Southern delegates, who would not surrender all the gains the small Southern farmers had achieved since the Civil War.[31] The Southerners were voted down, but events bore out only too well their predictions. Bryan went down in defeat, although he polled 6½ million votes, and with him went the Populist party. The party never recovered from the blow, although it remained in existence until 1912. The farmers were tired of the movement, perhaps, and disillusioned about its chance of success. At the same time, the Spanish-American War, entered into under the McKinley administration, united popular support around the war party, and, as both crops and prices began to improve, the farmers were fairly prosperous. With no grievances, it was hard to stay militantly organized.

LATER DEVELOPMENTS

After the decline of the Alliance and the Populist party, various farmers' organizations appeared. However, none became so influential as these groups, or showed so much promise of actually being in a position to achieve its goals through political means. Here we can mention only the most prominent of these organizations, most of which still exist. The Gleaners, the Equity Union, and the American Society of Equity were

[31] Edwards, *op. cit.*, p. 264.

relatively small, but the Farmers' Union, the Farm Bureau, and a few others gained enough importance to merit more detailed discussion.

The Farmers' Union

The Farmers' Educational and Cooperative Union of America was organized by a professional farmer, Newt Gresham, at Point, Texas, in 1902. Its appeal was not so much in its effort to relieve economic distress as in its being a secret order in a part of the country where farmers' movements of that nature were traditional. The movement, like the Alliance, was by no means exclusively, or even primarily, political, but it did contain important aspects of this nature. The principal objects of the organization were to work for the improvement of the credit and mortgage system in the South, to assist members in buying and selling, to educate farmers in methods of scientific agriculture, to systematize methods of distribution and production, to forbid speculation in farm futures, and to get prices guaranteed by the government to ensure a fair return for farm enterprises.[32]

The Farmers' Union was perhaps the most extreme of all the movements in its exclusiveness. The organization tried to prevent the infiltration into its ranks of businessmen, middlemen, and professional men, who had no interest in farming but a financial interest in good farmer contacts. Like the Alliance, the Union also sought to cooperate with labor in its days of importance. However, in recent years it has become decidedly less friendly with labor, and in general more conservative in its approach to a number of problems.

The Farm Bureau

The Smith-Lever Act, passed in 1914, provided for appropriations to county agricultural agents for the organization of farmers' groups through which the information from state land-grant colleges and the U.S. Department of Agriculture could be disseminated. One result was the development of the Farm Bureau movement, the most influential and important farmers' organization of recent years. The Farm Bureau is not a government organization, although its early impetus came from this direction. The organization of the Bureau places more emphasis upon the local unit than have other groups of this type. Its chief aims are the improvement of techniques of farming and the achievement of economic advantages. It works through elected candidates to improve the welfare of the local farmer. Unlike its predecessors, the Farm Bureau does not usually try to do much about determining elections but tends rather to act as a pressure group in the interest of farmers in state and national

[32] Hunt, *op. cit.*, pp. 43–56.

legislation. It is significant that it has been as potent a factor in determining the course of legislation on farm problems as any of the more spectacular organizations.

Perhaps the greatest distinction between this movement and the others is that the type of leadership is different. The farm movements discussed earlier were led by men who were dissatisfied with conditions as they were and wanted to reform them. The Farm Bureau derives its leadership for the most part from successful farmers in each community, and the difference in political approach stems from this basic difference in character.

The Nonpartisan League

The more dramatic types of farm movements have not been lacking in the past few decades. The Nonpartisan League of North Dakota and adjacent states, founded in 1915, became a potent political force in this area of the nation. Although it had at its peak only 235,000 dues-paying members, its aims were so exclusively of a political nature that its influence was extensive. The principle of the League was similar to that of the Farmers' Union and Alliance. It did not set out to be a political party, as its name suggests, but instead sought to ferret out and defeat those within existing political parties who were not friendly to its principles.

It is interesting to note that this organization developed during Wilson's administration, when much agrarian legislation was passed, and that it spread throughout the war years, when prices were high. As Bizzell points out, this does not mean that the League was dissatisfied with existing legislation but rather that it felt that much more remained to be done, particularly in wheat-growing areas.[33]

The Farm Labor Union of America

The Farm Labor Union of America was organized in east Texas after the price fall in cotton in 1920 and 1921. Like the Alliance and Farmers' Union it concentrated upon the conditions of the cotton farmer, with emphasis upon rural credit conditions. The organization spread throughout the large cotton-growing districts of east Texas and eastern and southern Oklahoma. Attempts were made to spread the organization eastward into the Old South in the manner of the two previous organizations of Texas origin, but they had little success.

The movement in Texas was concerned principally with two issues that are reminiscent of those of the Nonpartisan League. First, it demanded a system of state credit whereby tenant farmers and laborers

[33] Bizzell, *op. cit.*, pp. 179–180.

could buy land and homes with money advanced by the state on long-term loans. Second, it sought the exemption of farm and city homesteads from taxes, with concurrent heavy taxing of undeveloped lands in comparison to developed lands of the same type.[34] The organization was without any particular success in Texas. It succeeded in electing a governor in Oklahoma, but through difficulty created by the Ku Klux Klan, he was impeached and the movement collapsed.

The Past Three Decades

When the depression of the 1930s hit the farm population, suffering became more acute than at any time since 1900. In some areas it was probably more acute than ever before. There is no doubt that the 1932 presidential election represented a "revolt" on the part of farmers in nearly all parts of the country. Conditions were ripe for a revival of an agrarian movement comparable to the Grange, the Alliance, and Populism. It is a matter of record that the first steps toward some such movement had been taken before the election.

The idea of a Farmers' Holiday was initiated by the Farmers' Union early in the 1930s. Organized bands of farmers began to clamor for debt moratoriums and to use tacit threats of violence to halt foreclosures. In the spring of 1933, thousands of farmers attended a conference, referred to sometimes as the Farmers' Holiday Association, and drew up a four-plank program: (1) debt moratorium, (2) reduction of farm taxes, (3) lower interest rates, and (4) fixing of minimum prices by law. Actually, some violence was used in 1932 and 1933, both in interrupting milk deliveries and in preventing foreclosures.

Thus all the indications were that a large-scale tendency toward organization was under way, and there seems little doubt that another nationwide wave of agrarianism was about to develop. That it did not can be explained only by the immediate action of the Roosevelt administration, which, in those critical first months, made desperate efforts to meet most of the farmers' demands for relief of agricultural conditions. Since this time, these programs have been retained and regularly amended in an all-out attempt to prevent serious political defection on the part of farmers. These efforts, plus the generally prosperous times, have probably forestalled widespread discontent. Nevertheless, the major farmers' organizations continue to maintain active, aggressive political programs. In the concluding section of this chapter, we shall review the current legislative policies and programs of three of the more important farmers' organizations.

[34] Hunt, *op. cit.*, pp. 145–186.

A PREVIEW OF POSSIBLE FUTURE CHANGES

The current legislative programs and policies of national farm organizations are of great interest to students of social change. They not only portend the future of agricultural legislation to a very real extent but indicate the trend of important legislation in other areas. The present discussion is designed to acquaint the student with some of the more important policies of three of the largest and most powerful of these organizations—the Farm Bureau, the National Grange, and the Farmers' Union. The information presented is from publications of the national offices of these groups.[35]

Policies and Programs of the Farm Bureau

The Farm Bureau, as of 1957, represented some 1,587,107 member families in the forty-eight states and Puerto Rico. It is the largest general farm organization in the nation at the present time. The stated philosophy of the Bureau amounts to belief in the basic constitutional freedoms, separation of church and state, a strict competitive system, private property, decentralization of government, government by law invested in strong and responsible state and local units of government, avoidance of the evils of the planned economy as represented in socialism, communism, and fascism, and the danger of monopolies.

A major concern of the Farm Bureau at present is the creation and maintenance of farm prosperity through programs that will provide maximum individual freedom and private ownership and initiative and minimum Federal regulation. The farm policies that the Bureau has designed to achieve this objective stress, among other things, (1) wise use of natural resources through Federal programs of agricultural conservation, development of water projects with Federal aid, and the expansion of Federal power projects such as the TVA; (2) price support and production programs; (3) expanded research by the U.S. Department of Agriculture to enlarge markets, achieve lower production costs, and improve the quality of agricultural products; (4) an expanded agricultural extension service with primary supervision of the program at the local level; (5) farm credit adapted to farm needs at low interest rates.

In addition to its farm policies, the Farm Bureau takes a definite stand on certain national and international problems. For example, the Bureau

---

[35] See: *1957 Policies of the American Farm Bureau Federation,* American Farm Bureau Federation, Washington; *Summary of Legislative Policies and Programs of the National Grange for 1957,* The National Grange, Washington; and *National Farmers' Union Program for 1956–1957,* Farmers Educational and Cooperative Union of America, Denver.

favors: (1) continuing programs of technical assistance, trade, investment, and military aid to friendly nations; (2) continuation of the selective service program; (3) the right to work regardless of membership or lack of membership in any organization; (4) continued primary responsibility of states in the construction, administration, and policing of highways; and (5) control of schools remaining with the smallest unit of government capable of satisfactory performance.

The numerous other stated policies and programs of the Farm Bureau can be found in the 1957 statement of policy, referred to earlier.

Policies and Programs of the National Grange

The National Grange includes 7,200 local Subordinate Granges and has a membership of over 860,000 actual members in thirty-seven states. It is well represented in every part of the United States except the Deep South.

The Grange process purports to be democratic at all levels and bipartisan in so far as national-party affiliation is concerned. The policies of the Grange, like those of the Farm Bureau, encompass the broad scope of national and international affairs. Such widespread interest is explained in the following quotation from the aforementioned handbook on *Legislative Policies and Programs of the National Grange for 1957.* "Because the Grange is a farm organization, and for other reasons, Grange people are concerned with matters of world peace, education, taxation, military training and preparedness, civil defense, health, and many subjects in addition to agricultural development." The programs of the Grange are aimed at facilitating and maintaining the successful operation of our national economy and in so doing promoting the maximum in economic prosperity, progress, and freedom.

The agricultural policies of the Grange reflect its philosophy that family farms are the backbone of rural America. Among the farm goals of the Grange are: (1) specially designed production and marketing programs for individual commodities, (2) expanded research on agricultural production and marketing, (3) expansion of cooperative activity, (4) expansion of foreign and domestic markets, (5) increased credit and educational aid to farmers, (6) special assistance to farmers with substandard incomes, (7) continuing programs of land- and water-resource conservation and development, and (8) price-support programs for commodities when needed.

Other interests of the Grange include changes in the national transportation policy in the interest of freer competition, an expanded and more efficient highway administration, expanded radio and television coverage for rural America, a conservative tax program to end deficit financing and provide more equitable taxation, opposition to fair-trade laws, expansion of right-to-work laws, opposition to universal military training, and decentralization of certain government functions.

At the international level, the Grange favors the continued strengthening of friendly nations within the limits of moderate expense to the American farmer, the implementation of reciprocal trade on a mutually beneficial basis, and the strengthening of the United Nations.

These are some of the more significant aims of the National Grange. In closing this review of Grange policies, it is of interest to note that a final aim of the Grange is to make the corn tassel the national floral emblem.

Policies and Programs of the Farmers' Union

In 1957 the membership of the Farmers' Union was approximately 300,000 "working" farm families. The aims and principles of this organization resemble those of the Farm Bureau and the Grange in some ways but are quite different in others. A summary statement of the beliefs and philosophy of the Farmers' Union is as follows: "We seek an agriculture of farm families on family farms, prosperous, efficient, masters of themselves, good stewards of the soil they till, standing on their own feet and seeking nothing of any man except a fair and equal chance to use their abilities to the fullest in their own behalf as useful members of a democratic society."

The action program of the Union is set up to achieve this goal. The major policies recommended are: full, fair farm-parity income, expanded local and foreign markets, production and marketing goals, adequate crop insurance, liberal and expanded farm credit, investigation of market spreads, special low-income family-farm programs, and expansion of rural telephone and electrification programs.

An expanding full-employment economy is another major concern of the Farmers' Union. To achieve this aim, they are for improving the Employment Act, increasing the public-works programs, further development of power resources, decentralization of industry, doing away with "right-to-work" legislation, adjustment of tax burdens to ability to pay, and provision of adequate civil defense and disaster insurance. Other allied programs of special concern include the promotion of civil liberties and rights for all, social security for all, the administering of public and privately owned land resources in the interest of all, and the promotion of an agricultural and industrial balance.

From an international standpoint the Farmers' Union is concerned with waging peace. It would do this through an adequate national-defense program, universal disarmament, expansion of the United Nations, exchange of nonmilitary atomic materials and information, and programs of economic development in foreign countries.

Questions for Review and Discussion

1. Explain what is meant by the term *social movement*.
2. List and describe the various stages of a social movement.
3. Why is it rare for a social movement to reach the final stage?
4. Are farmers' movements genuine social movements? Defend your answer.
5. Select one of the major farmers' movements in this country and trace its origin, development, and success.
6. List the major policies and programs of the Farm Bureau, the Grange, and the Farmers' Union.

Selected References for Supplementary Reading

Green, Arnold W.: *Sociology*, 2d ed., New York: McGraw-Hill Book Company, Inc., 1956, pp. 530–538.

Heberle, Rudolf: *Social Movements*, New York: Appleton-Century-Crofts, Inc., 1951.

Taylor, Carl C.: *The Farmers' Movement, 1620–1920*, New York: American Book Company, 1953.

――― et al.: *Rural Life in the United States*, New York: Alfred A. Knopf, Inc., 1949, chap. 29.

CHAPTER 24   *Communication and Technological*
Change in Rural Society

Much human interaction involves the communication of ideas, facts, feelings, and information. In rural communities communication is becoming increasingly important because more knowledge is required to perform the tasks and make the decisions necessary in present-day living than was needed in past years.

Success or failure of crops and a profit or loss from farm products may be determined by whether the farmer has received timely information about these matters. Whether the family gets sound materials and equipment for the household and makes the best use of them depends upon the kind of information received about them. Likewise, the value of improvements in the areas of education, health, recreation, and community services is dependent upon how and to what extent information is communicated about them.

If the farmer and his family are to compete with other segments of the economy and enjoy the benefits of our advanced technological society, they must keep abreast of developments for the farm and the household. Acceptance of changes is an important process in itself and will be discussed in the following chapter. The present chapter deals more specifically with the role of communication in alerting farmers to new ideas, tools, and practices. In it we shall attempt to answer the following questions:

1. What is the nature of the channels of communication as they affect information about technological change?
2. What is the availability of different channels of information by locality, region, social status, and educational level?
3. What are the roles of different channels of communication in the process of change—
   a. with respect to type of information?
   b. with respect to type of change?

370

COMMUNICATION AND CULTURE

Before considering the specific problems of communication as related to technological change, it is necessary to review the influence of culture upon communication. How do the norms, values, and ideas of the people influence their acceptance of information from different sources? In answering this question, three direct ties between culture and effectiveness of communication in rural areas must be noted.

First, cultures in which a high value is placed upon familism and tradition as opposed to individualism and science are likely to be resistant to channels of communication originating outside the community. The reason for this attitude is that the acceptance of information from the outside world tends to disrupt tradition and family ties. Furthermore, the formalized agencies of communication represent secular values that are contrary to the values of familistic and localistic cultures. As a result of inability to identify with the objectives and interests of these agencies, rural people disregard them.

The acceptability of communications is also influenced by the extent to which the information being communicated supports such rural values as independence and self-reliance. This is a second problem. Communications from outside sources are likely to be rejected by those who place strong emphasis upon these values. The farmer who says, "No one is going to tell me how to farm," fits into this category. Such attitudes may be strong enough to produce resentment of any communication from outside sources which implies that changes should be made in ways of farming or living. This is most likely to result from the use of impersonal and one-way channels of information where there is little opportunity for the receiver to express his ideas and feelings about the change.

The semantics of communication is the third problem related to culture. Communication involves the use of words that are symbols of the speaker's meaning. The meanings of words are determined by the context in which the words are used. Communications are effective only in so far as the meanings of the communicator are conveyed to the receiver. Words must be used in the sense in which they are understood in terms of the local culture. This can best be assured in two-way communication in which there is an opportunity for "give and take" until a mutual understanding of the ideas and issues is reached.

THE CHANNELS OF COMMUNICATION AND THEIR USES

The channels of communication are of two main types: formalized agencies whose main purpose is to transmit information, advertising, or entertainment; and informal contacts that transmit information incidental to other functions which those contacts serve, such as friendship, mutual aid, and trade.[1] Certain channels of information, such as farm organizations, do not fit clearly into either of these two types. While they are formally organized groups, their main purpose does not include the dissemination of information. This function is usually secondary to the economic, political, and social functions of such organizations.

In a similar manner, certain public-action agencies, such as the Soil Conservation Service, the Agricultural Stabilization and Conservation Service, and the Farmers Home Administration, are important sources of certain types of information, although their main purpose is to provide certain other services for the farmer (see Fig. 38).

It is thus obvious that the formality or institutionalization of a channel of communication is a matter of degree. Furthermore, some of the formalized channels, such as the educational agencies, utilize both formal and informal means of communication. The nature of the important communicating agents in rural society with respect to their functions, their ways of communicating, and their accessibility is described below.

The Farm Family

In the past, most of the skills and knowledge of farm and household have been transmitted from father to son and from mother to daughter. This practice is still quite prevalent, as indicated by the fact that two-fifths of a sample of Wisconsin farm owners reported that they learned most about farming from their fathers or from their fathers and other sources equally.[2] Similarly, half the wives said they learned most about homemaking from their mothers and another one-third gave their mothers with another source as most important. At this point it is significant to note that the farm family plays a more important role in transmitting knowledge and skills to its younger members than many urban families. This is especially true of occupations for which knowledge is learned through apprenticeship, trade schools, or professional training.

To the extent that parents are the primary source of knowledge for the son and daughter on the farm, the opportunity for introducing new ideas and techniques is limited. In this situation, the teachings and practices of parents become more than mere techniques for doing things; they become the symbols of family pride and loyalty; fathers' and mothers' ways of doing things take on a "value" involvement (see Chapter 4).

The introduction of new ideas and techniques in farming and family

[1] E. A. Wilkening, *Acceptance of Improved Farm Practices in Three Coastal Plain Counties,* North Carolina AES Technical Bulletin 98, 1952, pp. 25–27.
[2] E. A. Wilkening, *Adoption of Improved Farm Practices as Related to Family Factors,* Wisconsin AES Research Bulletin 183, 1953.

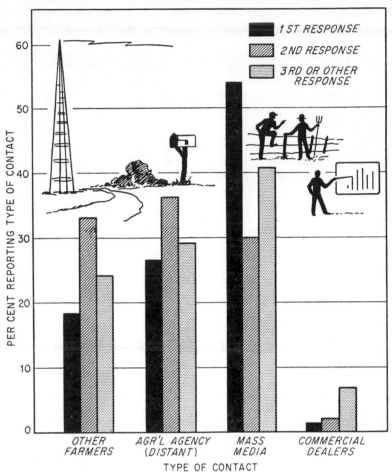

Figure 38. Percentage of 170 sample farm owners of Sauk County, Wisconsin, reporting three major types of contacts for most information and for additional information about new things in farming. (From E. A. Wilkening, *Adoption of Improved Farm Practices as Related to Family Factors*, Wisconsin AES Research Bulletin 183, 1953.)

living disrupts, in a sense, the authoritative role of family and kin as a source of knowledge. The father, for example, must be willing to admit, without a feeling of loss of pride or prestige, not only outsiders but also family members as sources of information about farm matters. This attitude is more likely to come about in an atmosphere of mutual respect and confidence among family members than in one characterized by subordination and father-centered decision making.

There is evidence that such a transition is occurring among many farm families. In the Wisconsin study previously mentioned, about half the operators with sons twelve years of age or over said their sons had encouraged them to make specific changes in their farms.[3] Many of the changes encouraged were practices the sons had learned about through vocational agriculture courses in high school or through the 4-H Club. About two-fifths of the same group of farm owners said their wives had encouraged them to make specific changes in enterprises or practices on their farms. Frequently such encouragement resulted from the wife's contacts outside the family or with radio programs or magazine articles.

Further evidence of this trend is found in Abell's study of Canadian farmers. She found that farm matters were discussed more frequently with wife and children than with anyone else.[4] No doubt much of this discussion involved the transmission of information that wife or son had gained through their individual contacts, both personal and impersonal. To this extent they are an important link in the communication of farm information.

Neighbors and Friends

Next to family members, the average farmer is in more frequent contact with neighbors and friends than with other persons. Most farmers have from three to six other farmers with whom they have frequent personal contact. Whether the contacts are nearby neighbors or friends outside the immediate locality varies with region and with socioeconomic status. Farmers of lower status are more likely to limit their contacts to nearby neighbors and to relatives who are not too distant. Those of higher status are less likely to limit their visiting and social contacts to those living in the immediate locality. For them, visiting and personal contacts are based upon mutual interest.

Whether based upon spatial proximity or mutual interest, this type of contact is characterized by informality and by a highly personal type of relationship. The contacts serve many functions, among which the transmission of information is only incidental, such as friendship, mutual aid, and recreation. Because of these basic functions of the neighborhood and clique group, they have a high degree of influence upon behavior. It is in such groups that attitudes are formed and behavior molded. Most people take into account "what the neighbors think" or "what my friends will say" before making decisions involving a change in behavior.

Neighbors and friends are highly important sources of information about farm and home matters. A North Carolina study revealed that neighbors ranked first as the source from which "most information" was

---

[3] *Ibid.*, p. 31.

[4] Helen Abell, *The Exchange of Farm Information*, Ottawa, Canada: Department of Agriculture, Marketing Service, 1953, p. 1.

obtained for seven out of eight improved practices studied.[5] Other studies in Iowa, Wisconsin, and Canada arrived at similar conclusions.[6]

Lionberger made an intensive study of the manner in which informal social groups (cliques, kinship groups, and work-exchange groups) affect the diffusion of farm information.[7] He found that informal groups operate both to facilitate and to hinder the transmission of farm information. Farm operators were much more likely to seek information from persons belonging to the same informal group than from persons outside the group. This was true for the social cliques as well as for the kinship, work-exchange, and other informal groups. Lionberger and Hassinger discovered that living in an "identifiable neighborhood" was likely to lead to seeking information from other farmers of the same neighborhood. Persons residing in nonneighborhood areas were more likely to rely upon institutionalized sources of information.[8]

Although neighbors and friends are very important sources of information about new ideas, a question arises regarding their reliability. This is an important question, since there is evidence that personal communication between neighbors and friends is more effective in influencing behavior than any other means.[9] Such communication is between social equals, and there is likely to be a high degree of identification in interests and objectives.

The implication of studies thus far is that neighbors and clique groups have limitations in transmitting information. In the first place, they usually lack access to information about technological change. In the second place, the information is quite frequently not transmitted objectively and completely. And the extent of information about new things is limited to the experience and contacts of the members of the group. Also, since the transmission of information about technological changes is not a primary function of this type of group, such information is likely to be incomplete or at least colored by the interests and sentiments of the individuals.

[5] Wilkening, *Acceptance of Improved Farm Practices.*

[6] Bryce Ryan and Neal Gross, *Acceptance and Diffusion of Hybrid Corn Seed in Two Iowa Communities*, Iowa AES Research Bulletin 372, 1950; Abell, *op. cit.;* and Wilkening, *Adoption of Improved Farm Practices as Related to Family Factors.*

[7] Herbert F. Lionberger, "The Relation of Informal Social Groups to the Diffusion of Farm Information in a Northeast Missouri Farm Community," *Rural Sociology*, 19: 233–243, 1954.

[8] Herbert F. Lionberger and Edward Hassinger, "Neighborhoods as a Factor in the Diffusion of Farm Information in a Northeastern Missouri Farming Community," paper presented at the meeting of the Mid-West Sociological Society, Madison, Wisconsin, May, 1954.

[9] See S. M. Eisenstadt, "Conditions of Communication Receptivity," *Public Opinion Quarterly*, 17:363–374, 1953.

Informal Leaders

What is the role of the informal leader, or the persons most frequently sought as sources of farm information? Are those who are influential in other affairs also influential in farm matters?

In a culture where social differences are not emphasized and in which there is access to many sources of information, leadership in farm matters, as in others, is clearly not highly centralized. Although certain individuals have a relatively great amount, influence is widely distributed among a large number of people.[10] For example, Lionberger found that of 279 farm operators in a community, over half were given by at least one other farmer as the person with whom he "talked most frequently about farm problems." [11] Twenty-two were mentioned by five or more farm operators in this connection, sixty were named by two to four, and seventy-two by one. Wilkening found a similar distribution among the "best farmers" in a survey of 200 out of 3,365 farmers in a southern county of Wisconsin. Allowing two designations, the 200 farm owners named 157 "best farmers they knew pretty well." Of this number 21 were mentioned by three or more, 36 were mentioned twice, and 100 were listed only once. This suggests the wide dispersion of persons who "influence" others in farm matters.

With such a widespread distribution of the persons to whom other farmers look for ideas and information, it is apparent that most of these persons do not know a great deal more than the persons who look to them. A general observation is that farmers seek others who are just above them, but not too far, with respect to prestige and economic status. The "best farmers" chosen by the Wisconsin sample were above average with respect to income and size of farm, although not much above. Lionberger found that the farm operators who were sought for farm information operated larger farms, had higher incomes, and had higher prestige than the average farmer of the community. They also were more active in all types of formal social organizations and were more likely to be leaders in educational and civic affairs. In both the Wisconsin and Missouri studies the influential persons had adopted more improved practices than had the noninfluential persons.[12]

Although further study is needed to determine the role of informal

[10] See Robert K. Merton, "Patterns of Influence: A Study of Interpersonal Influence and of Communication Behavior in a Local Community," in Paul F. Lazarsfeld and F. N. Stanton, *Communications Research 1948–49*, New York: Harper & Brothers, 1949.

[11] Herbert F. Lionberger, "Some Characteristics of Farm Operators Sought as Sources of Farm Information in a Missouri Community," *Rural Sociology*, 18:327–338, 1953.

[12] This is contrary to the findings of certain other studies.

leaders in farm matters, there is evidence that farmers with a wider range of influence are likely to obtain their information directly from the institutionalized sources of information and are the leaders in innovation. It is apparent that they look beyond their locality and identify themselves with nonlocal groups. Those with a smaller range of influence are less likely to be "progressive-minded"; they may identify themselves entirely with local concerns and lack interest in promoting change.

Community Contacts

Many of the contacts of the farmer extend beyond neighbors and close friends. The farmer of today has many contacts in the community in which he lives. These include his contacts for buying and marketing, education, and religious, social, and civic activities. Although many of these contacts are informal in nature, they cover a wider area than the immediate locality.

The fact that about half of 179 farm owners in southern Wisconsin gave "best farmers" who lived over two miles away is an indication that the farmers' contacts for farm matters extend beyond the immediate vicinity. Many of these contacts no doubt occur in the trade center or in connection with other community activities, such as church and school. In a study of a Missouri community, it was found that farmers who do not belong to identifiable neighborhoods most often meet other farmers in the trade center, along the road, at farm meetings, and in exchanging work.[13]

The dealer in farm supplies, the custom sprayer, and the veterinarian are commercial sources of information located within the community. Persons in such occupations are in a strategic position to supply information on technological changes involving the use of materials and equipment. They are frequently asked "how much," "what kind," and "how to do it" questions. In responding to these questions, the dealer draws upon the experiences of other farmers in the locality and the recommendations of manufacturers and colleges of agriculture. Frequently he is a farmer himself and is thereby in a position to give more weight to his own recommendations.

The influence of sales promotion in the adoption of hybrid corn has been demonstrated.[14] Salesmen were given as the source of "original knowledge" about hybrid corn by half the farmers interviewed in a survey in Iowa. One-third of the farmers cited salesmen as "most influential" in their adoption of hybrid corn. These findings suggest the importance of the commercial operator in influencing certain types of changes.

[13] Lionberger and Hassinger, *op. cit.*
[14] Ryan and Gross, *op. cit.*

Mass Communications

The communication of news, information, propaganda and entertainment has become highly institutionalized in most places in the United States. The mass media are themselves a product of technological development. The extent of coverage of the mass media—radio, television, newspapers, magazines, and other printed materials—varies with general technological advancement and with educational level. Today, few American farmers are without radio or television, a newspaper, and at least one farm magazine. In addition, many circular letters and pamphlets from public agencies and private concerns reach the farmer's mailbox.

The relatively low cost of the mass media as a way of disseminating information has led some to conclude that this should be the primary means used by educational agencies. But a closer look at the nature of the mass media as means of technological change reveals certain limitations.

The newspaper has long been recognized as a means of keeping informed about local and nonlocal events. Many weeklies and local dailies carry regular articles by extension agents or by farm reporters. Where such articles have been developed to include news and personal accounts of the experiences of farmers and their families, there is evidence of considerable influence as a source of new ideas in farming and homemaking. The newspaper is more likely to be an aid to other agencies of communication, such as the Agricultural Extension Service and the Colleges of Agriculture, than to be an important channel of information for technological change itself.

Radio and, more recently, television are important in disseminating information on changes in rural society. As with the newspaper, radio and television stations are usually business enterprises. The type of information transmitted about new technology is likely to be influenced by the need for stimulating and holding the interest of the listener or the viewer. Whatever is presented must have an appeal to a fairly wide audience. Market news and weather news have the widest appeal to the farm radio listener. Informational programs for the farmer and for the homemaker rate much lower in farm-family listening interest.[15]

Here also, the kind of material presented is limited by interest and ease of communication. Interviews with other farmers and housewives appear to have higher interest value than talks by the experts. The relating of local experiences with new practices and enterprises has more appeal than the report of an experiment. Yet, talks by experts who in-

---

[15] See, for example: Alvin L. Bertrand and Homer L. Hitt, *Radio Habits in Rural Louisiana*, Louisiana AES Bulletin 440, 1949.

clude the experiences of farmers with the results of experimental studies are very common. Timely information about the method of disease and insect control and about new crop varieties are adaptable to radio talks. In a North Carolina study, interviewees gave radio programs more than any other single type of contact as the source of "some information" about boll weevil control on cotton, blue mold control on tobacco, and improved permanent pastures.[16]

Farm papers and magazines reach most farm homes. They are of three main types: the national farm magazines, state magazines, and house organs of farm cooperatives, commodity organizations, and general farm organizations. The first and second types are most important in technological change. The farm magazine draws from a wide variety of sources of materials—the agricultural experiment stations, experts, and the experiences of individual farmers and farm families. They depend upon the prestige of the expert and the feature writer or departmental editor rather than upon that of local farmers. How a sample of North Carolina farmers obtained their information on eight farm practices is shown in Figure 39.

Farm magazines are accessible at a low cost and can be read at the convenience of the farmer. They cover a wide range of subject matter and are heavily illustrated. These features, no doubt, are responsible for the widespread mention of the farm magazines as a source of information about new things in farming. Studies in the Northeast and Middle West found farm magazines to rank first or second in frequency of mention as the main source of new ideas in farming. In areas of lower educational level, farm magazines are not so widely recognized as a primary source of new ideas and information.

Educational and Public Agencies

Much social and technological change is mediated through the schools and other institutions whose primary function is to transmit ideas and information about the new as well as the old. Public schools and colleges teach the principles of farming and homemaking in addition to many other disciplines. They instill in the student a respect for the experimental or scientific approach to these subjects. To the extent that they are successful in this endeavor, the student accepts experimental evidence and scientific principles as the basis for evaluating technological changes.

The change from *experience* to *experiment* as the basis for accepting farm technology is dramatically illustrated by the experience of the son who has attended the College of Agriculture and returns home to try

---

[16] Wilkening, *Acceptance of Improved Farm Practices*, p. 26.

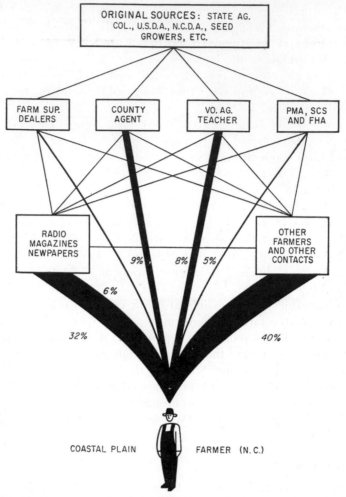

Figure 39. How a sample of 341 farmers in the Coastal Plain of North Carolina obtained their information about eight selected farm practices. (From E. A. Wilkening, *Acceptance of Improved Farm Practices in Three Coastal Plain Counties,* North Carolina AES Technical Bulletin 98, 1952.)

to get across some of the ideas he has learned to his father, who still relies primarily upon his own experience and that of his acquaintances.

Although the number of college-trained persons is small among the farm population, their influence in advancing new ideas and technology is likely to be considerable. Not only do they have more up-to-date knowledge, but they establish contacts with the colleges and with other agencies which provide continuous contacts for information about farm and household.

The Agricultural Extension Service is the agency most frequently identified with new ideas and information in farming. This agency, supported cooperatively by Federal, state, and local funds, has programs for farmers, housewives, and youth. Participation in its activities is entirely voluntary, and much of its work is done on an informal basis. For these and other reasons, more farm families of middle and higher socioeconomic status than of low status participate in the meetings and seek information through this agency. By means of radio, television, news articles, and other mass-communication media, the wider cross section of farm families is reached by the Agricultural Extension personnel.[17] An important characteristic of the Agricultural Extension Service in influencing technological change is its flexibility in the methods and techniques used. These range from personal consultation on the farm to the impersonal news article and circular letter. Also, much of this influence is indirect, exercised through consultation with leaders or organized groups and commercial firms. The influence of the Agricultural Extension Service in technological change cannot be measured by the extent of direct contact with the local agent. Studies in various parts of the country show that between 10 and 30 per cent of the farmers have at least occasional direct contact with their county agent.

Many public-action agencies are also influential in promoting technological change. Their influence is generally through special types of services rather than through educational programs as such. An illustration of this is the fact that the Soil Conservation Service was listed most frequently as the source of information about terracing in North Carolina, whereas, in the same study, the Production Marketing Administration was ranked high as a source of information about improved permanent pastures.[18] Other agencies given as sources of information about farm and home practices include the Farmers' Home Administration, the Rural Electrification Administration, the State Department of Agriculture, and public-health officials. These public agencies are in an advantageous position to provide information on the techniques and means of putting innovations into operation, although the initial information about them comes from other sources.

CHANNELS OF COMMUNICATION IN THE PROCESS OF CHANGE

The question arises in studying communication in connection with rural technological change, "Are different types of information received

[17] See Herbert F. Lionberger, *Low-Income Farmers in Missouri: Their Contacts with Potential Sources of Farm and Home Information*, Missouri AES Research Bulletin 441, 1949; and Herbert F. Lionberger, *Information Seeking Habits and Characteristics of Farm Operators*, Missouri AES Research Bulletin 581, 1955.

[18] Wilkening, *Acceptance of Improved Farm Practices*, pp. 26 and 63.

through different channels?" In other words, are farm people first informed about new ideas through different channels than those most influential in their adoption? Ryan and Gross, in their study of the adoption of hybrid corn in Iowa, found this to be the prevalent pattern. Salesmen, most of whom were farmers, were the dominant source of "original knowledge" about hybrid corn, whereas neighbors were "most influential" in the adoption of this practice. Wilkening found that, in North Carolina, more farmers heard about improved methods of blue mold control, improved permanent pastures, and hybrid corn through neighbors and other farmers than through any other single source, although neighbors and other farmers were given by an even greater number as the source of "most information" for blue mold control measures and for hybrid corn. In Wisconsin, one of the agricultural agencies was the most frequently mentioned source of first knowledge about 2-4-d weed control, although farm magazines were listed most frequently as the source of first information about grass silage. However, "other farmers" were cited most frequently as the source of "most information" about grass silage.

These findings suggest that awareness of technological change occurs through different sources, depending upon the region as well as upon the type of change. Also, the sources of "first knowledge" are frequently different from the sources of "most information" or "major influence" in adoption of the practice. As can be seen in Figure 40, the mass media, particularly the farm magazine and the radio, are relatively more important in first informing farmers about new practices than in providing the type of information needed upon which to evaluate and to learn how to perform an operation. Thus we may conclude that the one-way communication of the mass media is sufficient to provide initial information about new developments, but they are not so effective as other sources of information in the final decision of the farmer.

Thus the process of learning more about new changes and evaluating them requires discussion with someone who knows local conditions and who can answer specific questions. Two-way communication, as in personal contact with experts or with other farmers, is an important aspect of deciding upon a new idea and of putting it into practice.[19]

A second question that arises in studying communication in connection with rural technological change is, "At what point in the introduction of technological changes are different channels of communication utilized?" As one might expect, those who are among the first to adopt changes are more likely to get their information from sources originating outside the community—salesmen, radio programs, magazines, and

[19] See E. A. Wilkening, "Role of Communicating Agents in Technological Change in Agriculture," *Social Forces,* 34:361–367, 1956.

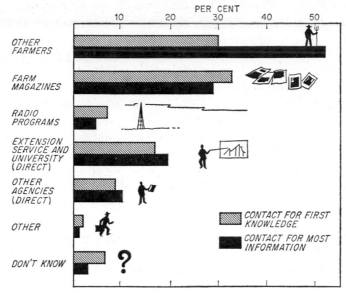

Figure 40. Percentage of 170 sample farm owners of Sauk County, Wisconsin, reporting different types of contacts as the source of first knowledge and as the source of most information about grass silage. (From E. A. Wilkening, *Adoption of Improved Farm Practices as Related to Family Factors,* Wisconsin AES Research Bulletin 183, 1953.)

agricultural agencies. Of the first 10 per cent to adopt hybrid corn in Iowa, about two-thirds said they were influenced most by salesmen. However, the latest adopters gave their neighbors as the source of major influence in their decision to use hybrid corn.[20]

The fact that later adoption of innovations is influenced by friends and neighbors does not mean that educational agencies cease to be important during the period of acceptance of an innovation. Acceptance is continuously accelerated by the educational and action agencies. But perhaps their role changes from that of setting up demonstrations and initiating the new practice to that of adapting the change to local conditions and appraising the result of local as well as nonlocal experiences with the practice.

Effectiveness of Communication

It is quite evident that different types of information sources are most effective for different types of technological changes. Furthermore, no one type of source is of equal effectiveness at all stages in technological change. An appropriate question, then, is, *"What kinds or combinations of information sources are most effective for what kinds of changes at*

[20] Ryan and Gross, *op. cit.,* pp. 684–685.

what stage in the process of diffusion?" The problem of determining the most effective information media is indeed a complex one. Only a few guiding principles for students will be suggested here.

1. Information transmitted through personal contact tends to be more effective than that transmitted through impersonal media. Related to this is the observation that two-way communication is more likely to influence behavior than one-way communication, even though the latter be through personal contact, as in group meetings.

2. Dependence upon sources of information outside the immediate locality is more likely to result in the adoption of technological changes than dependence upon neighbors. This principle appears to hold whether the outside sources of information are institutionalized agencies or other farmers. In the Wisconsin study previously cited, farmers giving "best farmers" living beyond a two-mile radius had adopted more improved practices than those giving "best farmers" living within a one-mile radius. Also, dependence upon educational agencies for information is associated with a higher adoption of technological changes.

3. The greater the number of sources of information reaching the farmer or homemaker, the greater the likelihood of his making changes in practices. This is in keeping with the idea that the acceptance of new ways requires not only one but several types of information over a period of time. Dependence upon several types of sources assures not only early thinking about the change but more complete knowledge of it. This includes the evaluation of its advantages and disadvantages, learning how to put it into operation, and understanding the reasons for the success or failure of initial trials.

4. Communication in general is effective in so far as it is oriented to the interests and needs of the receiver of the information. This depends upon the content of the information as well as upon the extent to which the communication allows for interaction. It is here also that confidence in and identification with the communicator is important. The receiver must accept and identify with the objectives of the communicating agent if the communication is to be regarded as a basis for action.

Questions for Review and Discussion

1. How is communication related to technological change in rural society?
2. Why is a knowledge of the culture in which a medium of communication operates important in understanding its success?
3. List in the order of their importance the channels of communication available to farmers in your area.
4. If you were a sales consultant to a manufacturer of agricultural products, how would you proceed to "sell" a new product in a given area?

Selected References for Supplementary Reading

Abell, Helen C.: *The Exchange of Farming Information,* Ottawa, Canada: Department of Agriculture, Marketing Service, Economics Division, 1953.

Bertrand, Alvin L., and Homer L. Hitt: *Radio Habits in Rural Louisiana,* Louisiana AES Bulletin 440, 1949.

Lionberger, Herbert F.: "Some Characteristics of Farm Operators Sought as Sources of Farm Information in a Missouri Community," *Rural Sociology,* 18:327–338, 1953.

Merton, R. K.: "Patterns of Influence: A Study of Interpersonal Influence and of Communication Behavior in a Local Community," in Paul F. Lazarsfeld and F. N. Stanton (eds.), *Communications Research, 1948–1949,* New York: Harper & Brothers, 1949.

Report of the Subcommittee on the Diffusion and Adoption of Farm Practices of the Rural Sociological Society, *Sociological Research on the Diffusion and Adoption of New Farm Practices,* Kentucky AES RS-2, 1952.

Wilkening, E. A.: *Acceptance of Improved Farm Practices in Three Coastal Plain Counties,* North Carolina AES Research Bulletin 98, 1952.

——: *Adoption of Improved Farm Practices as Related to Family Factors,* Wisconsin AES Research Bulletin 183, 1953.

CHAPTER 25 *The Process of Acceptance*
of Technological Innovations
in Rural Society

As indicated elsewhere, the technology of a society includes its techniques, its tools, and its materials for manipulating the physical world. The technology of rural society is of three main kinds, related to three aspects of the rural economy: technology of crops and livestock; technology of the preparation of foods and other articles for consumption; and technology of transportation and communication. The first involves the techniques and methods of farming; the second centers in the household; and the third applies to the movement of materials, equipment, or people and to contacts between people. The primary emphasis in this chapter will be upon technology relating to crops and livestock; this does not mean, however, that the other two are less important as a part of the technology of rural society.

TECHNOLOGY OF RURAL SOCIETY

The techniques and tools for farming have undergone great change since the first pointed stick was used to scratch the soil for planting seed. These changes have occurred over thousands of years, sometimes with and sometimes without conscious promotion. Development has been uneven, with little innovation in many parts of the world (such as the Middle East and parts of the Far East and Africa) within the past thousand years. In other areas the farmer has increased his output manifold in the past half-century, largely as the result of improved technology. This chapter is devoted to a discussion of some of the principles of technological change which apply to rural society and to farming in particular.

Types of Technological Innovations in Farming

Innovation represents a *qualitative* and not merely a *quantitative* change. A change in the amount of fertilizer applied to a crop would not constitute an innovation, whereas a change from organic to inorganic fertilizer would.

Innovations vary in both their intrinsic properties and their relationship to other aspects of the culture. On the basis of their intrinsic properties, innovations might be classified according to the changes they involve in: (1) amount of human effort required, (2) amount of capital or physical materials required, (3) manipulative skills involved, and (4) management ability required for achieving maximum benefits from the innovation. The first three of these properties can be indicated fairly objectively: for example, the labor, cost, and skill needed for the use of hybrid corn can be estimated within limits. The level of management ability required is more difficult to assess.

Innovations can also be classified according to their relationship to existing technology. Some innovations represent additions to or changes in existing farming or household operations. Changing from the dump hayrake to the side-delivery hayrake is an illustration of a change in an existing operation, that of raking hay. The use of the pressure canner instead of the open kettle in canning is a similar illustration in household technology. Other innovations are more or less independent of existing operations. Terracing and contour stripping, for example, represent new techniques not associated with previous operations. Relationship to existing technology has important implications for the rate of acceptance of innovations and for the sources of influence in acceptance.

Acceptance of Innovations as a Process

Innovations arise out of the on-going activities of man. They may occur without planning and incidentally to other activities, or they may occur as the result of consciously directed effort. Today, most innovations in the productive and consumptive activities of the farmer and his family are of the latter type. They are the product of the research efforts of the Agricultural Experiment Stations or of other public or private research institutions. The purpose of these research efforts is usually to develop techniques that allow the farmer and his family to do their work more efficiently or with less effort. *Efficiency* is thus the main criteria for the development of these innovations.

The relative advantages of the new as compared with the old technology constitute a condition affecting acceptance of change. In economic terms, this is the comparison of output per unit of input—the relative efficiency of the new item. The greater the efficiency of the new technology in producing returns in the form of economic or consumption goods or satisfactions, the greater the likelihood of its acceptance. An important qualifying condition of this principle is the relative ease with which the new technique can be demonstrated and the amount of time it takes to do this. The relative ease with which the advantage of hybrid corn could be demonstrated no doubt has influenced its rapid acceptance. On the other hand, the difficulty of demonstrating the advantage of strip-cropping or new crop rotations has made for slower acceptance of these practices.

This does not mean, however, that the acceptance of innovations is based entirely upon the efficiency of the new as compared with the old. If this were true, one would expect the new developments in farming and homemaking to be accepted as soon as their advantage over existing techniques was demonstrated. The gradual acceptance of most innovations suggests that many other factors influence acceptance. Even such simple innovations as hybrid corn required, on the average, five years for acceptance by Iowa farmers after they first heard about it.[1]

The act of adopting a new practice is the decision of an individual farmer, or householder, and his family and is preceded by a series of events or activities bearing upon the decision. They include: (1) the initial hearing about the practice; (2) learning about its features; (3) weighing the evidence, gathered through different sources, for and against its adoption; and (4) adopting the practice after organizing the time, labor, and materials required. The first two activities are distinguishable only in degree. However, hearing about a new practice is not always followed by learning more about it. Furthermore, adoption may be divided into two stages—trial adoption and complete adoption; this is shown graphically in Figure 41.

Viewed in this manner, the adoption of innovations is the result of a process occurring over a period of time. The time elapsing from initial knowledge until complete adoption may be a period of days or weeks for some individuals or many years for others. For still others, adoption never occurs.

The acceptance of innovations as a process is further described by the rate of acceptance over a period of time in a community or area. Plotted graphically, the cumulative number of persons adopting an innovation by years tends to follow a growth or S curve. This means that a period of slow acceptance is followed by a period of rapid acceptance until almost all the potential adopters have accepted the change.

[1] Bryce Ryan and Neal Gross, *Acceptance and Diffusion of Hybrid Corn Seed in Two Iowa Communities,* Iowa AES Bulletin 372, January, 1950, p. 678.

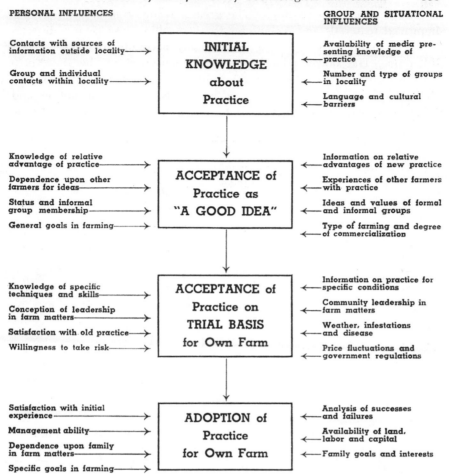

PERSONAL INFLUENCES

GROUP AND SITUATIONAL INFLUENCES

Contacts with sources of information outside locality——→

Group and individual contacts within locality———→

INITIAL KNOWLEDGE about Practice

←——Availability of media presenting knowledge of practice

←——Number and type of groups in locality

←——Language and cultural barriers

Knowledge of relative advantage of practice——→

Dependence upon other farmers for ideas——→

Status and informal group membership——→

General goals in farming——→

ACCEPTANCE of Practice as "A GOOD IDEA"

←——Information on relative advantages of new practice

←——Experiences of other farmers with practice

←——Ideas and values of formal and informal groups

←——Type of farming and degree of commercialization

Knowledge of specific techniques and skills——→

Conception of leadership in farm matters——→

Satisfaction with old practice——→

Willingness to take risk——→

ACCEPTANCE of Practice on TRIAL BASIS for Own Farm

←——Information on practice for specific conditions

←——Community leadership in farm matters

←——Weather, infestations and disease

←——Price fluctuations and government regulations

Satisfaction with initial experience——→

Management ability——→

Dependence upon family in farm matters——→

Specific goals in farming——→

ADOPTION of Practice for Own Farm

←——Analysis of successes and failures

←——Availability of land, labor and capital

←——Family goals and interests

Figure 41. The process of acceptance of new farm practices and factors influencing that process. (From E. A. Wilkening, *Adoption of Improved Farm Practices as Related to Family Factors,* Wisconsin AES Research Bulletin 183, 1953.)

A leveling off in the rate of adoption before approaching 100 per cent suggests that the change is not regarded as appropriate for the remaining portion or that there are barriers to communication of information about the change within the area (see Fig. 42).

A comparison of the rates of adoption of different types of innovations reveals certain variations in the process of acceptance. In a study of acceptance of certain improved farm practices in North Carolina, it was found that insect- and disease-control measures on cotton and tobacco, respectively, were accepted more quickly than hybrid corn or improved permanent pastures.[2] The greater recognition of the need for improved materials and techniques for controlling insects and diseases and the simplicity of the change probably accounts for most of this difference. The slower adoption of permanent pastures by the North Carolina farmers is related to the nature of the innovation. In this case the change involves operations and materials new to the cotton and tobacco farmer. This is in contrast to a change only in source and type

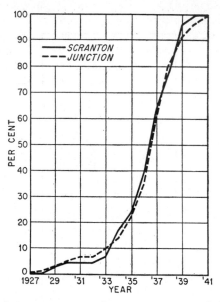

Figure 42. Cumulative percentages of operators accepting hybrid seed in two Iowa communities during each year of the diffusion process. (From Bryce Ryan and Neal Gross, *Acceptance and Diffusion of Hybrid Corn Seed in Two Iowa Communities,* Iowa AES Research Bulletin 372, 1950.)

of seed—hybrid corn—or a change in type of materials—new chemical compounds—for boll weevil control and for blue mold control. The rate of acceptance of innovations is the result of a number of factors: the recognized need, the amount of change involved, and external conditions that affect the need and ease in making the change. The latter include weather, the prevalence of disease and insects, and the economic factors that affect the costs and returns of the practice.

Despite differentials in rate of adoption, once an idea has been introduced and the process of innovation initiated in a given community, some people can be found at all the stages of the process of acceptance. These stages have been succinctly outlined by a subcommittee for

[2] E. A. Wilkening, *Acceptance of Improved Farm Practices in Three Coastal Plain Counties,* North Carolina AES Technical Bulletin 98, May, 1952, pp. 36–39.

the study of diffusion of farm practices of the North Central Rural Sociology Committee as follows.[3]

1. *Awareness:* At this stage the individual learns of the existence of the idea or practice but has little knowledge about it.

2. *Interest:* At this stage the individual develops interest in the idea. He seeks more information about it and considers its general merits.

3. *Evaluation:* At this stage the individual makes mental application of the idea and weighs its merits for his own situation. He obtains more information about the idea and decides whether or not to try it.

4. *Trial:* At this stage the individual actually applies the idea or practice—usually on a small scale. He is interested in how to apply the practice; in amounts, time, and conditions for application.

5. *Adoption:* This is the stage of acceptance leading to continued use.

TECHNOLOGICAL CHANGE AND THE FARM ENTERPRISE

The individual proceeds from initial knowledge to final adoption within a socioeconomic context. For the highly commercialized farmer, only a very small part of this context may be involved in his decision to adopt a new practice. His decisions are made primarily within the context of costs and returns. The adoption of a change in technology is governed primarily by its contribution to greater efficiency in production. Yet, even for the commercialized farmer, decisions in the area of technology are influenced by other than purely economic considerations. Changes in technology require knowledge, skills, adjustments in the farm enterprise, and frequently changes in relationships between the farmer and the tenant, the farm hand, the buyer, or other farmers.

The less commercialized the farm operations, the more likely it is that changes in technology will be influenced by noneconomic considerations. The more self-sufficient farmer uses technology not so much to make more money as to satisfy the direct needs of his family—for food and shelter, for example. To this extent he measures the costs and returns of technology not in terms of money but in terms of the available resources and the suitability of the product for family consumption. Hybrid corn has been rejected by the Spanish Americans of New Mexico and by some farmers in the South because of their objection to using it for human food. The variety of corn used in these sections of the country is selected because of its suitability for tortillas or corn bread as well as for livestock feed. Under these conditions, technological change is likely to be considerably affected by family tastes and interests. As one farmer remarked, "I am not interested in trying out new hybrid

[3] *How Farm People Accept New Ideas,* North Central Regional Publication 1, Special Report 15, Agricultural Extension Service, Ames, Iowa: Iowa State College, 1955, pp. 3–4.

strains and other new ideas. I want to make a living for my family and have a little to go on in my old age."

To a large extent, the slower acceptance of new technology by small farmers and by some tenant operators is no doubt due to lack of resources in the form of land and capital. In the North Carolina study previously mentioned, it was found that tenant operators and the operators of smaller farms were as favorable toward certain improved practices as the larger farmers and owners, although they had not adopted as many as the larger operators. The adoption of improvements on tenant-operated farms requires consideration of the costs and returns to both tenant and owner. Leases providing for compensation for improvements made by the tenant and for maximum security to both parties appear to be an important condition for adoption of changes on tenant-operated farms. In Iowa, where tenants are ordinarily more secure than in the South, there is no significant difference between tenants and owners in the adoption of hybrid corn.

Availability of credit for operating capital and government subsidies is also associated causally with the adoption of innovations and improvements in farming. Easy-term loans for operating capital through loan agencies, and subsidy payments through the Agricultural Conservation Program, have greatly facilitated the adoption of certain cropping and conservation measures on a national basis. The Rural Electrification Administration, by financing the extension of electricity to rural areas, has likewise been an important factor in the phenomenal increase in the use of electricity. Only 13.4 per cent of the nation's farms had electricity in 1930 as compared with 93 per cent in 1954.

Technological Change as a Function of Group Identification

As has been pointed out, people behave not as isolated beings but as members of groups having certain standards, values, and norms. The output of the factory worker is influenced by the standards set by his fellow workers, the violation of which is met with severe penalties. Similarly, the farmer is influenced by the norms and expectations of his family, his neighbors, and the members of the organizations to which he belongs. In making their decisions about farm matters, few farmers are independent enough to disregard the opinions of their neighbors, the demands of their families, and the expectations of the organizations of which they are members. To this extent the farmer's participation in various groups retards or accelerates change, depending upon how the change is interpreted by the group and upon the particular farmer's role in the group.

Participation in farm organizations (the Farm Bureau, the Grange, the Farmers' Union, cooperatives, and commodity associations) has been found to be consistently associated with adoption of recommended changes in farming. This is to be expected, since one of the functions of such organizations is the promotion of better farming methods. It is significant, however, that being identified with a group whose aims include the promotion of changes in farming is usually an indication of willingness to adopt such changes. Figure 43 illustrates this phenomenon.

Although participation in formal agricultural associations in general tends to be associated with a higher rate of adoption of innovations in farming, this relationship does not hold in the case of many other or-

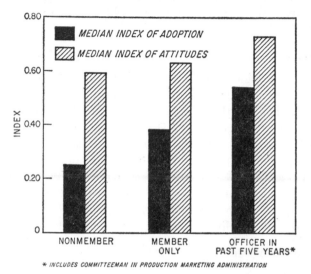

Figure 43. Median index of adoption of and attitudes toward eight improved farm practices of nonmembers, members, and officers in farm organizations. (From E. A. Wilkening, *Acceptance of Improved Farm Practices in Three Coastal Plain Counties,* North Carolina AES Technical Bulletin 98, 1952.)

ganizations. For example, church participation was not significantly associated with the adoption of improved practices in two sample groups of Wisconsin farmers. The studies to date suggest that to the extent that formal social contact is indicative of social status and of social contact outside the immediate locality, it is likely to be associated with the adoption of technological changes.

Thus it is obvious that the nature of the group with which the farmer or housewife identifies is likely to have a greater bearing upon the acceptance of technological change than general social participation. The farmer who identifies with the "good dairy farmers" of the community, county, or state is likely to make innovations faster than the farmer who merely has frequent social contacts. We shall not discuss the development of identification patterns here; however, such factors as early training experiences, personal association with farmers, and the reading of journal articles and other literature pertaining to the particular enterprise help to create a sense of identification.

There is evidence that the person who identifies primarily with the farmers of the immediate locality or kinship group is not likely to be strongly motivated to adopt changes in his farming enterprise. Those farmers most dependent upon neighborhood and kinship ties for visiting and exchange of work were less likely to have adopted improved farm practices.[4] Marsh and Coleman found in Kentucky that the norms of the locality make a difference in the adoption of recommended farm practices.[5]

The Informal Leader and the Innovator in Farm Technology

It would seem logical that the informal leaders in farm communities would promote the adoption of technological changes. The informal leader, as we shall use the term here, is one to whom two or more other farmers go for advice on or discussion of farm problems. One study reveals little difference between local informal leaders and other farmers in the extent of adoption of a group of farm practices.[6] On the other hand, the evidence available suggests that those persons who are "community-wide leaders" are likely to be among the first to adopt technological changes in farming.[7] Local leaders must conform to the values and standards of the locality and consequently do not push too far ahead of the group. Yet they are influential in spreading new ideas, after acceptance by the innovators and early adapters.

It follows then, that innovators are not necessarily influential persons locally in farm or in other matters. In fact, they are likely to be persons who are not closely bound by the locality group as leaders or as followers. They are likely to be of higher socioeconomic status than the average farmer of the area, or at least to aspire to higher status. They are likely to have interests and contacts outside the immediate locality and to be motivated more by material than by nonmaterial rewards. They may become known as persons who "always try out new things" or "are always experimenting with something." Their role is that of in-

[4] E. A. Wilkening, "A Sociopsychological Approach to the Study of the Acceptance of Innovations in Farming," *Rural Sociology*, 15:352–364, 1950.

[5] C. Paul Marsh and A. Lee Coleman, "The Relationship of Neighborhood of Residence to Adoption of Recommended Farm Practices," *Rural Sociology*, 19:385–389, 1954.

[6] E. A. Wilkening, "Informal Leaders and Innovators in Farm Practices," *Rural Sociology*, 17:272–275, 1952.

[7] Herbert F. Lionberger, "Some Characteristics of Farm Operators Sought as Sources of Farm Information in a Missouri Community," *Rural Sociology*, 18:327–338, 1953.

troducing new practices, which are then spread to others by personal contact or by the influence of the "informal leader" in farm matters.

The Family and Technological Change

The average farm is a family enterprise, and decisions on farm matters frequently involve other family members than the operator. How does the participation of family members in the farm enterprise affect the acceptance of technological changes?

The answer to this question, among others, was sought in a study of 170 farm-owner families in south central Wisconsin.[8] Although the sample is small, there is evidence that the family does influence the acceptance of recommended practices. For example, encouragement of sons to accept an active role in farm activities at an early age was found to be positively associated with acceptance of improved practices. Operators with children in 4-H or in vocational agricultural projects had also adopted more improved practices than had those without children in these organizations. Also, those farmers who indicated that their sons had encouraged new practices or other changes in the farm enterprise had adopted a greater number of improved practices. Farm operators also reported influence from their wives in making changes in the farm enterprise.

Many farmers, therefore, benefit by the participation of other family members in decision making on the farm. Working out satisfactory arrangements between father and son and between husband and wife for sharing in farm as well as household decisions appears to be an important consideration in encouraging technological change. It is significant that in those instances in which almost all decisions were made by the father, somewhat fewer innovations had been adopted.

Family goals or family values appear to have a greater bearing upon the adoption of changes in farming than does the nature of family relationships. Those operators placing a high value upon education for their children had adopted most improved practices in the Wisconsin study. This included favorable attitudes toward vocational agriculture for boys going into farming. On the contrary, placing higher value upon security in "owning one's farm free of debt" than upon education for children or upon other family goals was associated with adoption of fewer improved practices. This suggests that too much concern for security on the part of the farm family may retard the acceptance of new technology.

Making improvements and acquiring conveniences in the home goes along with the adoption of technological changes on the farm. This has

---

[8] E. A. Wilkening, *Adoption of Improved Farm Practices as Related to Family Factors,* Wisconsin AES Research Bulletin 183, 1953.

been demonstrated in several studies (see Fig. 44). Whether this relationship is a causal one or whether farm and home modernization are both the result of a general desire for material improvement is not

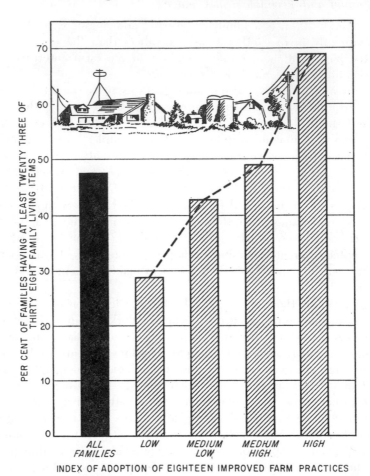

Figure 44. Percentage of 170 farm-owner families in Sauk County, Wisconsin, having at least twenty-three out of thirty-eight family living items according to index of adoption of eighteen improved farm practices. (From E. A. Wilkening, *Adoption of Improved Farm Practices as Related to Family Factors*, Wisconsin AES Research Bulletin 183, 1953.)

easily determined. Yet there is evidence that the desire for living conveniences and comforts provides motivation for the adoption of improvements on the farm. In the Wisconsin study, more farmers' wives than farmers said they would purchase farm machinery before household furniture, and a milk cooler before a home freezer, if there had to be a choice between the two.

Age and Education in Acceptance of Technological Change

Certain individual characteristics are associated with acceptance of change in farming methods and practices. Age and education, for example, which reflect different statuses and roles in the family and in the community, are related to the acceptance of innovations.

Generally, innovations are accepted more readily by the young than by the old. The exceptions to this case are probably due to the other correlates of age. Older farmers tend to have larger farms and more capital resources. These in turn influence adoption of those practices requiring land or capital resources. Younger farmers who wish to adopt new equipment or other practices, on the other hand, do not have the necessary land or capital resources.[9]

It is significant that younger persons do not accept new ideas when they are under the close control of parents and are dependent upon them. The failure to adopt new equipment or other changes in operations is attributed by many young men to being restrained by their fathers or fathers-in-law. Failure to turn over ownership or operation of the farm to the young son or son-in-law tends to extend this restraining influence. In his role as farm operator, the son, although he may be able, is frequently not allowed the freedom to make decisions involving changes in materials, equipment, or operations. This dilemma is forcefully demonstrated in the following quotation from the article, "My Farm Problem Is Dad." [10]

As he grows older he grows more complacent about things as they are, more reluctant about investing in "unnecessary" improvements, more resistant to change. The inefficient old barn is still solid. It is good enough. A nucleus of purebred cows would be fine but not worth the outrageous price. Fancy stock is a rich man's plaything. The big bull of a crawler tractor with labor-saving attachments I'd like to have is nonsense. Look what we've done with the two tractors we have.

Schooling is also associated with the adoption of innovations in agriculture. Both high school and college training are conducive to the acceptance of innovations. This is true in the area of household technology as well as in that of farm technology. The schools have institutionalized technological change in courses relating to farming and homemaking. In addition, formal education allows for the introduction of ideas and standards from outside the family and the locality group. These ideas provide the impetus as well as the rationale for accepting new technology. In such a situation the standards of farming and living of one's

[9] Wilkening, *Adoption of Improved Farm Practices*, pp. 45, 48–50.
[10] Anonymous, as told to Frank A. Cooper and reported in *Capper's Farmer*, March, 1955, p. 39.

peers replace those of one's family, and the school rather than the family becomes the source of standards and practices.

Cultural and Community Differences in the Acceptance of Innovations

Cultures and localities differ in the freedom allowed the innovator and in the conditions contributing to the acceptance of innovations. H. G. Barnett points out the difference in the degree of expectation of change in different cultures. The Navajo Indians welcome change and have continuously adopted alien elements in adjusting to the world about them. The Zuñi, nearby, take an ethnocentric view of their world and neither anticipate nor welcome change.[11] Studies by Hoffer, Kollmorgen, and Pedersen have demonstrated differences in the acceptance of farming practices among different cultural groups.[12] Germans have been found to be quick to accept soil-building practices. The Danish in a Wisconsin area had adopted more recommended practices than had the Polish in the same area at the time of the study. The Dutch of Michigan had adopted fewer approved celery-growing practices than had other farmers in the area.

An analysis of these and other studies of cultural groups suggests that differences in acceptance of changes in farming technology are associated with certain characteristics of the culture. For example, the degree of contact with the outside world, due to language or to lack of communication media, affects the acceptance of new technology. Value orientations that emphasize security and the past as opposed to success and the future make for greater resistance to change. On the contrary, emphasis upon individualism as opposed to familism is likely to be more conducive to change. Emphasis upon the nonmaterial or the sacred in a culture rather than the material or secular is likely to result in slower acceptance of technology.

Differences in the social structures of communities or localities also have significance for technological change: distinct differences in economic and social status appear to retard the extensive acceptance of improved farm practices. In North Carolina the neighborhoods with most stratification were slowest in their acceptance of improved practices. Social cleavages act as barriers in the communication of ideas associated with new technology and reflect differences in the appropriateness of

[11] From John Adais and Evon Vogt, "Navaho and Zuñi Veterans: A Study of Contrasting Modes of Culture Change," *American Anthropologist,* 51:547–561, 1949.

[12] C. R. Hoffer, *Acceptance of Approved Farming Practices Among Farmers of Dutch Descent,* Michigan AES Bulletin 316, 1942; Walter M. Kollmorgen, "The German Settlement in Cullman County, Alabama," and "The German-Swiss in Franklin County, Tennessee," Bureau of Agricultural Economics, USDA, Washington, 1941 and 1940 (processed); and H. A. Pedersen, "Cultural Differences in the Acceptance of Recommended Practices," *Rural Sociology,* 16:37–49, 1951.

specific items of technology. The small farmer does not necessarily regard equipment adopted by the large farmer as appropriate for his operations.

Questions for Review and Discussion

1. Describe the three main kinds of technology found in rural society.
2. Why is acceptance of innovations referred to in this chapter as a process?
3. List the stages in the process of acceptance of an innovation.
4. Discuss at some length the factors associated with acceptance of technology by farmers.
5. Would you expect an innovation equally useful in town and country to be more readily accepted by a rural community or by an urban community? Defend your answer.

Selected References for Supplementary Reading

Barnett, H. G.: *Innovation: The Basis of Cultural Change*, New York: McGraw-Hill Book Company, Inc., 1953.

Hess, C. V., and L. F. Miller: *Some Personal, Economic, and Sociological Factors Influencing Dairymen's Actions and Successes*, Pennsylvania AES Bulletin 577, 1954.

Pedersen, Harald A.: "Cultural Differences in the Acceptance of Recommended Practices," *Rural Sociology*, 16:37–49, 1951.

Ryan, Bryce, and Neal Gross: *Acceptance and Diffusion of Hybrid Corn Seed in Two Iowa Communities*, Iowa AES Research Bulletin 372, 1950.

Spicer, Edward H.: *Human Problems in Technological Change*, New York: Russell Sage Foundation, 1953.

CHAPTER 26   *Agricultural Technology*
             and Rural Social Change

The means by which innovations are brought to the attention of farmers
and the processes by which farmers accept them have been described in
the preceding two chapters. The present discussion is concerned with
the impact of such changes on rural social life in the United States.
Many factors, such as war and education, are instrumental in bringing
about changes in rural society, and in most instances it is impossible to
segregate the specific influences of any individual factor. The important
fact for this discussion, however, is that at present all factors work toward
the increasing use of technology, which is significantly related to rural
social change. Thus, in some respects this chapter is a summary of this
volume.

When people accept and use new discoveries or inventions, social behavior is inevitably affected to a greater or lesser degree. More often
than not, inventions have implications for social change far beyond their
immediate foreseeable effects. For example, the manufacturers of the
first automobiles would have had to be extremely farsighted to envision
the change in courtship patterns, among many other things, brought
about by this new mode of transportation. Technology always proves to
be an effective, many-faceted stimulus to changing society.

In this chapter the student will be introduced to some of the changes
primarily associated with the acceptance of technological innovations in
rural areas of the United States.[1] The purpose is to demonstrate the
process of social change as well as to acquaint the student with an in-
ventory of the most obvious of these changes. A brief look at certain

[1] In the context of this chapter, anything of a material nature which has utility
in the farm home or in the operation of the farm, whatever its function, is looked
upon as a part of agricultural technology. To illustrate, a mechanical cotton picker
is no more or less a technological item than a television set.

evidences of the change that is taking place will set the stage for the discussion.

The Mechanization of Agricultural Systems

The rate at which technology has proceeded can be demonstrated by reference to the pace at which agriculture has been mechanized. Two trends, one positive and the other negative, clearly illustrate the process of mechanization. The first is the increase in the number of tractors in the United States since 1910, and the second is the decrease in the number of work stock in the nation since that time.

In 1910, the first year in which tractors were counted, there were only 1,000 tractors in the whole of the United States. The increase in the ten-year period from 1910 to 1920 was phenomenal, as 246,000 tractors were counted in that year. This high rate of increase continued through the early twenties, although it slackened somewhat in the latter part of the decade. The depression of the mid-thirties did no more than momentarily slow down the rate of increase, and by the later thirties the trend had swung sharply upward again. It has continued to rise at a phenomenal rate ever since. For example, the average annual rate of increase was 210,000 tractors from 1940 to 1950. In actual numbers, the increase in tractors was from 1,545,000 in 1940 to 3,615,000 in 1950. By 1955 there were 4,800,000 farm tractors in the nation. The fact that this growth was accomplished in some fifty years demonstrates the speed at which mechanization has developed in rural areas of the United States. Table 25 shows the increase in the number of farm tractors and the decrease in the number of work stock since 1910.

The decrease in the number of work stock in the United States has paralleled the increase in the number of tractors and can be cited as further evidence of agricultural mechanization. In 1910, for example, there were well over 24,000,000 horses and mules in this country. This number increased during the next decade to something like 26,000,000 by 1920, the peak year for work stock. After this year there was a rapid decline. By 1930 only slightly more than 19,000,000 work animals were counted; in 1940 the number had decreased to around 14,500,000, and by 1950 there were only 7,781,000. In 1954, only a few more than 5,000,000 such animals were left, and many of these were doing only limited service as farm animals. It has been computed that each tractor in the nation as a whole displaces something like 3.5 work animals.[2] It is significant, in this context, to note the statement made by U.S. Department of Agriculture officials in their outlook report for 1956: "Tractors

[2] Harald A. Pedersen, "Mechanized Agriculture and the Farm Laborer," *Rural Sociology*, 19:144, 1954.

Table 25. Number of Farm Tractors and Work Stock in the United States in Selected Years, 1910–1954

Year	Tractors	Work stock
1910	1,000	24,211,000
1920	246,000	25,742,000
1930	920,000	19,124,000
1940	1,545,000	14,478,000
1950	3,615,000	7,781,000
1953	4,400,000 *	....
1954	....	5,035,000 *

* Latest available data.

SOURCE: *Farm Power and Farm Machines*, F.M. 101, USDA, BAE, Washington, 1953, p. 2; and *Agricultural Situation*, 38(8):3, 10, 1954.

and motor vehicles have become so numerous that horses or mules are no longer an important source of power on most farms." [3]

Other changes in agricultural technology have paralleled the changes noted above, as can be seen in Figure 45. These will suffice, however, to show the tremendous pace at which technological change has taken place. We turn now to some resultant changes of a social nature.

SOCIAL CHANGE IN RURAL AMERICA

Social interaction in rural areas falls logically into three categories: relations of people to the land, relations of persons to persons, and the institutional aspects.[4] These three categories provide an appropriate organizational frame of reference for the presentation of research findings and hypotheses concerning the impact of technology on rural social organization in the United States.

Changes in the Relationship of People to the Land

The important relationships between the population and the land center about the nature of property rights, the distribution of ownership and control of the land, and systems of land division and settlement patterns.[5] Technology has brought about changes in all these relationships. How-

[3] *Agricultural Outlook Charts, 1956*, Washington: USDA, Agricultural Marketing Service, Agricultural Research Service, 1955, p. 15.

[4] See T. Lynn Smith, *Sociology of Rural Life*, 3d ed., New York: Harper & Brothers, 1953, p. 197.

[5] *Ibid.*

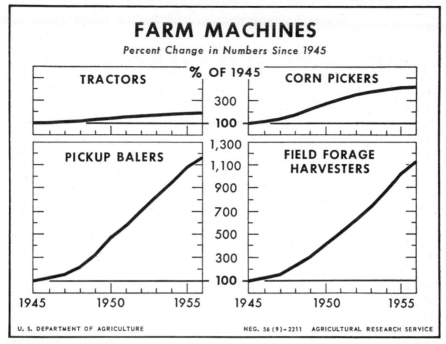

Figure 45. Increase in the number of selected machines on farms in the United States since 1945.

ever, it is in the first and second of these that most of the change in rural social organization appears to have occurred. In the distribution, ownership, and control of the land, several significant changes can be traced directly to the influence of technology. A brief review of these follows:

1. Technology has brought an increase in the average size of farms over the nation. There is conclusive evidence that mechanization is associated with increases in both total and cultivated acreages per farm.[6] This phenomenon is associated with the migration of many rural persons to urban centers. Most persons who leave rural areas do so because of the lure of high industrial wages or because they have been displaced by machines. Some, of course, such as Negroes in the South, leave for other reasons. When families migrate, their land is frequently

[6] See Otis Durant Duncan, "Economic Changes in American Rural Life," in *1955 Yearbook of Rural Education*, Washington: Department of Rural Education, NEA, 1955, pp. 316–325; Paul J. Jehlik and Ray E. Wakeley, *Population Change and Net Migration in the North Central States, 1940–50*, Ames, Iowa: North Central Regional Publication 56, Iowa AES Research Bulletin 430, 1955; Alvin L. Bertrand, J. L. Charlton, Harald A. Pedersen, R. L. Skrabanek, and James D. Tarver, *Factors Associated with Agricultural Mechanization in the Southwest Region*, Fayetteville, Ark.: Southwestern Regional Bulletin 6, Arkansas AES Bulletin 567, 1956; and Alvin L. Bertrand, *Agricultural Mechanization and Social Change in Rural Louisiana*, Louisiana AES Bulletin 458, 1951.

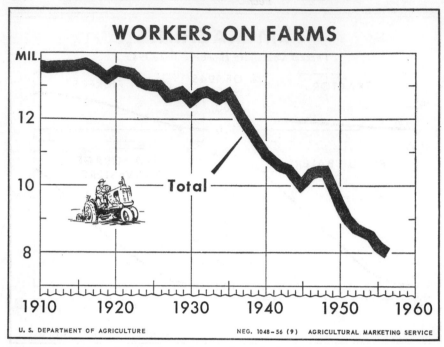

Figure 46. The decrease in workers on farms in the United States from 1910 to 1956.

absorbed into the bordering mechanized farm units, the owners of which are motivated in their purchase by the necessity to utilize equipment as efficiently as possible.

2. A direct outcome of the increase in size of farms is a decrease in the number of farms in the nation. It is, therefore, possible to assign to technology a direct causal relation to this phenomenon. Evidence of this trend is to be found in the various studies cited previously.

3. Technology is also associated with an increase in the proportion of owner- and part-owner-operated farms and a decrease in the number of tenants. Twenty years ago, social scientists were predicting that ownership of farms would fall to a few and that tenancy would increase to a dangerously high level. Today, thanks largely to mechanization, the trend is in the other direction, with farm ownership rather than tenancy increasing. It is interesting that the trend toward an increase in tenancy is apparently more true in the Cotton than in the Wheat and Corn Belts. The relatively sudden advent of technology in the cotton area probably accounts for this fact.[7]

---

[7] The historical background of the South explains why this region delayed its acceptance of technology. See Alvin L. Bertrand, "The Social Processes and Mechanization of Southern Agricultural Systems," *Rural Sociology*, 13:31–39, 1948.

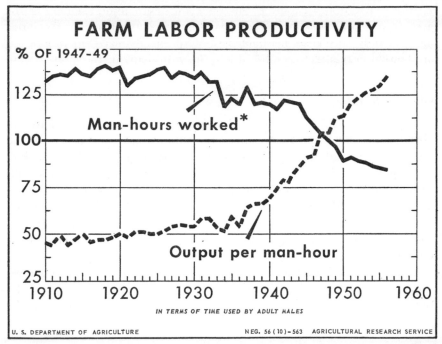

Figure 47. The increase in farm output per man-hour of work in the United States from 1910 to 1956.

4. Significantly, one of the most noticeable impacts of technology on agricultural systems is in the decrease of farm laborers. In fact, according to the conclusions of several studies, farm laborers have been affected more by technology than any other major tenure group. In this respect it is particularly noticeable that there is a lessening need for hired hands and for the use of women and children in the fields at rush seasons. Figure 46 shows the decrease in farm workers in the United States from 1910 to 1956, and Figure 47 shows the increase in output per laborer. It is also interesting that changes in labor housing and housing arrangements have come about as a result of the introduction of technology. In the large-scale farming areas of the South, for example, traditional sharecropper housing patterns are being abandoned in favor of housing more closely approximating urban standards. The tendency is for workers to be located nearer the center of activities and not scattered over the farm, as was usual under the old system. Interestingly, many workers have gone even further in the direction of urban patterns and do not live on the plantations at all but in nearby towns and villages, where they provide their own housing.[8] The land formerly occupied

[8] Pedersen, *op. cit.*, p. 151.

by the sharecropper cabins is put back into cultivation, increasing the acreage available for crops. Those workers who do remain on the farms are generally specialists in some part of the mechanized operation and are housed in relatively comfortable units with many of the modern conveniences.

Changes in Interpersonal Relations

The impact of technology on interpersonal relations has more importance than the average student of the subject has realized. This is the second general category of changes associated with technology. Among the changes of this nature are those classifiable as having to do with social differentiation, social stratification, the social processes, and sociopsychological characteristics. Rural sociologists and agricultural economists have studied the direct and indirect relationships of technology to changes of this nature throughout the nation. We shall review their findings here.

1. The mechanization of farming operations has had many repercussions in the number, distribution, and composition of the rural population (see Fig. 48). As has been pointed out, this fact is tied in with the

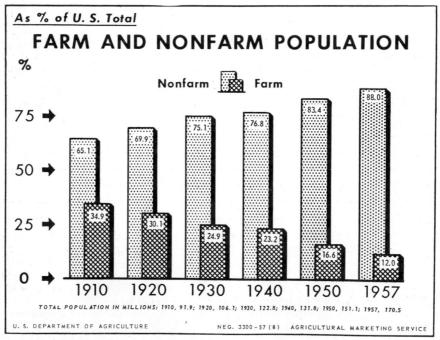

Figure 48. Decrease in the number of persons on farms in the United States from 1910 to 1957.

changing labor requirements in farm areas. The evidence available at present, although it is somewhat inconclusive, indicates that mechanization is associated with the general decrease in the rural population, a greater relative decrease of nonwhite farm operators, declining fertility among the farm population, a decreasing mortality rate in rural areas, and an increasing stability of occupancy among farm operators.[9] It is safe to state that all population changes have repercussions in person-to-person relations. These come about in terms of the socioeconomic and cultural adjustments that are made necessary.

Other changes of this general nature pointed out by several researchers are that larger numbers of persons of productive ages, more older persons, and more females remain in rural areas now than earlier.[10] The implications are similar for each of these groups in so far as interpersonal relations are concerned. Speaking broadly, technology has caused a reshuffling of the population and has produced important changes in rural personal-social structure. In this connection, it is of great significance that a smaller number of persons is producing the largest amount of food and fiber ever produced in the nation. Today, for example, one farm worker has an output sufficient to supply himself and approximately twenty others (see Fig. 49).[11]

2. Technology has been associated with distinct changes in the cooperative practices and conflict situations in farm communities. Evidences of the first are readily observed by persons traveling through the rural areas of the nation. Perhaps the most obvious change of this nature is the decrease in mutual-aid practices and informal cooperation. The tendency now, in the more highly mechanized areas, is for formal contractual relations to supersede these practices. Evidence of this type of change is especially noticeable in the great increase in formal labor arrangements. Formal organization of labor, because of specialization and an increasing division of labor, tends to intensify interpersonal relations. Durkheim called this *organic solidarity;* it has always been more characteristic of urban than of rural societies (see Chapter 2).

With regard to the process of opposition, the evidence indicates that such behavior in rural areas is becoming less direct and more impersonal. This means that disagreements are settled by arbitration or by the courts and recourse is had to violence less often than in the past. At the same

[9] Calvin L. Beale, "Population Trends and Distribution in Rural Areas," in *1955 Yearbook of Rural Education,* Washington: Department of Rural Education, NEA, 1955. pp. 299–306. See Chapter 5 for further documentation.

[10] Bertrand, *Agricultural Mechanization and Social Change in Rural Louisiana;* Robert T. McMillan, *Social Aspects of Farm Mechanization in Oklahoma,* Oklahoma AES Bulletin B-339, 1949; and B. O. Williams, "The Impact of Mechanization of Agriculture on the Farm Population of the South," *Rural Sociology,* 4:300–313, 1939.

[11] *Agricultural Outlook Charts,* p. 17.

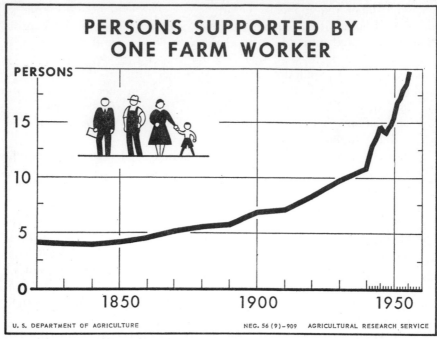

Figure 49. Increase in the number of persons one farm worker in the United States can support, from 1820 to 1956.

time, there is less conflict with the urban population than there was when rural interests were more strikingly different from urban ways.

3. Technology has had significant implications for patterns of rural social stratification. It has already been stated that technology tends to cause farms to develop along the lines of manufacturing concerns.[12] In this connection, social differentiation has become more complicated, with higher status being accorded to persons with technical skills, such as mechanics and tractor drivers. Symbols of success and prestige are also changing. For example, the number and kind of tractors the farmer owns may carry more weight than the number of workhands he employs.

4. The more technology there is in a farm area, the more urban characteristics its population will exhibit and the less intimate and personal their social relations will be. Although very few studies have taken primary cognizance of the sociopsychological effects of technology, the ultimate impact of innovations—on the farm and in the home—on the customs, beliefs, traditions, and attitudes of the people challenges the imagination. In fact, we saw in the preceding chapter that it has been empirically determined that technology has brought more "liberal" atti-

[12] See the description of the tractor farm in Harald A. Pedersen and Arthur F. Raper, *The Cotton Plantation in Transition*, Mississippi AES Bulletin 508, 1954.

tudes, less ritualism and fatalism, improved acceptance rates for new agricultural practices, and many other such changes.

Changes in the Major Social Institutions

Because of the great importance of social institutions, the influence of technology upon rural social institutions is of great significance in rural social change. Empirical evidence of change in social institutions in the nation is meager, however, and a great deal more study is needed in this area. Nevertheless, the direction of the changes that are taking place is clear.

1. First, with regard to economics, it has been found that the level of living of farm families is closely related to their command of technology.[13] In all studies touching on this subject, the conclusion has been that the percentages of farms with automobiles, electricity, running water, radios, telephones, and other indexes of levels of living are higher in mechanized localities than in nonmechanized areas. The states receiving central-station electricity are shown in Figure 50. It has further been determined that the amount of farm income available for family living usually increases directly with technological development.

2. Technology further shifts the whole structure of economic relationships in the direction of commercialization. What this means in terms of farm management is obvious. Research findings indicate that farmers shift the center of their activities from the smaller to the larger towns as they become increasingly dependent on specialized services. For example, when the purchasing of specialized supplies or the repair of machinery takes a farmer to a larger town, he tends to do his marketing of products and his shopping there. In some areas it has been noted that a complete shift in demand for consumer goods takes place with mechanization. This usually involves more sophisticated wearing apparel, food, and other consumption items. Certainly traditional economic landmarks, such as the general store and commissary, have become practically nonexistent in highly mechanized areas.

3. Although the relationship to technology has not been fully established, there is a trend toward a decrease in the number of rural schools and an improvement in the facilities and staffs of those schools that remain in the rural parts of the United States.[14] It is logical to expect that decreases in population brought about by mechanization and modern means of transportation would lessen the demand for schools in rural

[13] See Bertrand et al., *Factors Associated with Agricultural Mechanization in the Southwest Region,* pp. 7–8; and Duncan, "Economic Changes in American Rural Life," pp. 324–325.

[14] See Chapter I of *1955 Yearbook of Rural Education,* Washington: Department of Rural Education, NEA, 1955, entitled, "A Decade of Progress in Rural Education."

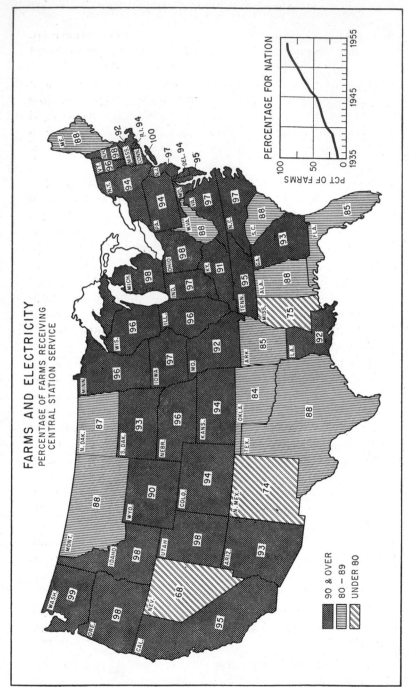

Figure 50. Percentage of farms receiving central-station electrical service in the United States by states, and the increase in the percentage of farms in the nation with electricity from 1935 to 1955. (U.S. Department of Agriculture, Agricultural Marketing Service.)

areas. It is also logical to expect that modern means of communication would increase the demand for adequate facilities and well-trained teachers.

4. As technology has caused a decline in the number and size of farm families, it has brought a decline in the number of rural churches. This trend, noted by several researchers, has also occurred in nonmechanized areas that have been depopulated for some reason.[15] Interestingly, it has been shown that the influence of the church on the remaining population also declines with an increase in mechanization.

5. As a result of the impact of technology, the farm family shows evidence of change from its traditional structure toward that of the urban family. This includes a trend toward medium size (large families are less common), less stability, and a shift from paternalistic authority to equalitarianism, among other things.[16] Thus the bonds holding the rural family together have loosened, as evidenced by the increased divorce rates and the parents' feelings that children today do not respect their parents as much as earlier generations did. The shift toward an equalitarian family is seen in the increasing interest the wife takes in major decisions having to do with the farm and home and the change in her role.

6. There is evidence that governmental and political institutions are undergoing changes as a result of technology. These changes fall under three main headings: (1) There is increasing consolidation, centralization, and integration of governmental activities. (2) Large-scale commercialized agriculture relies increasingly upon government assistance in production and price supports and is increasingly subjected to regulation by government. (3) As a result of the diminishing number of persons in agriculture, a realignment of political power is under way which would give the farm bloc less voice in local, state, and national affairs. The end results of these changes for the farmer are not clear at the present time.

7. Farm people in mechanized areas have increased their social activities more than those in areas where technology has had less impact. Research reports indicate mechanization is associated with more participation in such things as school activities, civic programs, and recreational activity.[17] One significant change is the movement from primary

[15] See Smith, *Sociology of Rural Life*, pp. 472–475, and J. L. Charlton, "Decline of the Church Serving Farmers," *Science Points the Way*, Arkansas AES Bulletin 453, 1944, pp. 16–18.

[16] Beale, "Population Trends and Distribution in Rural Areas," pp. 302–303, and Bertrand, *Agricultural Mechanization and Social Change in Rural Louisiana*, pp. 43–44.

[17] A summary review of these studies appears in Alvin L. Bertrand, "Rural Locality Groups: Changing Patterns, Change Factors, and Implications," *Rural Sociology*, 19:174–179, 1954.

to secondary, or special-interest-group, relationships in rural areas, which takes place as rural social participation becomes increasingly centered in nearby towns and cities.

8. Health facilities and public-welfare activities are directly associated with mechanization. In this connection, it is sufficient to say that it has been shown that the number of persons per doctor and other medical personnel varies directly with the degree of mechanization.

Conclusion

The impact of technology on rural social organization can best be summarized in general terms. Many areas, of course, are still in the pre-technology stage, and the remaining areas have yet to achieve their full potential in technological development, if, indeed, such a level can ever be reached. Nevertheless, from the standpoint of the average rural neighborhood or community in the region, technology means, in the terminology of Durkheim, the organization of society on an organic rather than a mechanistic basis. Thus groups are held together, or maintain cohesion, because of division of labor and specialization of tasks rather than because of homogeneity of character. In the terminology of Tonnies, what is taking place is the transition from *Gemeinschaft* relations (those developing unconsciously or subconsciously) to *Gesellschaft* relations (those entered into deliberately for the achievement of recognized ends). The followers of Cooley might describe the impact of technology as changing group relationships from the primary type (those based on intimate, face-to-face contact) to the secondary type (those based on special interests). Whatever the terminology, technology in rural society undoubtedly has produced a trend toward fewer personal relationships.

Questions for Review and Discussion

1. What indications do we have of the rate of mechanization of agricultural systems in the United States?

2. Is it possible for social change to come to rural areas without creating problems?

3. What are some of the most important changes that have already taken place in rural areas of the nation?

4. In your opinion, what will be the end result of current trends in rural social change?

5. Select a rural community familiar to you and name the changes that have taken place in it in the past ten years.

Selected References for Supplementary Reading

Bertrand, Alvin L.: *Agricultural Mechanization and Social Change in Rural Louisiana,* Louisiana AES Bulletin 458, 1951.

Bertrand, Alvin L., J. L. Charlton, Harald A. Pedersen, R. L. Skrabanek, and James D. Tarver: *Factors Associated with Agricultural Mechanization in the Southwest Region,* Fayetteville, Ark.: Southwestern Regional Bulletin 6, Arkansas AES Bulletin 567, 1956.

Jehlik, Paul J., and Ray E. Wakeley: *Population Change and Net Migration in the North Central States, 1940–50,* Ames, Iowa: North Central Regional Bulletin 56, Iowa AES Bulletin 430, 1955.

McMillan, Robert T.: *Social Aspects of Farm Mechanization in Oklahoma,* Oklahoma AES Bulletin B-339, 1949.

CHAPTER 27 *Rural-urban Interaction and Rural Social Change* *

The fact that the rural segment of the population has been set apart for special and intensive study in this book might lead the student to lose sight of the interaction between rural and urban society. The assimilative and acculturative processes operating in connection with rural-urban contacts are explored in this chapter. The phenomena involved in these processes hold the key to much of present-day social change in rural areas. This discussion completes the picture presented in the preceding chapter of factors associated with rural social change.

Definitions

The overlapping and merging of the major residential segments of our society have been studied by a number of scholars, who have used a variety of terms and concepts to describe the nature of the processes they have discovered. A knowledge of these terms and concepts is essential to an understanding of the discussion that follows.

The terms *urbanization* and *ruralization* connote one-directional cultural influence, from urban to rural in the one case and from rural to urban in the other. *Rurbanization* is a more general term, implying that rural-urban contacts result in integrative influences that are not necessarily characterized by dominance of one or the other segment of society. This concept is related to the term *suburbanization* but is not so ecologically oriented.

Suburbanization is generally used as a demographic-ecological term. It implies a residential movement into the suburbs, or the residential

* The author wishes to express with gratitude his indebtedness to Drs. Charles H. Coates and Wayne C. Rohrer for their aid in defining this approach to rural social change.

adjuncts of cities. Terms such as *urban fringe* and *dormitory towns* are often used in studies of suburbanization.

A final term to be introduced at this point is *sub-urbanization,* which is very nearly a new concept. It is used to connote a situation in which there are multifaceted rural-urban contacts that are urban dominated. The concept of sub-urbanization does not imply a one-way process, as ruralization and urbanization do. It merely acknowledges one-way (urban) dominance. It is no doubt true that a sub-ruralization process is operative in certain places, but the term does not appear in the literature pertinent to interchanges of rural and urban cultures.

The terms suburbanization and sub-urbanization may be differentiated more fully as follows. Suburbanization studies generally seek mechanical explanations for movements such as growth of population, growth of automobile transit, changing fashions in housing construction, and ecological invasion.[1] Sub-urbanization studies allow for subjective explanations of these trends as well, taking into account such factors as human likes and dislikes, desires, fears, and knowledge. They allow for the fact that people act in terms of what they want, their knowledge of how to get what they want, their resources for getting it, and their subjective evaluation of their chances for getting it.[2] Although people act individually, their actions assume mass proportions as one person after another, because of a similarity of attitudes and desires, follows a given pattern. For example, one can explain on this basis why a majority of new suburban homes in certain areas are ranch-type houses.[3] Action can also be taken collectively, as when a suburban community resists incorporation because of a fear of increased taxes.

This distinction between these two types of studies is not an attempt to discredit the many fine studies of suburbanization and the urban fringe. These works make a definite contribution to sociological knowledge. At the same time, they should be distinguished from studies of sub-urbanization, which attempt to show urban culture as dominant in its contact with rural culture, whereas suburbanization studies, as mentioned previously, emphasize the redistribution of population into suburbs.

These terms are not used extensively in the discussion that follows. However, the student will recognize the two concepts, particularly in relation to the phenomena of assimilation and acculturation.

[1] For example, see: Henry S. Shryock, Jr., "Population Redistribution Within Metropolitan Areas: Evaluation of Research," *Social Forces,* 35:157–158, 1956.

[2] For the sociological definition of human motivation, see: Kingsley Davis, *Human Society,* New York: The Macmillan Company, 1949, chap. 5.

[3] Russell Lynes, *The Tastemakers,* New York: Harper & Brothers, 1954, chap. 14.

RURAL-URBAN EXCHANGE

This chapter is principally devoted to outlining the nature and types of rural-urban contacts and their influence as it appears in rural social change. For the most part, interaction of this type is integrative in nature and has the effect of bringing ruralites and urbanites closer together in their behavior patterns. The important fact for this discussion is that, to the extent that farm people accept the ways of city people, rural social change occurs. There is a reverse process, of course, but it is not discussed in this book. In this first section, the major means by which rural change can be effected are reviewed.

Rural-urban Migrants

As we saw in Chapter 5, the urban population of the United States has had a consistent growth. In 1950 there were 84.5 million persons living in 168 standard metropolitan areas, and 14 standard metropolitan areas had 1 million or more residents. Generally, all these areas grew about one and one half times as fast as the nation as a whole during the decade 1940–1950.[4] The fifty largest cities in the United States are shown in Figure 51. The significant fact for this discussion is that, in achieving this growth, urban areas drew heavily on rural areas. Rural migrants become exposed to city life in all its varied aspects and communicate their new experiences to relatives and friends still residing in rural areas. In so doing they set up a potential for rural change.

Urban Technological Dominance

Urban dominance is more than a matter of superiority of numbers of people; technologically, it extends into the areas of industry, manufacturing, business, transportation, communication, government, and education, among others. One would expect such technological superiority in the major residential segment of the national population, of course. This technological dominance serves as a vast potential for cultural change. As one sociologist put it,[5]

The city has the prestige of power and wealth and specialized knowledge. It holds the key of finance. It is the market to which the ruralite must turn in order to buy and sell and borrow. Its people, habituated to many contacts, have the advantage, when city and country meet, of being more articulate, more expansive, and, superficially at least, more alert.

---

[4] U.S. Bureau of the Census, *Census of Population: 1950,* vol. II, part 1, Washington, 1953.

[5] Robert MacIver and Charles Page, *Society,* New York: Rinehart & Company, Inc., 1949, p. 330.

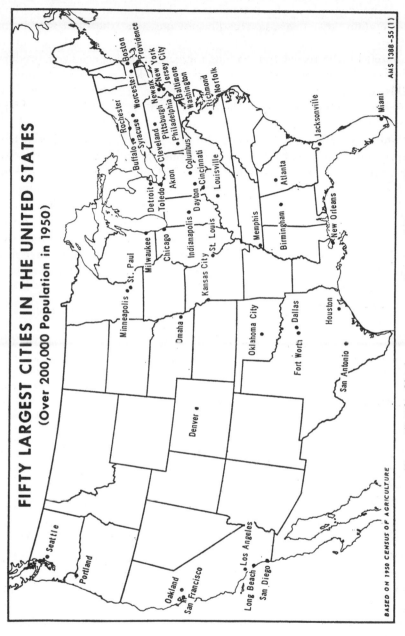

FIFTY LARGEST CITIES IN THE UNITED STATES
(Over 200,000 Population in 1950)

Seattle
Portland
Oakland
San Francisco
Long Beach • Los Angeles
San Diego
Denver
Minneapolis • St. Paul
Milwaukee
Chicago
Omaha
Kansas City
Oklahoma City
Fort Worth • Dallas
San Antonio
Houston
Detroit
Toledo
Akron
Indianapolis
Dayton
Cincinnati
Columbus
Louisville
St. Louis
Memphis
Birmingham
New Orleans
Atlanta
Jacksonville
Buffalo
Rochester
Syracuse
Cleveland
Pittsburgh
Worcester • Boston
Providence
Newark • New York
Jersey City
Philadelphia
Baltimore
Washington
Richmond
Norfolk
Miami

BASED ON 1950 CENSUS OF AGRICULTURE

AMS 1388-55 (1)

Figure 51. The fifty largest cities in the United States, 1950.

417

The sheer weight of its technological development gives the urban world certain advantages, not readily obvious, over the rural world. Industrialization, for example, results in larger agricultural markets. This is illustrated by the recent tremendous increase in the specialized production of eggs, dairy products, fruits, and vegetables for urban consumers. In this regard, it is significant that the total farm output today has increased about 60 per cent over the output of 1910, due primarily to technological changes stemming largely from experimentation by Federal and state agricultural experiment stations. It is significant that urban markets dictated the nature of the developments and provided the necessary technological base. As noted in the last chapter, when the urban-developed power sources were finally made available to the farmer, in the form of the tractor and other machines, the resulting shift from horses and mules was phenomenal. The change also profoundly affected farming enterprises, as 70 million acres formerly used to grow feed for farm animals were converted to other crops. Such changes brought manifold changes in farm organization, resulting in greater urban technological influence. In Mighell's words, the commercial farm of today is: [6]

. . . a biological manufacturing plant. . . . In many respects the technological organization of commercial farms is more intricate and involved than that of industrial plants . . . to the extent they are crop producers their visible manufacturing plants consist of fields. . . . Here they place their genetic materials and add fertilizer, pesticides, and other inputs. They power-tool the soil, power-harvest the products, and take them to concentration points for packaging and shipment.

The technological "revolution" going on in rural areas has been extensively discussed in other chapters. Its dependence on urban technology is so obvious as to need no further elaboration.

Urban Economic Dominance

The economic dominance of the urban world can best be seen in terms of competition for property in land. Property is defined as the control of the use of a thing or process, and land is one kind of property. Every society defines what constitutes property, how and to what purpose it is controlled, and the sentiment with which it will be regarded. For us, property means for the most part utility. It is to be manipulated and used in the way that is most likely to bring profits. It is not a thing in itself, and we do not attach a sentimental value to it. Land, therefore, is appropriated for the most efficient and profitable use. Because greater profits accrue from urban usages, land is made urban or remains rural

[6] Ronald Mighell, *American Agriculture: Its Structure and Place in the Economy,* New York: John Wiley & Sons, Inc., 1955, p. 15.

according to its utility for urban activities. Urban communities are located with relation to natural resources, breaks and crossovers in transportation facilities, defensible positions, and trade areas. Such factors, of course, cannot be considered apart from technology, but granted a particular technological level, we can presume that potential land use will be decided by urban needs, which in our society has meant gradual encroachment upon farm lands. This trend obviously increases the potential for change in rural areas.

The evaluation of rural land has a second dimension also. The utility (or value) of farm land is dependent upon the accessibility of urban markets. Thus it can be said that the type of farming and the social and economic organization of farm communities are geared to outside (urban) demands. For example, the political behavior of rural segments of the population reflect their economic conditions, which in turn are related to their markets. All in all, the potential for change deriving from urban economic dominance is no small one.

FACTORS AND TRENDS IN RURAL SOCIAL CHANGE

Three types of factors are primarily involved in rural social change. These are the channels through which change may be effected, the processes or trends that speed or retard cultural contacts, and the types and degrees of motivation for change. The preceding section concerned potential channels of change. The present section and the one that follows it are devoted to the second and third categories of factors involved in rural social change, the trends and processes relating to cultural contacts being considered first.

Urban Ecological Processes

The nineteenth-century city was a highly concentrated and centralized community whose economy and ecological patterns were founded upon water and steam power. Today's city is moving rapidly towards organization according to a decentralized and deconcentrated ecological pattern. A great economic and social upheaval is thrusting the city's residents, services, businesses, and industries out beyond its confines into its suburbs, into the lesser cities that form a ring around it, and into the interstitial open country and the outlying rural areas. Its radius of activity is now several hundreds of miles.

Consequently, urban influence in the twentieth century can be summed up in the concept of the metropolis, which is an "extensive community (ecological area) composed of numerous territorially specialized parts the functions of which are correlated and integrated through the agency of a central city." [7] Bogue states that the whole United States is encompassed in a system of metropolitan communities (ecological areas). The central city dominates in wholesale and service activities all segments of the metropolitan area. In retail activities it dominates only the urban fringe, or the area within a 45-mile radius, since the nature of the retail process requires close proximity to buyers. Studies show that the manufacturing influence from the city extends up to 65 miles. In each case, it appears most likely that the economic activities of the regional hinterland are accommodated to the central city and feature cooperative specialization rather than competitive similarity. That is, each lesser center manufactures and sells products that complement rather than compete with the objects made and sold in the central city.

Distance is not the only factor that causes variation in the degree of metropolitan influence on rural areas. Areas lying along the major transportation lanes between major cities and nearby urban centers tend to take on urban patterns more quickly and completely than outlying areas. This demonstrates that urban ecological processes are important to rural social change. This fact is further verified by the demographic studies of the outward movement of population from the central city. [8]

The most significant aspect of this interchange of population between the central cities and their rings (hinterland) from the standpoint of the distribution of population is that whereas the rings contain almost one-half (45.6 per cent) as many people as the central cities they sent less than one-fifth (18.5 per cent) as many migrants to the central city as they received from them. This intra-metropolitan migration was, therefore, predominantly a one-way outward movement.

The same author discovered a tendency for intermetropolitan migrants to seek a hinterland residence instead of a central city residence.

Farm Tenure Trends

By census definition, a part-time farmer is one who does 100 days or more of nonfarm work during any one year. A residential farm is one for which the reported income from the sale of farm products is not more than $250. As shown in Chapter 8, in 1950 there were 639,230 part-time farms and 1,029,392 residential farms. Together they made up 31 per cent of all farms. Significantly, about 35 per cent of the residential farms reported no sale of farm products.

---

[7] Donald Bogue, *The Metropolitan Community*, Ann Arbor, Mich.: Horace Rackham School of Graduate Studies, 1949. The concept of the community is erroneous, as only ecological variables are mentioned.

[8] Warren Thompson, *Migration Within Ohio, 1935–40*, Miami, Ohio: Scripps Foundation, Miami University, 1951, p. 18.

The bulk of part-time and residential farms are in the South, particularly in the Appalachian Mountains. To a considerable extent, they represent people combining farming with work in lumber camps and mills, furniture factories, coal mining, textile mills, and smaller industries.

In part-time farming the economic and family-life patterns become more and more conditioned by urban society, because of continued association. One study of part-time farming reports that higher social status results from this partial shift to urban employment.[9] Home ownership is more common than among industrial workers, and part-time farmers hold positions of leadership more frequently and participate more in organized community affairs.

As indicated in previous discussions, estimates of future agricultural trends indicate increased mechanization, increased yields, and smaller rural populations. These factors will not only produce out-migration of the farm population but also more part-time farming. At the same time, the practice of part-time farming or extensive gardening frequently represents the reverse process and involves an exurbanite. These practices are encouraged by some industries in an effort to stabilize a highly mobile labor supply. The hope is to anchor their workers to the community through landownership and labor expenditure. In some cases, urbanites turn to part-time farming for fear of industrial layoffs or cutbacks.

Whatever the source of part-time and residential farmers, the significance of this trend remains clear: the part-time farmer and his family increasingly participate in the urban social world.

Mass Communications

Mass-communications media serve to draw the farmer's attention to the urban world. News from the radio stations covers first the national and international scene and then the local city or metropolitan news. In either case, urban values are touted. For example, it may be noted that farm reports are sponsored by farm appliance and service agencies. These advertisers consult agricultural-experiment-station studies of rural-farm radio-listening and television-viewing habits before selecting time spots. In addition they consult similar sources for information concerning farmers' entertainment preferences in order to present the most attractive front possible for their commercials.

Advertisers generally do not beam specific appeals to farmers but instead treat them as an integral part of the massed United States audience. Automotive agencies, for example, do not single out the specific

[9] R. H. Allen et al., *Part-time Farming in the Southeast*, Washington: WPA Research Monograph IX, 1937.

needs and tastes of the typical family farm to stress in their advertising. They prefer to associate their product with the generalized American liking for speed and power and therefore show their car doing such things as zooming up a mountain.

At the same time, the subject matter for most radio, television, magazine, and movie offerings draws upon universal American values. Love and its problems, family life and its problems, quiz games, rags-to-riches wish fulfilment, and the heroic man of rugged virtue are standard subjects. It is frequently only in terms of background and minor characteristics of the actors that anything less than universal cultural values enters the picture. Significantly, at this level the values are likely to be urban-metropolitan. With this locale as the setting, the characters more often than not take on urban-metropolitan traits. Rural elements are portrayed, of course, but often with an urban tie in, that is, the small-town or country boy or girl comes to the city to make good. Western themes are, perhaps, an exception; however, they represent such a stereotyping of values as to be almost beyond reality.

Although the influence of mass media has not been thoroughly studied in relation to rural social change, its importance is clear. The basic research problem is to determine the critical threshold, the point at which one is actively motivated to respond to stimuli. As with advertising, it is not enough to make your audience remember the slogan associated with the product; it is necessary to make them go out and buy the product. Mass-communications media bombard the farmer and others alike with positive assertions of universally held cultural values, and in so far as they are successful, the farmer is blended into the broader American society. Many American values are of rural origin, of course, but in the course of time these values have achieved a sophistication somewhat removed from the extreme rural interpretation, and rural views may be in the process of changing to conform to the remodeled version.

SOCIO-PSYCHOLOGICAL ASPECTS OF RURAL SOCIAL CHANGE

Rural social change does not come about through the mere happenstance of cultural contact. The persons in contact must want to change or be willing to accept the change desired by others. The ruralite will accept urban values and standards as his own only when he "wants" urban things. On the other hand, the current "flight from the city" is occurring because urbanites favor and desire certain elements of rural life. In this section we shall discuss the desire for urban conveniences and glamour and the converse tendency toward rural romanticism as motives for rural social change.

The Appeal of Urban-innovated Conveniences

The tremendous improvements in rural levels of living are mute evidence of the appeal of urban-innovated "conveniences" to rural people. Level of living, as noted before, is a technical term referring to the ownership and use of certain facilities and equipment. In the sense in which it is used here, it refers to the possession and use of such things as piped running water, indoor toilets, electric lighting, and telephones.

In the past, innumerable analyses have called attention to the disparity between the levels of living of farm families and city families.[10] Level-of-living trends are probably one of the best measures of the acceptance of certain more or less urban values by rural people. In the years from 1920 to 1956, the number of farms reporting electric lighting rose from 10 per cent of all farms to 96 per cent. The ownership of automobiles rose from 31 per cent to three-fourths of all farm operators. More drastically, in the period 1950 to 1956 the per cent of farm families owning television sets rose from 3 per cent to 53 per cent.

The Tenacity of Rural Idealism

Many of our basic institutions in the United States reflect our rural heritage. Jefferson's concept of democracy involved a great number of farmers whose independence and democratic outlook sprang from their private ownership of the land and their independence of action and responsibility. Jacksonian democracy has been pictured as a rebellion against the oligarchic tendencies of Eastern urban thought, reflecting the enfranchisement of the farmer-frontiersman. It was a further step in promoting rural leadership in national affairs. Similarly, the Grange, the Farmers' Alliance, and other protest movements of the late nineteenth century provided the political impulse that led to popular election of senators, referendum and recall, and antitrust laws (see Chapter 23).[11] Our idealized picture of political campaigning is still "stump-speaking" and small-town general-store "politicking." The current practice of delivering presidential campaign addresses at the National Plowing Contests in Iowa is more than an effort to secure the "farm vote"; it is an attempt of candidates to become identified with the small-town and rural heritage of America and with the common man and to demonstrate an interest in machinery and the land.[12]

[10] For example, see: Edgar A. Schuler and Walter C. McKain, Jr., "Levels and Standards of Living," in Carl C. Taylor et al., *Rural Life in the United States,* New York: Alfred A. Knopf, Inc., 1950, chap. 17.

[11] For a statement of the relationship between family farm values and political development in the United States, see: Joe R. Motheral, "Land Tenure Policies and the Political Development of the United States," paper delivered at the International Political Science Association, Geneva, 1956.

[12] See the reported conversation of Governor Thomas E. Dewey in John Gunther, *Inside U.S.A.,* vol. 2, New York: Harper & Brothers, 1957, pp. 1–2.

Even the most urban people reflect a rural heritage in thought, speech, and ideals. Adolf Tomars has defined a number of attitudes and habits reflecting rural heritage, such as the preference for single as opposed to multifamily housing and for fireplaces as esthetic objects, the use of rural objects, possession of folk wisdom, and use of proverbs couched in rural terms.[13]

The novel and poetry also make possible continued familiarity and identity with the American rural scene. In much of our literature, rural life is portrayed as a way of life in its own right and also as a background against which to appraise the basic American beliefs and values. Pulitzer-prize novels concerning rural life include *One of Ours* (Cather, 1924), *The Able McLaughlins* (Wilson, 1925), *So Big* (Ferber, 1925), and *Early Autumn* (Bromfield, 1927). Other fine works concerning American rural life include: Johnson's *Now in November*, Davis's *Honey in the Horn*, Westcott's *The Grandmothers*, Meigs's *Wild Geese Flying*, de la Roche's *Jalna*, Garland's *Daughter of the Middle Border*, Cannon's *Red Rust*, Cather's *My Antonia*, Glasgow's *Barren Ground*, Suckow's *Country People*, Eastman's *Hundred Maples*, Carroll's *As the Earth Turns*, Rölvaag's *Giants in the Earth*, Walker's *Fireweed*, Kantor's *The Voice of Bugle Ann*, Rawlings's *South Moon Under*, Steinbeck's *The Grapes of Wrath*, Frederick's *Green Bush*, Scarborough's *Can't Get a Red Bird*, and Miller's *Lamb in His Bosom*.[14]

The poems of Whittier, Riley, Whitman, Sandburg, Benét, Frost, and Coffin all reflect American rural life and heritage. Some may seem overdone to the modern reader, but each calls up treasured impressions of past and present rural life.[15]

We can conclude that, as a society, we have a tremendous idealistic association with nature and with farm and small-community living. This evaluation and the approval of urban living standards cited earlier appear to constitute two great "psychological" forces in rural change, one favoring change and one opposing it. In the following section we shall consider these evaluations in terms of the expressed attitudes of farmers and exurbanites.

Rural and Urban Attitudes Affecting Social Change

In response to questioning as to why they moved to the city, rural migrants give economic reasons first—jobs, money, and the fact that there

---

[13] Adolf S. Tomars, "Rural Survivals in Urban Life," *Rural Sociology*, 8:378–386, 1943.

[14] Caroline B. Sherman, "Rural Fiction as Interpreter of Rural Life," *Rural Sociology*, 2:36–45, 1937.

[15] See the discussions of Lewis Cheresman, "Rural Life in Modern American Poetry," *Rural Sociology*, 3:48–56, 1938; and F. Van Wyck Brooks, *The Flowering of New England*, New York: E. P. Dutton & Co., Inc., 1936.

are limited prospects, or none, on the farm. Personal reasons are the glamour of the city, modern conveniences, the new and exciting, the chance for more numerous social contacts, and marriage prospects. In summary, urban life has an appeal because it offers a chance to live and a chance to "live."

On the other hand, the urbanite who moves to the rural-urban fringe does so in order to get away from the city. He mentions more family life, a better environment for rearing children, neighborliness, gardening, and a slower tempo of life.

Both the farmer and urbanite appear to agree that those things valued most in our society—wealth, material possessions, comforts, power, and success—are to be found in the city. When these values are obtained, or at least partially so, then values associated with rural life are sought. These values can be viewed as ideals that are outweighed by the more "real" and "basic" economic values that motivate both residential mobility and acculturation. This is neither a denial of rural values nor an indication of diminished belief about its pleasures. It is a pragmatic response to the fact that in our society we do not live for the situation or for sentiment; we live for our prospects, for success in material things, and for prestige. And these, we believe, are to be found in an urban way of life. If we cannot live in the city, or if we wish to avoid some aspects of city life, we transpose to a rural setting as many elements of urban life as possible.

Rural Social Change in Perspective

Perhaps it would be wise at this point to remind the student that the point of view of the authors of this book is that rural-urban differences form a continuum. Because of this, the process of sub-urbanization holds no threat that persons concerned with agriculture and rural life—including rural sociologists—will be put out of business. Whatever the direction of change, there will always be a segment of the society which is, relatively speaking, more rural than urban.

Questions for Review and Discussion

1. Distinguish between suburbanization and sub-urbanization as the concepts represented by these terms are used in this chapter.

2. Briefly review the evidences of urban cultural dominance in this country.

3. Define the term *ecology* and list several urban ecological processes.

4. Explain the role of mass communication in rural social change.

5. Can you find evidence of rural idealism in even the most urbanized areas? Explain.

6. In your opinion, will the United States evolve into a "mass" society, culturally homogeneous? Why?

Selected References for Supplementary Reading

Bogue, Donald J.: *Metropolitan Decentralization,* Oxford, Ohio: Miami University Press, 1950.

Keats, John: *A Crack in the Picture Window,* Boston: Houghton Mifflin Company, 1957.

Landis, Paul H.: *Rural Life in Process,* 2d ed., New York: McGraw-Hill Book Company, Inc., 1948, chap. 17.

Seeley, John, R. Alexander Sims, and Elizabeth W. Loosely: *Crestwood Heights: A Study of the Culture of Suburban Life,* New York: Basic Books, Inc., 1956.

Sullenger, T. Earl: *The Sociology of Urbanization: A Study of Rurban Society,* Ann Arbor, Mich.: Baun-Brumfield, Inc., 1956.

PART SEVEN

Rural Sociology in Perspective

It is now about fifty years since the inception of rural sociological research in the United States. The time is fitting for an evaluation of the
developments and trends in and the contributions of this relatively young
discipline. This has been the objective of Chapter 28, the final one in this
volume.

CHAPTER 28 *Rural Sociology at Mid-century*

Rural sociologists, like specialists in other fields, periodically evaluate the state of their discipline. Such an evaluation can be made by counting the number of professionally trained people working in the field, by tallying the courses taught and research bulletins or articles published, or simply by measuring the extent to which the general public understands, supports, and makes use of the findings presented by the specialists.[1] For our purposes, however, the importance of rural sociology at mid-century can best be understood against a background of some of the major trends on the horizon. These fall conveniently under three headings: the changing scope of rural sociology, its connection with the developments of social science theory and methodology, and its usefulness in the solution of everyday problems.

THE CHANGING SCOPE OF RURAL SOCIOLOGY

It is a paradox that rural sociology is increasing in importance at the very time when the farm people of the United States are decreasing in actual numbers and as a proportion of the total population. This is to be explained, of course, by the changing scope of rural sociology. First, however, it will be helpful to review some facts presented in earlier chapters which would appear to be a source of grave concern to those whose chief occupation is the study of American rural life.

In 1920 the rural-farm population made up 29.9 per cent of the total population of the United States; in 1950 it comprised only 15.3 per cent. But the

[1] For a realistic but somewhat discouraging picture (from the standpoint of the rural sociologist) as of 1948, see: Bonney Youngblood, "The Status of Rural Sociological Research in the State Agricultural Experiment Stations," *Rural Sociology,* 14:111–115, 1949. For an optimistic view as of 1950, see: C. Horace Hamilton, "Some Current Problems in the Development of Rural Sociology," *Rural Sociology,* 15:315–321, 1950. Hamilton also reviews briefly the report prepared by the Farm Foundation Committee on the status of rural sociology.

rural-nonfarm population was more than holding its own: in 1920 it made up 19.1 per cent of the total population, and in 1950, 20.7 per cent (see Chapter 5).

In 1953, rural-farm families totaled 5,452,000, or only 13.3 per cent of the total of 41,020,000 families. This represented a drop of approximately 800,000 families in eight years. The farm family continued to be larger than other families, averaging 4.04 persons as compared to 3.53 persons for the United States as a whole (in 1953).

The family farm, which has traditionally been viewed as the backbone of American agriculture, is losing its importance in the economy of the country.

In a nonstatistical sense, as pointed out in Chapter 4, it is safe to assume that a distinct set of values will soon be a memory and no longer a fact in American rural life.

Many other facts have been cited in earlier pages to show that farm people are becoming increasingly like urban people and that centralized control—much of it necessary in the world of today—is making itself felt in local government, economic matters, medical care, special-interest groups, and a number of other areas.[2] The city rather than the countryside appears to be the main center of power. In view of these and other trends, one can justifiably ask whether the scope of rural sociology is shrinking to the vanishing point, holding steady, or expanding. Four important considerations provide an answer to this question.

Changing the Emphasis of Studies

Granting that the farm population has been declining, there will always be an irreducible number of persons—say, from 12 to 20 million—for whom agriculture is a means of livelihood. As it becomes gradually more commercialized, farming may be less a "way of life" than it has been, but those engaged in it will continue to constitute a very important element in American society. Farm people are the first line of economic defense in that they produce the food and fiber on which our nutrition and much of our industry depend. Rural sociologists will continue to make their contribution by studying what is happening to social relations affecting farm people. Such studies are even more important in times of cataclysmic change in order that those concerned with problems and policies will have reliable information on which to base their decisions.

Increasing the Comprehensiveness of Studies

Rural sociology would continue to advance, even if it did no more than increase the number and comprehensiveness of its studies of farm

[2] For an excellent discussion of these and related matters, see: Howard W. Beers, "Rural-urban Differences: Sôme Evidence from Public Opinion Polls," *Rural Sociology,* 18:1–11, 1953.

people, despite the fact that these constitute only one-eighth of the total population. This is because there is an increasing demand for detailed information about the remaining rural people. An examination of the bulletins of any agricultural experiment station will show that the rural-sociology staffs of these stations have not even begun to make comprehensive studies of the rural life of the various states. Limitations on funds and personnel have done much to prevent this. Every staff has investigated some aspects very thoroughly; furthermore, the variety of topics treated by rural sociologists is tremendous, although many of these topics have been covered or touched upon by the staffs of only a few experiment stations. Rural sociologists in years to come may well find themselves studying in greater detail more topics related particularly to farm people, the study of whom has just begun in some states. One situation that gives impetus to this broadened scope is the long-time acceptance and, one might say, even the institutionalization of the study of rural life. Both at the national and at the state level, many administrators of programs affecting rural people have become accustomed to using the facts that rural social scientists present—although not to the extent that many social scientists would wish. Their demands upon rural sociology can be expected to continue.

Changing the Focus of Studies

The focus of rural sociology is not necessarily limited exclusively to rural-farm people, even though their way of life may have been the basic subject matter in the past. Today the rural sociologist also has a legitimate interest in the nonfarm person who is settling in the countryside. This movement from the city to the suburbs, and even to the fringes beyond the suburbs, as the previous chapter has shown, is one of the most dramatic and significant facts of contemporary American life. The rural sociologist has as much to contribute to the study of this change as any other social scientist. As a matter of fact, studies by rural sociologists of suburbanization and of the so-called urban fringe have been pioneering landmarks in the field. It is no wonder, then, that when a large industry moves to a rural area, rural sociologists are asked to make a study of the social impact of the move. What happens to family life, recreation, religion, and local government when many farm people turn to industry for part-time employment and when some even abandon farming altogether but remain in the community and drive a long distance to work? What steps can be taken to prevent major dislocation of the local institutions when such a change is under way?

But rural sociologists are well aware that many problems are much too complex to be covered completely by any one discipline, a fact which explains why, from time to time, rural sociologists work in co-

operation with other social scientists who are interested in suburbanization from the standpoint of local and regional planning, metropolitan
dominance, and the political problems of taxation and providing educational, health, and welfare services.

It seems likely that rural sociologists, because of their ability to see
and analyze the rural dimension, will participate even more fully in the
study of human relationships in those communities which are not altogether rural but which are not yet caught up in the direct, almost
daily influence of the metropolis. This includes a large proportion of
people now classed as urban (by a necessarily arbitrary census definition) but who would feel ill at ease, initially at least, if suddenly transplanted to such large centers as New York, Chicago, or Los Angeles.

Contributing to the Understanding of Other Rural Societies

If the movement to the suburbs and the fringe is one of the most
spectacular contemporary social developments in the United States, then
the most far-reaching world-wide political fact of the second quarter of
this century has been the rise of the United States to a position of world
leadership. This fact has had its impact on all the social sciences, including rural sociology. At the end of this century, scholars reviewing
the achievements of rural sociology throughout the twentieth century
may quite possibly rank at the very top of these achievements the contribution made by rural sociologists to the understanding of other societies, in most of which the majority of the people are rural. The assistance rendered has not been merely that of interpreting these foreign
societies to American governmental leaders and to other interested Americans; it has, even more significantly, meant an interpretation of the rural segment of other societies to their own ruling groups, which had
formerly been ignorant of or oblivious to the rural people. Several American rural sociologists within recent years have had the distinction of
being the first to teach courses, deliver lectures, or write books on the
rural sociology of particular foreign countries. In some cases, these efforts have represented the first application of this social science to the
study of rural phenomena in the history of the country. The demand
for those with the skills and experiences of the rural sociologist in overseas programs continues to grow, and U.S. government agencies experience difficulty in filling all their positions. One of the areas of greatest
expansion is community development, since programs related to this field
are being carried out in almost every country where the United States
has a foreign-aid arrangement. International agencies such as the Food
and Agriculture Organization periodically seek rural sociologists to render services requested by member governments.

Outlook for the Future

Clearly, the scope of rural sociology is changing. Most rural sociologists in the years ahead will continue to concentrate on the social relations of American farm people, including in their research numerous investigations of the phenomena of suburbanization and the movement of urban people to the countryside. As in the past, some will serve as specialists in certain problem areas, such as health, communications, migration, personality development, and community life, and bring the sociological approach to bear upon the solution of these problems. Some American rural sociologists will make the study of foreign peoples their lifework, learning the languages and acquiring the other skills needed for effective scholarship and practical counseling on action programs such as those in village improvement. At the same time, increasing numbers of rural sociologists whose permanent connection is with an American university, government agency, or some other organization will spend one, two, or three years in a foreign setting, where they will make available their special knowledge to those seeking to apply social science to the problems of their countries.

DEVELOPING SOCIAL SCIENCE THEORY AND METHODOLOGY

Any social science discipline can be viewed not only in terms of its subject matter, which has just been discussed, but also in terms of the stage of development of its basic theory and methodology. As was pointed out in an introductory section on the scientific method, sciences are built upon hypotheses that have been empirically verified. What has been tested and observed is classified and described in an orderly fashion and is added to the body of knowledge made available to others who might wish to reexamine the whole problem anew.

Rural sociology, like any specialty within the broad field of sociology, must derive most of its theoretical orientation from the parent discipline; at the same time, it is in position to make important contributions to the general body of sociological theory. It does so in two ways: first, the rural sociologist may formulate hypotheses or propositions of such basic importance that they eventually become a central part of the body of theory; second, he may test the existing propositions, devising new methods for doing so.

The Focus of Rural Sociological Research

For the most part, rural sociologists, though they recognize the need for thorough grounding in general theory, do not concentrate primarily upon the formulation of theory as an end in itself. For that matter, relatively few general sociologists work exclusively in the area of theory and methodology, a fact which would also hold true of most other specialists studying the family, criminology, the community, and the like. This has been particularly true, however, in the case of rural sociological research, since it tends to be problem-focused. The problem upon which the rural sociologist focuses may be some aspect of rural life which has become or is expected to become a cause of concern to someone—for example, to those who administer agricultural or educational programs, managers of farm cooperatives, rural church leaders, or industrialists closely following size and competencies of possible labor supply. Or the problem may be of more theoretical than immediately practical interest—for example, the applicability of the Freudian theories of personality to the rural people of a given region—and may therefore be a subject that has significance to the researcher but not to the general public.

In studying a problem, the rural sociologist first reviews the available hypotheses and findings drawn up by others. In examining these, he may put some of the propositions together into new combinations, involving a creative act that contributes to general theory; but this is usually done primarily to help him toward an understanding of the problem he has set for himself. After he has completed his research he may need to suggest new hypotheses to account for the behavior he has observed.

The Theoretical Contribution of Rural Sociologists

By far the greatest contribution rural sociologists have made to general theory and methodology is their testing of existing theories and the working out of new research techniques to accomplish this. To the uninformed student, many of the rural sociological studies describing social characteristics of a single county (or several counties) may seem unimportant or at least unexciting. But upon closer examination, it is evident that such unpretentious studies may present evidence to show that some specific widely accepted sociological proposition does not apply to that case, thereby forcing those formulating a theory either to sharpen their definitions, revise their statements, or abandon them altogether. No one study in itself would necessarily cause such revision, but when several studies presenting the same findings appear in succession in different states, the effect is decisive. A second result of even a limited investigation and publication of findings is to provide data for social scientists who are trying to work out broader generalizations to apply to related topics. Since this is the way a science grows there is no substitute for the patient accumulation of data by careful, well-explained methods.

In their efforts to test theory and to solve problems, the rural sociologists have made use of a wide variety of methods, showing some to be appropriate and others to be not very useful. They have also developed indexes and scales of several kinds, some of which have been widely adopted. They have concerned themselves with sampling techniques, the use of questionnaire material, and the problems of bias in the field interview. Some have tried the projective techniques of the psychologist, or the statistical analyses employed by agricultural economists in types of farming studies, and the numerous rates and ratios relied upon by the demographer in his effort to predict population growth.

Support of Rural Sociological Research

These research concerns of rural sociologists must be seen, however, against the background of the type of financial support they receive, since the development of any science bears some relationship at least to the questions asked by those who "foot the bill," particularly in these days of costly team research. Here again two considerations are worthy of note.

Support from Public Funds. Much research in rural sociology is financed by public funds, a fact which partially explains the concentration of many rural sociologists on the description of the current scene rather than on general theory. Federal funds channeled through the state experiment stations support projects that have a direct or implied connection with problems of rural people. There are regular stages through which a federally financed project goes in the state agricultural experiment station before being reviewed by the Office of Experiment Stations in the U.S. Department of Agriculture in Washington. One must conclude, therefore, that to some extent, political, or at least bureaucratic, decisions play some part in influencing both the content and methods of rural sociology today; but one cannot conclude that any Federal agency is "dictating" developments in this field of study. A very delicate three-way balance is maintained between the scholar (with his belief in freedom of scientific endeavor), the state experiment station (jealous of its own autonomy), and the Federal government (with resources to be placed at the disposal of competent specialists). A foreigner who seeks to equate an American state with a province of his own country, the latter being chiefly an administrative division of the central authority, will miss altogether the sense of individual freedom which the experiment-station sociologist enjoys because of this three-way balance.

Support from the Foundation Grants. Foundation grants of various kinds are having a marked effect on the field of rural sociology in that they provide an opportunity for those who are interested in the theoretical aspects of the subject to work more actively in general theory. Such grants have also made possible the coming together of rural sociologists on a regional basis to explore some common area of interest, such as migration or diffusion of farm practices, with the result that definite hypotheses take shape for later testing by those who have met together. Grants for additional study and attendance at summer seminars concentrating upon statistics or selected interdisciplinary problems bring competencies and insights into rural sociology as they would for any specialized field of study. Because of the many opportunities of this sort now available and because of the type of training he is now receiving in graduate school, the rural sociologist today makes much use of, and in turn contributes his part to, general sociological theory, which cuts across all the sociological specialties such as rural sociology. This trend is also encouraged by the fact that there now exists many relatively new approaches to the study of the group, the community, culture, social change, and society as a system, which, though considered a part of general theory, have a direct bearing upon the immediate research problem of the rural sociologist.

APPLICATION OF RURAL SOCIOLOGY TO EVERYDAY PROBLEMS

Rural sociologists through the years have been recognized as social scientists interested in the application of their findings to everyday life. Not merely as public-spirited citizens but as professional sociologists they have generally manifested a lively interest in efforts to deal with some of the perennial problems of our time. As has been pointed out in earlier chapters, this is a part of the tradition of the field.[3] In addition to the research role already discussed, there are at least three professional roles that rural sociologists play in applying their science to everyday problems: first, they play the educational role, or interpret the findings of social science in order to give others a better understanding of rural society; second, they play the policy role in the sense of making definite recommendations with respect to policy decisions; third, they play the action role and apply their knowledge of group behavior and community processes to programs designed to solve the problems with which the people around them are concerned. A look at each of these roles affords

---

[3] Bruce L. Melvin refers to this as follows: "Out of the resultant drive to better rural conditions rural sociology came into existence as a discipline in college teaching and as a subject for research supported by funds made available through the agricultural experiment stations. Increasingly the subject became functional. Its findings were used, along with those of other fields of research, by the Cooperative Extension Service, in the educational program for farmers." "Rural Sociology in a Chaotic World," *Rural Sociology,* 16:58, 1951.

additional information about the standing of rural sociology at mid-century.

The Educational Role

Many rural sociologists teach. Most of those who do so offer courses in the colleges of agriculture throughout the country. A study of their course titles, however, reveals that they are interested in sociological areas broader than the rural scene of their own particular state, thereby underlining their identity with general as well as rural sociology. Rural sociology is also taught in many other types of schools, frequently by those who are trained in another sociological specialty but wish their students to understand the importance of rural patterns in the past and present.

For some rural sociologists, the state is the classroom and the entire farm population are potential pupils. These are the extension sociologists who work with groups of farmers and their wives and children in programs of home and community development, in the teaching of new recreational skills, and from time to time in helping other extension workers, not trained in the social sciences, to understand some of the social realities that determine the success of their programs. The extension sociologist is basically an educator.

An assessment of the educational role of rural sociologists at mid-century would indicate that staffs in this field are primarily engaged in the educational role, if extension is included as education. The Farm Foundation Committee study, published in 1950, indicates that at that time in 40 institutions providing complete reports about the activities of 139 rural sociologists, there were 52 full-time equivalents in teaching, 52 in research, and 35 in extension work. The customary pattern, however, is for most rural sociologists not assigned to extension work to do both classroom teaching and research, with the result that they feel closely identified with both roles.

Not only as teachers in the classroom but by means of their speeches and writings rural sociologists seek to create a better understanding of the social world about them. Only as the results of research are communicated to those who can profit from the findings are practical values achieved. Although the rural sociologist has written many books, bulletins, and journal articles,[4] he had failed, at mid-century, to interpret sufficiently to the public the nature of the contribution he has to make.

---

[4] The latest tally of publications by rural sociologists in land-grant colleges for the 1938–1947 period showed 1,149 publications: 429 bulletins and circulars, 399 papers in technical journals, and 321 articles of a miscellaneous character. These do not include the important contributions of rural sociologists not affiliated with land-grant colleges, nor do they take account of the accelerated productivity since 1947.

Once the public understands this contribution, rural sociology can advance more rapidly, for it will then have the additional public support it needs.

The Policy Role

A significant number of rural sociologists go into administrative positions both in the universities where they have taught and as officials of state and national government. As administrators, they are often involved in policy determination as well as in policy implementation. But this administrative role is not essentially a sociological role. The rural sociologist plays his policy-making role when administrators request him to conduct a study, draw up findings, and then make recommendations on which the administrator or a policy-planning board can base their decisions. For example, for rural planning and zoning, boards need basic current data about populations, occupations, attitudes, and social changes if they are to act intelligently. Such facts must be not only presented but also interpreted so that their significance for planning will be clear.

For example, the extension of the various provisions of the social security program to cover different types of rural people had to be considered in the light of the facts. In several states rural sociologists made field studies to determine the financial status of the older people and the effects of including them under the social security program. To the extent that they were asked to give their recommendations about what should be done, they were playing a policy role. This is one way of applying research findings to daily needs. It means stepping out of the "neutral" role of the scientist and taking a stand for or against an idea or an issue, something rural sociologists have been willing and able to do in a number of cases without jeopardizing their position as sound research scholars.

The Action Role

A role of ever-growing importance to the rural sociologist is that of assisting in programs of local improvement, by whatever name they may be called (see Chapter 7). He does this chiefly as an individual with professional training and insight which can be applied to the solution of the problems he faces. Such contributions are being made in at least two ways: The first is through special programs set up at the university or by the agency for which the rural sociologist works. When these programs are sponsored by the State Extension Service, they are called Farm and Home Development programs. Other such programs deal with community development and still others with depressed agricultural areas. The chief point is that those in charge of these programs are committed to helping local people improve their situations. What may appear at first to be merely a technological problem of demonstrating simple agricultural techniques may turn into a problem of human motivations and social organization. This is where the rural sociologist steps into the picture to help those in charge deal with the human side of the equation. He works, then, as a specialist along with other specialists, but his field of competence lies in the analysis of social relations, a basic ingredient in any program of community change. Rural sociologists, therefore, are being called for varying periods of time from their research and their classroom teaching to assist extension sociologists in carrying out action programs.

The second contribution of rural sociologists to problem solving is made through programs that are devised and promoted by private groups not connected with the institution or agency where the rural sociologist is regularly employed. Programs of mental health sponsored by mental-health associations, programs of community improvement sponsored by private utility companies or local civic clubs—to mention but two examples—demand the assistance of those who understand the processes through which society operates. Increasingly, persons conducting such programs are turning to the rural sociologist and, where the size of the program justifies it, even adding a trained sociologist to the staff. Because of the type and quality of his training, the rural sociologist usually does some preliminary research before swinging into action, a characteristic that tends to distinguish him from the promoter or reformer, who may let his own enthusiasm serve as a substitute for the basic facts.

These examples do not begin to exhaust the ways in which the knowledge and techniques of the rural sociologist can be applied; they do, however, indicate some of the areas in which he is frequently asked to play an "action" role.

Conclusion

If one were to ask the members of the Rural Sociological Society of America, almost 500 in number, to specify in order of importance the sociological roles they prefer to play, the chances are that the research role would prove an overwhelming favorite, the teaching role (including extension) would come next, and the other two—policy and action roles—would dispute for third and fourth places. This rank order reflects the basic theme of this entire book: rural sociology is a specialty within social science, which is distinguished from the humanities by its emphasis upon the scientific method. It seeks to deal with observable and measurable phenomena in so far as possible, recognizing that many facets of social relations cannot yet be fully captured by present-day methods but may some day be definable by such methods. But the rural sociologist, even in viewing some of these less tangible facets (such as values), by virtue of his mental orientation seeks the objective as opposed to the intuitive and the repetitive pattern of behavior rather than the unique, and is willing to abandon a preconceived notion when the facts show it to be unfounded. He also seeks to apply his discoveries to help solve problems in rural areas both in the United States and in other countries.

Questions for Review and Discussion

1. In the light of your studies of recent trends, do you believe that rural sociology is here to stay? Defend your answer fully.

2. List the more conspicuous changes in rural sociology over the past twenty-five years.

3. Looking into the future, what types of problems will concern rural sociologists of your generation?

4. List the benefits that a student may derive from a course in rural sociology.

Selected References for Supplementary Reading

Brunner, Edmund deS.: "The Growth of a Science: A Half-century of Rural Sociological Research in the United States," New York: Harper & Brothers, 1957.

Duncan, Otis Durant: "Rural Sociology Coming of Age," *Rural Sociology*, 19: 1–12, 1954.

Hamilton, C. Horace: "Some Current Problems in the Development of Rural Sociology," *Rural Sociology*, 15:315–321, 1950.

Kaufman, Harold F.: "Rural Sociology, 1945–55," *Sociology in the United States of America*, Hans L. Zetterberg (ed.), Paris: United Nations Educational, Scientific, and Cultural Organization, 1955, pp. 104–107.

Melvin, Bruce L.: "Rural Sociology in a Chaotic World," *Rural Sociology*, 16: 56–62, 1951.

Name Index

441

Subject Index